ROYAL RIVER

POWER, PAGEANTRY AND THE THAMES

Sponsored by

BARCLAYS

Guest curator
DAVID STARKEY

Edited by
SUSAN DORAN
with ROBERT J. BLYTH

ROYAL
MUSEUMS
GREENWICH

SCALA

Published on the occasion of the exhibition
Royal River: Power, Pageantry and the Thames
at the National Maritime Museum, Greenwich,
London, 27 April–9 September 2012

First published in 2012 by
Scala Publishers Ltd
Northburgh House
10 Northburgh Street
London EC1V 0AT, UK
www.scalapublishers.com

In association with the National Maritime Museum,
Greenwich, London www.rmg.co.uk

ISBN 978 1 85759 752 3 (hardback)
ISBN 978 1 85759 700 4 (paperback)

Project management by Sandra Pisano
Copy editing by Janet Ravenscroft
Design and typography by Isambard Thomas, London
Front cover title lettering by Land Design
Printed in China

10 9 8 7 6 5 4 3 2 1

Inside covers (endpapers on hardback edition):
Aqua Triumphalis (see pp.54–55)
p.1: Prince Frederick's barge (see pp.148–49)
p.2: Greenwich Hospital from the north bank of
the River Thames, detail (see pp.132–33)
p.7: Royal opening of the National Maritime
Museum, 27 April 1937 (detail of C9138-2)

NOTES ON CONVENTIONS

The information in the catalogue has been given as
fully and accurately as possible, but some areas of
uncertainty inevitably exist.

*Catalogue entries have been compiled in the
following order:*

Title of the object is shown in bold type.

Date of the object where known. Square brackets
indicate the original date of publication.

Inscriptions are given where they add
to the meaning of the object.

Artist/ maker/ author and their dates
or school or place of origin where appropriate
or certain.

Media and dimensions,
height × width × depth.

Collection and reference number
where documented. Full lender and picture credits
are detailed on p.292.

Text. Details of provenance will be given here
where they add to the meaning of the object.

Literature. Up to four works have been selected
for some objects. The full reference appears
in the bibliography.

Each catalogue entry is followed by the initials
of its author(s). The abbreviations are explained
on p.282.

ACKNOWLEDGEMENTS

Many people have contributed to the success of the *Royal River* exhibition
and to the publication of this book. The editors would like to thank all of
the contributors to the catalogue for their hard work in meeting various
production schedules. We are particularly grateful to David Starkey for his
support and assistance in organising the structure of the book. Oliver Craske
and Sandra Pisano at Scala Publishers and the designer, Isambard Thomas,
showed patience and understanding in seeing this complex project through
to completion. At the National Maritime Museum, the production of the
catalogue was most efficiently co-ordinated by Rebecca Nuotio and Kara Green,
who were assiduous in maintaining a strict adherence to deadlines. We are
indebted to John McAleer for his considerable help at the proof-reading stage;
and to Kris Martin, the exhibition curator, and Matt Lawrence, the exhibition
project manager, for their invaluable assistance. Picture research was skilfully
undertaken by Melanie Oelgeschlager; and we are grateful to the teams in
the Museum's photo studio and conservation department for their efforts
in preparing material for publication.

More broadly, this catalogue reflects the extraordinary wealth of objects
brought together for the *Royal River* exhibition. We are indebted to the many
lenders to the exhibition who have supported the exhibition and the
accompanying catalogue. In particular we must thank Her Majesty The Queen
and the staff of the Royal Collection (especially Jonathan Marsden, Sir Hugh
Roberts, the Hon. Lady Jane Roberts and Desmond Shawe-Taylor), John
Somerville, the senior curator of the Lobkowicz Collections, and the staff
of the many livery companies of the City of London. The exhibition was made
possible by the provision of insurance through the Government Indemnity
Scheme. The National Maritime Museum would like to take this opportunity
to thank the Department for Culture, Media and Sport and the Arts Council
England for providing and arranging this indemnity. The *Royal River* exhibition was
generously supported by Barclays. To everyone involved – in roles large and small,
acknowledged and unacknowledged – we extend our thanks and gratitude.

Susan Doran and Robert J. Blyth, Oxford and Greenwich, 2012

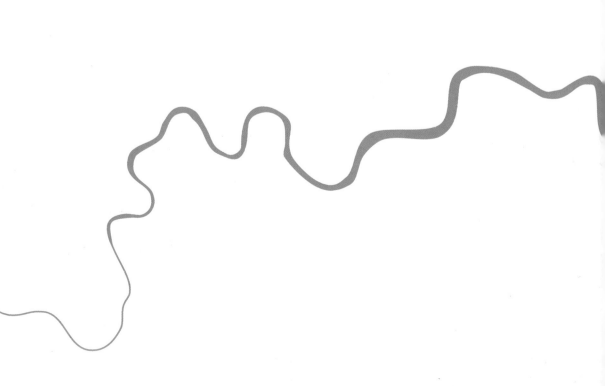

BUCKINGHAM PALACE

The Duke of Edinburgh has been a trustee and patron of the National Maritime Museum for nearly 65 years. My own association with Greenwich is even longer. I well remember, aged eleven, accompanying my father to the opening of the Museum seventy-five years ago. When the King and Queen stepped ashore at Greenwich, as monarchs have done for centuries, they approached the great riverside buildings in the way intended: from the Thames.

I am delighted that the National Maritime Museum has chosen to celebrate the Diamond Jubilee with its *Royal River* exhibition. It explores themes – power, pageantry and the Thames – that lie at the heart of the prospect and purpose of Greenwich, which this year has become a Royal Borough. In many ways, *Royal River* also illuminates the wider history of the United Kingdom from the Tudor age to the present.

I hope that all those who visit the *Royal River* exhibition may come to appreciate the extraordinary and varied role the Thames has played in British history, and its contribution to national life.

Elizabeth R

MUSEUM FOREWORD

On behalf of the Trustees, the Director and the staff of the National Maritime Museum, I would like to take this opportunity to congratulate Her Majesty The Queen on the occasion of her Diamond Jubilee. The Queen has visited the Museum many times during her long and illustrious reign. His Royal Highness The Duke of Edinburgh, the Baron Greenwich, has continued to provide the Museum with invaluable support and guidance for nearly sixty-five years: as a Trustee from 1948 and as Patron from 2000. Together, they have witnessed every milestone in the life of the Museum.

This year sees the seventy-fifth anniversary of the opening of the Museum. As the first major exhibition in the Museum's Sammy Ofer Wing, *Royal River* marks the next stage of its development. This exhibition has been made possible by the kind help and support of a significant number of individuals and lending institutions in this country and overseas. I am especially pleased to thank Her Majesty The Queen for the unprecedented number of objects lent by the Royal Collection.

The Museum is grateful to Barclays for its generous support of, and enthusiastic commitment to, the exhibition. I must also thank David Starkey, who has guided and shaped the exhibition with members of the Museum's staff, and Susan Doran and Robert Blyth, who haved edited this catalogue.

The Rt Hon. The Lord Sterling of Plaistow, GCVO, CBE
Chairman of Trustees

SPONSOR'S FOREWORD

I am delighted Barclays is sponsoring *Royal River: Power, Pageantry and the Thames* at the National Maritime Museum. The Museum has always exhibited with distinction on the topic of Britain and the sea, showing the contemporary significance of maritime events and the stories of this island nation. *Royal River* is a fitting way for the National Maritime Museum to celebrate its 75th anniversary and Her Majesty Queen Elizabeth II's Diamond Jubilee.

Royal River will attract visitors from London and across the world to remind them about London's greatest 'thoroughfare' – the River Thames. The river has played a crucial role for trade and finance in London, of which Barclays has been a part for over 300 years.

The new *Sammy Ofer Wing* has spectacularly changed the National Maritime Museum with a new entrance for visitors, breathtaking architecture and superb facilities. It provides a wonderful space for the Museum to hold leading exhibitions such as *Royal River* and we're excited to sponsor the first of these.

With artefacts gathered from collections across the world, *Royal River* promises to be a unique and insightful exhibition.

Barclays is committed to supporting the communities we serve. Sponsorship of *Royal River* enables us to partner with a treasured arts organisation; help enhance the experience of thousands of visitors; and provide a fitting tribute to Her Majesty Queen Elizabeth II on the occasion of her Diamond Jubilee. On behalf of all Barclays colleagues around the world, I hope that everyone who attends enjoys this wonderful exhibition.

 BARCLAYS

Marcus Agius,
Group Chairman, Barclays

LONDON, FLOWER OF CITIES ALL: ROYAL RITUAL AND THE RIVER

DAVID STARKEY

William Dunbar's eulogy, 'London, thou art flower of cities all', was first performed – perhaps declaimed, perhaps set to music – as the highlight of the Lord Mayor's Christmas festivities at the Guildhall in 1501. It is one of the great City poems; it also translates into verse (the best, incidentally, to be written in English since Chaucer, whom Dunbar revered) the themes of this exhibition. Especially the lines on the Thames, which has a whole stanza to itself:

> Above all rivers thy river hath renown
> Whose boreal streams, pleasant and preclare [very clear]
> Under thy lusty walls runneth down
> Where many a swan doth swim with wings fair
> Where many a barge doth sail and row with are [air]
> Where many a ship doth rest with top royal
> Oh town of towns, patron and none compare
> London thou art the flower of Cities all.

Here is a vision of the Thames as it once was and which we seek to evoke again: a riverscape of vast and lazy meanders, where land met water and noble buildings rose from the river and great gardens swept down to it; a river busy with shipping and teeming with life, at once a setting for pomp and pageantry and pleasure, and the everyday artery and life-blood of the City, a scene worthy of the pen of Thomas Wyatt and Edmund Spenser, of the music of Handel and the brush of Canaletto and Turner.

And all gone in the space of a few decades from 1830 to 1860. rst it was polluted by rampant population growth and industrialisation, which built over its gardens, stained its buildings and befouled its water and air. Then it was obliterated by the embankment of the Thames, which cut the river off from the City and left some of its noblest buildings – like Somerset House – stunted and stranded. Only at Greenwich itself, appropriately enough, can we see something of the old Thames, with the grandest combination of water, landscape and architecture in England.

It is one of the great views of the world and a miraculous survival; it is also a reminder of what we have lost.

Dunbar, on the other hand, represents as good a beginning as any for our story. He had arrived in London on 20 November 1501 as a member of the suite of a Scottish embassy. The Scots were received into the City at Bishopsgate, 'and from thence conveyed with many noble men and jolly gallants through the high streets unto St John's in Smithfield and there lodged'.[1] The embassy came to negotiate the marriage of James IV of Scotland to Henry VII's eldest daughter, Margaret. But its members reached London in the middle of the celebrations of what seemed at the time to be a much greater union: the wedding of Arthur, Prince of Wales to Katherine of Aragon. The bride made her entrée to London on 12 November and the wedding itself took place at St Paul's Cathedral on the 14th. The festivities continued with four more days of jousting and feasting and dancing at Westminster, and concluded with a grand river procession to Richmond, whence most of Katherine's escort took leave and departed for Spain.

It was probably the most magnificent and protracted celebration that London had ever seen. And Dunbar had a grandstand seat. The Scottish embassy were official guests at the second day of the jousts and there is every reason to suppose that Dunbar, an eager and curious observer, joined the throng at the rest. And what he saw undoubtedly conditioned his poem, especially the river procession on the 26th.

First, the King dined with the bride and groom at the palace. Then the whole Court embarked at Westminster Stairs for Richmond, 'whither the mayor with his brethren and a certain of the worshipful fellowships of the City in barges and great boats garnished with sundry instruments of music gave their attendance'.[2]

The procession seems to have passed off without incident, unlike the earlier water procession which had escorted Katherine from Paul's Wharf to Westminster on the 16th. Once again, the flower of the City had turned out in all their finery 'in barges garnished with banners and other cognizances of their crafts and all instruments of music'. But the Mercers, who were the first in the order of precedence of the City livery companies or guilds, let the side down by turning up in a barge that 'was not garnished and appareled according unto their worship, nor so well as other, which were of less authority'. The Lord Mayor, 'grievously discontented' with this insult to his authority and the dignity of the City, ordered the Mercers home and subsequently arraigned and fined them.[3]

So the Lord Mayor, Sir John Shaw, a Goldsmith and the nephew of an earlier and even more distinguished Lord Mayor, Sir Edward Shaw, was a martinet, which is not a bad

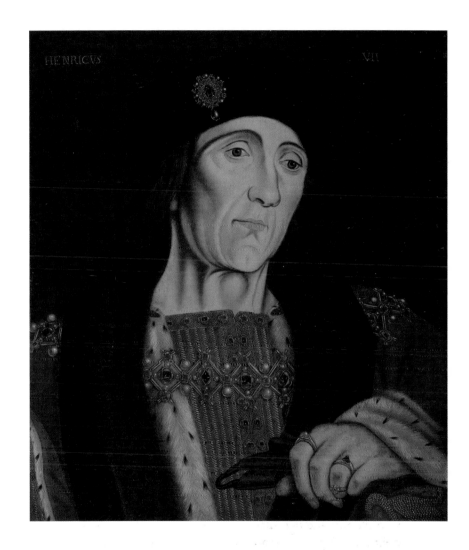

Fig. 1 Henry VII, oil on panel, English school, *c.*1505.

National Maritime Museum, Caird Collection, BHC2762.

temperament for one who aspires to marshal complex ceremonial. He was also an innovator.

He had shown his colours at his inauguration. The inauguration took place each year on 29 October, when the Lord Mayor-elect processed to Westminster to be sworn in at the Court of the Exchequer. For almost the last fifty years the procession had been by water. But Shaw added a refinement. Hitherto the Lord Mayor and aldermen had walked from Guildhall to embark at the riverside. But Shaw insisted that they ride. Maybe, one of his fellows speculated cruelly, it was because 'he was little of stature'; or, a better reason, 'for more honourable guise hereafter to be used'. He also held his feast in the Guildhall, whereas previously it had been the practice for the mayor to entertain in his own house or livery hall. To make this possible, he had kitchens and other offices added on to the Guildhall, and secured contributions from the livery companies to build them. Soon, the Lord Mayor's Guildhall feast became part of immemorial custom. But, at the time, Shaw's 'invention of tradition' seemed 'full raw and far out of order for that business'.

No wonder, with such an assertive incumbent, that Dunbar's poem ends with a stanza devoted to the pre-eminence of London's Lord Mayor 'above all mayors as master most worthy':

> Thy famous mayor, by princely governance,
> With sword of justice thee ruleth prudently;
> No lord of Paris, Venice or Florence
> In dignity or honour goeth to him nigh.

Shaw thus takes his place, not only as a notable, if cantankerous, City figure, but also as one of the founders and shapers of the 400 years of civic pageantry whose rise, zenith and decline are charted by Ian Archer in this volume. Much more important in our story, however, is another of Shaw's contemporaries: Henry VII (fig. 1).

Henry too was a ceremonialist, who managed and invented pageantry and on a vastly grander scale. He personally marshalled the procession at the creation of his second son, Henry, as Duke of York. He and his advisers invented the red rose, one of the most resonant emblems in English history, as the symbol of the house of Lancaster. And he seems to have been the first to make the River Thames

HENRICVS · VIII   ANG · REX.

feature regularly in royal pageantry. He ended his first progress in June 1486 with a waterborne procession from Richmond to Westminster. The mayor and livery companies met him in their barges at Putney and escorted him for the rest of the journey; on his arrival, the citizens, grouped in their companies, also formed a kind of guard of honour within the palace precinct, lining his route from Westminster Stairs to St Margaret's Church. Similar, even more elaborate, displays were laid on for Henry's Queen, Elizabeth of York, when she went by water from Greenwich to the Tower two days before her coronation in November 1487, and for his eldest son, Arthur, when he was taken from Richmond to Westminster for his creation as Prince of Wales two years later.[4]

The eve-of-coronation procession for Elizabeth of York is especially noteworthy, since a direct comparison is possible with the coronation festivities of the two preceding Queens Consort, Margaret of Anjou in 1445 and Elizabeth Woodville in 1465. Both traversed a similar route, Margaret travelling to the Tower from Eltham, and Elizabeth Woodville from Greenwich. But both processed by land: Margaret was given a grand civic welcome at Southwark; while the mayor, aldermen and leading citizens rode out to meet Elizabeth Woodville at Shooters Hill before escorting her to the Tower via Southwark and Gracechurch Street in the City.[5]

Elizabeth of York's water procession from Greenwich was thus a deliberate break with earlier practice; it also turned out to be the invention of a new tradition that gave rise to some of the most splendid river spectacles of the following centuries. But here the innovator was not Henry VII but his second son and eventual successor, Henry VIII (fig.2).

Unlike his father, Henry VIII was not a natural innovator, in ceremony or anything else. Instead, it was the extraordinary pattern of his later marriages that made him so. Hitherto, it had been the invariable practice that a queen consort was crowned. If the royal couple were already married at the time of the king's accession, there was a double coronation; if the marriage took place subsequently, the queen was given a separate coronation ceremony. Henry VIII followed this precedent with his first wife, Katherine of Aragon. The two were married on 11 June 1509, and crowned together a fortnight later on the 24th in a ceremony that was magnificent but entirely traditional in form. It is especially

striking from our point of view that there were no river processions, either for the King or Queen.

The coronation of Henry's second, deeply contentious Queen, Anne Boleyn, presents a marked contrast. The couple had married bigamously on 25 January 1533; on 23 May, Henry's marriage to Katherine of Aragon was declared void and five days later his marriage to Anne valid. This opened the way – just – to Anne's coronation on 1 June. In these circumstances, the precedent of the separate coronation of Henry's mother, Elizabeth of York, in 1487 proved a godsend and it was followed to the letter – and especially in the matter of the river procession from Greenwich to the Tower. As in 1487, the procession delighted the eye with banners, pennants and streamers and the ear with extravagantly large numbers of musicians. The same prominence was given to the so-called Bachelors' barge, which was lavishly decorated and carried the main group of instrumentalists. And, on both occasions, the Queen was received at the Tower with a public demonstration of affection from the King: in 1533 the couple even embraced and kissed.

There were variations of course: in 1487 the Bachelors' barge had also carried a Red Dragon belching fire and smoke; in 1533, the Dragon had its own separate pyrotechnic boat, which, complete with wildfire and guns noisily firing blanks, headed the procession. Indeed, ordnance, which Henry VIII had done so much to foster in England, assumed a thoroughly modern role in this reception for his second Queen: the ships moored along the route fired salutes as Anne's procession rowed past and the Tower greeted her with its mighty guns.

But the most important innovations were organisational. Great pains were taken to preserve the good order of Anne's procession: the barges were directed to keep a distance of two lengths between them and three fast craft with 'officers' on board were provided to police the arrangement. Nearly three centuries later, the solemnity of the river procession for Admiral Nelson's funeral was to be preserved by very similar means. Finally, the arrangements make clear how far civic and royal ceremonial interlocked: the mounting of Anne's river procession was delegated to the Lord Mayor by the King's letters and the City consciously modelled the resulting show on the Lord Mayor's annual water procession to Westminster for his inauguration.[6]

The result was a waterborne triumph. Indeed, it was carried to such pitch of splendour that it threatened to overshadow the subsequent traditional land procession through London in which the new Queen, though pregnant, reclined in a horse-litter dressed in virginal white and with her hair round her shoulders in the manner of a bride.

Henry was to have four more wives. But none of them was crowned. Instead they were given various forms of inauguration which, in the case of three of them, featured a river pageant. On Whitsunday 1536, three years to the day since Anne's coronation, Jane Seymour was proclaimed Queen at Greenwich. Three days later, the King and his new Queen, attended by the lords and followed by the guard in a great barge, went in triumph by water from Greenwich to Henry's new palace of Whitehall: vessels at anchor in the Thames fired their guns; the imperial ambassador greeted them with ordnance and music at Rotherhithe; the artillery of the Tower saluted them as they rowed past and music sounded as they shot London Bridge.[7]

A notable omission was any contribution from the City. Perhaps events had moved too fast for one to be organised. But in any case the omission was made good in 1540 for the inauguration of Henry's fourth Queen, Anne of Cleves. Once again, the scene was Greenwich: she was greeted by the citizens, both on water and on land, when she first entered the palace; she was married on the Feast of the Epiphany and processed as a bride in cloth of silver, with her hair down and a jewelled circlet woven with rosemary on her head; and on 4 February she and Henry made the now customary water procession to Westminster. All the familiar elements were present: the Lord Mayor and livery companies in their barges; salutes from shipping and the Tower ('above a thousand chambers of ordnance, which made a noise like thunder'); the shooting of London Bridge.[8]

A mere six months later, in August 1540, Henry married Katherine Howard at Hampton Court, where she was proclaimed Queen the same day. Decency, however, required a longer interval before the new Queen was honoured with a water procession. It took place the following year in March 1541. The procession, with the King and Queen in one barge, also went in the opposite direction, downstream from Westminster to London Bridge, beyond which it was greeted by the mayor and livery companies, past the Tower with its ordnance and the shipping with its sounding guns, and so to Greenwich.

The sense of going though the ceremonial motions is manifest. As, strikingly, is a clear understanding of their significance. 'This', the chronicler noted, 'was the queen's grace's first coming to London since the king's grace married her.' In other words, shooting London Bridge and being received by the City barges had become a new kind of entrée into the City and new form of popular recognition.

But even this was denied Henry's sixth Queen, Katherine Parr, who was merely proclaimed after her marriage, also at Hampton Court, in 1543.[9] The pageantry was, as Simon Thurley points out in his essay below, underpinned by the practicalities. By the turn of the fifteenth century, all the major royal palaces – Hampton Court, Richmond, Westminster/Whitehall and Greenwich – clustered in and around London and all were on the Thames, which formed the natural means of communication between them. The palaces put their best faces towards the river and most of them rose directly from its waters. Their water gates became major architectural features and the royal barges were more and more elaborately decorated.

But the 1560s, as Thurley emphasises, saw an important change. Comfortable sprung coaches first appeared in England and were soon all the rage. Roads replaced the river as the preferred form of transport and, as they did so, the principal entrances to the royal palaces were reorientated from the water to the landward side.

It was a transport revolution; what has not been properly noticed is that it threatened to bring about a corresponding revolution in ceremony. Indeed, under Elizabeth I, the revolution took place. Elizabeth I was the most famously ceremonious monarch in English history and her progresses are the stuff of legend. But, as far as I can tell, she never took part in a major Thames pageant. When Elizabeth opened Parliament, she rode or went in a coach (fig.3). When the citizens came to Greenwich to honour the Queen, they marched by land and mounted a muster in the park. Even when she celebrated the aquatic triumph of the Armada, she did so on land, with a procession from Somerset House to St Paul's. The procession took place on 24 November 1588 and,

Fig.3 *IIII of Spades. Queene Eliz: Riding in Triumph through London in a Chariot drawn by two Horses and all ye Companies attending her wth their Baners*, printed playing card, *c*.1588.

National Maritime Museum, PAD0181.

significantly, the royal coach had a starring role second only to the Queen's own. Called 'a chariot-throne', it featured 'four pillars behind to have a canopy, on the top whereof was made a crown imperial, and two lower pillars before, whereon stood a lion and a dragon, supporters of the arms of England, [and was] drawn by two white horses'.[10]

But if Elizabeth ignored the river for her ceremonies, the Stuarts took to it once more and with a vengeance. The explanation, as it had been under the earlier Tudors, was marriage. Henry VIII used the river to inaugurate queens that he could not, or would not, crown. The Stuarts used it, *faute de mieux*, to honour queens who themselves would not be crowned or even married in England, since they were Catholic and England was Protestant.

Most extreme was the case of Henrietta Maria, the Queen of Charles I. It was the first time that a Catholic princess had been married to a Protestant king and the papacy imposed stringent conditions. The girl herself (she was only fifteen) had also been brought up in the strict piety then fashionable at the French court and she continued to be under the influence of her Oratorian confessors in England. The result was a sort of ceremonial hunger-strike. Henrietta Maria not only refused to be crowned by a Protestant prelate (though the marriage treaties clearly envisaged some form of coronation); she also flatly refused to attend her husband's coronation, even in the specially screened traverse, or enclosure, which had been prepared for her. Charles, who took his coronation very seriously, was deeply offended.[11]

It was the same with her marriage. Henrietta's only form of marriage with Charles was a wedding by proxy at the doors of Nôtre Dame in Paris. The proxy, the Duc de Chevreuse, and the Protestant English ambassadors were then left *outside* while Henrietta Maria and the French went *inside* to celebrate the nuptial mass. Once in England, Henrietta Maria submitted to a blessing with her husband, but no more.

In these circumstances, the revival of inauguration by a Tudor-style water procession made complete sense. The only innovation was to extend the route. The couple boarded the royal barge at Gravesend and were then rowed upstream amid the scenes of popular rejoicing described in the chapter by Julie Sanders. The ships fired salvoes and the Tower its thunderous salute; the crowds cheered; the couple shot

Queene Eliz: Riding in Triumph through London in a Chariot drawn by two Horses and all ý Companies attending her wth their Baners

London Bridge and landed at Whitehall Stairs – just as Henry VIII and four of his queens had done, and for much the same reasons.

Almost forty years later, Catherine of Braganza, the Catholic bride of Charles II, was more accommodating and the couple were married in person: twice in fact, as a secret Catholic wedding ceremony was complemented by a public Protestant one. But still there were limits and there was no question of a Catholic consort undergoing a Protestant coronation. So, once again, a river procession was used as a form of inauguration.

The procession, *Aqua Triumphalis*, was reckoned to be the most magnificent of all such ceremonies. It contained many customary elements, in particular the reception of the royal couple by the Lord Mayor of London and the London livery companies in their barges. That was the corporate City. But the physical City – of brick and stone and teeming multitudes – was missing. Earlier river processions, with their route past the Tower and the symbolic shooting of London Bridge, had been water entrées into this real City. As such, they had substituted very effectively for the traditional eve-of-coronation procession on land from the Tower, through the City and to Westminster.

But in 1662 such symbolism, like the City itself, was missing. Instead the route of the water procession was far upstream to the west, from Hampton Court to Whitehall. This section of the Thames, with its banks lined with royal parks, was indeed *the* royal river. But why ignore the City? Convenience? Or fear of how the Protestant City might greet another Catholic queen?

With the accession of James II, both the King and his Queen, Mary of Modena, were Catholic. Hitherto, Catholicism had been an insuperable obstacle to a Protestant coronation. Now the obstacle was overcome by the simple expedient of omitting the Anglican communion from the service and both the King and Queen were crowned in a magnificent ceremony on 21 April 1685. There followed two days of celebrations on the river: a water procession on the 22nd and an aquatic firework display from pontoons moored in the Thames on the 23rd.

The firework display, with its great illuminated image of 'Monarchy', was splendid. But the route of the river procession, from Whitehall to Westminster, was even shorter than in 1662. It was also, as it had been from the days of Henry VIII, a substitute. Hitherto, and for generations, James's predecessors had shown themselves to their people in the eve-of-coronation landward procession from the Tower to Westminster. James did not and perhaps dared not. Instead he made do with processing along a few hundred yards of the river.

Was the monarchy shrinking too?

Three years later, it was all over. James fled ignominiously from his kingdom to exile in France and the throne was offered to his elder daughter Mary and son-in-law William of Orange. And they were as vehemently Protestant as James and Mary of Modena had been Catholic.

These revolutionary events were regularised by the Bill of Rights of 1689. First the Bill declared 'it … inconsistent with the safety and welfare of this Protestant kingdom to be governed by a popish prince'. Then it made the prohibitions necessary to enforce the principle: henceforward, no Roman Catholic could inherit the kingdom, nor could any king or queen marry a Roman Catholic.

The thoroughgoing Protestantisation of the monarchy effected by the Bill of Rights marked an epoch in royal ceremony. There would be no more Catholic queens consort; no more refusals to be married or crowned by Protestant rites and so no further need for informal inauguration ceremonies. The principal casualty was the grand royal river procession: none was needed and none was held.

Other contemporary events conspired further to divorce the monarchy from the river. Most important was the great fire of 1698 which destroyed the riverside palace of Whitehall. The official seat of the Court now became the landlocked St James's. Other important royal residences, like Kensington were also inland and even Hampton Court, the starting point for so many magnificent river pageants, lost its water gate, which was first converted into a bijou residence for Queen Mary and later demolished.

As had first been prefigured under Elizabeth I with the invention of the sprung coach, roads – and in particular the King's Road, the monarch's private thoroughfare from Chelsea to Hampton Court – had finally replaced the river as the principal royal artery.

The divorce of the Crown and the Thames was not absolute of course. But monarchs, like their subjects, now used the upper reaches of the river largely for entertainment and retreat: it was the setting for elegant river parties, like the one for which Handel's 'Water Music' was written, or for the sylvan delights of George III's palace and pleasure gardens at Kew.

Nor did other, non-royal river ceremony die a sudden death. It was kept alive by a vainglorious City and the competitiveness of its livery companies; by the identification of the British élite with that earlier, ceremonious state, the waterborne republic of Venice, and by their employment of Venetian painters, like Canaletto, who transmuted the Thames into the Rialto. The rise of Britain's naval and imperial power helped too, since it turned the Thames from a royal highway into the gateway to the world and its riches, which poured like tribute into the wharfs and warehouses of the Pool of London.

To all of this, the solemn river pageant of Nelson's funeral, described by Timothy Jenks in his essay, was at once the apogee and the beginning of the end. Within less than fifty years, Spenser's 'sweet Thames' had become the dark and turbid stream of Dickens and Doré; its palaces and pleasure gardens a memory and its ceremonies scarcely that.

Except at Greenwich. Here in this exhibition we complement what survives with what can be reconstructed and evoke once more the Royal River for the right royal celebrations of Queen Elizabeth II's Diamond Jubilee.

And so our story comes full circle: the first Elizabeth abandoned the Thames for her coach; the second returns to it for a new royal river pageant to commemorate her sixty years upon the throne. The pageant may not match the glories of the past, but it will mark an important stage in London's long-overdue rediscovery of its river. As, and we hope more lastingly, will this exhibition.

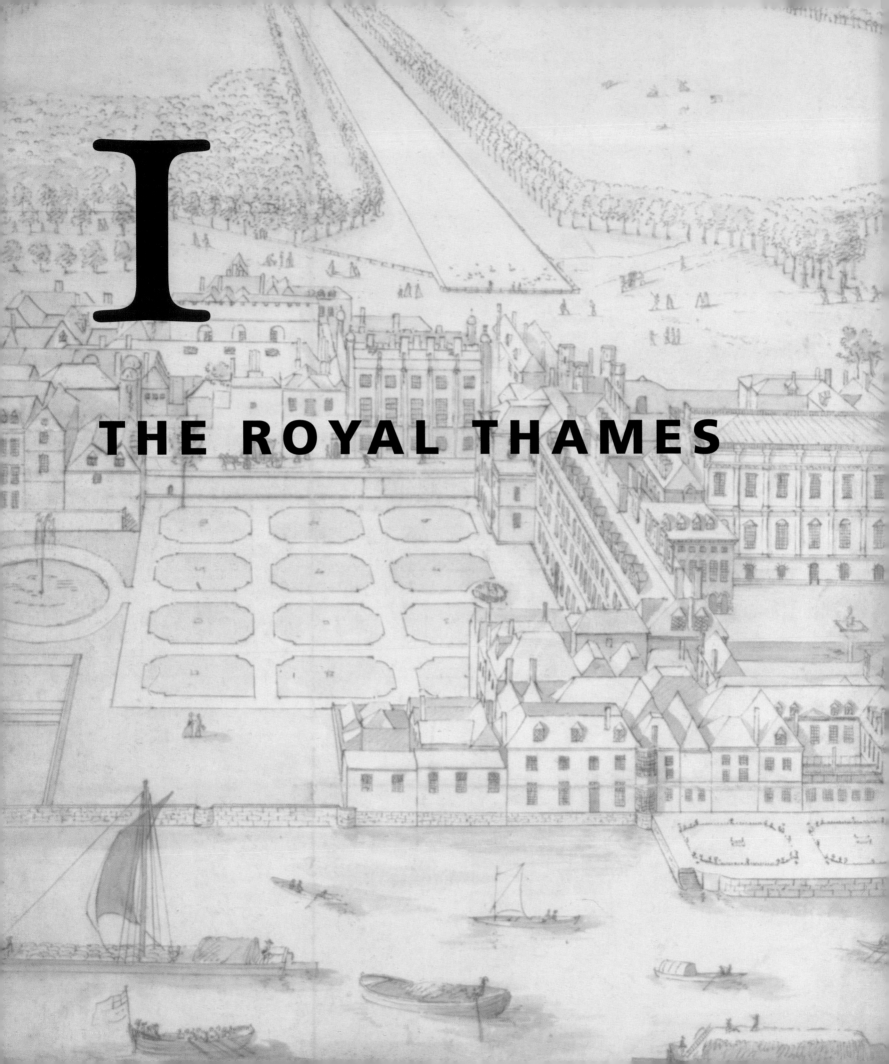

I

THE ROYAL THAMES

THE VANISHING ARCHITECTURE OF THE RIVER THAMES

SIMON THURLEY

The Thames exercised a decisive influence on the architecture of royal and aristocratic houses in London from the early Middle Ages. In the reign of Elizabeth I, however, changes took place that fundamentally altered the spatial relationship between the river and the great houses that lined it. These developments were important as they help to explain the evolution of London, the shifting priorities of the monarchy and our complex relationship with the river.

The Tudor and Stuart royal court was not a monolithic body. Rather like today it was a conglomerate made up of a number of separate households, the principal one being the king's, with smaller ones for the queen and the royal children. In the case of Henry VIII, for example, the King's household was, of course, the largest, numbering perhaps 800 people in the winter; in summer it was slightly smaller at around 600. The Queen's household was a scaled-down version of the King's and numbered perhaps 120. The royal children – Mary, Elizabeth and Edward – had households in miniature.

None of these households was sedentary: they moved from place to place by barge, by horse, by litter and by cart. In the winter these movements were essentially confined to the royal palaces known as the standing houses. These were at Greenwich, Richmond, Hampton Court, Windsor and Whitehall, all situated on the River Thames. In summer, the Court moved further afield in search of good hunting. The summer houses, or lesser palaces, were smaller but set in hunting parks or forests. It was very rare for all the royal households to be in a single location at any one time. In fact, it is likely that only Whitehall was really capable of accommodating the whole royal family, and only then by most of the household members staying in inns and taverns nearby.

As a result, from the 1530s until its destruction by fire in the 1690s, Whitehall was the pivot upon which royal life turned and the Thames was the lubricant that enabled it to move. Whitehall Palace was, from the outset, architecturally integrated with the river. The site of what became Whitehall had originally incorporated three public rights of way from King Street (the road from Westminster to Charing Cross) to the riverfront. Each of these had a public bridge, or landing stage, at its end that allowed the inhabitants of Westminster access to the river. In 1530 one of these, at Endive Lane, was closed off when Henry VIII bought up the medieval tenements that lined it and incorporated the lane into his new palace. The second lane that ran along the southern boundary of Scotland Yard was absorbed by the palace and, while remaining accessible to the public, became Whitehall's waterside goods entrance known as the Whitehall Stairs. Thus, throughout the palace's history there was a narrow public right of way running from the street, through the screens passage of the great hall, behind the chapel and kitchens to the river. In 1532, a large royal coat of arms was erected over the landing stage in case anyone was in any doubt as to whom it belonged.

Clearly the public wharf would not do as a royal entrance and Henry VIII commissioned a new private bridge in 1530. When completed, this was the most elaborate and magnificent of all the landing stages along the central section of the Thames. Supported on beautifully made stone cutwaters, the timber-framed structure had two storeys with a terrace on its roof. Stairs led up from the river into the first-floor gallery, which connected directly with Henry's own lodgings. The King's barge moored here regularly, but it is clear that in the later sixteenth and into the seventeenth century the barges of leading courtiers were also permitted to dock at the privy stairs. Indeed, ordinary watermen were allowed to disembark their passengers at the privy stairs on the strict condition that they did not loiter waiting for a return fare.

Whitehall was the headquarters for the royal barge. In 1532, a long narrow dock was dug in Scotland Yard for it but when, in 1536, a new barge was made the dock was enlarged and a superstructure erected over it. The King's bargemaster and his oarsmen had offices and storerooms nearby. On major ceremonial occasions the royal barge, its satellites and the barges of the aristocracy were all pressed into service. For instance, in 1522, during the reception of the Habsburg Emperor Charles V and his retinue, thirty magnificent barges collected the party from Gravesend and conveyed them to Greenwich.

In the 1540s, Henry VIII extended Whitehall further south by cannibalising yet more land and absorbing a third lane leading to the river at Lamb Alley. At first this provided access to the Thames for Henry's builders but, in due course, it became another private landing stage leading to the orchard and later to the bowling green.

In the sixteenth century, Whitehall was thus entirely focused on the river for access to the palace by the monarch, courtiers, suppliers and workmen via three stairs or wharfs. The principal landward gate – the Whitehall or Palace Gate – was used regularly, but provided access to the slow, crowded and dirty streets of Westminster. Those who wanted to preserve their dignity, to transport large or heavy objects, or to move rapidly used the river.

Ice was the biggest enemy to this smooth communication. The Thames was particularly prone to freezing upstream of London Bridge because its narrow arches restricted the flow of the river. In 1515, the ice was so thick that when it broke up it carried away five arches of the bridge. On these occasions the royal family, courtiers and ambassadors resorted to horseback. Moving from Whitehall to Greenwich by horse was not easy. The best solution was to cross the Thames by horse ferry at Westminster rather than to ride through the City and cross at London Bridge. Nevertheless, with the river frozen in 1536, Henry VIII and Queen Jane rode through the City over London Bridge to reach Greenwich.

Ice was not the only drawback to river travel, for the tides had to be considered as well. Until the eighteenth century the river was tidal at least as far as Hampton Court and often as far as Windsor. Tidal variation could be as much as 23 feet and the average at London Bridge was 15 to 23 feet. Moves between palaces were therefore always planned in relation to the tide. Sir John Finet, Charles I's Master of Ceremonies, set out from Gravesend in October 1631 in a flotilla of six royal barges aiming to get to London. The tide, however, was turning and the wind was against them and even the barge with twelve oars was unable to make headway. So the party had to disembark at Greenwich and transfer to coaches to complete its journey, which took three hours. Consequently, brief trips from Whitehall to Greenwich or Hampton Court often had to be prolonged to take account of the tide. It was for this reason that Henry VIII installed a clock at Hampton Court in 1541 that told the time of high and low tides at London Bridge.

Despite these problems, from the early Middle Ages anyone with any means travelled around London by river. But in the 1550s there was a social revolution that had far-reaching effects. The invention of the carriage was a boon for travellers, as for centuries people had been trying to devise a vehicle that could move at a trot without pulverising its occupants. In the 1550s, a new type of carriage that had originated in Hungary appeared in England. Instead of the passenger compartment resting directly on the axles, the new Pomeranian coach was slung on leather braces and by the 1620s, on occasion, on steel springs. This gave a much smoother and more comfortable ride. The first new coaches arrived in London in around 1555; by 1600 their use was no less than a craze and by 1620 coach-making was one of the most lucrative industries in the capital. The finely carpentered carcasses were upholstered with luxurious silks and velvets costing perhaps twice as much as the £50 expense of the body work. While this was clearly out of reach for most people, it was a sound investment for the very rich, as a single coach could carry a lady, her maid and four children with only two horses and a coachman.

Before the introduction of the carriage there were few horses stabled in London, but from the 1660s for every carriage there had to be at least two horses. Stables and coach houses were built at each of the royal palaces and at all the great aristocratic mansions from the 1670s. The new coach house at Hampton Court survives today overlooking the green. It was built next to the existing Tudor stables.

The construction of stables and coach houses was neither the primary nor the most important effect of the rise of the coach. Carriages also affected the orientation of the great town houses. As we have seen, Whitehall Palace was built to face the river not only in an architectural and aesthetic sense but in an intensely functional sense, too. This was the same for all the other royal palaces and, in particular, for the large aristocratic mansions that were built along the Strand from the 1550s onwards. Anybody making the journey from the Tower of London to Whitehall in the middle of Elizabeth I's reign would have passed the magnificent water stairs of a dozen great houses. Of all of these only the York Water Gate now remains, marooned in Embankment Gardens near Charing Cross Station. Erected in 1626–27, it originally gave access to the Duke of Buckingham's mansion, York House.

With the advent of the coach there was a collapse in water carriage, fury from the watermen, and a re-orientation of the great houses from the river to the street. While households might retain barges for occasional formal use or for recreation, the fashionable way to move about town was now by road,

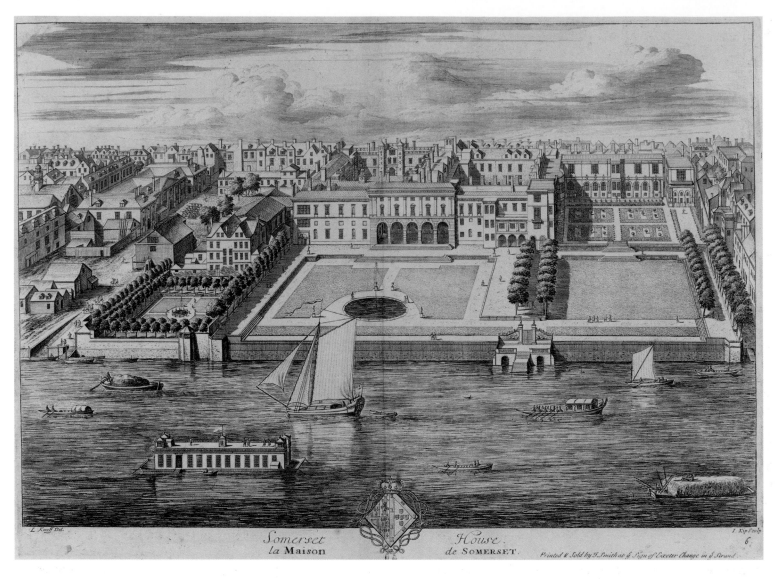

Somerset House.
la Maison   de SOMERSET.

and houses had forecourts and gatehouses specifically designed for carriages and the newer ones had no formal access to the river.

The proliferation of coaches led to a drastic improvement in the road network round London: for twenty to thirty miles outside the capital the roads were now excellent. A coachman might make twelve miles an hour on a good stretch but a more realistic average was six. The effects of the coach on the environs of London were huge: it was now possible to go out to Richmond or Greenwich for dinner by road and return the same evening. More importantly it allowed aristocrats to go to Highgate or Wimbledon, villages far from the river. Thus the invention of the coach liberated the aristocracy, the gentry and the richer merchants from reliance on the river. Houses could now be built across the Thames basin and not only on the riverbanks. In fact by the 1630s most aristocrats lived in the suburbs rather than the city. Some of their houses were on the river, but many were not. For the houses that remained on the river there were some significant changes. In this context it is worth comparing the royal houses of Somerset House and Hampton Court.

Edward Seymour, Earl of Hertford and later Duke of Somerset, was one of the courtiers of Henry VIII who, after the Reformation, acquired former Church property on the Strand. On the site of Chester Inn and Worcester Inn (the former residence of the Bishops of Carlisle) he constructed a fine residence for himself which was not completed before his fall from power. Although Somerset House fell into royal hands after Seymour's death, the house only really became an important royal palace in the reign of James I when it was Anne of Denmark's official residence (fig. 4).

There is no doubt that it was Anne who transformed Somerset House into one of the great buildings of seventeenth-century England: great architecturally, but also important as a cultural centre and as one of the pivots upon which royal London turned. Reconstruction works started in 1609 and continued for nearly five years. Ultimately the cost of completing and furnishing Somerset House was well over £45,000, making it the single most important royal domestic architectural work of the early Stuart period. In comparison, Inigo Jones's Banqueting House at Whitehall cost £15,000.

Fig.4 *Somerset House*, by Leonard
Knyff, engraved by Jan Kip, *c*. 1720.
National Maritime Museum, PAH2184.

Fig.5 (overleaf) *Graenwich*,
by Wenceslaus Hollar, printed by
Peter Stent, London, *c*.1642.
National Maritime Museum, PAJ2421.

Early in the reconstruction, the mason-turned-architect Robert Smythson visited what was by then generally regarded as the most exciting architectural commission of the age. Smythson seems to have had access to the plans as well as to the site itself. The product of his visit was a careful survey of the building and its site. This includes details of the gardens that adjoined the Thames. It shows two embarkation points: one simply labelled 'stayrs' and the other 'Quenes staires'. The stairs led into the gardens and to a raised terrace that presumably doubled as a flood embankment on the riverside. The Queen's stairs were Anne's privy entrance to the palace. From the riverside a 190-feet-long covered walkway led to the corner of the Queen's gallery, which contained private stairs leading up to Anne's innermost lodgings. Significantly, Smythson took the trouble to show the stairs inside the palace on his survey, thus emphasising the key royal route from the river to the Queen's lodging.

Wenceslaus Hollar's bird's-eye view of the west central district of London shows Somerset House as it was in around 1660. Since Queen Anne's time there had been some changes, but the essentials were the same. Clearly labelled are both the public and private wharfs and stairs. The public had access to the river immediately to the east and west of the royal palace. On the west there was a right of way through Somerset Yard, which was the palace's service yard but, by the 1660s, it contained stables and coach houses as well as the traditional stores and kitchens. Here Somerset Wharf was available for freight. Next to it were Somerset Stairs for passenger traffic. To the west was Strand Bridge, another passenger terminal reached by a narrow alley from the Strand. Between the two were the privy stairs for Somerset House. But it is fairly clear that even in the 1660s English Queens wanted a usable and architecturally pretentious water gate at their house.

The history of Hampton Court shows how things changed. The palace there was begun in the fifteenth century but was hugely extended by Cardinal Wolsey. On Wolsey's fall it became a royal palace and was extended to become Henry VIII's principal country residence. In 1536, the King began the construction of a structure known as the Water Gallery at the south end of his gardens next to the river. This remarkable building was part landing stage, part barge house and part pleasure pavilion. It allowed the royal barge to moor under cover and Henry to disembark in privacy and comfort. From this river terminal a network of covered galleries delivered him to his private lodgings. Throughout the early Stuart period and into the Restoration, the gallery retained its function as the principal point of arrival for those travelling by water.

However, by the reign of Charles II, the normal means of transport from central London was by carriage and the Water Gallery was used for ceremonial occasions only. The arrival of Catherine of Braganza in 1662 illustrates just how much things had changed. The new Queen arrived at Hampton Court from Windsor in a vast carriage procession that swept in through the west gatehouse into the inner court where she alighted. Catherine and Charles remained at Hampton Court while Whitehall was made ready for them and the welcome ceremonies prepared. The plan was to arrive at Whitehall by river and in readiness for this the Tudor Water Gallery had been modernised and redecorated. A gilded wrought-iron balcony ten-feet wide and five-feet deep had been inserted in the window above the landing stage, and the great room which opened on to it was refurbished. On the day appointed for the royal party's entry to London, the riverbanks were crowded with soldiers and spectators as the King and Queen, the Duke and Duchess of York, Prince Rupert, his brother Prince Edward and the Countess of Suffolk, together with hundreds of household officials and courtiers, embarked for Whitehall. A huge and magnificent flotilla sailed with the tide from Hampton Court and arrived at the Whitehall privy stairs in utmost splendour.

It was therefore right at the start of Charles II's reign that the river's primary function for the monarchy finally shifted from the practical business of everyday transport to monarchical ceremony. The Countess D'Aulnoy records an excursion from Whitehall to Hampton Court to honour the Prince of Neuburg in 1675:

> Barges were waiting, dressed with flags both striped and embroidered, & hung with brocaded tapestries of rose colour & silver, their decks spread with Persian carpets, with a gold ground. When all the court had taken its place an advance was made up the grand river Thames ... The air resounded with agreeable symphonies.

On reaching Hampton Court the party disembarked and the entertainment began.[1]

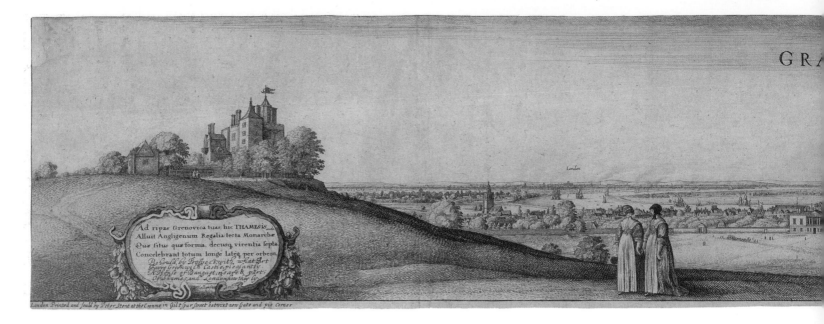

The coronation of James II in 1685 set the seal on the river being a ceremonial rather than a functional aspect of Whitehall Palace. His coronation was minutely documented at his own request by the herald Francis Sanford, who included large-scale plates of the feast and popular celebrations afterwards. James II saw his accession to the throne as a translation from a naval to a regal Crown: exchanging the position of Lord High Admiral for King. Thus the river had special connotations and the procession of barges and the firework display centred on Whitehall were important elements. The old Tudor privy stairs were an inadequate centrepiece for such magnificent occasions, and as the great painting of the Lord Mayor's river procession shows, spectators could not easily or safely witness processions from them. So it was James II's coronation that contributed in part to a radical refashioning of Whitehall's riverside to accommodate its enhanced ceremonial role. In 1691, orders were given for a new terrace to be built in front of the Queen's new privy lodgings at Whitehall. This was to be a garden 285-feet long and 70-feet deep built against the old Tudor waterfront jutting into the Thames. Elegant curving steps and a central privy landing stage provided ceremonial access to the river for Queen Mary.

It is this terrace that was to form the backdrop to river festivities such as the magnificent firework display of 1713 to celebrate the so-called general peace ushered in by the Treaty of Utrecht. Even after Whitehall was burnt by fire in 1698, and the monarchy moved its official seat to St James's, the terrace was used by the aristocratic tenants for fireworks and other riverside entertainments.

It was Whitehall that, until its destruction, retained this ceremonial function. At Hampton Court there was a different story. As William III modernised and rebuilt Hampton Court in the 1690s, the Water Gallery was first converted into a private pleasure pavilion for Queen Mary and was then demolished after her death and replaced by a garden. At this point William filled in the Tudor moat at the west front and a large turnaround (or sweep) was constructed for the use of coaches. This was essentially a cobbled circle protected by stone bollards in front of the gatehouse that allowed coaches to turn easily. Henceforth, everyone arrived by road and, when the Court was in residence, the west front was clogged by hackney coaches waiting for a fare from courtiers attending Privy Council meetings. In 1701, coaches were provided at state expense for the Lords of the Treasury when they met at the palace: an early example of an official chauffeur-driven service for politicians. A turnaround was a new invention probably imported from Holland, where there had been one at William's house of Honselaersdijk since the 1660s; its introduction at Hampton Court finally modernised access to the palace, setting the seal on the dominance of the carriage.

The history of Whitehall and Hampton Court shows that by the reign of William III both the functional and the architectural relationship between the river and royal palaces had changed forever. However, this leaves the question of Greenwich (fig.5). Between 1512 and about 1530, Greenwich was the most important royal residence in England. The residential parts of Westminster Palace had burned down in 1512 and Henry VIII settled on Greenwich, with its extensive recreational facilities, as his principal seat. Greenwich was thus the location for the great set-pieces of Henrician diplomacy. It was at Greenwich in August 1518 that Henry VIII received the two papal legates, Cardinals Campeggio and Wolsey, standing in the great hall surrounded by most of the prelates and barons of the realm. It was at Greenwich, too, in May 1527, that the reception of the French ambassadors took place following the signing of the Treaty of Perpetual Peace in Westminster.

In the Tudor period it is hard to deduce a rigid mechanism for the welcoming and reception of ambassadors. On arrival,

diplomats were normally greeted by a Gentlemen Pensioner at a convenient location to the east of London, often at Gravesend. From this point the ambassador would be escorted in a cavalcade into the City of London and on to Whitehall. James I, however, brought a new formality and organisation to diplomatic activity. He needed to. He had three children – Henry, Elizabeth and Charles – upon whose marriage prospects rested the future of the Stuart dynasty and that of the country as a whole. That future would have to be secured through diplomacy. James I created the post of Master of Ceremonies, responsible for all aspects of diplomatic ceremonial, following the practice of most Continental monarchies. The post was inaugurated at Greenwich on 21 May 1603 with a stipend of £200 a year, making it one of the highest rewarded court posts. The creation of a new court post was only one consideration: James also needed to recalibrate his royal residences to give each a specific and distinct role in diplomatic protocol.

While Whitehall was to remain the ultimate theatre for diplomatic ceremonial, Greenwich's role was reserved for the welcome ceremonies. During James's reign a formalised sequence of three welcomes was devised for the most prestigious diplomats. The first would be at Gravesend, where the Master of Ceremonies presented a welcome to the visiting diplomat. This done, the ambassador would remain at Gravesend while the Master of Ceremonies returned to Court to determine who was the most appropriate peer to present the second, more formal welcome in the King's name and to arrange barges and coaches to convey the embassy. For the most important ambassadors, the second welcome would take place at Greenwich Palace before the ambassador transferred to the King's barge. For others this speech might be made on Tower Wharf before they transferred to a cavalcade of carriages surrounded by courtiers and City aldermen. After this, all ambassadors had their first reception at Whitehall.

Thus, in February 1633, the King of Poland's extraordinary ambassador, the twenty-year-old Janush Radzivil, son of the Duke of Birze, arrived at Gravesend where he was received by Sir John Finet, the Master of Ceremonies. The following day Radzivil was conveyed to Greenwich where he was met by Robert Rich, the second Earl of Warwick (attended by his son); the Scottish peer, Thomas Hamilton, Lord Binning and Byres; William, Lord Paget and seventeen gentlemen of the Privy Chamber. These dignitaries accompanied Radzivil in the King's barge to Whitehall.

Why Greenwich was chosen as the place for these receptions is obvious. Its position on the river to the east of London made it the natural place for important visitors to transfer to the royal barge and its flotilla of small boats to travel to the Tower. At the same time, the opportunity was taken to deliver a series of welcome speeches and ceremonies. The first important Jacobean usage of Greenwich was for the reception of Christian IV of Denmark in 1606. On this unusual occasion, James I and Prince Henry were waiting in the royal barge at Gravesend for the Danish King. They were rowed together to Greenwich, where Christian was reunited with his sister, Anne.

This very specific usage explains the attempts after the Restoration to rebuild Greenwich as a palace designed to facilitate diplomatic ceremonial. Charles II commissioned John Webb to design an architectural scheme that related to the river in such a way as to form an auditorium for diplomatic entries. But this project, incomplete apart from the King Charles block, was the last time an English royal palace was designed to relate specifically to the Thames. That it was appropriated as a seamen's hospital is most fitting and today the buildings of Greenwich fossilise the otherwise lost relationship between architecture, ceremony and water that lay at the heart of royal and aristocratic life for so long.

BETWEEN COUNTRY, COURT AND CITY: ART, THE THAMES AND THE TIDES OF ROYAL POWER

SARAH MONKS

On 29 May 1533, Anne Boleyn was carried by boat from Greenwich to the Tower of London just before her Westminster coronation as Queen Consort to Henry VIII. As described by an early historian, it was a spectacle orchestrated 'by all the crafts of [the City of] London' and led by the Lord Mayor's barge 'adorned by flags and pennons hung with rich tapestries, and ornamented on the outside with scutcheons of metal, suspended on cloth of gold and silver'. Ahead of this travelled a gunboat on which 'a dragon pranced about furiously, twisting its tail and belching out wildfire', while to the left of the Mayor's barge another boat carried a large *tableau vivant* bearing Boleyn's arms: 'an artificial mountain, having on its summit a wheel of gold, whereon was perched a white falcon crowned and surrounded by garlands of white and red roses ... and on the mountain sat virgins who sang and played sweetly'.[1]

Clearly, the presentation and framing of royal ceremony within the City called for extravagant works of design, material expenditure and craftsmanship, especially on the Thames, whose open expanse allowed public spectacle to receive a more elaborately choreographed form and a greater audience than within the capital's narrow streets. Before painting and independent sculpture became established as the proper focus for artistic ambition in England, it is towards these pageants that we should look for the forms of art's relationship to the Thames. There were increasingly elaborate processions on the Thames for the marriages of Henry VIII and Anne of Cleves in 1540, of James I's daughter Elizabeth and Prince Frederick in 1613, and of Charles I and Henrietta Maria in 1625. Here, art's role, as manifest in the pageant, was to dramatise the symbolic resonance of these marriages. The dramatic restatement of unity between the neighbouring cities of London and Westminster was undoubtedly one of the most potent. Clearly, the City of London's representatives were prepared to expend substantial amounts of money, material, skill and labour on their displays. Thus, while we should understand these as rhetorical expressions of overt loyalty and obligation, we should also take them seriously as investments from which some return was expected by their many and varied participants. For such displays – with their banners, gowns and gilded barges – made a spectacle of the City's mercantile power, giving it dazzling visible form in a way that highlighted the extraordinary financial, material and artisanal resources to which this alternative, and often competing, metropolitan power base had access. Advertising the quality of stock and skills possessed by merchants and their guilds, the lavish ceremonies arranged and ornamented by these men demonstrated Londoners' allegiance to, and necessity within, royal spectacle. In effect, that spectacle – and, as Charles I's reign would establish, the material conditions of royalty itself – depended upon City commerce, profits and largesse for its proper manifestation. 'The Lord Mayor's water-procession on the Thames' (c.1683) [see cat.no.47] presents us with a riverscape filled with City barges and attendant vessels, the whole a testament to the wealth and rich regalia upon which London's merchants could draw to display their own power and permanence before the Crown, signified by the buildings of Whitehall seen beyond. Whether in the wedding processions noted above, the Lord Mayor's annual voyage to pledge allegiance to the Crown at Westminster, royal funerals and coronations, or the associated ceremonial entries of both monarchs and foreign dignitaries staged until the mid-eighteenth century, the ties between Court and City – and hence between Crown and subjects – were dramatised in exuberant form. Running like a silver thread between them was the Thames, London's major thoroughfare, upon which many of these spectacles took place as, at once, their support and their conduit.

Another version of the Thames ran alongside this imagery of state pageant within sixteenth- and seventeenth-century English culture. Staged beyond the river's urban reaches (most often upriver, beyond the tidal effects of the sea), this other Thames formed a telling counterpart to the spectacle of business presented on City waters, and was created through river poetry where it set the scene for a vision of courtly leisure and pastoral myth. In John Leland's *Cygnea cantio* (1545) – an early example of the form dedicated to his patron Henry VIII – swans serve as surrogate spectators of the Thames along which they glide from Oxford to Greenwich, the sights they see prompting reveries upon the river's historical associations.[2] In this poem and those that followed – in particular, 'De Connubio Tamae et Isis' in William Camden's *Britannia* (1586), William Vallans's *A Tale of Two Swannes* (1591) and Edmund Spenser's *Prothalamion* (1596) – the Thames doubles as a symbol of both natural harmony and natural force, integrating subsidiary rivers as it runs smoothly but with increasing strength along its winding course. As such, the Thames offered its early poets metaphors of natural (that is, easy) confluence with, and submission to, a beautiful and irrepressible power, metaphors which were appropriate to the celebration of both courtly marriage and Tudor rule.[3] The reassuringly constant qualities of the river before Teddington – where it turns tidal – served as both soothing preface to, and telling contrast with, the expansive force of the Thames at London, whose glittering banks could be described as the culminating glory of the natural landscape, or the site of its urban corruption. And while swans' attentiveness to beauty and vaunted immortality had long made them figures for poetry, their regal bearing, brilliant hue, and seemingly faithful coupling also made them appropriate symbols for Tudor royalty.[4] River poets such as Michael Drayton turned the placid and sylvan qualities of the upstream Thames into the home of swan-like nymphs and a mirror for, and tribute to, an Elizabethan regime for which comparable qualities could therefore be claimed, justifying the courtly use of these reaches as sites of leisure and rural retirement:

> O thou fayre silver Thames: O cleerest chrystall flood,
> *Beta* alone the Phenix is, of all thy watery brood,
> The Queene of Virgins onely she:
> And thou the Queene of floods shalt be …
> Range all thy swannes, faire Thames together on a ranke,
> And place them duely one by one, upon thy stately banke …
> Goe passe on Thames and hie thee fast unto the Ocean sea,
> And let thy billowes there proclaime thy *Betas* holy-day.[5]

Crowned with both ships and swans, the Thames itself became a monarch among rivers in sixteenth- and early-seventeenth-century English poetry, its various associations with power prompting picture poems of extraordinarily rich allusion:[6]

> But now this mighty Flood, upon his voyage prest
> (That found how, with his strength, his beauties still increas'd
> From where brave Windsor stood in tiptoe to behold
> The fair and goodly Thames, so far as ere he could,
> With kingly houses crowned, of more than earthly pride,
> Upon his either banks, as he along doth glide)
> With wonderful delight, doth his long course pursue …
> Then Westminster the next great Thames doth entertain:
> That vaunts her palace large, and her most sumptuous fane:
> The **land's** tribunal seat, that challengeth for hers,

> The crowning of our kings, their famous sepulchres …
> And on by London leads, which like a crescent lies,
> Whose windows seem to mock the star-befreckled skies:
> Besides her rising spires so thick themselves that show
> As do the bristling reeds within his banks that grow:
> There sees his crowded wharfs, and people-pestered shores,
> His bosom over-spread with shoals of labouring oars:
> With that most costly [London] bridge, that doth him most renown,
> With which he clearly puts all other rivers down.[7]

The Thames is here personified by Drayton as a presiding river god in whose wake London has become a bustling city to rival Rome in power and splendour; in such poetry, as in its classical precedents, rivers 'doe the earth enrich and beautifie'. Poets – notably Spenser in *The Faerie Queene* (1596) – drew upon those precedents to imagine Father Thames himself, 'fresh and jolly' in a robe embroidered with waves 'glittering like Christall glas', and attended by the gods and nymphs of all the oceans, rivers and streams at his marriage to the Medway. The regal status of Spenser's Thames is underlined not only by the crown of London's towers upon his head, and the subsidiary Thames Valley rivers who serve as his pages, but also by the respect paid to him as 'their principall' by all the major rivers of Britain.[8]

Yet, despite such poetry and the evocative images it conjures, the Thames was rarely depicted in English art before the late seventeenth century. An anonymous diptych at St Faith's Church in Gaywood, Norfolk, shows both the discovery of the Gunpowder Plot in 1605 and the arrival of Elizabeth at Tilbury in 1588. In it, the Thames's estuarine waters appear as the necessary feature with which to locate the Queen's decisive appearance among her subjects, yet those waters quickly and abruptly open out to the much broader seascape on which the Spanish Armada is shown being defeated. We might take its abbreviated treatment in English painting of this period to suggest that the Thames was an ambiguous element within the native landscape, for artists and their patrons. Neither land nor sea, a conduit to other places and momentary and poetic states, the river's flowing form may have been difficult to equate with the imagery of stability and fixity that characterised English painting during this period. But without pictorial conventions and contexts for its closer depiction, the riverscape remained beyond the scope of English painting. Our thoughts and perceptions are necessarily shaped by the languages we speak, and find expression as meaningful

Fig.6 George III with the River Thames, bronze, by John Bacon the Elder at Somerset House.

Conway Library, A2/234.

statements only through the shared grammar and vocabulary we have at our command. The visual arts are no exception. A compelling imagery of the Thames may have been offered by Elizabethan poetry and state pageant alike but, without the means and the requirement for that imagery's translation into pictorial forms, artists cannot be expected to have produced it.

Only with the arrival of artists and images from elsewhere – in particular from the Netherlands and Venice, where artistic forms for the meaningful visual depiction of riverscapes and waterside cities had already been developed – were the resources available for the Thames's emergence as a significant element within painting.

An extraordinary if indirect instance of this river's integration into art is Orazio Gentileschi's 'The Finding of Moses' (*c.*1630–32), one of four history paintings commissioned from the artist and his daughter Artemisia by Charles I following their arrival in England from Italy. This painting celebrates the birth of the King's first son, and was hung in the great hall of the Queen's House, Greenwich. There, the outstretched arms (and, in one case, intense gaze) of the two standing figures to the right, a more prominent feature of the composition than their narrative role demands, emphasises their significance. What they gesture towards is not the English riverscape that appears as the distant backdrop to the finding of Moses (a fanciful variation perhaps on the view towards Greenwich from the opposite bank). Instead, those figures seem to point to the Thames itself, running beyond a window adjacent to the painting's intended location. Gentileschi's painting therefore drew comparisons between its biblical subject matter – the salvation of a child destined to lead his people to safety – and the contemporary setting of a kingdom whose reigning dynasty had been secured with the birth of a male heir.[9]

In this painting, the Thames is referred to as both the site and the authenticating guarantee of the Stuart dynasty's flowing lineage. Fifty years later, the river would again be

called on to support – and perhaps to redirect – that lineage in Caius Gabriel Cibber's statue of Charles II (1681), which originally stood on a high pedestal with personifications of 'the four principal Rivers of England' (the Thames, Humber, Severn and Tyne) in Soho Square, where the statue alone remains.[10] Named King's Square by its developers (a brewer and a bricklayer), this was one of several simultaneous property developments in London's West End, all of which were residential squares built speculatively with an élite clientele in mind. Competing developers needed to set an exclusive tone for their squares if they were to attract significant residents and rents. Publicly associating one's square with the most prestigious individual in the land was evidently a means by which that character might be articulated, even if, as in this case, the elegant townhouses themselves were of increasingly shoddy build. Hence this former scrap of pasture, leased out by Charles II, gained both its regal name and its regal statue (the first to be placed in a London square) as well as the titled residents who made it one of the most fashionable addresses in late-seventeenth-century London.[11] The square's central focus was Cibber's large and ambitious sculptural group. It consisted of a fountain where each of the four rivers was illustrated by figures (the Thames as 'an Old Man and a Young Virgin') around which fish and urns poured water into a pool below.[12] Any resemblance to Gianlorenzo Bernini's spectacular Four Rivers Fountain (1648–51) in the Piazza Navona – the grandest square in Rome, a city where Cibber had studied for several years around 1650 – was surely intentional. Yet the differences between them are telling: Bernini's river gods represent the four corners of the world beneath an obelisk, and the whole piece is symbolic of the Roman Catholic Church's global ambitions. Cibber's rivers were all English and reclined beneath a king in contemporary armour whose right hand originally clutched a baton of command with some determination. Charles II's unusual depiction here is significant given the fierce contemporary criticism of his readiness to forge peaceful alliances with Catholic France. At least twelve of the square's titled residents were parliamentary opponents of the King's pro-Catholic, pro-French tendencies, the arbitrary character of his rule, and his openly Catholic heir, the Duke of York. These residents were also supporters and associates of the man whom many people believed should have been Charles II's successor: his illegitimate son, the Protestant Duke of Monmouth, a military commander of considerable renown whose mansion in King's Square was begun in the same year as Cibber's fountain. Perhaps Cibber's statue depicts both the King *and* the pretender to his throne (an apparent lookalike), the former shown as the belligerent figure many wanted him to be, the latter in regal guise for those who cared to discover him there. Certainly, by surrounding this figure with allegorical representations of English rivers, Cibber's fountain suggested that the King's proper interests and heavenly mandate lay within the four compass points of Protestant England rather than Catholic France, a nation which seemed to threaten the natural bounty and unity of England symbolised by the water pouring from the rivers' urns. As one of Cibber's inscriptions had it, 'Famously, the Thames is supplied with goods from around the world, but even more famously, the Thames cares for its Charles.'[13]

In King's Square, the King was framed by his own realm, rather than vice versa, in a monument that proposes a more interdependent relationship between monarch and kingdom – represented by its rivers – than Charles II was prepared to admit. By 1789, when John Bacon the Elder's sculpture, 'George III with the River Thames' was installed in the courtyard of Somerset House, the close bonds between Crown and state had long been established as the basis of the British constitution (fig.6). Recently completed and situated by the Thames, the new Somerset House was the purpose-built headquarters for Britain's naval, tax and cultural bureaucracy, and hence the location from which much of George III's rule over his dominions and imperial territories was administered. Bacon's large bronze sculpture served as the fitting centrepiece to this complex, since it shows the King with his hand on the Roman tiller symbolic of state leadership, while the prow of a Roman vessel and the British lion beside him symbolise the state's powers and its strength. Below reclines the figure of Father Thames with an urn and the cornucopia or horn of plenty for which Bacon had, like Cibber, drawn on river personifications in Roman sculpture both ancient and (in Bernini) modern. As a whole, Bacon's sculpture suggests that George III, his governments and his forces will direct London's constantly flowing and bountiful energy with the intelligent

poise suggested by the King's pose and classical toga, as well as the smooth virtuoso surfaces of Bacon's bronze. Yet the distance between King and Thames remains as striking as it was to Bacon's contemporaries. While the river god points downwards in a gesture which highlights 'the putredinous pool of stagnant rain water' – the mere 'effluvium' of the 'swinish democracy of the realm' – that originally lay beneath them both, the figure of George III appears to be concerned only with 'the exits and entrances of the clerks and watchmen [of Somerset House], as if he kept a day-book to check their time'. For this satirist, the King appeared 'bronzed' to what really threatened him: the force of democratic and republican sentiment which seemed increasingly to be shared by members of Britain's lower classes, in the aftermath of the French Revolution.[14] A work commissioned by the Treasury at considerable public expense and intended to promote confidence in the success with which national and imperial affairs were being conducted, Bacon's sculpture could also seem to refer all too clearly to the realities of its contemporary context. For 'bronzed' means 'unfeeling', a reference perhaps to George III's psychological state following the public revelation of his mental illness in 1788. Softly posed and improbably youthful, Bacon's statue of the King seems lost in a fantasy land of ships and lions, made gothic by the dynamism and grotesqueness ('so frightful a figure' in the words of Queen Charlotte) of Father Thames below.[15]

The tension found in Bacon's sculpture between the high and the low, and between élite visions and grotesque realities, also characterised the pictorial representation of the urban Thames as that developed during the eighteenth century. As the British art world expanded in the seventeenth century, so did the market for its output. London-based artists increasingly found and created a speculative demand for views of recognisable urban landscapes with which buyers were most likely to identify and with which they might easily live. The Thames riverscape was an ideal subject in this regard, especially since many of these artists' potential customers could be expected to have gained their income from the commercial and political activities on its banks. Following his arrival in London, the Dutch landscape painter Hendrick Danckerts worked for royal command and royal servants alike, producing images such as 'Greenwich from the Park showing

the Queen's House' (*c.*1670) for both sets of patrons (fig.7). Whether this painting was intended for Charles II or, as is traditionally believed, the clerk to the Navy Board, Samuel Pepys, its vision of a distant city viewed across a winding Thames dotted with passing shipping would long be repeated in British paintings and prints as testament to that vision's appeal to the broad range of the picture-buying public. See, for example, J.M.W. Turner's 'London from Greenwich Park' (1809). In such paintings, the Thames is to be appreciated as a conduit for the trade and power of London, seen both in its entirety and at a cultural and geographical remove thanks to the elevated viewpoint offered by the bucolic and royal confines of Greenwich Park.[16]

The opposition hinted at here between the clean white architecture and healthy verdant surroundings of Greenwich, and the dark menacing sprawl of London is a materialised version of that between the rural and the urban Thames proposed in English poetry. Such an imagery is itself to be distinguished from the topographical depiction of the city's riverscape, which began to appear in the wake of popular map-printing projects. Samuel and Nathaniel Buck's *A Long View of London* (1749) therefore explores the pictorial possibilities contained within maps such as John Ogilby and William Morgan's enormous *London &c. Actually Survey'd* (1682). Consisting of five printed sheets that combine to make up a detailed panoramic survey of the city as seen from the south

bank of the Thames, the Bucks' view pays little heed to the riverscape's moral or social meanings. No building or detail seems to have been too humble for inclusion by the Bucks, whose greater concern for topographical accuracy over the social or historical importance of particular structures was such that they were prepared to advertise the mundane site from which the views had been taken: one Mr Scheve's sugar warehouse. Such an apparent regard for objective observation would, however, be given significant cultural meaning in the hands of Canaletto, who had arrived from Venice in 1746 and would spend the next nine years working in Britain. He was an able and noted practitioner of *vedute* painting, a Venetian pictorial tradition in which elevated yet detailed perspectives of that city were provided for the many élite tourists who, visiting for the first and often only time, formed a ready market for visual mementos. These men understood that the point of Venice was, however, not only its varied and historical cityscape but also the internal harmony with which 'La Serenissima' had been led by its large yet close-knit body of aristocrats, who made up its republican government. And while Canaletto's scrupulous gaze gave expression to the freedoms with which mercantile wealth had been allowed to flourish there – each palazzo marked by its owner's concern for individual distinction in ways that Canaletto's *camera obscura* technique was able to record – his soft palette, large skyscapes and regard for detail suggest an overarching social harmony. At once busy and calm, Venice appears in Canaletto's imagery to be a city in which liberty and community have been reconciled as rich and poor residents alike go about their business alone, in small groups or in corporate splendour beneath the same golden skies and upon the same body of water: the Grand Canal.

Canaletto's imagery had great significance for his British patrons, as the extent of their investment in his work makes clear. These individuals were often members of an aristocracy that shaped itself around ideals of élite communal government and its harmonious social effects. Under their patronage, this republican vision (in the classical, Italianate sense rather than the modern revolutionary one) of the well-run state was translated by Canaletto into forms of the Thames in images such as 'The Thames from Somerset House towards Westminster' (fig.8). Produced for his great patron Joseph Smith, the British Consul in Venice, this painting depicts the river as a surface for free traffic, juxtaposing ceremonial and commercial barges, which are much closer to us and hence appear larger. Furthermore, that traffic also consists of the free social and visual interaction between people of separate rank, such as the foreground incident in which a London waterman looks across or perhaps swears (his profession being notorious for foul language and egalitarian sentiment) at the well-dressed individual who steers a little too confidently and self-consciously across his path, in his own boat. The two are clearly distinguished by dress and attitude but otherwise share the same pictorial space, waters and air in a landscape of simultaneous contrasts and serenity. Open, free and regulated only by mutuality, the river in Canaletto's work represents a particular ideal of what public street life might be like in modern London. The liberty found there spills over into, and from, the city itself, where a washerwoman might share a pavement with a fashionable lady and where a mechanical tower used to draw drinking water (its obelisk-like form carefully delineated towards the right-hand side) might exceed in stature the monuments of Church, Crown and state seen beyond. The sole determining factor here is the imagined viewpoint of the artist himself, not the power structures on to which he seems to look, in an imagery which downplays – and therefore makes unproblematic and 'natural' – the presence

and effect of those structures within the lives of the city's inhabitants. In turn, the city is presented to us as an object for aesthetic appreciation, its inhabitants shown gazing and conversing upon both the riverscape and that recent marvel of engineering, Westminster Bridge. Otherwise, the signs of the commercial and industrial modernity which underpinned this wealthy city are consigned to beyond the frame, together with its unpleasant effects upon the architecture, lives and waters of the Thames. Power is subsumed and softened by art in Canaletto's work, and downriver and upriver values are reconciled in a world of subtle spectacle that is at once sublime and beautiful.

As 'Westminster Bridge with the Lord Mayor's procession' (1747) [see cat.no.48] indicates, Canaletto found much of the riverscape's sublimity and beauty in the signs of its material improvement. Cutting a swathe across both the Thames and Canaletto's canvas, the new Westminster Bridge appears lit by brilliant sunshine, which allows us to see both the cleanness of its stone forms (prematurely completed by the artist) and the sheer size of its arches, whose breadth and depth are further demonstrated by the three City barges shown turning within them. Beyond, the ancient roofline of Westminster and the gilded extravagance of the foreground barge appear above and below the bridge respectively: they represent the public government and private finance that, together, made this feat of engineering possible. Only obliquely, if at all, do we see evidence of royal power, which Canaletto's Whig patrons believed should act as a silent partner in this vision of communal power and its material benefits.

By the late eighteenth century, the increasingly polluted and noxious state of Thames water meant that this vision, so central to modernity, became hard to maintain. Just as Britain's monarchs were increasingly and popularly understood to be individuals with personalities and personal problems rather than transcendent state figureheads, so the Thames became less a surface for spectacle than a body with many undesirable properties.[17]

Nineteenth-century artistic attempts to celebrate the Thames's appearance as a site of royal and civic pageantry seem often to have struggled with the river itself. John Constable's 'The Opening of Waterloo Bridge, Whitehall Stairs, June 18th 1817' (1832) is a case in point. Like Canaletto's

painting of Westminster Bridge, Constable's image celebrates the construction of a new river crossing. Unlike Canaletto's painting, Constable's image presents the bridge at a considerable remove and off to the right-hand side, where the Mayor of London's barge is also relegated. There, innumerable smoking chimneys contrast with the leafy surroundings and classically inspired forms of the élite residences seen on the opposite bank, where the painting's central motif is located. This is the embarkation of the Prince Regent and his military retinue at Whitehall Stairs prior to the official opening of the bridge. Constable therefore established a clear pictorial opposition between disorderly urban industry to the right and the flourishing forms of natural order to the left, the latter a site of royal event and loyal celebration. What he seems to have been less clear about, judging by the painting's convoluted thirteen-year-long gestation, is the proper viewpoint – and with that, the proximity to the Thames – from which this scene should be surveyed, finally introducing a foreground parapet which situates the viewer in a garden rather than on or above the river. In the many versions and sketches Constable produced along the way, the foreground river is itself often drawn or painted with thick clotted marks and in dark colours, creating an effect to contrast with the white tones and languid strokes of the distant waters.[18]

In William Holman Hunt's 'The Sea-King's Peaceful Triumph on London Bridge, 10th of March, 1863 (London Bridge on the night of the marriage of the Prince and Princess of Wales)' (1863) [see cat.no.225], those waters became even more occluded and contrasted in their treatment: a glimpse of cool blue at distant left; a slice of boiling red to our lower right. Half-Hogarth and half-Valhalla, Hunt's painting focuses on the spectacle of street celebrations marking the Prince of Wales's marriage to a Danish princess ('the sea-king's daughter' in Tennyson's words).[19] Those celebrations take place on a bridge that appears, not as a subject in its own right, but as a vehicle for their theatrical pageantry, for their undirected social form, and for Hunt's capacity to forge metaphors of cross-cultural unification out of a river crossing. Yet the bridge's ghostly, mist-shrouded character is significant because Hunt's painting seems haunted by the imagery with which London's sewers, water mains and river embankments were then being depicted, as massive engineering projects finally set about sanitising the Thames.[20] More spectral still are the pictorial traditions it leaves behind (Canaletto in particular) and the absences at its heart: a royal presence and the thread of a river. As the bearded figure peering into the scene from the right-hand edge suggests, and the wide-eyed rapture of a young woman towards its left seems to demonstrate, the crowd has become its own flowing and unstoppable spectacle.

STAGING THE RIVER

JULIE SANDERS

The river danced in the early modern period. Sometimes it quite literally danced or performed, as when the Thames was festooned for royal, ceremonial or civic pageantry. With flags, ensigns and bunting dressing the scene, the river performed the role of stage, its waters crowded with ceremonial barges and specially decorated small ships, or pinnaces, crowded with participating nobles and dignitaries, musicians and performers or simply waterborne spectators of the festivities. The firing of ordnance or the constant release of fireworks as part of the spectacle heightened the intensity of the moment by adding a potent soundscape. The river danced in a more stylised sense during the frequent court masques at the early Stuart courts. In these theatrical events, noblemen and women adopted roles as real rivers, their costumes artfully designed to suggest the watery element through headpieces fashioned from coral and shell, and shimmering taffeta embroidered to capture the effects of light on water.

In 1610, Princess Elizabeth (fig.9), the only daughter of James I and Anne of Denmark, played the part of the River Thames in Samuel Daniel's court masque *Tethys' Festival*, which was staged at Whitehall Palace. Tethys is Queen of the Ocean, wife of Neptune, and in this respect we can see how the overall iconography and symbolism of this masque appealed to the fondness of James and Anne for depicting themselves in political speeches and events as joint rulers of the oceans. In the masque, Tethys leads thirteen nymphs representing the various rivers of the three kingdoms of England, Scotland and Ireland over which the royal couple had dominion.

Tethys' Festival is a striking instance of physical geography made real, as well-known rivers including the Trent, the Derwent, the Severn and the Lea were made manifest through dance, costume and the actual body of the performer. But the masque also constituted an embodiment of more cultural, and indeed political, understandings of regional geography as each of the courtly ladies who took their place as one of the river nymphs performed a river 'appropriate either to their dignity, signories, or places of birth'.[1] Lady Arbella Stuart played the main river of her East Midlands domains, the Trent; the Countess of Arundel performed the Arun, a river that runs close by Arundel Castle; the Countess of Essex, fittingly enough, played the Lea; and it was the royal princess herself, Elizabeth, who played the chief river, the 'stately' Thames.[2]

We might deduce that this early experience of courtly masques for the young Stuart princess inspired in her a very special relationship with the capital's river, since the Thames would become a chief focus of the celebrations staged in 1613 to mark her marriage to Frederick V, the Elector Palatine. The celebrations for that particular royal wedding included Frederick's formal arrival at and entrance into Whitehall as the finale of a water-based procession along the Thames and the staging of a mock sea-battle, or *naumachia*, between the English and the Turks. The river-based section of the festivities was then repeated and refracted in the themes and motifs of masques and entertainments commissioned for evening performances at Whitehall, including Francis Beaumont's *Masque of Truth*, which had at its heart the dramatic conceit of a union between personifications of the Rivers Thames and Rhine. This nuptial strand of imagery spoke volumes about the hopes of a European dynasty that were invested in the young couple: ultimately it was an ill-fated match, as Frederick's assumption of the Crown in Bohemia would plunge Europe into military crisis and force his eventual exile from that country to the Netherlands, with Elizabeth in tow. This imagery also mobilised the still-potent memory of Elizabeth's brother, Prince Henry, heir to James I's throne who had died the previous year. The river in these events proved to be a vehicle, both literal and metaphorical, for staging the nation's sense of self and this idea was regularly re-enacted in numerous waterborne greetings staged on behalf of visiting foreign ambassadors.

A linking of river space with royal ceremonial in the early seventeenth century was, of course, not a novel thing and was founded on a firm base of precedents, practices and traditions. Anne Boleyn's coronation in 1533 had, for example, included entertainments on the Thames, featuring a 'foyst garnished with banners and streamers'.[3] Nearly a century later those same traditions were visible in the celebrations held to commemorate the marriage of Charles I, newly ascended to the throne in 1625, and his French bride. *A True Discourse of all the Royal Passages, Triumphs and Ceremonies observed at the contract and marriage of the High and Mighty Charles, King of Great Britaine and the most excellentest of Ladies, the Lady Henrietta Maria of Bourbon*, a descriptive pamphlet published that same year, gives detailed accounts of a procession by

Fig.9 Princess Elizabeth, aged seven,
oil on canvas, by Robert Peake, 1603.
National Maritime Museum, BHC4237.

water: how the royal couple embarked upon a barge to take them to the City and how gun salutes accompanied their journey up the Thames. One contemporary participant, Dr Meddus, paints a vivid picture in personal correspondence of the scene, from the impressive number of boats and wherries visible on the Thames, down to the detail of the symbolic colour of the outfits worn by the King and the Queen, and the particular weather events that day:

> The last night, at five o'clock, (there being a very great shower) the king and queen, in the royal barge, with many other barges of honour, and thousands of boats, passed through London bridge to Whitehall; infinite numbers, besides those in wherries, standing in houses, ships, lighters, western barges; and on each side of the shore, fifty good ships discharging their ordnance, as their majesties passed along by, as last of all, the Tower did … the king and queen were both in green suits. The barge windows, not withstanding the vehement shower, were open.[4]

In the case of these royal wedding celebrations, nobility gathered on bridges and wharfs as the audience for a quasi-theatrical performance; so many gathered there in fact that accidents ensued. The aforementioned pamphlet, *A True Discourse*, notes that: 'The throng of spectatours was so great, that about two hundred being in a shippe that lay almost drie, and leaning against the Wharfe, they with their waight / and motion ouerthrew the shippe into the Thames'.[5] Dr Meddus confirms that occurrence when the postscript to his letter reveals that he was on the very boat that went down: 'Our ship, whereupon stood above a hundred people, not being balanced nor well tied to the shore, and they standing all upon one side, was overturned and sunk – all that were upon her tumbling into the Thames, yet was not any lost that I can hear of.'[6]

In 1662, the marriage of Charles II to Catherine of Braganza was celebrated by the City of London with water processions, full-scale entertainments and pageant barges hosted by the guild companies that were a deliberate restoration of these earlier practices following the hiatus of the English Civil War and the Commonwealth. The print version of this particular event, John Tatham's *Aqua Triumphalis* (fig.10), describes not only the appearance of the most impressive of the ceremonial barges but also the 'drolls' performed by actors pretending to be watermen and mariners at various staging points along the Thames. Tatham himself wrote central speeches of praise addressed to the monarchs as they progressed from Putney to the private water stairs of Whitehall Palace, and which were delivered by personified rivers, including Isis and the Thames.

As well as the river performing a role as chief actor in these formalised royal ceremonies, it is worth noting that many of the main royal residences at this time were themselves Thameside palaces, from Whitehall to Denmark House (later Somerset House) on the Strand to the Queen's House at Greenwich. *Aqua Triumphalis* draws attention to this fact when Father Thames is accompanied by water nymphs whose headwear represents the palaces of Greenwich and Windsor respectively.[7] Unsurprisingly these households regularly staged their own relationship to the river both through their self-conscious architecture and the theatre events they hosted. In 1592, for example, Greenwich had been the site of a performance of John Lyly's *Gallathea*, a play deeply invested in riverine themes, including the threat of flood, which was a regular experience for Londoners at this time. There is an intriguing connection to be made, then, between these sites and spaces and those of the commercial theatres on the Bankside, such as the Globe, where Shakespeare staged so many of his plays, and where the sound of the Thames just outside the theatre walls was a permanent sensory presence for spectators and performers alike. The practices of theatre and river were deeply interwoven in the first half of the seventeenth century.

While not royal events *per se*, the annual Lord Mayor's 'shows' were clearly crucial complements and counterparts to the monarchy's more infrequent engagement with the river as a performative space. The overlap of the rituals attached to the mayoral procession – with its journey to Westminster by decorated barge with various escort ships in tow and the use of fireworks, ordnance and music to create aural and visual effects – with the waterborne royal progresses are self-evident. Prominent playwrights of the day, such as Thomas Dekker, John Webster and Thomas Heywood, collaborated directly with skilled craftspeople and 'artificers' to create additional scripted 'shows'. These theatrical set-pieces were self-aware combinations of land-based and water-based scenes, often performed at pageant stations.

The artificers worked for several weeks leading up to these events to create often large-scale, theatrical props such as classical sea-horses drawing full-size chariots, pageant ships or alternative vessels that enabled lavish sea-fights to be staged or, indeed, enabling a 'paper whale' to sail upriver spouting fireworks. This particular instance of the 'whale' was presumably a papier-mâché creation. The playwright James Shirley alludes to this kind of waterborne prop as a common occurrence in the river sections of mayoral shows in his *A Contention for Honour and Riches* in 1633, when a country gentleman called Clod mocks the pretensions of a London merchant:

> the next day after Simon and Jude [the shows took place on 29 October, the day after the feast of St Simon and St Jude]; when you goe a feasting to Westminster with your Gallyfoist and your pot-guns, to the very terror of the Paper-whales, when you land in sholes, and make the understanders in Cheapside, wonder to see the ships swimme upon men's shoulders.[8]

The latter reference is to the fact that the boats and ships that appeared in these civic entertainments were not limited to the river-based section of the performance; several of the smaller pageant ships were, according to extant records, wheeled or carried in by several men to the banqueting halls where some of the later ceremonial took place. This is an example of the ways in which the 'work' cultural and actual – of the river permeated London spaces other than the Thameside edges from which spectators (including Shirley's Cheapside 'understanders', a somewhat sarcastic allusion to the capacity of popular audiences to comprehend the full import of these highly symbolic and allegorical performances) witnessed events such as these. It flowed into the halls and palaces of élite culture and into mainstream commercial theatres, not least through acts of quotation, allusion and literal re-stagings.

If the ceremonial life of the Thames circulated in the everyday culture of the city, not least in terms of the printed texts which regularly offered detailed narrative descriptions of these 'shows' and comparable royal events, it was nevertheless punctuated at every turn by the working life of the river. For the Thames *was* a working river: a trade river on whose waters could be witnessed, on a daily basis, the theatre of commerce, as cargo ships arrived and departed laden with goods or with the spoils of the global activities of exploration. In this way, the river was constantly being connected to the offstage space of the sea and through that action to the wider world in which London is self-consciously attempting to position itself at this time as the financial and political centre. The aforementioned paper whales performed a similar function of making meaning, by bringing into the central zone – that is to say the area of the river and therefore of the city past the significant entry point of London Bridge – objects suggestive of worlds elsewhere, not least the working townships of Spitsbergen and the Arctic North, where the whaling industry was developing at a rapid pace in the early decades of the seventeenth century. London Bridge was a low-slung portal; for that reason, only smaller pageant ships like the barges or the 'galley foist', a diminutive version of a fully rigged sailing ship, could gain access. Appearances in this central zone of the Thames were therefore automatically understood as symbolic and performative, from paper whales to pageant ships alike.

The artificers who fashioned the material props for these river theatricals were employed by particular livery companies, such as the Drapers, the Ironmongers or the Fishmongers. The content of the shows tended to reflect their commissioning context, with work for the Fishmongers, for example, being particularly engaged with topical questions of fishing rights and piracy. There were other ways, however, in which these shows also embodied the daily life of the Thames, connecting the particular calendar days of high ceremonial with the more quotidian activities of the City's inhabitants and its visitors. The staged 'scene' of multiple boats on the river that could be viewed by audiences for royal processions and Lord Mayor's shows were not so far from the everyday appearance of a busy river like the Thames, when there would have been dozens of ships, boats and wherries performing the business of the City and of global trade. Along with them were all the waterside activities of the loading and unloading of commodities and the sounds of the watermen plying for trade to taxi people around. A particularly popular fare was from the Blackfriars wharf across to the Bankside to watch plays at the Globe and other playhouses. The livery companies, which frequently hired these same watermen to row the pinnaces and barges used for the Lord Mayor's shows, provide another connecting fibre between the everyday and the ceremonial.

One particularly prominent family of artificers, Gerard Christmas and his sons John and Mathias, connect most tangibly the working life of the River Thames with its dramatic and ceremonial personae. In 1614, Gerard was appointed carver to the Navy with responsibility for the decoration of ships. This was an important role in an era when maritime policy was at the heart of any monarch's sense of national identity. The decorous appearance of ships was a key political statement of strength and intention. Simultaneous to his work on the great warships of the English Navy at this time, Christmas also worked on designing and building sets and props for the Lord Mayor's pageant; by 1621, he was in charge of the whole operation. This joint identity, naval and theatrical, was continued by his sons throughout the 1630s and culminated in their work on one particular ship, the *Sovereign of the Seas*, that was intended to be the jewel in the crown of Charles I's revived and regenerated Navy. A brief account of the life of this ship is a fine indicator of the blurred lines between shipbuilding regimes and theatre in this period. It also allows us to register another, often neglected, part of the Thames, its dockyards at Blackwall, Woolwich and Deptford (where the Christmas family was based), and to discover yet another way in which theatre, and theatre of a distinctly royal nature, took place on the river in the early seventeenth century.

The building of the *Sovereign of the Seas* in the 1630s was overseen by Phineas Pett at Charles I's behest following a visit to Woolwich in 1634 to witness work on another warship, the *Leopard*. Even in this royal visit to witness shipbuilding we can begin to identify intriguing confluences between this skilled manual craft and the idea of performance. This is underscored by the fact that Charles also commissioned Pett to build a scale model of the *Sovereign*, which he regularly displayed to visiting ambassadors at Hampton Court. Throughout the mid-1630s the construction of the ship was a subject of much excitement and even the topic of pointed allusions in a play by Richard Brome in 1635, *The Sparagus Garden*, where a china-shop owner dreams of going to see the 'new ship'.[9] What is significant about a female citizen aspiring to tour a warship in dock is the clue it gives us to royal engagement with the space and site of the docklands. Rebecca Brittleware – for that is the rather apt name of Brome's character – is aspiring to behave like the Queen. Henrietta Maria, like her husband, frequently

Fig. 10 John Tatham, *Aqua Triumphalis...*, published by T. Childe and L. Parry, London, 1662.

British Library (see page 55/cat. no. 20).

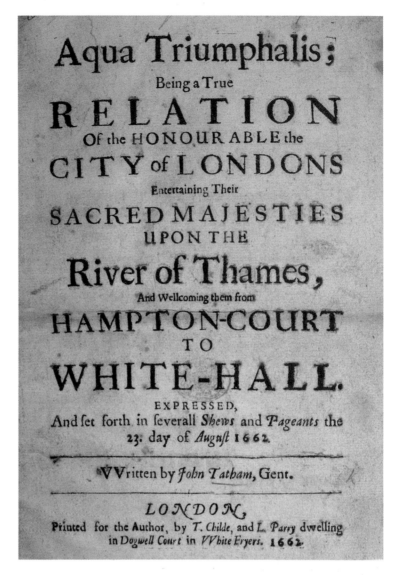

inspected new ships both during construction and prior to launch. In the case of the *Sovereign* there is a surviving pamphlet written by the playwright Thomas Heywood, who worked with the Christmases to produce the mottoes and emblems that adorned the interior of the ship in the same way that he collaborated with them to produce a series of Lord Mayor's shows during this same decade.[10] The pamphlet serves as a veritable guidebook to the ship's meanings and might well have been used on just such a royal tour.

The theatricality of ships has long been understood by those familiar with maritime culture. Shakespeare's *The Tempest* opens on the deck of a ship in the eye of a vicious storm and we have records of actual shipboard theatrical performances by English mariners at this time. In 1607, for example, *Hamlet* was performed on the *Red Dragon*, an East India Company ship that was then anchored off the coast of Sierra Leone. But what is less often recorded in these observations is how the Thameside docks themselves served as sites of theatre, an alternative Bankside and site of royal ritual. This reading is supported by surviving fragments from an early-seventeenth-century entertainment that were uncovered in papers in the National Library of Wales by Peter Beal. The manuscript contains three songs attributed to one 'Townshend', possibly Aurelian Townshend, a masque writer for the Caroline court in the 1630s. It is the content of the masque that is hinted at in these songs which is intriguing for our context. The first song, possibly conforming to the traditions of a comical antimasque, is performed by a 'rabble' of mariners. At the very least, this suggests a Thames-related theme. Critics have deduced from the song that, after a 'disorderly dance' by the mariners, a ship or 'barke' is blown to shore laden with a precious cargo, the contents of which are listed (and possibly directly represented in the masque) and include gold, diamonds, raw silk and sugar, all familiar items and objects from the trading life of the Thames.[11] As a result of this concentration on trade goods, some interpreters have suggested that this piece of theatre was staged at the behest of the Merchant Adventurers' Company but Karen Britland has recently argued that the songs may be a partial trace of an entertainment staged at Blackwall on yet another ship, the *Neptune*, for Henrietta Maria in 1627. On 13 March 1627 we know that the Queen dined at Blackwall aboard the ship,

which belonged to the Earl of Warwick, who had just been granted a commission to attack the Spanish fleet at sea. Britland speculates that this was exactly the kind of event at which a short entertainment might have been staged, not least for someone strongly associated with the patronage and performance of plays.

Even if the specific connection with the mariners' song and dance must remain hypothetical, in the public and publicised nature of the Queen's banquet on board the *Neptune*, a visible endorsement of Warwick's commission, we can still acknowledge another resonant example of the River Thames acting as the host to royal theatricals. This further serves to confirm the potency of the idea of the river as a vehicle for early modern theatricals, from the open barge of royal wedding ceremonials to the galley foists and pageant ships of Lord Mayor's Day; from the dancing rivers and mariners of Stuart masque culture to the real labour and material landscapes of the working river. In all of these examples and many more, the River Thames performed cultural and actual work, engaging with the practical and the spectacular aspects of river life in a powerful and enduring combination.

TUDOR POWER ON THE THAMES

I

Seating plan for the royal banquet, Greenwich

7 July 1517
Ink on paper, 385 × 265 mm
College of Arms, MS M8 fol. 65v

Tournaments were colourful and noisy affairs that attracted great crowds, but in the evenings a small and select company of nobles and ambassadors would attend the night's entertainment. At the joust held at Greenwich on 7 July 1517, the King entered the lists and was awarded the honours of the day jointly with the Duke of Suffolk. The seating plan for the King's table at the banquet held that evening has survived. It shows that seated at the top, from left to right, were Cardinal Wolsey, Queen Katherine, Henry VIII, the King's sister Mary, and the Imperial ambassador. Along the sides sat the French ambassador and members of the nobility. In the centre of the hall was a stage on which boys provided musical entertainment during the meal. 'Great was the sumptuousness of the repast, and the profusion of plate', wrote the Venetian ambassador. The food came sculpted as animals or castles, and was served on golden dishes. The guests remained at the table for seven hours and then danced till dawn. [SD]

LITERATURE: Starkey (ed.), *Henry VIII*, p. 46.

The Tudor monarchs owned several palaces on the Thames, which they transformed into impressive, fashionable structures that displayed the dynasty's power and prestige. Greenwich Palace came to be their favourite out-of-town residence, because it was close to their administrative centre at Westminster yet sufficiently far away from the smells and diseases of London. It was also conveniently sited on the southern bank of the Thames with good access to the Dover road.

Henry VII first turned the modest building at Greenwich into a grand palace and altered its riverside appearance by covering the frontage with a facing of red brick. Later, Henry VIII, who based himself at Greenwich for twenty years after a devastating fire had destroyed the Palace of Westminster in 1512, built facilities there for hunting, pleasure and feats of arms; his buildings included a tiltyard in the grounds, new stables, forges and a banqueting hall. Even after his new palace at Whitehall was built, Henry spent much time at Greenwich, holding great jousts in the newly built tiltyard in front of ambassadors, courtiers and other guests. To forge armour for such occasions, a Royal Armoury was established at Greenwich and manned by 'Almains', craftsmen from the Low Countries and northern Germany.

Another symbol of Tudor royal power on the river was the Navy. From the mid-fifteenth century, the Navy began to grow in size and required facilities on shore to build, maintain, supply and repair ships. The reign of Henry VIII saw these shore establishments placed on a permanent footing, with the dockyards at Woolwich (1512) and Deptford (1513) becoming two of the largest. They were placed on the south bank of the Thames, near the palace at Greenwich, where it was easy to get the materials to furnish the warships and craftsmen to build them. Woolwich dockyard was chosen as the site to build Henry's largest warship, the *Henry Grace à Dieu*, popularly known as the 'Great Harry', which was launched in 1514. Deptford dockyard had become the Navy's principal yard by the end of Henry VIII's reign. A navy was a magnificent symbol of royal power and Henry commissioned the construction of forty-six heavy ships, all ornately decorated and built high for dramatic effect. [SD]

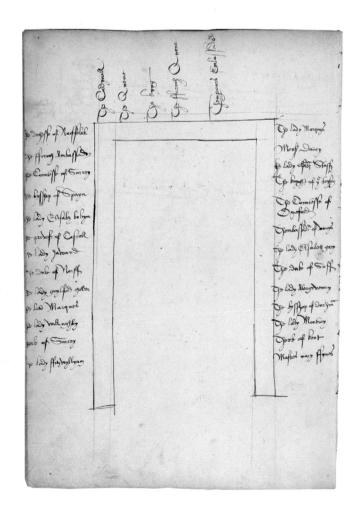

2

Tournament score cheque, Greenwich

19–20 May 1516
Ink on paper, 437 × 307 mm

College of Arms, Tournament cheque 1c

In 1515 Henry uprooted some orchards behind Greenwich Palace to lay down his first permanent tiltyard. It contained two five-storey viewing towers, a spectators' gallery, a display area for armour and a disguising house (a theatre for pageants). Jousting was a very popular sport in early Tudor England and provided splendid occasions for impressing foreign ambassadors and visitors. This score card illustrates the system of scoring for tilts. In a tilt, individual contestants charged towards each other on horseback along either side of a barrier and had to break a lance on an opponent or dismount him. The column on the left lists the names of the 'challengers' (here led by the King and the Duke of Suffolk); that on the right lists the 'defenders'. Next to each name is a rectangular box in which is marked the outcome of each joust. A stroke on the upper line records a strike to the head of an opponent, on the lower to the body; if the mark bisects the line, the lance has been successfully broken. The number of strokes on the line to the right of each box records the number of runs each jouster made. [SD]

LITERATURE: Starkey (ed.), *Henry VIII*, p.46; Rimer, Richardson and Cooper (eds), *Henry VIII*, p.139.

3

The 'Anthony Roll'

1546
ANTHONY ANTHONY (d. 1563)
Ink and colour on vellum, 5080 × 711 mm
British Library, Add. MS 22047

This roll was one of three compiled by Anthony Anthony, a clerk in the Ordnance Office. Together they provide a pictorial record of Henry VIII's Navy at the end of his life. The illustrations and details of the fifty-eight ships are interspersed with a list of their seamen and armaments. This picture is from the second roll showing galleasses: large, fast, heavily armed three-masted ships. At 450 tons, the *Anne Gallante* was the heaviest galleass in Henry's Navy and carried 250 men. It is likely that the roll was designed for display rather than to provide a simple inventory. [SD]

LITERATURE: Knighton and Loades, *Anthony Roll*, *passim*.

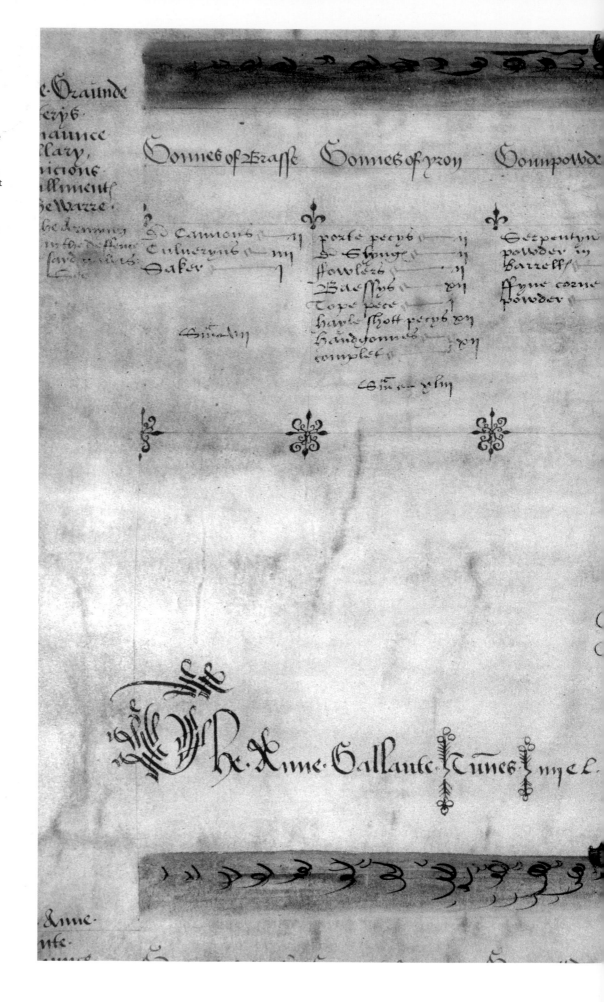

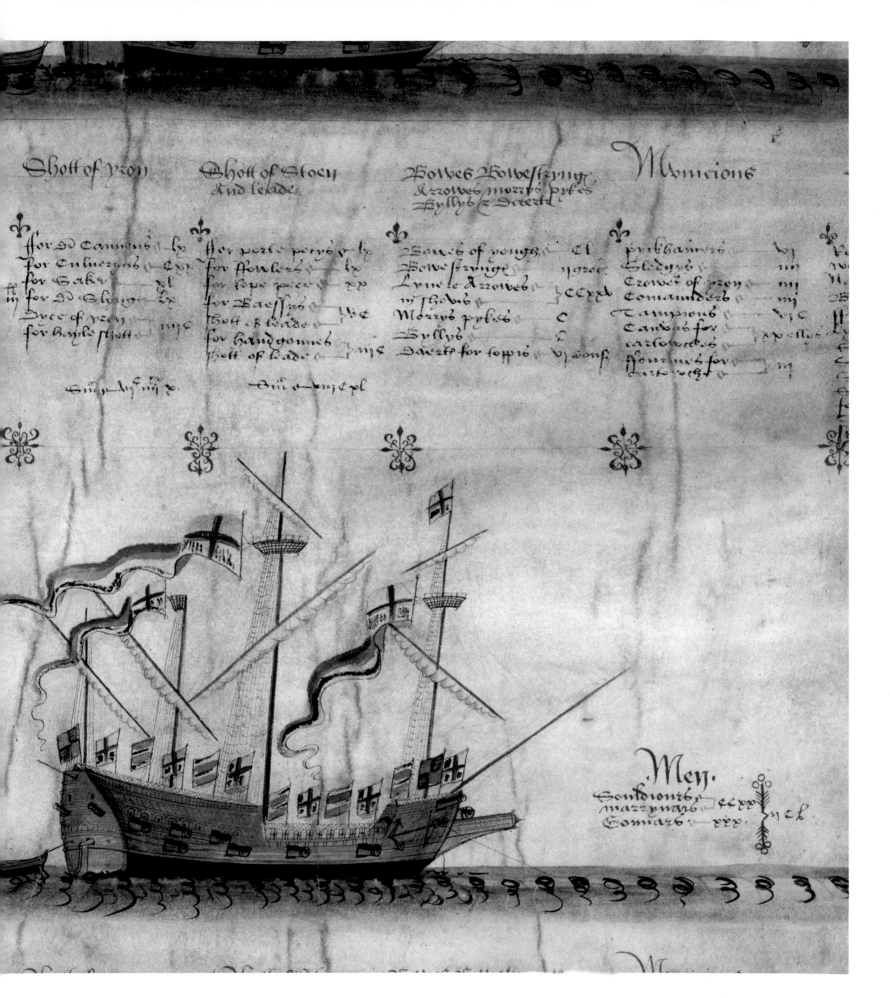

ANNE BOLEYN'S CORONATION, 1533

4
Medallion of Anne Boleyn

1534
Lead, 39 mm (diameter)

British Museum, M.9010

The one firm contemporary likeness of
Anne is this portrait medal of 1534.
Around the edge is the inscription: 'The
Moost Happi. Anno 1534' and on the left
is 'A.R.' standing for *Anna Regina*.
Although the nose is badly damaged,
Anne's long oval face and high cheek
bones are evident. The medal may have
been struck to commemorate Anne's
coronation, but some historians believe
that the occasion was the anticipated
birth of Anne's second child in the autumn
of 1534. Anne's miscarriage would explain
why multiple copies have not survived.
[SD]

LITERATURE: Ives, *Anne Boleyn*, pp.41–42.

During the Tudor period, royal processions on the Thames were quite
frequent, displaying the dynasty's power both to the onlookers who
lined the riverbanks and to readers of the pamphlets that described the
magnificent spectacles. One such procession was devised when Henry
VIII's second wife Anne Boleyn was crowned Queen of England on
Whitsunday, 1 June 1533 at Westminster Abbey. Three days before the
coronation, Anne was conveyed by river from Greenwich to the
Tower in a grand river procession. At the Tower, she was met by
the King who performed coronation rituals, including the creation
of eighteen Knights of the Bath, and after a short stay in the Tower
Anne embarked on a second procession – this time by road – to
Westminster, while Henry went by barge to York Place at
Whitehall.

Both coronation processions were designed to encourage and
demonstrate popular support for the King's new marriage. In the
eyes of many, Henry was still the husband of Katherine of Aragon,
even though their union had been declared invalid earlier in May by
Thomas Cranmer, the newly appointed Archbishop of Canterbury.
Queen Katherine, Pope Clement VII, and many others in England and
abroad did not recognise the annulment or Henry's marriage to Anne.
The King was therefore determined that his court and the City of London
would show great honour to the new Queen in a public arena.

At the time of the coronation Anne was visibly pregnant and on 7 September
she gave birth to a daughter, Elizabeth, at Greenwich Palace. No son followed, and
after a miscarriage in early 1536 the King began to have doubts about the validity of
this marriage too. On 2 May, Anne was arrested and charged with treason, adultery
and incest. Although she put up a good defence, the judicial decision of guilty and
sentence of execution were predetermined. Anne was beheaded at the Tower of
London on 19 May 1536. [SD]

5
Miniature of Anne Boleyn

c. 1525–27
Attributed to LUCAS HORENBOUT (d. 1544)
Watercolour on vellum and card,
42 mm (diameter)

Duke of Buccleuch and Queensberry

Born around 1500, Anne was the younger
daughter of Thomas Boleyn, Earl of
Ormond and Wiltshire, and Elizabeth, the
daughter of the second Earl of Norfolk.
After spending eight years in royal
households on the Continent, Anne
returned to England in 1521 as a
sophisticated court lady, well versed in
French manners. Despite her charm, she
did not attract the King's attention until
1526. Initially Henry hoped to make Anne
his mistress, a replacement for her sister
Mary Boleyn. However, after Anne
repeatedly rejected his advances, Henry
proposed marriage and began the process
of divorcing his wife. The two eventually
became lovers in December 1532 and were
secretly married the following January,
when Anne was already pregnant. Though
not conventionally beautiful, Anne was
said to have had dark and attractive eyes,
thick dark hair and an elegant neck. This
miniature is allegedly of Anne, but the
face shape depicted here is very different
from the likeness in the contemporary
medal (left). [SD]

LITERATURE: *Oxford DNB*; Ives, *Anne Boleyn*,
pp. 52–56; Bernard, *Anne Boleyn*, pp. 19–20, 196–200.

6
Miniature of Henry VIII

c. 1525
Attributed to LUCAS HORENBOUT
Watercolour on vellum and card,
44 mm (diameter)

Duke of Buccleuch and Queensberry

Shortly after his accession in April 1509,
Henry VIII married Katherine of Aragon,
the widow of his elder brother Arthur.
During their marriage, Katherine was
pregnant possibly seven times, but she
produced only one surviving daughter,
Mary, and by 1525 the Queen was past
child-bearing age. Henry came to believe
that their failure to produce a male heir
was a punishment from God, because he
had contravened scripture in taking to
bed his brother's one-time wife. This
conviction grew in intensity once Henry
fell in love with Anne Boleyn. However,
the Pope would not grant Henry an
annulment for fear of offending
Katherine's nephew, Emperor Charles V.
Convinced that popes could not set aside
scripture, Henry broke with Rome and in
1534 was declared Supreme Head of the
Church of England in the Act of
Supremacy. [SD]

LITERATURE: *Oxford DNB*; Wooding, *Henry VIII*,
pp. 47–51, 119–69.

7
Anne Boleyn's Book of Hours

Early sixteenth century
Flemish school
Leather, gilding, parchment, ink,
205 × 283 mm (open)

British Library, Kings MS 9, fol. 94

Books of Hours were personal prayer
books that usually contained a collection
of texts, prayers and psalms to be read at
different hours of the day in private
devotions. This is one of the three
surviving Books of Hours that belonged to
Anne Boleyn. Inside are scribbled
messages exchanged between Anne and
Henry. In his note, Henry wrote of his love
for Anne (in French) on a page depicting
the Man of Sorrows. Anne chose to write
a reply on a picture of the Annunciation,
signifying that she would be able to give
Henry the son and heir he so much
desired. Her response in doggerel English
offered the promise: 'Be daly prove you
shall me fynde/ To be to you bothe
lovynge and kynde.' [SD]

LITERATURE: Ives, *Anne Boleyn*, passim; Doran, *Man
and Monarch*, p.117; Carley, *Books of Henry VIII and
his Wives*, pp.105–06.

8
Music book written for Queen Anne

1533–35
Possibly compiled by
MARK SMEATON (c.1512–36)
Ink on paper, 285 × 190 mm

Royal College of Music, MS 1070, p.4

This music book opens with a motet,
which was probably composed for Anne's
coronation festivities, and contains
altogether thirty-nine Latin motets and
three French chansons by Franco-Flemish
composers. The manuscript is of mediocre
quality – unfinished, frequently corrected
and made from paper not vellum – and it
may have been compiled for Anne by
Mark Smeaton, a musician of the King's
Privy Chamber. On page four, an
illuminated initial shows a falcon
(Anne's badge) attacking a pomegranate
(Katherine's badge).

Three years after the coronation,
Smeaton was arrested and tortured so
that he would admit to committing
adultery with Anne. Others accused of
the same offence denied it, but Smeaton's
testimony condemned Anne and she was
executed in May 1536. He met a similar
fate. [SD]

LITERATURE: Lowinsky, 'A music book for Anne Boleyn',
pp.160–235; Ives, *Anne Boleyn*, pp.295–97.

9
Chape

c. 1533
Inscribed: '+RAF+FEL+MIGAM+'
Silver-gilt, 42 × 53 × 7 mm
Museum of London, 90.295

This sword-belt chape (a cover for the ends of belts) depicts the emblems of Henry VIII and Katherine of Aragon: a Tudor rose (on the left) and a pomegranate (on the right). In the centre is a gilded figure of St Barbara. We can see from the inscription that the chape was originally worn by Ralph Felmingham, Sergeant-at-Arms for Henry VIII, and it may have been a New Year's gift to him from the King. It was found on the Thames foreshore at Vintry and was possibly discarded around 1533, when Henry took a new bride. At that time, any sign of loyalty to Katherine became dangerous. [SD]

10
The noble tryumphaunt coronacyon of quene Anne

1533
WYNKYN DE WORDE (d. 1534/5), London
Printed paper, 188 × 139 mm (closed)
British Library, C.21.b.24

To circulate a positive description of Anne Boleyn's coronation, the London printer Wynkyn de Worde produced this pamphlet shortly after the festivities. It consisted of eleven typeset pages with a woodcut of a courtly scene on the front cover. Presumably the loving couple on the right is supposed to depict the King and Queen. The account is an official version of the event and Anne's popularity was by no means as great as was implied here. Describing the river procession of the afternoon of 29 May 1533, the author comments especially on the City Company barges 'splayed with goodly banners fresh and new' and the noise of the gunshots as Anne passed by in her 'rich barge among her nobles'. [SD]

LITERATURE: Pollard (ed.), *Tudor Tracts*, pp. 11–12.

ℭ The noble tryum-
phaunt coronacyon of quene Anne,
wyfe vnto the moost noble kynge
Henry the. viij.

Q. Anne Bullen the second wife of K. Henry 8 was
Crowned at Welfm' on Whitfonday the firft of Iune
Anno Domini. M.D.XXXIII

This Triumph is fet forth at large in Stowes Chronicle

THE PALACE OF WHITEHALL

Inigo Jones (1573–1652) was born in London, where he may have trained as a joiner. After some time in Italy, he turned to architecture in 1606 and then gained the post of Surveyor of the King's Works which he held from 1615 to 1643. He had previously spent another year in Italy with the Earl of Arundel, studying ancient and Renaissance architecture. Between 1619 and 1622, Jones built the Banqueting House, Whitehall, the setting for many of his later masques. A loyal adherent of Charles I, Jones suffered greatly in the Civil War. After his death, unmarried, the efforts of his pupil and principal heir, John Webb, ensured Jones's enduring influence on the development of classical architecture in England.

Rysbrack's original terracotta bust (now at Chatsworth House), was made about 1725 for the Earl of Burlington. The history of this version before 1948 is still untraced and whether by Rysbrack or by an early copyist remains uncertain. [PVDM]

The Palace of Whitehall was built on the river in the heart of Westminster outside the City of London. The building, originally known as York Place, had been the London residence of the Archbishop of York, but Henry VIII appropriated it after the fall of Cardinal Wolsey in 1529 and began an ambitious and expensive project to extend and improve the building. Henry aimed to make it match or surpass in magnificence the fashionable and sumptuous palaces commissioned by his great rival Francis I of France. However, during Henry's lifetime, the palace remained something of a building site and it was left for Elizabeth I to complete. Nonetheless, covering twenty-three acres, Whitehall was Henry's largest and most important palace by the end of his reign. It provided him not only with a grand setting for Court and government occasions but also facilities for recreation, including four tennis courts, a bowling alley, a cockpit and parks where he could hunt. For easy access by water, a new dock was built by the river with a barge house to provide shelter for the royal barge.

During James I's reign, the architects Inigo Jones and John Webb drew up plans for a huge new palace to be constructed at Whitehall. In fact, only the Banqueting House was built, but James I intended this to be the ceremonial centre of a new palace. Designed by Inigo Jones and completed in 1622, the Banqueting House was the first purely Renaissance building in England, impressive in its uncompromising classicism. After James's death, Charles I commissioned Peter Paul Rubens to paint a magnificent ceiling which celebrated his father's wise rule and achievements: 'The Union of the Two Crowns' (England and Scotland), 'The Peaceful Reign of James I' and 'The Apotheosis of James I'. Somewhat ironically, Charles was executed on a scaffold erected just outside the Banqueting House on 30 January 1649.

Shortly after his return from exile in 1660, Charles II gave thought to redesigning the Palace of Whitehall, but the Great Fire of London put paid to his plans; all available money and men had to be employed in the rebuilding of the City. James II, though, was determined to rebuild the palace and Christopher Wren was commissioned to design a new range of buildings that would include new apartments for the Queen, a new Council Chamber, and a new Roman Catholic chapel. Work was rapid: the chapel was used for the first time on Christmas Eve 1686 and the Queen's apartments were completed by January 1687. Despite James's initial pretensions to build an English Versailles, the architectural style was both modest and English. Nonetheless, the chapel at Whitehall was a symbol of the Roman Catholicism that many Londoners found offensive and was to be the cause of James's downfall. [SD]

12

The Whitehall Mural: Henry VII, Elizabeth of York, Henry VIII and Jane Seymour

1667
REMIGIUS VAM LEEMPUT (1607–75);
after HANS HOLBEIN THE YOUNGER (c. 1497–1543)
Oil on canvas, 889 × 992 mm

Royal Collection, RCIN 405750

For his Privy Chamber in Whitehall, Henry VIII commissioned Hans Holbein the Younger to create a mural with life-size figures of himself, his parents and his wife Jane Seymour, the mother of his only son, Prince Edward. The painting included Latin verses directing praise at the two Kings but ranking Henry VIII's achievements higher than his father's. Henry's majestic figure dominates the painting and was said to overawe spectators. In 1667 the Flemish artist Remigius vam Leemput (an assistant of Van Dyck) made a copy of the mural at the command of Charles II. The commission was opportune, as Whitehall Palace burned down in January 1698 after a laundry maid left washing to dry before an open fire. [SD]

13
Designs for the proposed new palace at Whitehall for Charles I

c. 1637–39
JOHN WEBB (1611–72)
Pencil on paper, 342 × 445 mm

Worcester College, University of Oxford, H&T 28

Webb was a pupil of Inigo Jones and was married to his master's cousin, Anne. When Charles I came to the throne in 1625, he was keen to rebuild the rambling Tudor palace at Whitehall. An initial scheme was devised by the French architect Isaac de Caus, but the King lacked the necessary funds. Charles returned to the idea in the mid-1630s and commissioned Jones to develop a massively ambitious proposal. Webb produced these designs for the river façade of a new Whitehall Palace under Jones's supervision. Again, a shortage of money and the deteriorating political situation meant the plans were shelved.

But Charles would not let go and, in 1647, when a parliamentary prisoner at Carisbrooke Castle on the Isle of Wight, he somewhat optimistically asked Jones and Webb to consider a third scheme. Ultimately this too came to nothing, halted by the King's execution. Nevertheless, Webb continued to plan, refining his ideas for the palace while working on other projects. He presented a proposal to Charles II, but it was not adopted. The King did, however, select Webb to design the new palace at Greenwich. [RB]

LITERATURE: *Oxford DNB*; Thurley, *Whitehall Palace*, pp. 65–67.

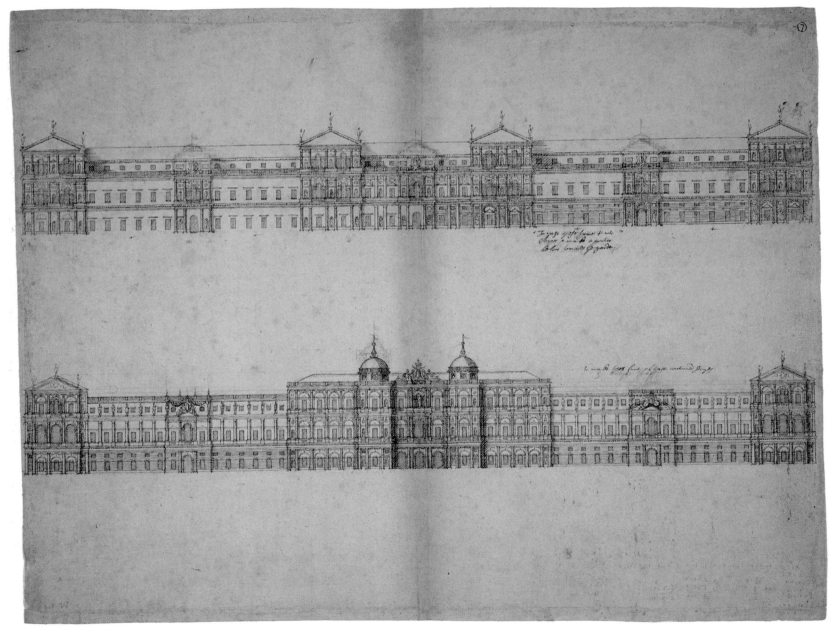

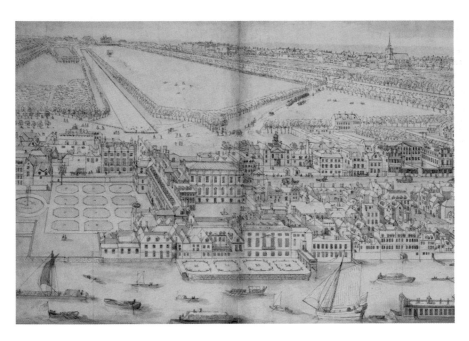

14
Aerial view of Whitehall Palace from the east

c 1695
LEONARD KNYFF (1650–1722)
Paper and ink, 560 × 800 mm

City of Westminster Archives Centre, E134.1 (024)

Leendert Knijff (known as Leonard Knyff) was born in Haarlem, the Netherlands, but frequently worked in London for extended periods, painting and drawing portraits, animal scenes and topographical subjects. This view shows Whitehall from an imagined aerial perspective. Additions to the complex had been made by Wren during the short reign of James II, including new apartments for the Queen and a Roman Catholic chapel. Following a fire in 1691, which destroyed much of the older Tudor residence, James's daughter Mary II (1662–94) made improvements to her own quarters and commissioned the terrace garden that can be seen overlooking the river. A much more serious fire on 4 January 1698 destroyed the residential part of the palace. It reignited the following day, consuming most of what remained: the Banqueting House was saved through great effort. [RB]

LITERATURE: *Oxford DNB*; Thurley, *Whitehall Palace*, pp.97–103.

15
The Apotheosis of James I

Mid-seventeenth century
Inscribed in the lower left margin:
'P.P. RUBENS PINXIT' and 'LUCAS VORSTERMAN IUN. SCULP.'
LUCAS VORSTERMAN II (1624–after 1666); after PETER PAUL RUBENS (1577–1640)
Etching, 303 × 201 mm

British Museum, 1873-0809.818

Peter Paul Rubens's celebration of the Stuart vision of kingship on the ceiling of the Banqueting House at Whitehall survives as one of the most dazzling examples of the cosmopolitan patronage of the Stuart court. The ceiling centres on the Apotheosis of James I, in a large oval (depicted in Vorsterman's etching), surrounded by the various benefits of Stuart rule, including personifications of Wise Government stamping out Rebellion, and Liberty trampling Avarice. The ceiling was commissioned by Charles I, during Rubens's brief visit to England in 1629–30, and completed in the artist's studio in Antwerp before being rolled and transported to London in boxes. The finished canvases were installed in 1636.

Rubens recognised the commercial and artistic importance of printmaking, and supervised closely the reproduction of many of his paintings, retouching proofs where necessary. Lucas Vorsterman the Elder was among the first and most prolific engravers hired by the artist. This etching was made by Vorsterman's son and pupil, Lucas the Younger, probably from an oil sketch for the central oval of the ceiling at Whitehall that remained with the artist (now in the Tate Collection). [RJ]

CATHERINE OF BRAGANZA'S *AQUA TRIUMPHALIS*, 1662

16

Porringer commemorating the marriage of Charles II and Catherine of Braganza

c. 1662
Lambeth pottery
Tin-glazed earthenware, 190 mm (diameter)
Fitzwilliam Museum, C.1427-1928

This porringer, a shallow vessel from which broth or porridge was eaten, is part of a surge in celebratory display pieces produced in the wake of the Restoration in 1660. It was probably made to commemorate the marriage of Charles II and Catherine of Braganza two years later. Referred to as a bleeding cup elsewhere, the porringer is a refined piece, often called English delftware, which was made for the wealthy middle-classes. It is decorated with painted portraits of the King and Queen with their initials 'CR' and 'KR' above. [KM]

LITERATURE: Rackham, *Catalogue of the Glaisher Collection*, nos. 207, 1427.

During the reigns of the later Stuarts – Charles II and James II – the Thames again became a stage for royal river processions and pageants. One of the most spectacular took place on 23 August 1662 when Charles presented his new wife, the Portuguese Infanta Catherine of Braganza, to Londoners in a procession along the Thames from Hampton Court to Whitehall. Known as *Aqua Triumphalis*, this show was described by John Evelyn in his diary as 'the most magnificent Triumph that certainly ever floted on the Thames'. According to Samuel Pepys some 10,000 barges and boats formed part of the procession. As the procession moved along the river to 'the sound of trumpets and other musick', it encountered pageants organised by the City livery companies, which were performed on barges anchored in the middle of the river. Being both foreign and Catholic, Catherine was regarded with suspicion in London and was a somewhat unpopular choice of Queen with many of her English contemporaries. However, the marriage settlement had been very profitable for king and country: England received an unprecedentedly large dowry of about £333,000 and the important trading posts of Tangiers in North Africa and Bombay in India. In return, England offered Portugal help in maintaining its independence from Spain. Despite her loyalty and genuine affection for Charles, Catherine's failure to provide an heir and her subsequent implication in several Catholic plots, meant the Queen never won the heart of the nation. [SD & KM]

17
Miniature of Charles II

c. 1665
SAMUEL COOPER (1609–72)
Watercolour on vellum and card, 83 × 66 mm

National Maritime Museum, Caird Collection,
MNT0188

Charles was the eldest of Charles I's three
sons, all of whom were driven into
European exile by the Civil War. Although
crowned King in Scotland in 1650
following his father's execution in 1649,
Charles's attempt to retake England from
Parliament was defeated at the Battle of
Worcester in 1651. The death in 1658 of
Oliver Cromwell as Lord Protector,
without a credible successor, led to
Charles's restoration in 1660 as King of
England, Scotland and Ireland. Cooper, a
nephew of the miniaturist John Hoskins
the Elder, became the leading practitioner
of his age. After the Restoration, Cooper
did numerous studies of Charles II,
including the King's profile used on the
new coinage, and in 1663 was appointed
King's Limner. Unlike many others by
Cooper, this miniature is not signed,
which has traditionally left an element of
doubt over his authorship, though its
quality suggests no great reason for this.
[PVDM]

18
Miniature of Catherine of Braganza

c. 1660
Attributed to DAVID DES GRANGES (c. 1611–
c. 1672); after DIRCK STOOP (c. 1610–c. 1685)
Watercolour on vellum laid on card with
a gesso back, oval, 56 × 44 mm

Royal Collection, RCIN 420101

This miniature is after a portrait by the
Dutch artist Dirck Stoop, who worked for
the royal court in Lisbon from 1659 and
accompanied Catherine of Braganza to
England in 1662. Stoop's picture was sent
to England by the Portuguese ambassador
shortly after the Restoration, when
Charles II was considering Catherine as his
Queen. On seeing the painting the King is
said to have hesitantly remarked 'that
person cannot be unhandsome'.

The miniaturist, probably David Des
Granges, an English painter of French
descent, may well have copied Stoop's
portrait while it was in the Palace of
Whitehall. Catherine is about twenty-two
years old and shown dressed in the
conservative style of the Portuguese royal
household. This was at odds with the
sumptuous and sometimes daring fashions
popular with women of the English court.
When Catherine arrived in England her
unusual dress and appearance were
mocked; her black clothes apparently
inspired the King to remark that he had
been sent a bat. Yet Catherine quickly
adopted English fashion and in a letter
to his sister, Charles later wrote, 'she hath
as much agreeableness in her looks as
I ever saw'. [KM]

LITERATURE: MacLeod and Alexander, *Painted Ladies*,
p.83; Reynolds, *Sixteenth- and Seventeenth-Century
Miniatures*, no. 101.

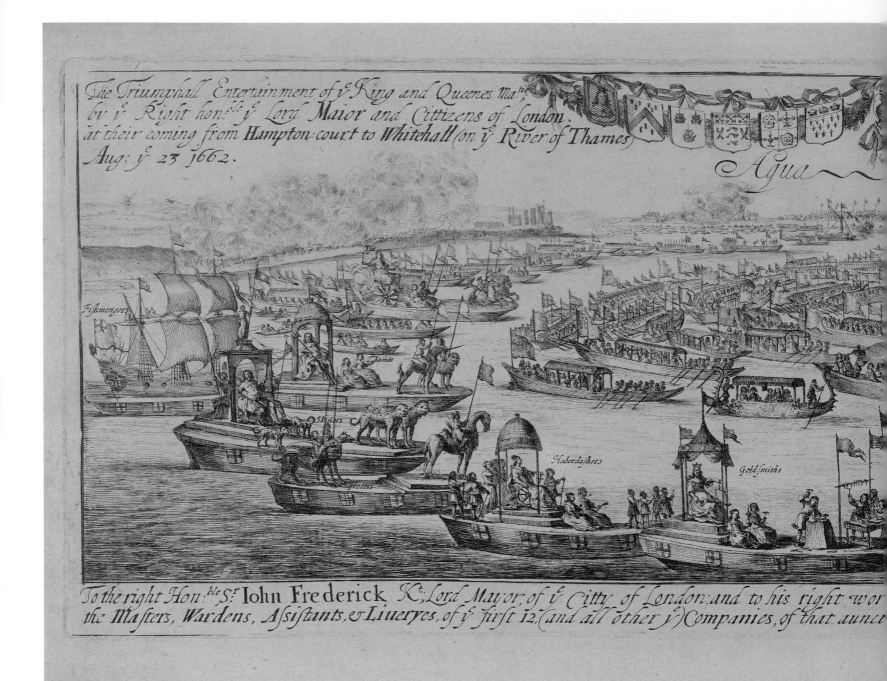

The Triumphall Entertainment of ye King and Queenes Matie; by ye Right honble ye Lord Maior and Cittizens of London, at their coming from Hampton-court to Whitehall (on ye River of Thames) Aug: ye 23 1662.

Aqua

Fishmongers
Thames
Skinners
Haberdashers
Grocers
Goldsmiths

To the right Honble Sr Iohn Frederick Kt; Lord Mayor, of ye Citty of London: and to his right wor the Masters, Wardens, Assistants, & Liueryes, of ye first 12 (and all other ye) Companies, of that aunct

19

Aqua Triumphalis

1662
DIRCK STOOP (c. 1610–c. 1685)
Etching on paper, 235 × 587 mm

National Maritime Museum, PAH4104

On 13 May 1662, Catherine arrived in Portsmouth from Lisbon on board the *Royal Charles*. She had never met the King and was unable to speak a word of English. The couple married in the town a week later in a secret Catholic ceremony followed by a public Protestant service. On 23 August 1662 they made their state entry into London, travelling by river from Hampton Court to the Palace of Whitehall in a carefully orchestrated procession. This etching is one of a series that record Catherine's journey from Portugal to England, ending with her *Aqua Triumphalis*. At the centre is 'Ye King's barge' and just ahead is the

barge of the Lord Mayor, Sir John Frederick, crowded with musicians and the aldermen and sheriffs of the City. In the foreground are the elaborately dressed pageant barges of the livery companies including, as identified by Stoop, the Mercers, Drapers, Merchant Taylors, Goldsmiths, Haberdashers, Skinners and Fishmongers. Each of these carries a figure which was the focus of the Companies' pageants. An ostentatious display of support for the new Queen, Catherine's *Aqua Triumphalis* recalled a tradition of magnificent public processions that came to prominence during the reigns of Elizabeth I and James I. [KM]

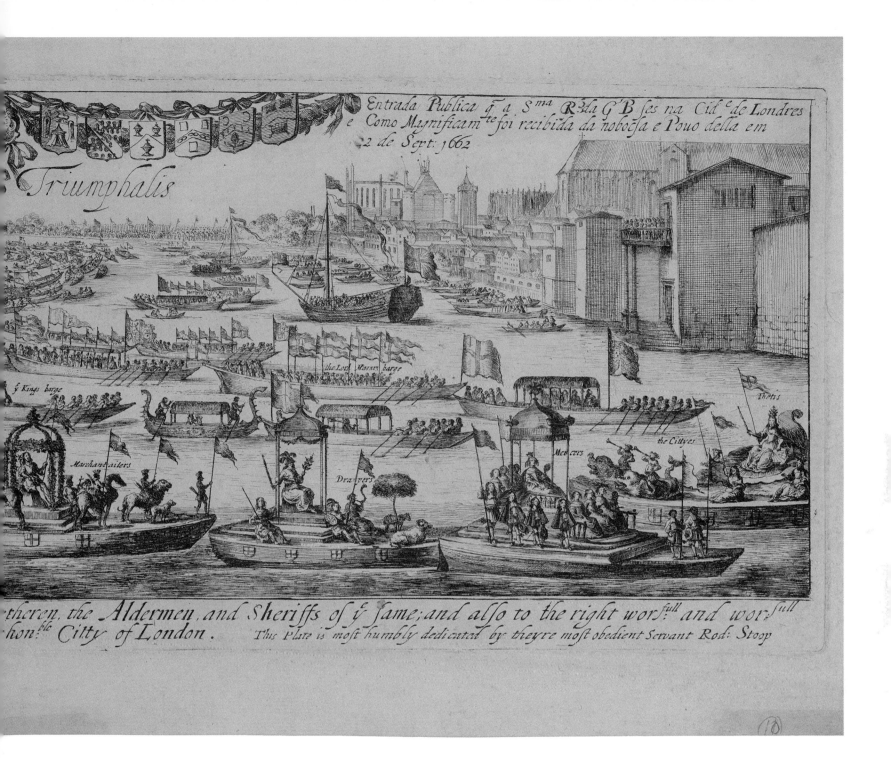

Entrada Publica q̃ a Sᵐᵃ R̃ᵈᵃ G'B̃ ſes na Cidᶜ de Londres e Como Magnificamᵗᵉ foi recibida da nobeſa e Pouo della em ²2 de Sept: 1662

Triumphalis

ſ Kings barge · Marchant tailers · the Lord Mayors barge · Drapers · Mercers · the Cittyes · Thetis

...theren, the Aldermen, and Sheriffs of ŷ ſame; and alſo to the right worſᶠᵘˡˡ and worſᶠᵘˡˡ honᵇˡᵉ Citty of London. This Plate is moſt humbly dedicated by theyre moſt obedient Servant Rod: Stoop

20 (see fig.10/page 37)

Aqua Triumphalis; Being a True Relation of the Honourable the City of Londons Entertaining Their Sacred Majesties Upon The River of Thames, And Wellcoming them from Hampton-Court To White-hall...

1662
JOHN TATHAM (fl. 1632–64), London
Printed book, 293 × 182 mm
British Library 11E i 42

Between 1657 and 1664, the poet and dramatist John Tatham produced eight annual pageants for the Lord Mayor's procession. These included a land and river procession, and all but one was entitled *London's Triumph*. A staunch royalist, Tatham also produced *London's Glory Represented by Time, Truth, and Fame*, a pageant to welcome Charles II returning from exile in 1660 and *Aqua Triumphalis*, the City's magnificent tribute to Catherine of Braganza two years later.

This pageant pamphlet is an 'order of service' for Catherine's river procession. It includes details of the three main pageants written for the King and Queen, which were performed during the procession at Chelsea, between Vauxhall and Lambeth, and at Whitehall. These publicly declared Catherine's suitability as Queen and the importance of a strong alliance between England and Portugal. Allegorical representations, including Father Thames and Isis, addressed the royal couple with dedicatory speeches and poems, while music, song and dance were performed by Thames watermen and sailors. The pamphlet also details some of the pageants performed by the principal City livery companies on barges, or 'floats', anchored along the processional route. [KM]

LITERATURE: Maidment *The Dramatic Works of John Tatham*, p.ix–xii.

IN·GOD OVR·TRVST IS·ALL

21

Decoration from the barge cloth of the Pewterers' Company

1662
Workshop of JOHN BEST (d. 1677)
Applied work in woollen cloth with embroidery in long and short and satin stitches in crewel wools on a modern ground, 1150 × 1120 mm (inner frame dimensions)
The Worshipful Company of Pewterers

The barge cloth was the most important part of a suite of textiles used to decorate royal and City barges at river processions and pageants. It was central to the display of identity and power, forming a canopy and tester on which the royal or company coat of arms was prominently displayed and against which a throne or cushion would be set.

The records of the Worshipful Company of Pewterers show that just over two weeks before the *Aqua Triumphalis* it was 'ordered and agreed upon … that 12 new [probably painted silk] Banners bee bought to adorne ye barge at ye recepc[i]on of the King and Queene by water from Hampton Court to White Hall', and it is likely that this woollen barge cloth was commissioned around the same time.

The bill for the barge cloth shows that it cost £38 18s 9d (almost £3000 today), of which the largest share, £24 (about £1840), was for John Best's exquisite embroidery of the Company's arms flanked by the date '1662'. The decoration from the Pewterers' cloth is a remarkable survivor of the Great Fire, which destroyed the original Pewterers' Hall, a later Company fire and the Blitz. [KM]

LITERATURE: Wardle, 'A Rare Survival', *passim*; Palmer, *Ceremonial Barges*, p. 76.

22

Charger commemorating the marriage of Charles II and Catherine of Braganza

1662
WILLIAM PETTIFER
Engraved pewter, 520 mm (diameter)
The Worshipful Company of Pewterers

By the seventeenth century, England led the way in the production and export of high-quality pewter. Domestic items – plates, dishes, cups and flagons – made of pewter were not uncommon even in more modest households. This large display plate or charger is engraved with 'wriggle-work' decoration, with the Royal Stuart coat of arms at the centre, the 'CR' cipher and royal motto. The Latin inscription, *Vivat Rex Carolus Secundus Beati Pacifici* ('Long Live King Charles II of Blessed Peace'), has been incised close to a broad rim of floral decoration that is also adorned with four roundels, two of which contain full-length depictions of Charles and Catherine. [KM]

THE GREAT FROST FAIR OF 1683-84

23

Great Britains Wonder: or, Londons Admiration. Being a True Representation of a Prodigious Frost…

1684
Printed by R. WALTON, London
Letterpress, 550 × 394 mm

British Library, 82.I.8 (16)

This print, showing a view from the centre of the river, depicts the Middlesex shore from Arundel House to the eastern end of the Temple. It gives a view of Essex House, with its round-headed arch, and the three groups of stairs serving it and the neighbouring buildings of Arundel House and the Temple. On the river, popular entertainments of the period, including bull-baiting and skittles, are in progress. Gallants promenade in fashionable dress, wearing wigs and carrying swords; ladies are shopping. The doggerel verse below marvels that the Thames has become both a fair and a market, attracting thousands of customers daily. [ML]

Before the demolition of the old London Bridge in 1831–32 and the construction of the embankments from the 1860s, the River Thames was broader than today and flowed more slowly. Winters were harsher in the 'Little Ice Age' from the mid-fourteenth to the nineteenth century, and the Thames occasionally froze over. Hawkers, entertainers and stallholders were always quick to exploit the phenomenon and frost fairs were held on the ice. The most famous frost fair took place from late December 1683 until 6 February 1684 when the Thames was completely frozen for nearly two months. In London the ice was eleven inches thick.

Charles II was a frequent visitor to the frost fair, and a card commemorating his visit on 31 January still exists. He, his Queen and other members of the royal family were said to have been present when an ox was roasted whole on the ice and to have eaten part of it. Hackney carriages took people over the frozen river as if on land. A double row of booths was built on the river called 'Temple Street', running from Temple Stairs across to the south bank, containing coffee houses, inns and souvenir shops. A printer called Croom made good money by charging 6d for souvenir cards printed at his press on the frozen river with the customer's name and date of purchase. On the surrounding ice there was a variety of entertainments, including music, puppet shows, ox-roasting, bear-baiting, football and even hunting when a fox was set loose for the King and companions to pursue. Thames watermen, unable to follow their usual trade, instead sold food and alcohol on the river. Many others whose work was disrupted by the hard frost just made the best of a bad job and threw their energies into enjoyment. The unusual weather conditions encouraged an atmosphere of unrestrained, Saturnalian revelry on the river but, throughout, the poor suffered miserably both from the biting cold and from the rising prices of basic provisions. As vessels carrying supplies could not pass beyond London Bridge, the freeze caused serious economic dislocation.

The diarist and lawyer Dudley Ryder was 'extremely struck' by the appearance of the frozen Thames during the frost of 1715–16:

> It is all froze over, but by the snow and tide, which has broke the ice and heaped it one upon the other, it looks the most wild and confused sight I ever saw. It looks as if there had been a violent storm and it had froze the waves, just as they were justling [sic] and beating against one another, and the billows and foam and white froth were grown stiff as they were at the height of their hurry.

The last great frost fair was in 1814 when there were swings, sliding-barges, merry-go-rounds and even donkey rides on the Thames. [ML & SD]

Great BRITAINS WONDER:
OR, LONDONS Admiration.

Being a True Representation of a Prodigious *FROST*, which began about the beginning of *Decemb.* 1683. and continued till the Fourth Day of *February* following. And held on with such violence, that Men and Beasts, Coaches and Carts, went as frequently thereon, as Boats were wont to pass before.

There was also a Street of Booths built from the *Temple* to *Southwark*, where were sold all sorts of Goods imaginable, namely, Cloaths, Plate, Earthen Ware, Meat, Drink, Brandy, Tobacco, and a Hundred sorts of other Commodities not here inserted. It being the Wonder of this present Age, and a great consternation to all the Spectators.

Arundel House.   Essex-Buildings.   The Temple.

BEhold the Wonder of this present Age,
A Famous *RIVER* now become a Stage.
Question not what I now declare to you,
The *Thames* is now both *Fair* and *Market* too,
And many Thousands dayly do resort,
There to behold the Pastime and the Sport
Early and late, used by young and old,
And valu'd not the fierceness of the Cold;
And did not think of that Almighty Hand
Who made the Waters bare, like to the Land:
Thousands and Thousands to the River flocks,
Where mighty flakes of Ice do lye like Rocks.
There may you see the *Coaches* swiftly run,
As if beneath the Ice were Waters none;
And sholes of People every where there be,
Just like to Herrings in the brackish Sea;
And there the quaking Water-men will stand ye,
Kind Master, drink you Beer, or Ale, or Brandy:
Walk in, kind Sir, this Booth it is the chief,
We'l entertain you with a slice of Beef,
And what you please to Eat or Drink, 'tis here,
No Booth, like mine, affords such dainty cheer.
Another crys, Here Master, they but scoff ye,
Here is a Dish of famous new-made Coffee.
And some do say, a giddy senseless Ass
May on the *THAMES* be furnish'd with a Lass.
But to be short, such Wonders there are seen,
That in this Age before hath never been.
Before the *Temple* there a Street is made,
And there is one almost of every Trade:
There may you also this hard Frosty Winter,
See on the Rocky Ice a Working-*PRINTER*,
Who hopes by his own Art to reap some gain,
Which he perchance does think he may obtain.
Here is also a Lottery and Musick too,
Yea, a cheating, drunken, leud, and *debauch'd crew*.
Hot Codlins, Pancakes, Duck, Goose, and Sack,
Rabit, Capon, Hen, Turkey, and a wooden Jack.

In this same Street before the *Temple* made,
There seems to be a brisk and lively Trade:
Where e'ry Booth hath such a cunning Sign,
As seldome hath been seen in former time;
The *Flying Piss-pot* is one of the same,
The *Whip* and *Egg-shell*, and the *Broom* by name:
And there if you have Money for to spend,
Each cunning Snap will seem to be your Friend.
There may you see small Vessels under Sail,
All's one to them, with or against the Gale,
And as they pass they little Guns do fire,
Which feedeth some, and puffs them with desire
To sail therein, and when their Money's gone,
'Tis right, they cry, the *Thames* to come upon.
There on a Sign you may most plainly see't,
Here's the first Tavern built in Freezeland-*street:*
There is Bull-baiting and Bear-baiting too,
That no Man living yet e're found so true;
And Foot-Ball play is there so common grown,
That on the *Thames* before was never known;
Coals being dear, are carry'd on Mens backs,
And some on Sledges there are drawn in Sacks;
Men do on Horse-back ride from shore to shore,
Which formerly in Boats were wafted o're:
Poor people hard shifts make for livelihoods,
And happy are if they can sell their Goods;
What you can buy for Three-pence on the shore,
Will cost you Four-pence on the *Thames*, or more.
Now let me come to things more strange, yet true,
And question not what I declare to you;
There Roasted was a great and well-fed Oxe,
And there, with Dogs, Hunted the cunning Fox;
Dancing o'th' Ropes, and Puppit-*plays* likewise,
The like before ne'r seen beneath the Skies;
All stand admir'd, and very well they may,
To see such pastimes, and such sorts of play.
Besides the things I nam'd to you before,
There other Toys and Baubles are great store;

There may you feast your wandring eyes enough,
There you may buy a Box to hold your Snuff;
No Fair nor Market underneath the Skies
That can afford you more Varieties;
There may you see some hundreds slide in Skeets,
And beaten paths like to the City Streets.
There were *Dutch* Whimsies turned swiftly round,
Faster then Horses run on level Ground:
The like to this I now to you do tell,
No former Age could ever parallel;
There's all that can supply most curious minds,
With such Varieties of cunning Signs,
That I do think no Man doth understand,
Such merry Fancies ne'r were on the Land;
There is such Whimsies on the Frozen Ice,
Makes some believe the *Thames* a Paradice.
And though these sights be to our admiration,
Yet our sins, our sins, do call for lamentation.
Though such unusual Frosts to us are strange,
Perhaps it may predict some greater Change;
And some do fear may a fore-runner be
Of an approaching sad Mortality:
But why should we to such belief incline?
There's none that knows but the blest pow'r *divine*
And whatso're is from *Jehovah* sent,
Poor Sinners ought therewith to be content;
If dreadful, then to fall upon the knee,
And beg remission of the DEITY:
But if beyond our thoughts he sends us store,
With all our hearts let's thankful be therefore.
Now let us all in Great *Jehovah* trust,
Who doth preserve the Righteous and the Just;
And eke conclude Sin is the cause of all
The heavy Judgements that on us do fall:
And call to mind, fond Man, thy time misspent,
Fall on thy knees, and heartily Repent,
Then will thy Saviour pitty take on thee,
And thou shalt live to all Eternity.   *Finis.*

Printed by M. Haly, *and* J. Millet, *and sold by* Robert Walton, *at the Globe on the North-side of St. Pauls-Church, near that end towards Ludgate; where you may have all sorts of Maps, Coppy-Books, and Prints, not only English, but Italian, French, and Dutch. And by* John Seller *on the West-side of the Royal-Exchange.* 1684.

59

24

Frost Fairs on the Thames, with Old London Bridge in the distance

c. 1685
English school, formerly attributed
to JAN WYCK (c. 1645–1700)
Oil on canvas, 641 × 768 mm

Yale Center for British Art, B1976.7.113

The smog-filled sky in the painting substantiates the diarist John Evelyn's description of the heavy pollution caused in London when smoke could not escape upwards through the freezing air. He complained that the air was so full of the fumes and reek of coal fires that people could hardly breathe. The painting shows the variety of transport on the frozen Thames, including numerous carriages and boats on wheels or transformed into sledges but still with sails hoisted to benefit from the wind. A 'street' of stalls and booths can be seen in the foreground, with crowds of spectators forming makeshift arenas beyond; the houses and shops of the old London Bridge are visible on the horizon. To the left, visitors step gingerly on to the ice from a water gate.
[ML]

25

Pen portrait of Charles II

1684
JOHN SEDDON (1643/4–1700), London
Engraving on paper, 289 × 207 mm

British Museum, Gg,4F.77

Charles II attended the frost fair on the Thames in late January 1684. He was accompanied by his wife, Catherine of Braganza, his brother James, Duke of York, and James's pregnant daughter Princess Anne and her husband, George of Denmark. The royal party are said to have joined in with the festivities, purchasing small souvenir tickets printed with their names and eating roast ox, which was cooked on the ice. This portrait of Charles II in ornamental penmanship was one of many popular souvenirs made at the fair by entrepreneurial printers who set up their presses on the ice. Selling personalised certificates, ballad sheets and royal portraits, which might cost up to 6d each, could prove a lucrative business, purportedly earning printers up to £5 a day. The artist, calligrapher John Seddon, was master of Sir John Johnson's Free Writing School in London's Foster Lane, where he wrote a number of copy books for students, including *The pen-man's paradise* (1695). These demonstrated his immense talent for exuberant calligraphic flourishes made with a single pen stroke.
[KM]

LITERATURE: Schneer, *The Thames*, pp. 75–80; *Oxford DNB*.

26
Souvenir spoon

1684
Inscribed: 'bought at the faire kept upon
the Midle of ye Thames … in the great
frost on the 29 of January 1683/4'
Silver, 200 × 48 × 25 mm

Museum of London, 79.484

This souvenir spoon was engraved at one
of the booths on the Thames during the
frost fair of 1683–84. This costly item
indicates that the fair attracted wealthy
visitors, and that the frozen river created
an impression strong enough to make
people want to commemorate their visit
with a precious silver object. By inference,
the event was not only important to the
individual but also to the community and
the nation.

This is a trefid spoon: flat-handled
with a stem that widens at the top and
has two notches that form it into a three-
lobed shape. This pattern was introduced
into England when Charles II returned
from exile; it had a comparatively short
life, falling from favour in the early
eighteenth century. [ML]

27
Souvenir mug from the 1683–84 frost fair

1684
Inscribed on a silver mount: 'Bought on ye
Thames ice Janu: ye 17 1683/4'
Glass and silver, 58 × 70 × 40 mm

Victoria and Albert Museum, C.156-1997

One of the most important surviving
souvenirs of the terrible winter of 1683–
84, this mug was probably engraved at the
point of purchase at one of the booths on
the river. It is a miniature replica of the
glass mugs used for strong ale in the
period, and was made in London, perhaps
in Southwark, using the same method to
create the ribbing on the base and to fix
the handle on the side as would have
been used for a full-size cup of this type.
The cup would have been termed a 'toy',
meaning that it had no practical use other
than being a child's plaything. [ML]

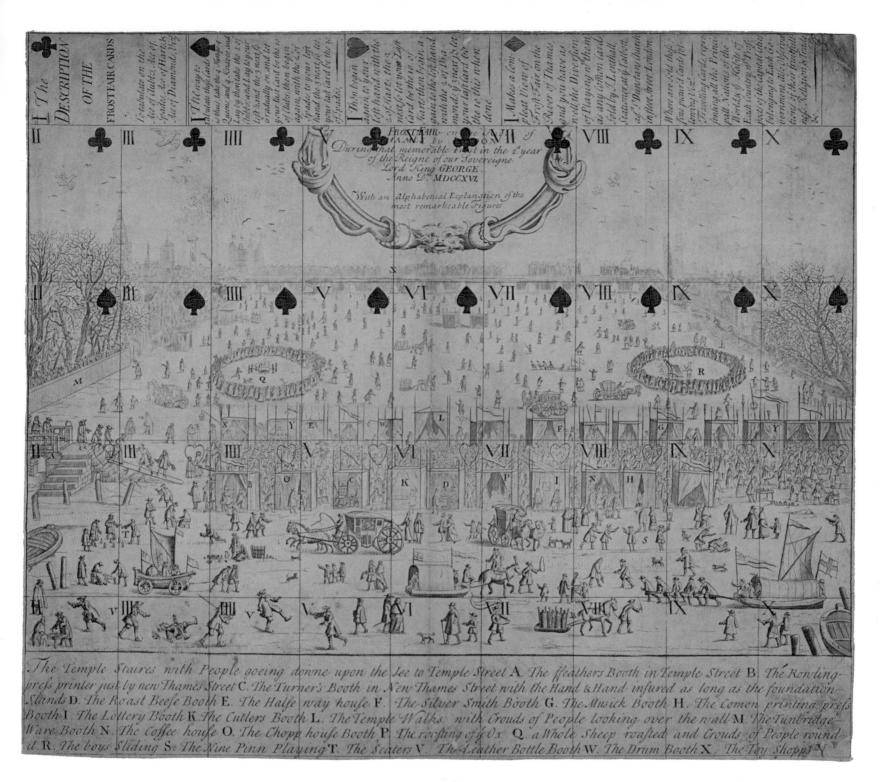

28

The Description of the
Frost Fair Cards

1716
Printed by JOHN LENTHALL (*fl.* 1670–1716),
London
Engraving on paper, 430 mm (width)

The 1683–84 frost fair remained a topic
of popular interest into the next century.
This print has been divided into forty-five
playing cards with instructions in the top
margin and a key to the various booths
and activities on the river at the bottom.
The print shows people descending
Temple Stairs to the central street of
booths crowded with customers. Towards
London Bridge, spectators form circles
to watch blood sports. John Lenthall,
a stationer and printer operating from
Fleet Street, specialised in the production
of playing cards. [ML]

THE CORONATION
OF JAMES II, 1685

29
Miniature of Mary of Modena

Seventeenth century
NICHOLAS DIXON (b. c.1645)
Watercolour on vellum and card,
22 mm (diameter)

Duke of Buccleuch and Queensberry

Maria Beatrice, or Mary (1658–1718), from the Italian duchy of Modena, wished to take the veil and enter a convent. Instead, in 1673 aged just fifteen, she became wife to the widowed James, Duke of York. His Catholic conversion was then little known but – as heir apparent to his brother Charles II – he still needed to father a legitimate male heir, since he had two daughters only. The wedding took place by proxy at Modena, and Mary first met James on reaching England. It nevertheless proved a successful match: the new Duchess was attractive and characterful, and while not bred for court life she learnt rapidly.

Although fertile, miscarriages and infant deaths left Mary childless by the time of her husband's accession. In June 1688, however, she gave birth to a surviving son, James Francis Edward Stuart – later the Old Pretender (d.1766). By then, a Protestant cabal was already negotiating with James II's Dutch son-in-law, Prince William of Orange, to replace him on the English throne. After William's bloodless invasion, James and Mary fled to the protection of Louis XIV of France, who granted them the Palace of St Germain-en-Laye as a court in exile. Both – and a final daughter, Louisa Maria Teresa (1692–1712) – subsequently died there. [PVDM]

LITERATURE: *Oxford DNB.*

In the later years of Charles II's life, with no legitimate Protestant heir likely and fears of increasing Catholic influence on the Court, parliamentary factions desperately tried to force through the exclusion of the openly Catholic James, Duke of York, from the succession. Although a Catholic consort, like Catherine of Braganza, could be tolerated, the prospect of a pro-French, Catholic sovereign was too much for some Protestants to bear. Their efforts, however, were unsuccessful and in 1685 James II of England and VII of Scotland succeeded to the throne with his second wife, the Catholic Mary of Modena, at his side.

At first there was significant popular support for James from a population keen for stability. He capitalised on this by swiftly arranging a grand coronation which would confirm his legitimacy as Stuart heir and King. On 23 April, just over two months after Charles II's death, James and Mary were crowned in a lavish ceremony at Westminster Abbey, which, significantly, omitted the Anglican Communion. Several days of public rejoicing accompanied the event, including a great river procession and spectacular fireworks on the Thames. Celebrations only served as a diversion to the Catholic problem, however, and the King's popularity soon waned as he began to introduce concessions to prominent Catholics.

When Mary gave birth to a son in June 1688, a Catholic line of succession seemed assured. Alarmed about the future, a group of English noblemen invited Prince William of Orange (the Protestant husband of James's elder daughter Mary by his first marriage) to come and save England from 'popery and slavery'. For William, the prospect of a Catholic succession that would ally England with France against the Netherlands persuaded him to act. He invaded England in December 1688 but met no resistance. James fled the country, leaving the throne vacant for William and Mary to fill. These events became known as 'the Glorious Revolution'.

[KM, PVDM & SD]

30
Miniature of James,
Duke of York, later James II

1670–72
SAMUEL COOPER (1609–72)
Watercolour, gilt, velvet, 78 × 64 mm

National Maritime Museum, Caird Collection, MNT0191

James II (1633–1701) was the second son of Charles I, who appointed him Lord High Admiral in 1638. He resumed the post at the Restoration in 1660 until debarred from office, as a Catholic, by the Test Act of 1673. On becoming King in 1685, James's political inflexibility and Catholic bias rapidly lost him initial support and in 1688 he was deposed. His attempts – with the aid of Louis XIV – to dislodge his successors, William III and Mary II, soon failed and James later died in French exile. However, 'Jacobite' plots continued around his son and grandson, the Old and Young Pretenders, until their cause was effectively extinguished at Culloden in 1746. [PVDM]

LITERATURE: *Oxford DNB.*

31

Chalice and paten belonging to James II and VII

1686–87
Silver-gilt, chalice, 277 mm (height);
paten, 158 mm (diameter)

National Museums Scotland (on loan from the Scottish
Roman Catholic Hierachy), Q.L. 1970.11 (chalice), Q.L.
1970.12 (paten)

Under the influence of his mother
Henrietta Maria, James became
particularly interested in the Roman
Catholic faith during his time of exile
in France (1649–60). He eventually
converted to Catholicism around 1668.
On becoming King, James had the Chapels
Royal furnished with new altar plate,
enabling him to take Holy Communion
according to that faith. This paten for the
bread and chalice for the wine are part of
the surviving pieces from the Chapel Royal
at the Palace of Holyroodhouse in
Edinburgh. Bearing James's cipher, they
were both made and bought in London
by the Lord Chancellor of Scotland, the
Earl of Perth. He recorded that on
'23 November 1686, The Kings Yaught
arrived from London at Leith with the
Popish altar, vestements, images, Priests
and other dependers for the Popish
Chapell in the Abbey'. It is likely that
these pieces were part of that cargo.

During the Glorious Revolution in 1688,
the chapel was the focus of an attack on
the palace by an anti-Catholic mob. Much
was destroyed but these pieces were
rescued, together with other plate, by
a priest who fled the city. [KM]

LITERATURE: McRoberts and Oman, 'Plate made
by King James II and VII', pp. 285–95.

32

Commemorative dish of James II's coronation

c. 1685
WILLIAM TALOR
Lead-glazed earthenware, 438 mm (diameter)

Manchester Art Gallery, 1923.145

Commemorative wares showing James
and his consort, Mary of Modena, were
produced by potters across England to
mark the coronation. This slipware display
dish, or charger, made and signed by
Staffordshire potter William Talor, is
believed to show the Archbishop of
Canterbury, William Sandcroft, steadying
the crown on James II's head as it
appeared to slip during his coronation.
This widely reported event was seen by
some to be a bad omen for James's reign.
Traditionally an inexpensive rural pottery,
slipware is decorated using different
coloured slips, or liquid clays, which are
trailed across the surface to form patterns
and pictures. There appear to have been
several families making these large royal
commemorative chargers, most notably
the Toft family. An almost identical dish to
this is in the collection of the Fitzwilliam
Museum in Cambridge [KM]

33

James II's coronation cup and cover

c. 1685
Inscribed: *Hoc obtinui / Ex in Aug: Iac: 2.d / Et Mar:
Ap: 23.85.* ('I obtained this from the Coronation of
James II and Mary, April 23 1685')
Silver-gilt, 130 mm (height)

Victoria and Albert Museum, M.34:1-2008, M.34:2-2008

This cup is made from the recycled silver bells
and stave mounts that adorned the canopies
carried above the heads of James II and Mary
of Modena during their coronation procession.
This explains the flat-chased decoration of four
figures carrying a canopy on both cup and
cover. The honour of carrying the canopies was
given to the Barons of the Cinque Ports,
freemen of the port towns of Hastings,
Romney, Hythe, Dover and Sandwich on the
south coast, in recognition of their role in
supplying ships and men to defend king and
country. After the ceremony they were given
the bells and canopies to share among
themselves. The opposite side of the cup is
inscribed with a cartouche enclosing the coat
of arms of the Draper family of Winchelsea,
two members of which carried the canopies.
The overall style of the ornamentation reflects
the emerging fashion at this time for exotic
Chinese-style decoration, or chinoiserie. [KM]

LITERATURE: Morton, *Triumphs of the Silversmith's Art*,
pp. 8–9; Murdoch, 'A silver cup commemorating the
coronation of James II', *passim*.

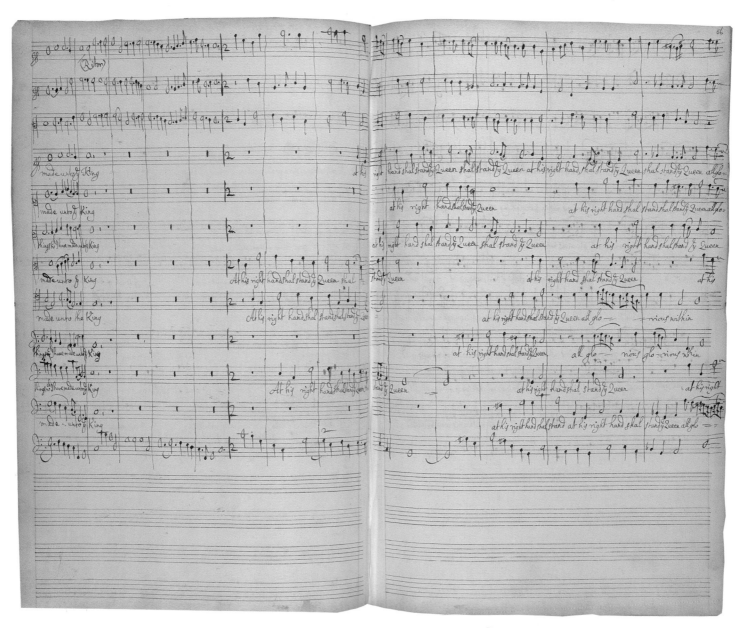

34
Trumpet

1666
Inscribed on the decorated silver
garland around the bell: 'AUGUSTINE DUDLEY
1666 LONDINI FECIT'
AUGUSTINE DUDLEY (fl.1635–96), London
Copper alloy with silver mounts,
146 × 713 mm

Museum of London, 64.147

Sixteen trumpeters played at the
coronation of James II. They walked
towards the front of the procession from
Westminster Hall to the Abbey, and later
performed fanfares from the west gallery
of the Abbey during the coronation
service. This trumpet is of the type played,
although those used at royal occasions
would have been made entirely of silver
with a fabric banner hanging from the
upper yard. The cordage and tassels are
original.
  Just two instruments made by City of
London trumpet-maker Augustine Dudley
are known to exist, and both are in the
Museum of London's collection (the other
dated 1651). Like many trumpet-makers
working in precious metals during this
period, Dudley was a member of the
Goldsmiths' Company. He served his
apprenticeship under Thomas Cooke and
received his freedom of the Company in
1644. Dudley attained the position of
Warden of the Goldsmiths in 1681 and
was Prime Warden from 1693. [KM]

LITERATURE: Byrne, 'The Goldsmith-Trumpet-makers of
the British Isles', pp.76–77; Halfpenny, 'Four
Seventeenth-Century British Trumpets', p.51,
Halfpenny, 'Musicians at James II's Coronation',
pp.106–08.

35
Autographed manuscript for 'My heart is inditing of a good matter'

c.1690
HENRY PURCELL (1659–95)
Ink on paper, 420 × 520 mm
British Library, R.M.20.h.8, fols 55v–56

As Keeper of the King's Instruments and
Organist of the Chapel Royal, Henry
Purcell composed music for royal
birthdays, coronations, funerals and even
the fortuitous escape of the King from a
shipwreck. In 1685, he was commissioned
to write music for the coronation of James
II. This included his most ambitious
anthem 'My Heart is Inditing', with music
set to an adapted version of Psalm 45 and
the Book of Isaiah. Written for eight-part
choir, strings and organ, it is Purcell's
longest anthem and represents one of the
most extravagant pieces ever composed
for a coronation. It was sung by the Choir
of the Chapel Royal in Westminster Abbey
while Mary of Modena, crowned and
anointed, was being conducted to her
throne alongside the King. This makes the
words 'at his right hand shall stand the
Queen, all glorious within' somewhat apt.
This anthem is contained in an incomplete
volume of compositions for Charles II and
James II, begun around 1681, and
transcribed in Purcell's own hand. [KM]

LITERATURE: Fellowes, English Cathedral Music,
pp.172–74; Shay and Thompson, Purcell Manuscripts,
pp.5, 127–28, 130.

36
Violin made for the Stuart household

c.1685
Attributed to RALPH AGUTTER (fl.1680s), London
Sycamore and pine wood, 585 × 205 × 38 mm
Victoria and Albert Museum, 34-1869

Soon after the Restoration, Charles II
formed an ensemble called the 'Twenty-
four Violins' which was a central feature
of court life. As well as supplying dance
music, playing as the King dined and
welcoming him as he arrived at the
palace, the violinists were a vital
accompaniment to state occasions,
including coronations, diplomatic visits
and royal weddings. Under James II, they
were subsumed into a larger baroque
orchestra.
  The Stuart coat of arms incorporated
into the ornately carved back of this violin
has led some to suggest that it belonged
either to Charles II or James II. The
presence of the arms and the exquisite
workmanship, attributed to London
instrument maker Ralph Agutter, make
it highly likely that the violin was used in
the royal household in the 1680s. [KM]

LITERATURE: Baines, Non-keyboard Instruments,
pp.16–17; Holman, Four and Twenty Fiddlers, pp.282,
305–07, 417

37 (above)

Fireworks on the Thames celebrating the coronation of James II

1685

WILLEM VAN DE VELDE, THE ELDER (1611–93)
Graphite, pen and ink, with wash on paper,
228 × 876 mm

National Maritime Museum, Caird Collection, PAJ2541

The festivities for James II's coronation began on 23 April 1685 with a short river procession from the Palace of Whitehall to Westminster. The following day, the celebrations reached their climax with a magnificent firework display on the Thames attended by the new King and Queen. This scene shows the Thames at Whitehall with boats and barges full of spectators crowding the river. The decorated pontoon, the central focus of the display, can be seen to the right.
[KM & RB]

38 (below)

The decorated pontoon before Whitehall

1685

WILLEM VAN DE VELDE, THE ELDER
Graphite, pen and ink, with wash on paper,
280 × 1060 mm

National Maritime Museum, Caird Collection, PAJ2562

Willem van de Velde's drawings were made while the Dutch artist was working for the Stuart court. He was a witness to the events on the river. This drawing shows the pontoon in greater detail to the left, delineating some of the grandeur and symbolism of its decoration. The great flotilla of small craft, some flying flags, banners and pennants, fills the right of the drawing.
[KM & RB]

39

A Representation of the Fireworks upon the River of Thames ... at their Majesties Coronation

From FRANCIS SANDFORD (1630–94), *The History of the Coronation of James II and of Queen Mary* (London, 1687)
Etching on paper, 428 × 446 mm

London Metropolitan Archives, SC/GL/PR/W2/WHI

This etching, one of twenty-seven, is taken from Sandford's beautifully illustrated record of the coronation and associated ceremonies. Sandford, a herald (Rouge Dragon pursuivant) at the College of Arms, spent two years working on the enormous book with fellow herald Gregory King. The completed volume was something of a failure, being produced just a year before James II fled the country. It shows in detail the pontoon on the river, decorated with figures representing 'Monarchy' (*MONARCHIA*) and the 'Father of the Country' (*PATER PATRIÆ*), and the extravagant royal firework display. [KM & RB]

LITERATURE: *Oxford DNB.*

HAMPTON COURT AND QUEEN MARY

40
William III

Seventeenth century
SIR GODFREY KNELLER (1646–1723)
Oil on canvas, 1479 × 1255 mm

National Maritime Museum, Greenwich Hospital
Collection, BHC3094

Born into the House of Orange-Nassau,
William III (1650–1702) ruled Britain
jointly with his wife, Mary II, until her
death. As a Protestant, he participated in
wars against the Catholic Louis XIV of
France, and many people heralded him as
a champion of their faith. As well as a
soldier, William was a patron of the arts.
After Mary died, William ruled alone but
his popularity soon plummeted. During his
last years William also suffered from
melancholia and ill health. Nevertheless,
his reign was largely successful: he resisted
the French domination of Europe and
established the Protestant succession in
England through the Act of Settlement
of 1701. In March 1702, William died of
pneumonia, a complication from a fall
while riding at Hampton Court. [AM & SD]

LITERATURE: *Oxford DNB*; Thurley, *Hampton Court*
pp. 172–74.

William III and Mary II moved into Hampton Court soon after their coronations to escape the London smog that exacerbated William's asthma. However, the Tudor palace had been badly neglected over the previous forty-five years and was in need of major rebuilding, modernisation and refurbishment. Furthermore, the palace was inconveniently sited, hours away from the government at Whitehall, and the royal couple had to live for most of the week at Kensington, two miles from the centre of London where the air was also cleaner, and use Hampton Court as a weekend home, summer residence and place for entertaining guests.

Early in 1689, the monarchs commissioned Christopher Wren to redesign Hampton Court. Their aim was to demolish the original Tudor palace and rebuild it in the much grander and more fashionable baroque style of Continental courts. Wren's original plan was to sweep away all but the great Hall of the Tudor palace. While work continued on the main building, Mary concentrated her attention on the conversion of the Tudor water gate into a pleasure house on the Thames. This Water Gallery was the only building at Hampton Court to be completed before Mary's death. On the ground floor was a dairy with running water, as well as a bedroom, bathroom and withdrawing room. Mary used the gallery for dining from 1692 until she died on 28 December 1694. At Mary's death the building work at Hampton Court ceased, partly because of William's grief but largely as a consequence of escalating costs. Between April 1689 and March 1694, £131,000 had been spent on the new apartments. Work was only resumed in 1698 when peace abroad freed up William's finances. Two years later, the King's apartments were finished and William returned to Hampton Court. [SD]

41
Queen Mary II

Seventeenth century
SIR GODFREY KNELLER
Oil on canvas, 1480 × 1242 mm

National Maritime Museum, Greenwich Hospital
Collection, BHC2853

Mary (1662–94) was the eldest daughter
of James, Duke of York, later James II, by
his first wife Anne Hyde (1637–71). Aged
fifteen, Mary married the much older
William of Orange in 1677 and went to
live in The Hague until 1688, when she
and her husband took the throne
following the flight of her father.
Although she reigned as joint sovereign
with her husband, she received no
substantive regal power. Nevertheless,
she proved to be both astute and
successful. She was behind the rebuilding
of Hampton Court and strongly supported
the development of a Seamen's Hospital in
Greenwich. However, Mary did not see the
dream completed: she died of smallpox in
December 1694 at the age of thirty-two.
[AM & SD]

LITERATURE: *Oxford DNB*; Thurley, *Hampton Court*,
pp. 172–74.

42
Milk pan from Mary II's dairy

c. 1689–94
Made by ADRIANUS KOCX (d. 1701),
'Greek A' factory, Delft, the Netherlands;
designed by DANIEL MAROT (1661–1752)
Tin-glazed earthenware, painted in blue,
474 mm (diameter)

Victoria and Albert Museum, C.384-1926

This is one of a set of milk pans made for
Mary's ornamental dairy that was housed
in the ground floor of the Water Gallery
at Hampton Court Palace. Dairies like this
were viewed as a particularly appropriate
female occupation, having a specific focus
on healthfulness, cleanliness, sobriety
and productivity. After her death, *King
William's Royal Diary* (1705) noted that
Mary 'was so far from being fond of great
Dainties, that I heard her once say, That
she could live in a Dairy'. The dairy was
a place of retreat for the Queen where,
as her health was never strong, she
could regularly take the course of milk
prescribed by her doctors. Special milk
pans designed for the dairy by Daniel
Marot featured pastoral scenes and some,
like this one, echoed the Asian influences
of her blue and white ceramics collection.
[AM]

LITERATURE: Martin, 'Interiors and interiority in the
ornamental dairy tradition', p. 361.

44
Blue and white japanned table

c. 1690
Attributed to DANIEL MAROT
Wood, gesso, gilt, marble,
800 x 1200 x 700 mm

Compton Verney, CVCSC: 0249.B

Mary worked very closely with Marot on
the design of the Water Gallery interiors.
The result, according to Daniel Defoe, was
that 'she ordered all the little neat curious
things to be done which suited her own
conveniences, and made it the pleasantest
little thing within doors that could
possibly be made'. The design for this
table reflects the baroque style promoted
by designers like Jean Le Pautre at the
French court, under whom Marot trained.
Although the paintwork has been
restored, the original japanned colours
and gilding would have been very vivid,
creating the effect of gilt-mounted
porcelain. [AM & SD]

LITERATURE: Thurley, *Hampton Court*, p. 172.

43
Delftware tile from the Water Gallery at Hampton Court

c. 1694
Made by ADRIANUS KOCX,
'Greek A' factory, Delft, the Netherlands;
designed by DANIEL MAROT
Tin-glazed earthenware, painted in blue,
610 × 610 × 23 mm

Victoria and Albert Museum, C.13-1956

While Hampton Court Palace was
undergoing extensive rebuilding and
refurbishment, Mary took up residence in
the Water Gallery, described by the writer
Daniel Defoe as 'a building formerly made
use of chiefly for landing from the river'.
Here she displayed her beloved blue and
white delftware and porcelain collections,
as Defoe noted, 'the like whereof was not
then to be seen in England'. The interiors
were designed to reflect their colour
scheme. These tiles by Daniel Marot – an
influential designer who worked first at
the court of Louis XIV and later for
William and Mary at Het Loo Palace,
Apeldoorn in the Netherlands and then in
England – were used in a set of four either
as a door or fireplace frame. [AM]

45
Bust of Sir Christopher Wren

Eighteenth century
After EDWARD PIERCE (c. 1635–95)
Marble, 710 × 530 × 200 mm
Royal Institute of British Architects, SCU/WREN/2

The architect, mathematician and astronomer Christopher Wren, was massively involved in the rebuilding of London after the Great Fire of 1666, which included, of course, his masterpiece, St Paul's Cathedral. He helped to redesign and build much of Whitehall Palace, although his work was destroyed in the blaze of 1698. Under the patronage of William and Mary, Wren began work at the palaces of Hampton Court and Kensington, employing red brick dressed with Portland stone. The vast south façade at Hampton Court is a testament not only to his skill in planning large-scale projects, but also to the continuing influence of Versailles on the English court. In 1694, Wren was commissioned to design the Royal Hospital at Greenwich, developing John Webb's abandoned palace for Charles II. He produced the final scheme by 1698.

The original version of this bust by Edward Pierce (or Pearce) is in the Ashmolean Museum, Oxford. It is widely regarded as the finest English portrait bust of the later seventeenth century, and certainly the most revealing representation of Wren. [RB]

LITERATURE: *Oxford DNB.*

46
Hampton Court Palace from the south

c. 1702
LEONARD KNYFF (1650–1722)
Pen and ink with wash on paper, 412 × 585 mm
British Museum, 1961-0408.1

Knyff almost certainly drew this detailed bird's-eye view of Hampton Court Palace in connection with his work for *Britannia Illustrata*, first published by David Mortier in 1707 with engravings by Johannes (Jan) Kip. The view, with the Thames in the foreground, shows the completion of Wren's baroque south façade with the old Tudor palace behind. The gardens are laid out in the popular and elaborate Franco-Dutch style. The Privy Garden stretches down to the river; to the east is the Fountain Garden designed by Daniel Marot. The labyrinth can be seen to the north. The Water Gallery, in which Queen Mary resided during Wren's work, was demolished as part of the scheme. [RB]

2

THE LORD MAYOR'S PROCESSION

THE CITY OF LONDON
AND RIVER PAGEANTRY, 1400–1856

IAN W. ARCHER

The City of London, declared Richard Burton in a commonplace in 1684, owed 'its glory and riches and many other blessings to the excellent river of Thames'.[1] The river provided the gateway to the international trade which fuelled the City's growth, and it was a vital supply line for the provision of foodstuffs and other necessaries. From the twelfth century, the City fathers had exercised jurisdiction over the river from Staines to Yantlee Creek and the Medway, a distance of some seventy-eight miles. Although they were frequently contested by the Lord Admiral and the Lieutenant of the Tower, the City's rights were jealously guarded, and the aldermen regularly sought to maintain navigation by removing fish weirs and other obstructions. The Thames figured powerfully in the iconography of the City, as the urban panoramas, which became fashionable from the mid-sixteenth century, usually took a viewpoint that foregrounded the river and the bridge. Londoners praised their river above all others. In 1629, the playwright Thomas Dekker, drawing on the urban mythology of London as having been founded by refugees from Troy, imagined that the Ganges, Nile and Euphrates would 'weep out their eyes/ mad that New Troy's high towers on tiptoe rise/ to hit Heaven's roof'.[2]

It is unsurprising then that the river should have featured so prominently in civic pageantry. By the mid-sixteenth century the river played a critical role in the festivities which accompanied the installation of the Lord Mayor on 29 October. He was accompanied by the liverymen of the City's trade guilds in their barges to and from Westminster for his oath-taking in the presence of the Barons of Exchequer, before processing through the City streets to Guildhall, his route punctuated by various edifying pageants. But the water procession seems to have originated as an economy measure, replacing the more expensive processions on horseback from 1453 rather to the chagrin of the Crown. Although there were occasional water processions before that year, for example in 1422 when the recent funeral of Henry V perhaps made excessive pomp both unseemly and too costly, it was the draper mayor, John Norman who instituted the regular use of barges in 1453. Over the course of the sixteenth century, the pageantry associated with the mayor's inauguration became ever more elaborate. Professional dramatists, acting alongside artificers specialising in scenic invention, were employed by the sponsoring company to lay on spectacles that combined powerful visual and poetic effects. The shows were probably at their zenith in the early seventeenth century with companies spending sums of the order of £1000 on the spectacle. They were interrupted during the Interregnum, but revived at the Restoration. Always rather rumbustious occasions, and characterised by an increasingly staid panegyric mode at odds with the realities of the deep political divisions in Restoration London, they were falling out of favour with polite society. Samuel Pepys dismissed the shows as 'poor and absurd' and on another occasion as 'very silly'.[3] The land shows were abandoned in the early eighteenth century, but the river processions continued until 1856, and it is from the eighteenth century that we can enjoy some of the most spectacular visual representations.

It is noteworthy that the Crown also seems to have begun to make more use of the river for spectacle from the later fifteenth century, and that the citizens were heavily involved. Pageantry associated with royal entries to the capital had tended to make use of London Bridge in the past, but increasingly the Crown turned to water shows. In 1486, Henry VII was escorted from Fulham or Putney to London by the citizens in their barges 'with shooting of wildfire';[4] in the following year Henry's Queen, Elizabeth of York, processed by water from Greenwich to the Tower on 23 November in preparation for her coronation; the livery companies provided barges and music, but there was also

> a barge garnished and apparelled, passing all other, wherein was ordained a great red dragon [the Tudor emblem] spouting flames of fire into [the] Thames. And also many other gentlemanly pageants well and curiously devised to do her Highness sport and pleasure with.[5]

We know nothing of what those 'gentlemanly pageants' consisted (the word could be used for highly decorated banners as well as a staged show), but Anne Boleyn's coronation water procession is better documented. Preceding the Mayor's barge was a galley foist (a small escorting ship) with large amounts of ordnance and a great dragon; on board there were 'monsters and wildmen casting fire'. There were other barges to the right and left of the Mayor's, that on the left carried a show featuring 'a mount and on the same stood a white falcon crowned upon a rote of gold environed with white roses and red, which was the queen's device: about which mount sat virgins singing and playing sweetly'. On the right side was the Bachelors' barge (batchelors were the junior householders below the livery) hung with rich cloth of gold and silk, and festooned with flags and banners showing the devices of the company of Haberdashers and those of the Merchant Adventurers (the Mayor's companies), and at the stern two great banners of the arms of the King and Queen.[6]

The various royal celebrations of the 1530s seem to have persuaded the aldermen that they should provide their own barge rather than bidding against the companies to hire one. The 1540 barge was the first of many, and by the middle years of Elizabeth's reign the Master of the Barges (a new civic appointment) was maintaining two barges, one presumably acting as the state barge, and the other used to carry juries on the courts of conservancy through which London's river jurisdiction was maintained. By the end of the seventeenth century there were three city barges, of eighteen, eight and four oars respectively, and this pattern was sustained throughout the following century. In addition to its use on Lord Mayor's Day, the great barge was often called upon for receptions of visiting dignitaries, and in the rituals of the Thames conservancy.

But the inauguration of the Lord Mayor remained at the heart of the civic ritual calendar. In the later fifteenth and sixteenth centuries the livery companies continued to hire their barges, usually from leading aristocratic figures or sometimes the Crown. These barges were decorated in ways that identified them with the individual crafts, with large banners bearing the arms of the company as well as of the Crown and the City. There was always musical accompaniment, usually trumpets, drums and fife; and there was a great deal of noise from the galley foist, which set forth incessant gunfire. We hear of a galley foist with twenty cannon as early as the Merchant Taylors' show of 1556; the Ironmongers in 1609 had a vessel 60 feet long 'well rigged with 16 bases and 10 small shot'.[7] Banks of cannon were also placed at strategic points along the river, variously on the Bankside in Southwark, at Lambeth and at Paul's Wharf. A Venetian observer captured the powerful visual and aural impact of the water procession in 1617:

A dense fleet of vessels hove in sight, accompanied by swarms of small boats … The ships were beautifully decorated with balustrades and various paintings. They carried immense banners and countless pennons. Salutes were fired, and a number of persons bravely attired played on trumpets, fifes and other instruments … the discharges of the salutes were incessant.[8]

The noise would have reached a crescendo at the point where the Mayor disembarked at Westminster and landed again at Paul's Wharf to tremendous salutes. Some felt that the noise detracted from the more uplifting elements of the spectacle. Dekker complained that 'their thunder [according to the galley foist fashion] was too loud for any of the Nine Muses to be bidden to it'.[9]

But there is relatively little evidence for dramatic water shows as part of Lord Mayor's Day until the early seventeenth century. The Goldsmiths recorded in 1545 that the Masters of the Company's Bachelors 'had the oversight of payment of all the charges of *the pageants for the barge* with all the other charges thereto belonging', but it is not clear whether these were constructed tableaux such as were provided in the royal shows of 1487 and 1533, or merely banners.[10] The mid-century diarist Henry Machyn does not record water shows in his account of the river processions, though he does mention the pageants that greeted the Mayor on his return to the City. The typical elements in the processions at this time were the galley foist, the musicians and the gaily decorated barges. Here is Machyn's account of the water procession for 1555:

The 29 day of October there were two goodly pinnaces decked with guns and flags and streamers, and a thousand pensells, the pinnaces painted, one white and blue, and the other yellow and red, and the oars and guns like colour; and with trumpets and drums, and all the crafts in barges and streamers; and at the nine of the clock my new lord mayor and the sheriffs and the aldermen toke barge at the Three Cranes with trumpets and shawms, and the waits playing; and so rode [rowed] to Westminster, and took his oath in the Exchequer, and all the way the pinnaces shooting of guns and playing up and down; and so after came back to Paul's Wharf, and landed with great shooting of guns and playing.[11]

The shows became more complex in the years after 1585, and it is from this period that we find water shows as an integral part of the dramatic scheme. The Thames was an appropriate setting for pageants celebrating the riches that

Fig.11 Quarter badges from the
Fishmongers' Company barge, 1773.
The Worshipful Company of Fishmongers
(see page 102/cat.no.62).

Golden Fleece
(1623) features a galley
(the *Argo*) bearing the enchantress
Medea who, having withheld the golden
fleece for so long, is willing to grant it to the
Drapers to adorn their arms. She is accompanied by her
daughter Queen Irene, and by Jason, Hercules, Telemon,
Orpheus, Castor and Pollux who are 'armed with fair gilt
armours, and bearing triumphal lances, wreathed about with
gilded laurel and curious shields, all carrying the impresa of
the golden fleece'. The galley is rowed by 'six tributary Indian
kings … all of them wearing their tributary crowns and
antickly attired in rich habilments'.[14]

The water devices often required elaborate structures and
special effects. In *Metropolis Coronata* (1615), the first mayor Fitz-
Alwin delivers a speech to the incoming mayor from a tiered
'sea-chariot … shaped like to a whale or the huge Leviathan
of the sea', which also bore eight royal virtues and the figures
of Time and Fame.[15] The Ironmongers' records for 1609
reveal that a whale was used on the river. It was 'to row with
fins open for fireworks at the mouth, and water vented at the
head', all controlled by an operator inside the whale.[16]

Water shows were a feature of some of the early
Restoration processions, notably in the appearance of Oceanus
and his accompanying nymphs on a floating stage near
Whitehall in 1660 (a speech was delivered celebrating river-
borne commerce), but by the 1670s the pageantry was scaled
back. On several occasions we are told that two pleasure boats
rigged and manned like men-of-war, and decked with flags and
streamers, were moored off the Temple: as the Mayor passed
they volleyed forth with gun salutes. But there were no more
water shows.

It was in the early seventeenth century too that the
companies first began to acquire their own barges, rather than
hiring them each year. The Clothworkers acquired their first
barge in 1618, the Mercers in 1632, the Drapers in 1633, the
Fishmongers in 1634, the Merchant Taylors in 1640, the
Haberdashers, Skinners and Goldsmiths in 1656, and the
Leathersellers in 1664. It seems that it was becoming difficult to
hire barges and get service of the required quality. The
Vintners moaned in 1612 that the cost of hiring was high, and
that for want of a good barge members of the Company were

flowed to the City through its trade, whose reach was truly
global. Anthony Munday's *Chruso-thriambos: the Triumphes
of Golde* (1611) performed for a Goldsmith Mayor describes
a procession of 'sundry ships, frigates and gallies', one
of which bore an Indian king and his queen; there were
numerous skirmishes between the vessels on the way to
Westminster, 'each gallant having his Indian page attending
on him, laden with ingots of gold and silver, and those
instruments that delved them out of the earth'.[12] As the Mayor
approached the waterside in 1613 he found 'the river decked in
the richest glory to receive him; upon whose crystal bosom
stands five Islands artfully garnished with all manner of Indian
fruit trees, drugs, spiceries; and the like, the middle Island with
a fair castle especially beautified'.[13] Munday's *Triumphs of the*

in fear of their lives and much disgraced. In 1633 the Drapers asserted that they could seldom get a good barge. The Merchant Taylors complained in 1639 of their 'great want of a barge for the Company's decent and convenient passage by water'.[17] There was also, as in all areas of guild activity, an element of emulous rivalry. When the Haberdashers were considering a barge of their own in 1638, it was specified that it should be of similar dimensions to those of the Fishmongers and Drapers with eighteen oars. The drive to own a barge had predictably enough been led by the 'Great Twelve' companies, but in the later seventeenth century the so-called inferior companies were imitating them. The Armourers acquired a barge in 1658, the Bakers and Pewterers followed in 1662, the Stationers and Apothecaries in 1673, the Tallow Chandlers in 1675. When the Apothecaries ordered their first barge in 1673, they instructed that it should be 'as large and good in all respects whatsoever as the barge lately built for the Company of Mercers', the premier livery company.[18] Rivalry between the companies threatened the sedate order that was the ideal of all civic ritual. Elaborate instructions were issued to ensure that the companies processed according to their order in the precedence of civic hierarchy with fixed distances between the barges: 'no barge should row nearer to another than twice the length of the barge upon a great pain', it was ruled in 1533.[19] Nonetheless, there were still episodes like that in 1638 when the Drapers overtook the Lord Mayor's barge, landing at Westminster 'before the lord mayor and aldermen were landed, the lord mayor's barge being almost out of sight rowing towards Westminster'.[20] The exuberance of the day overcame strict civic protocols.

Maintaining a barge required considerable investment, because few lasted longer than thirty years. The Merchant Taylors' first barge was acquired in 1640 but had to be replaced in 1669, the bargemaster having declared that the old one was 'so rotten that he dare not adventure the company therein';[21] there were further renewals in 1687, 1718, 1764 and 1800. The Stationers replaced the hull of their 1673 barge in 1700, and ordered new barges in 1723, 1766, 1790 (involving a new hull, but with redecoration costing more than the original 1766 barge), and 1826. The Goldsmiths built barges in 1656, 1682, 1708, 1745, 1777 and 1823. Direct comparison of costs is difficult

because of the need to distinguish between the costs of constructing the barge and the costs of carving, painting and decoration, which could be substantial. Abraham Tue, shipwright of Southwark, received £98 13s 4d for the Merchant Taylors' barge in 1639–40; gilding and painting by John Terry cost a further £17, and the total bills came to just over £120. The Company paid £197 1s for the 1669 barge, £110 in 1687 (but excluding the painting), and £171 in 1718. In 1764 the Merchant Taylors received three bids for the building of the barge between £640 and £660; they went for the highest bidder, Thomas Searle. The bill for painting by Nathaniel Clarkson on this occasion came to £316 3s, and the total cost of the barge was just over £1000. In 1800 the barge cost £1607, of which £1321 was for construction and the rest for decoration. Given that overall prices had only doubled between 1650 and 1800, these figures suggest that there were considerable increases in real costs over the period. That the companies should have continued to invest in such expensive ceremonial paraphernalia suggests that their commitment to pageantry and its associated costs remained high throughout the eighteenth century.

There were considerable incidental expenses associated with the acquisition of a barge, not the least of which was the requirement for a barge house. Several companies leased land for barge houses from the Archbishop of Canterbury or the Duchy of Cornwall at Vauxhall or Lambeth; there were other barge houses at Chelsea, most notably the Apothecaries' whose physic garden was located there. The Stationers were paying a rent of £12 between 1680 and 1685, and 25 guineas a hundred years later. It cost the Barbers £244 to build their barge house in the 1660s. Some companies like the Mercers, Fishmongers and Clothworkers at Vauxhall were able to share facilities. There were also implications for the companies' salary costs. The barges were maintained by a bargemaster and his mate. Bargemasters had livery provided by the company: a silk gown, sash and cap being provided for the Merchant Taylors' appointee in 1718, while the Vintners' man was given a wine-coloured coat with flat silver buttons; their status was also marked by the distinctive silver badges with the arms or emblems of the company, several of which survive. Although bargemasters were paid annual retainers (usually £4 per annum in the seventeenth century, but as much as £10 per annum by 1800), the posts tended to remain in the possession of individual families. The bargemaster was responsible for keeping the barge in good repair and hiring the watermen to row the barge each year. The oarsmen would wear coats of blue cloth and distinctive red caps; small badges might be worn on their sleeves or in their caps.

The barges themselves tended to be between 60 and 80 feet in length and were usually powered by nine oars on each side. They became longer as time went on: the Goldsmiths' 1656 barge was 62-feet long, that of 1682 was 73 feet and that of 1745, 75 feet and 4 inches. The earliest barges perhaps just had an awning to protect the liverymen from the elements; later ones were equipped with cabins (or 'houses' as they were called) which became progressively larger (around 35 feet in length in the eighteenth century) and more sumptuously decorated. The decoration of the barges made repeated reference to guild iconography, including references to patron saints, guild legends, relevant classical deities and the beasts which acted as supporters to their coats of arms. In planning a barge in 1638, the Haberdashers proposed a carving of the Company's arms with the supporters on the stern, a figure of St Catherine four feet high, two sea nymphs two feet and ten inches high, and the King's arms over the Master's seat. The Apothecaries' 1673 barge was carved with unicorns on either side of the entrance to the cabin, and a rhinoceros above the door; the Company's arms adorned the stern. When it was replaced in 1727, the cabin was decorated with figures of the Four Seasons, Apollo and Aesculapius (the deities associated with healing), Hercules, Industry, and Neptune and Thetis drawn by a sea chariot. The Vintners' barge commissioned in the following year included carvings of the Four Seasons, Fame, and St Martin on horseback. In 1745, the Goldsmiths required a carving of their patron saint, Dunstan with his crozier and tongs, as well as two figures of Britannia, and two unicorns bearing the Company's arms. Some of these carvings, such as the Haberdashers' St Catherine, the Ironmongers' St Lawrence, the Goldsmiths' St Dunstan, and the Fishmongers' St Peter, as well as several panels of coats of arms, were rescued from the barges when these were eventually sold, and survive to adorn the Company's halls (fig. 11).

One of the most detailed programmes for the decoration of a barge comes from the pen of Nathaniel Clarkson (1724–95), a coach painter who became an assistant of the Merchant Taylors' Company and drew up the decorative scheme for the Company's 1764 barge. Clarkson eschewed the representations of deities 'which have no affinity with a company of the city of London' in favour of historical subjects, including Henry VII's grant of the charter of 1504, and the occasion in 1607 when the clerk presented Prince Henry with a roll of the names of kings and nobles who had been members of the Company in the past. The door panels were decorated with figures representing the Four Continents; other panels showed the Thames and Isis, 'being the two great rivers by which the riches of the four quarters of the world are brought to this great city', and the Dignity and Opulence of the city:

represented by a woman crowned with a tower holding the praetorian wand in her right hand on which is the cap of liberty, at a distance a ship, bales of goods lying by her; two boys one of which embraces a stork signify the harmony and union of the city of London.[22]

Here was a classic loyalist narrative of harmony between City and Crown, internal peace and a flourishing trade spreading over the world, sustained by the river.

To judge from the warnings in the 1790s that 'particular notice' would be taken of companies which did not give attendance, it seems that enthusiasm for the river procession was waning. The Haberdashers had disposed of their barge as early as 1753 on grounds of economy. Although from the 1760s some companies were making occasional use of their barges for pleasure trips for their members to Richmond, Twickenham and Shooters Hill, a company barge was a pretty expensive luxury, given that it was likely to be used a couple of times a year only. Increasing river pollution made the trips rather less salubrious than they had been. There were occasional river processions associated with the Crown, but they were no longer well supported: only four companies accompanied William IV to Greenwich in 1835, and the occasion was marred by a spat over precedence between the Goldsmiths and Mercers. By the early nineteenth century, reports that a barge was decayed was more likely to result in the conclusion that the barge be abandoned rather than a contract for a new one being issued. In 1817, the Apothecaries' barge was 'in ruinous condition and full of water'; it was reported that it could be repaired for £329, but the Company decided to sell it off instead.[23] The upcoming expiration of the Drapers' lease on their barge house in 1831 occasioned some hard thinking. The cost of a new barge would be £2000; building a new barge house an additional £2000; maintenance costs ran at £180 per annum. In 1829 the Company sold its barge for £35. The Finance Committee of the Merchant Taylors reached similar conclusions in 1837, and although its report was initially rejected, the writing was on the wall; with maintenance costs running at £250 per annum the Company decided to sell off its barge in 1846. Some company barges enjoyed an after-life as floating barge houses for viewing races on the river at Oxford. The Merchant Taylors sold their barge to Oxford University Boat Club in 1846, which later passed it to University College; the Goldsmiths sold their barge in 1848 to Oriel; the Stationers' barge eventually found its way to Exeter College.

As the companies gradually fell away, the Lord Mayor's procession became a rather tawdry affair. In 1830 there were just twelve companies in the procession, four years later only six. The last river procession on Lord Mayor's Day was held in 1856. It may be that the City's abandonment of the traditional pageantry had been precipitated by Parliament's recent attack on the Thames conservancy, the City's independent jurisdiction over the river, but the ceremonies were already unviable because of the loss of company interest.

CITY AND CROWN

The Crown and the City of London had a close and symbiotic – if sometimes tense – relationship. The monarch depended on the City for loans and taxes, and sometimes the City was required to store grain for distribution to the poor during times of dearth. The City received its charter of incorporation, and hence derived its right to self-government, from the sovereign. All the livery companies, which regulated London's crafts and trades, were in possession of their own royal charters of incorporation. The Crown also granted companies the right to bear a coat of arms.

The Lord Mayor of London was considered the monarch's representative, even substitute, in the City. A new mayor was elected every year on Michaelmas Day (29 September), and on 29 October he would travel to Westminster to swear an oath of allegiance before the monarch or royal judges. Following the calendar reform of the mid-eighteenth century, the oath was sworn on 9 November. For 400 years, from 1453 until 1856, the Lord Mayor's annual journey to Westminster was made by barge. He would be rowed upstream, accompanied by his aldermen and officers and followed by representatives of the principal livery companies in their barges. The procession was colourful and noisy: barges were decorated with banners and the arms of their companies, while drummers and trumpeters played in each barge, musketeers onboard fired volleys into the air, and fireworks were set off from the riverbanks. Following the oath-taking, the Lord Mayor returned to the City, disembarking near St Paul's from where he was escorted to the Guildhall in another grand procession. After a great dinner at the Guildhall and an afternoon service marking the inauguration at St Paul's, the entire procession would accompany the new Lord Mayor to his home by torchlight. [SD]

47
The Lord Mayor's
water-procession on the Thames

c.1683
English school
Oil on canvas, 1518 × 2610 mm

Royal Collection, RCIN 402608

The Lord Mayor's procession depicted in this river view of Whitehall Palace and the Banqueting House is assumed to be that of 1683, when Sir Henry Tulse 'went by water, accompanied by the late Lord Mayor, the new recorder, aldermen, and sheriffs, and attended by diverse of the companies in their barges; their majesties and the duke of York being upon the leads [flat roof] at Whitehall when they passed by'. As in the written record, the river appears crowded with company barges and that of the City of London carrying the new Lord Mayor which passed the viewer at close range. The artist has placed great emphasis on the display of company flags, further heightening the sense of drama. The barges of the Apothecaries, Fishmongers, Goldsmiths, Mercers, Skinners, Vintners and Weavers can be identified. [JGM]

LITERATURE: Millar (ed.), *Tudor, Stuart and Early Georgian Pictures*, cat.no. 441.

48
Westminster Bridge with the Lord Mayor's procession, 29 October 1746

1747
GIOVANNI ANTONIO CANAL,
known as CANALETTO (1697–1768)
Oil on canvas, 959 × 1276 mm
Yale Center for British Art, B1976.7.94

Canaletto's view of the river procession conveying William Benn, the new Lord Mayor of London, to take his oath of office, displays the event in all its festive, colourful and decorative detail. The livery company barges are being rowed upstream away from the viewer, but the Lord Mayor's barge has turned in the centre foreground, presenting itself as the painting's key narrative feature. Seen from an elevated viewpoint above the river, the brightly lit Westminster Bridge spans the picture plane. Together with the buildings on either bank behind it, the bridge forms an elaborate backdrop for the busy display of barges and rivercraft of all sizes decked out splendidly for the Lord Mayor's Day. However, the bridge was not completed until 1750, at least three years after this painting was produced and Canaletto has incorrectly imagined its finished appearance, adding statues of Thames and Isis over the central arch.

Canaletto arrived in England in 1746 and he probably painted the Lord Mayor's procession for the Whig George Garnier to hang *en suite* with three Venetian views at Rookesbury Park in Hampshire. Intentionally likening the picture in colour scheme and composition to a depiction of 'The Bucintoro at the Molo on Ascension Day', the artist is satisfying his Whig patron's admiration for the political structure of the Venetian Republic: by creating a visual kinship between the civic events on display and more specifically the Lord Mayor's barge and the *Bucintoro* (a ceremonial Venetian vessel), Canaletto is aligning the cities of London and Venice. [JGM]

LITERATURE: Beddington (ed.), *Canaletto in England*, no. 23; Redford, *Venice and the Grand Tour*, pp.76–78.

49
Charter of the Worshipful Company of Clockmakers

1631
Text composed by THOMAS COPLEY;
illumination by JOHN CHAPPELL
Illuminated manuscript on vellum,
965 × 832 mm

The Trustees of the Clockmakers' Museum

Signed on the King's behalf on 22 August
1631, this fine illuminated charter
established the Clockmakers' Company –
'The Master, Wardens, and Fellowship of
the Art or Mystery of Clockmaking of the
City of London' – as a separate entity
following a long wrangle with the
Blacksmiths. The charter, in common with
others issued to the livery companies,
allowed the new body to regulate the
horological trade of the City and, in this
case, within a surrounding radius of ten
miles. The first master of the Company
was David Ramsay (c. 1575–1660), who
was chief clockmaker to James I. Thomas
Copley, who composed the text of the
charter, was appointed as first clerk of the
Company by Charles I. John Chappell was
paid £4 in 1634 for illuminating the
manuscript. [RB]

50
Merchant Taylors' Company mace

Sixteenth century
Silver, parcel gilt with iron core,
498 mm (length)

The Worshipful Company of Merchant Taylors

The mace of the Merchant Taylors'
Company was carried in the various land
and water processions on Lord Mayor's
Day. Other items of Company regalia were
also displayed, including the beadle's stave
and a number of silver-mounted ivory
hammers. Processing by water had its
disadvantages: a hammer is alleged to
have been lost overboard, and a similar
fate befell the beadle's stave in 1835,
requiring the Company to spend
somewhere between £35 and £39 on
a suitable replacement. The mace was
luckier and indeed is a rare survivor of
the 1666 Great Fire of London, which
destroyed the Merchant Taylors' Hall.
Engraving on the foot of the mace shows
the Paschal Lamb and flag within a
radiant solar border. This heraldic insignia
was introduced in the 1481 grant of arms.
The arms on the top, however, are from
the second grant of 1586, when the flag
was dropped because of its Catholic
associations. It must presumably have
been added at some point between that
date and the mention of the mace in the
plate inventory of 1609. [RB & SD]

LITERATURE: Fry and Tewson, *Illustrated Catalogue*,
pp. ix, 11–13, 17, 22.

51
John Norman

c. 1450
ROGER LEIGH (*fl.* 1450)
Watercolour, 350 mm (height)

London Metropolitan Archives, k1306391

Before the mid-fifteenth century the Lord
Mayor would walk or ride to Westminster
to take the oath. The first Lord Mayor
to go by water along the Thames was
probably John Norman (d. 1468), who is
shown here in his Alderman's robes. He
may have chosen to travel by barge in
1453 on account of his age and infirmity.
The new mode of processing clearly
proved popular, for Londoners requested
that it be continued. John Norman was
a draper by trade. Before his election
as Lord Mayor, he was a sheriff and
Alderman, and also represented the
City in Parliament. [RB]

Fig. 12 Ferdinand Philip, sixth Prince Lobkowicz, oil on canvas, attributed to Martin van Mytens the Younger.

The Lobkowicz Collections, LR4618.

52

London: The Thames on Lord Mayor's Day, looking towards the City and St Paul's Cathedral

Before 1752
GIOVANNI ANTONIO CANAL,
known as CANALETTO (1697–1768)
Oil on canvas, 1185 × 2375 mm

The Lobkowicz Collections, LR5516

More than any other view of the Thames painted by Canaletto between 1747 and 1755, this depiction of Lord Mayor's Day captures the sense of pomp and grandeur attached to the pageant, which took place annually on 29 October. Looking downriver from the south bank, the panorama of the Thames and the City of London unfolds across the picture plane in front of the viewer. In the spectacular procession, the gilded barges of the livery companies, bedecked with colourful standards and pennants and surrounded by numerous smaller vessels, travel upstream past the mighty, sunlit structure of St Paul's Cathedral. Church spires and the Monument accentuate the cityscape beyond with London Bridge visible in the distance. Evidence of the 'working' river, in the form of riverfront warehouses and wharfs, has been captured in Canaletto's characteristic architectural detail, setting the procession against the source of much of the City's great wealth. There is a strong sense of movement and occasion, echoing some of the artist's best-known Venetian scenes, with oars being pulled, salutes fired and a great multitude of spectators in boats and wherries following the event.

This painting was acquired, and most probably commissioned, by Ferdinand Philip, sixth Prince Lobkowicz (1724–84) (fig. 12). The young prince visited London in 1745 to buy horses, remaining intermittently until the summer of 1748; for some of his stay he was accompanied by the composer Christoph Willibald Gluck (1714–87), whose musical career had begun in Lobkowicz's Vienna Palace orchestra. At this time, political difficulties arising from the War of the Austrian Succession (1740–48) made it necessary for him to leave Bohemia. (His most valuable estates were in Silesia, which Frederick II of Prussia had annexed, and since Lobkowicz risked their confiscation if he protested, he fell from favour with Empress Maria Teresa of Austria.) In London, the Prince had an introduction to Charles Lennox, the second Duke of Richmond (1701–50). It was through Richmond (or very possibly the Venetian ambassador's wife, the Contessa di Colalto, with whom he was soon having an affair) that he met Canaletto, who had arrived in London in May 1746. It seems fairly certain that Lobkowicz purchased 'London: The Thames and the City of Westminster from Lambeth' (fig. 13), having seen the work in Canaletto's studio in late 1746 or early 1747. He then presumably commissioned, or perhaps saw the very early preliminary work for, the St Paul's view that became the highly animated pendant to the more tranquil Westminster scene. Unlike many of Canaletto's British clients, Lobkowicz was in no immediate rush to take the paintings into his possession and, therefore, the artist may not have completed the second work until around 1750, or even slightly later. The pair was

finally sent to Roudnice Castle in north Bohemia, being delivered in 1752.

From a long line of intelligent, cultured and politically influential forebears, Ferdinand Philip was particularly learned and cultivated, with numerous diverse interests and talents. Upon his arrival in London, he struck up a close friendship with the Duke of Richmond's daughter, Lady Emily Lennox, upon whom he made a considerable impression: she described him as 'a giddy, good-natured, wild young man as any in the world'. Despite society gossip, nothing came of their relationship, which was, in any case, founded as much on mutual acquaintances and a shared ability to speak French as on any romantic attachment; Emily subsequently married James Fitzgerald, twentieth Earl of Kildare, later the first Duke of Leinster. In 1767, during a visit to Vienna, her son, William Fitzgerald, decided to see what news there was of Prince Lobkowicz. William discovered that he had retreated to the country, where he was 'now quite alter'd; instead of being gay and lively, he lives at home and sees nobody'. Emily had clearly known Lobkowicz at what proved to be his youthful best.

The lasting legacy of the Prince's visit to London is a unique pair of Canaletto's finest paintings of London, demonstrating both the artist's technical abilities and the precocious taste of the young Prince Lobkowicz. Until its display in the *Royal River* exhibition, this extraordinary painting of the Thames had not been seen in London, or indeed outside of Bohemia, since it was dispatched from Canaletto's studio nearly 260 years ago. [RB & JGM]

LITERATURE: Martineau and Robison (eds), *The Glory of Venice*, no. 133; Baird, 'Letters of introduction', *passim*; Fitzgerald, *Emily, Duchess of Leinster*, pp. 14–15, 123.

Fig.13 London: The Thames
and the City of Westminster from
Lambeth, oil on canvas, by Antonio
Giovanni Canal (known as
Canaletto), 1746–47.

The Lobkowicz Collections, LR11559.

CEREMONIAL BARGES AND LIVERY

53
City of London bargemaster's coat and breeches

1840–50
Wool, silk and silver
Museum of London, 86.429a&b

The bargemaster oversaw the oarsmen on the Lord Mayor's state barge. The Lord Mayor's procession was not the only time that the barge was used. In the 1840s, *The Times* reported such diverse events as 'Grand Aquatic Entertainments' on the river in the summer months, and the use of the barge to transport the Lord Mayor to a number of Conservancy Courts, to assess the state of the riverbanks, held along the Thames from Chelsea to Greenwich. This uniform dates from that period. [AM]

The livery companies of London have a long history. Beginning in the early Middle Ages as religious foundations, they soon came to regulate and monopolise the crafts and commerce of their members. During the fourteenth century their members began to wear a distinctive – and often brilliantly coloured – surcoat, known as a livery. Early in the reign of Henry VIII, London's Court of Aldermen assumed the right to control the grant of livery, to limit the number of liverymen within each company, and to rank the companies in order of precedence. In 1516, the order of precedence of forty-eight livery companies was fixed; those ranked in the first twelve became known as the 'Great Twelve'.

Most of London's livery companies owned or hired barges for use in the annual Lord Mayor's Day procession and special royal events on the river. The crew usually comprised a bargemaster, his mate and sixteen to eighteen oarsmen. The vessels were elaborately painted and decked out with many flags and banners to make a colourful presence on the river. At the stern there was space for musicians. The various barges of the participating companies displayed their coats of arms and patron saints in the river procession. From the mid-sixteenth until at least the mid-eighteenth century, a ceremonial armed escort accompanied them; these ships were also painted for the occasion and carried many newly painted shields. The sailors were bedecked with ribbons in the colour of the livery company from which the Lord Mayor had been elected that year. [SD]

54

Trumpet banners of the Skinners' Company

Inscribed: 'To God Only Be All Glory'
Textiles, 880 × 1030 mm (framed)

The Worshipful Company of Skinners

The Skinners' Company began as a guild of furriers, engaged in the sale and manufacture of furs for garments and trimmings. It received its first charter from Edward III in 1327; its current arms, shown on the trumpet banner, were awarded in 1634. It alternates in precedence with the Merchant Taylors' Company, coming either sixth or seventh. The shield is speckled to represent the ermine's winter coat and topped with three ducal coronets, emblematic of the fur's use. It is supported by a lynx on the left and a sable marten on the right; a further lynx forms the

crest. Lynx was a highly esteemed fur and could not be worn by anyone beneath the rank of earl.

The Skinners continued to employ their barge throughout the first half of the nineteenth century, attending the opening of the New London Bridge in 1831 and that of the Coal Exchange in 1849. The barge was sold in 1858 and used as a houseboat by Queen's College, Oxford. Music and ceremonial saluting were an important part of the Lord Mayor's Day procession. Liveried trumpeters with their banners, for example, were often hired for the celebrations. The lavish decoration of items as seemingly trivial as trumpet banners gives an indication both of the importance placed on the processions and of their extraordinary visual splendour.
[RB]

LITERATURE: Palmer, *Ceremonial Barges*, p.42.

55
Barge crew jacket of the Weavers' Company

Textiles

The Worshipful Company of Weavers

This striking blue and yellow uniform was worn by the barge crew of the Weavers' Company. The Weavers are the oldest recorded City livery company, going back to the reign of Henry I (1068/9–1135). Although they are forty-second in the order of precedence for the Lord Mayor's procession, two companies of the 'Great Twelve' – the Mercers and the Drapers – have their origins with the Weavers' Company. [AM]

LITERATURE: Palmer, *Ceremonial Barges*, pp. 121–22.

56
Bargeman's cap

Velvet, metal thread, leather and fur with a gilt badge, 155 × 220 × 280 mm

The Worshipful Company of Skinners

This is one of four surviving caps worn by the barge crew of the Skinners' Company. The crown of the cap is adorned with the gilt badge of the lynx, which is the crest of the Company's coat of arms. The Skinners hired a barge for the early river processions but built their own barge in 1656 at a cost of £114 10s. [AM & SD]

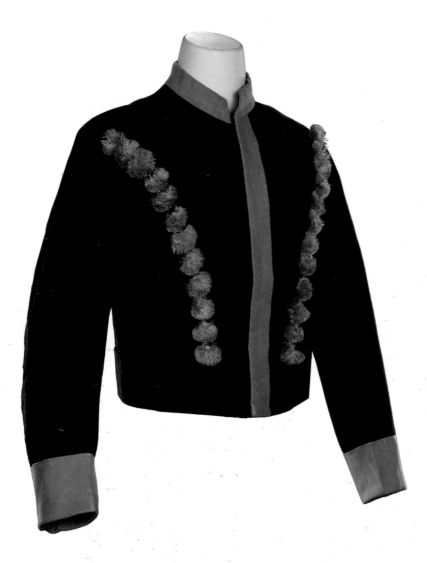

57 (left)

Waterman's coat and badge (V.I.P. crew)

1827
Textiles, silver

The Company of Watermen and Lightermen
of the River Thames

58 (right)

Watermen's Company bargemaster's coat, badge and hat

1984
Wool, metal thread, silver

The Company of Watermen and Lightermen
of the River Thames

The waterman's coat was worn during the Lord Mayor's procession of 1827; the bargemaster's coat is a modern version following the historic livery design. In that year Matthias Prime Lucas, Master of the Vintners' Company and also on the court of the Watermen's and Lightermen's Company, was Lord Mayor of London. According to *The Times* (10 November 1827), his pageant was the 'most glorious for many years'. However, the same was not true of the Guildhall banquet that followed. Towards the end of the great meal – during which abundant game, turtle and fine wines were served – a large board, supporting a lamp in the form of an anchor, crashed on to the heads of the Lord Mayor and his party. As *The Times* report continued:

> Dukes, judges, servants and trumpeters were intermixed and looking with astonishment in each other's faces. Fortunately, the Lady Mayoress sustained no injury besides the fright and the total derangement of her dress by the oil. The Lord Mayor did not escape quite so well: his head was a good deal lacerated by the broken glass; but the board having fallen obliquely, seems to have spent its force innocently upon the chairs.

Lucas thus narrowly avoided the dubious accolade of leaving office before drinking the last toast of his inauguration dinner.
[AM & RB]

59 (below)
Model of the Shipwrights' Company barge

c. 1780
Painted oak, brass, glass,
265 × 1075 × 180 mm, scale 1:16
National Maritime Museum, Caird Collection, SLR0544

The Shipwrights' Company dates back to at least 1387 when it was first mentioned as a fraternity in honour of St Simon and St Jude, both of whom were associated with boats. The Company's arms depict the hull of a ship on a sea. The crest is Noah's Ark resting on the mountains of Ararat, with the motto 'Within the Ark Safe for ever'. There is no record of the Shipwrights either owning or hiring a barge themselves, although they would have undoubtedly built and supplied barges to the other livery companies for various ceremonial and festive occasions on the river. This model illustrates the typical design of many of the livery barges with their distinctive clinker construction of overlapping planking, the long raking bow and broad shallow mid-section, all of which derive from the Thames 'wherry' hull form. It has a large and ornately decorated cabin with three pairs of carved animals, references to Noah, and figures representing the saints. The barge was pulled by sixteen oarsmen and steered by the bargemaster on a raised platform behind the cabin. [SS]

LITERATURE: Palmer, *Ceremonial Barges*, pp.22, 140.

60 (right)
Model of the Fishmongers' Company barge of 1773

1937
CHARLES WHITTAKER
Wood and other materials,
1200 × 330 × 200 mm, scale 1:24
The Worshipful Company of Fishmongers

The Fishmongers' Company, which tightly controlled the quality and sale of fish within the City, existed as a body long before Edward I granted its first charter in 1272. With more than half the year consisting of fast days on which meat could not be consumed, fish was a hugely important part of the diet in the Middle Ages. As a result, the Fishmongers' Company became immensely wealthy and was included as one of the 'Great Twelve', the leading City livery companies. The model represents the last of the Fishmongers' barges, which was broken up in the 1850s. [SD & RB]

61

Carved tail-piece from the Merchant Taylors' barge

1800
Carving by MESSRS BATTEN AND GLOVER, Horseferry, Rotherhithe; original painting and gilding by MESSRS FAIRCHILD AND SARNEY, 202 Bishopsgate Without
Painted and gilded wood, 2440 × 1950 mm

The Worshipful Company of Merchant Taylors

The Merchant Taylors' Company, a trade association of tailors and linen armourers (men who made padded tunics worn under armour), received its first charter from Edward III in 1327 and was one of the 'Great Twelve'. The present coat of arms, granted in 1586, shows a pavilion in imperial purple with gold, and lined with ermine, between two similarly decorated mantles with a lion passant. The crest depicts the Lamb of God on a green mount surrounded by a radiant border of sunbeams. The supporting camels relate to the silk route and the Company's far-flung trade. The motto is *Concordia parvæ*

res Crescunt: 'With harmony small things become great'.

In 1799, the Merchant Taylors' barge, in use since 1764, was deemed unserviceable and a new vessel was ordered from Richard Roberts of Lambeth. Consequently, the Master informed the Lord Mayor elect, Harvey Christian Combe, that the Company was unable to take part in the annual river procession. Roberts charged £1321 to build the new barge, which was 79-feet long, requiring an extension of the Company barge house. In addition, the magnificent tail-piece, in the form of the Company's coat of arms, cost £130 with a further £45 18s 6d spent on its decoration. Maintaining the barge proved increasingly costly until eventually prudence prevailed. The barge was given up in 1846 and sold for £63. The tail-piece was preserved and now hangs prominently on the grand staircase of the Merchant Taylors' Hall in the City of London. [RB]

LITERATURE: Sayle, *Barges*, pp.28–38; Palmer, *Ceremonial Barges*, p.46.

62

Carvings from the Fishmongers' Company barge

1773
Painted and gilded wood, quarter badges, 1320 mm (length); tail piece, 1676 × 1245 mm

The Worshipful Company of Fishmongers

On the tail-piece are the arms of the Company, granted in 1512 at the time of its union with the Stockfishmongers, who dealt with dried fish. It shows three dolphins between two pairs of stockfish wearing crowns and three pairs of keys of St Peter, the Company's patron saint. The crest consists of a pair of arms holding an imperial crown aloft; a merman and mermaid are supporters, holding respectively a falchion (a short sword) and a mirror. The motto reads: 'All worship be only to God'. The carved angels, or heralds, were quarter badges (see pp.82–83). [RB]

LITERATURE: Palmer, *Ceremonial Barges*, p.33.

63 (opposite)

Bargemaster's badge of the Goldsmiths' Company

1761
JOHN PAYNE (fl. 1751–79), London
Silver-gilt, 237 × 214 mm

The Worshipful Company of Goldsmiths

One of the 'Great Twelve' livery companies of the City of London, the Goldsmiths received its first royal charter in 1327 from Edward III. The Company had responsibility for testing the quality of gold and silver. After 1478 these precious metals had to be marked in the Goldsmiths' Hall: the origin of the term 'hallmark'. This badge displays the Company's coat of arms, granted in 1571. It incorporates the leopard's head, which has been the mark of the Goldsmiths since 1300. The Company's first barge was built by Edmund Tue in 1656 at a cost of £100. Its sixth and last barge, built by Couthorpe of Rotherhithe in 1824 for £1575, was sold off in 1845. [SD & RB]

LITERATURE: Palmer, *Ceremonial Barges*, pp. 38, 150.

64

Bargemaster's badge from the Grocers' Company

1759
W.G., London [probably WILLIAM GRUNDY (fl. 1743–79)]
Silver-gilt, 247 × 202 mm

The Worshipful Company of Grocers

The Grocers' Company began as the Guild of Pepperers, dating from the early twelfth century. It received its first royal charter from Henry VI in 1428 and was ranked second, behind the Mercers, in the 1516 order of precedence. The arms on the bargemaster's badge were granted in 1532. Two griffins support a chevron between nine cloves; the bridled camel on the crest carries bags of pepper, representing trade with the East. The Grocers took part in a great many water processions before selling their last barge in 1845. In 1889 it was decided to dispose of the bargemaster's coat. The same fate befell the badge, the beadle considering it to be of little worth. Eventually, it was recognised as valuable silver, and a jeweller in Cheapside sold it back to the Company. [RB]

LITERATURE: Palmer, *Ceremonial Barges*, p. 26.

65

Bargemaster's badge of the Stationers' Company

1680
WILLIAM GAY (d. 1687), London
Silver, 227 × 190 mm

The Worshipful Company of Stationers and Newspaper Makers

Founded in 1403, the original members of the Company were text writers, illuminators, bookbinders and some booksellers. The Company received a royal charter in May 1557, by which time print had largely replaced manuscript production and printers dominated the Company. The Company had a long tradition of employing barges on the Thames. They built six in total: the first costing £187 in 1679–80 and the last £1785 in 1826. In 1680, the Company spent £4 18s 9d on an arm badge for John Barrow, their first bargemaster, who was paid an annual salary of £4. Members of the Barrow family served the Company in this role for seventy-five years. In 1849, it was deemed 'inexpedient to retain the use of the Company's barge' and the vessel was sold for £105 and subsequently hired to Exeter College, Oxford. [RB & SD]

LITERATURE: Osborne, *State Barges of the Stationers' Company*, pp. 7, 15, 17, 40.

66

Bargemaster's badge of the Barbers' Company

1735
ROBERT LUCAS (fl. 1726–39), London
Silver, 210 × 190 mm

The Worshipful Company of Barbers

In 1462 Edward IV incorporated the Company of Barbers, whose members practised minor surgery and dentistry as well as shaving. The Company of Barbers and the Surgeons Guild were amalgamated by Act of Parliament in 1540. The badge here shows the arms of the Company granted in 1569. They are quartered with a cross and a lion passant, and consist of crowned double roses and chevrons between fleams. These were razor-sharp instruments used in blood-letting, and relate to the Company's association with surgery. The Barbers usually hired barges, having their own only between 1662 (undoubtedly commissioned for Catherine of Braganza's *Aqua Triumphalis*) and 1698. The 1662 barge cost a total of £210 to build, equip and decorate. The bargemaster's badge was purchased from Newton's of Lombard Street in the City for £4 11s 6d. [RB & SD]

LITERATURE: Palmer, *Ceremonial Barges*, p. 80.

67
Waterman's badge of the Merchant Taylors' Company

1791
Silver-gilt, 100 × 100 mm

The Worshipful Company of Merchant Taylors

When processing on the Thames, the livery companies engaged watermen to row their barges and provided badges to identify the crew. The Merchant Taylors' badge depicts *Agnus Dei* (the Paschal Lamb, or Lamb of God), which is associated with the Company's saint, John the Baptist, and forms the crest of its coat of arms. [RB]

68
Drapers' Company bargemaster's badge and oarsmen's badges

1671 and c.1792
Silver-gilt, bargemaster's badge, 218 × 184 mm; oarsmen's badges, 64 × 78 mm

The Worshipful Company of Drapers

The Drapers' Company, which received its first charter from Edward III in 1364, regulated the buying and selling of cloth within the City. Its arms, depicted on the central bargemaster's badge, consist of three clouds issuing sunbeams mounted by triple crowns, which represent the Virgin Mary, the Company's patron saint. The arms were granted in 1439. The bargemaster's badge cost £5 8s when purchased in 1671. The initials of various holders of the post are scratched on the reverse. The twenty-two oarsmen's badges (which were worn in their caps) feature a ram, part of the addition to the arms granted in 1560. The Company sold its last barge in 1829. But a shallop, of the design built for Mary II in 1689, was purchased in 2003 and now serves as the 'Drapers' barge'. Copies of the badges were commissioned for the oarsmen and the bargemaster to wear. [RB]

LITERATURE: Palmer, *Ceremonial Barges*, pp.30–31.

69
Bargemaster's badge of the Clothworkers' Company

1787
HENRY GREEN (*fl.* 1786–95), London
Silver, 242 × 213 mm

The Worshipful Company of Clothworkers

The Clothworkers' Company was formed by an amalgamation of the fullers and shearmen, both groups involved in finishing cloth. The Company received its royal charter from Henry VIII in 1528. The coat of arms, granted in 1530 with additions in 1587, shows two habicks, or double-ended hooks, used to secure stretched cloth, and a teasel, employed to raise the nap. The arms are supported by griffins and mounted by a ram crest. In 1782, the Company's barge was damaged in a collision with a lighter on Lord Mayor's Day, resulting in an order to limit the Clothworkers' consumption of wine while afloat. The Company gave up its barge in 1799, borrowing one from the Phoenix Assurance Company in 1803 and hiring another in 1850: on both occasions Clothworkers were appointed Lord Mayor. [RB]

LITERATURE: Palmer, *Ceremonial barges*, pp.64–65.

70
Waterman's badge

1736–37
WILLIAM LUKIN (*fl.* 1699–1751), London
Silver, 260 × 200 mm

National Maritime Museum, XXX2240

This arm badge was worn by watermen of
the Admiralty barge, which was based at
Somerset House from the late eighteenth
century. The gilt anchor and cable on a
red enamel ground are set in an elaborate
cartouche teeming with naval emblems
and motifs, comprising a shell, dolphins,
flags, cannon and numerous navigational
instruments. [RB]

71
John Dards, Fishmongers' Company bargemaster

E.F. LAMBERT (*fl.* 1823–46)
Oil on canvas, 1050 × 840 mm (framed)

The Worshipful Company of Fishmongers

John Dards was the bargemaster of the
Fishmongers' Company from 1807 until
1837. He is shown wearing the silver arm
badge of 1730. Standing high in the stern
of the barge, Dards had the considerable
responsibility of steering the vessel
(barges were notoriously difficult to
handle) and to ensure the order of
processional precedence was maintained.
His thirty years in the post suggest that
Dards was a skilled waterman. Little is
known of the London-based artist E.F.
Lambert, but he almost certainly exhibited
this portrait at the Royal Academy in 1829
with the title 'A City barge master in his
civic costume'. [RB]

72 (left)
St Dunstan from the Goldsmiths' Company barge

c. 1745
Gilded wood, 1730 mm (height)
The Worshipful Company of Goldsmiths

73 (below)
Coat of arms from the Goldsmiths' Company barge

c. 1745
Gilded wood, 1575 × 1200 mm
The Worshipful Company of Goldsmiths

The gilded arms and figure of St Dunstan are decorations from the fourth Goldsmiths' Company barge, built by John and Edward Hall of Southwark in 1745. The barge was commissioned for the mayoralty of Sir Richard Hoare (1709–54), a member of the Company, who was the grandson of the founder of Hoare's Bank in the City of London.

Dunstan (909–88) was a monk who rose to become Archbishop of Canterbury. He also worked as a goldsmith and jeweller, hence his role as the Company's patron saint. The long tongs represent this work, but also refer to Dunstan confronting the Devil in the form of a beautiful maiden:

> St Dunstan, as the story goes,
> Once pull'd the devil by the nose
> With red-hot tongs, which made him roar,
> That he was heard three miles or more.

[RB]

74
St Catherine from the Haberdashers' Company barge

c. 1656
Gilded wood, 1270 × 610 × 640 mm (approx.)

The Worshipful Company of Haberdashers

The Haberdashers' Company received its first grant of arms in 1446 and a Charter of Incorporation two years later. Their patron saint is St Catherine of Alexandria, an early fourth-century martyr, sentenced to death on a breaking wheel. She features in Thomas Heywood's pageant – *Londoni speculum: Or, Londons mirror* – written to celebrate the inauguration of Richard Fenn, a Haberdasher, as Lord Mayor in 1637. The Haberdashers hired a barge to escort Anne Boleyn for her coronation in 1533, but built their own barge in 1656. The figure of St Catherine was commissioned at this time. [RB & SD]

LITERATURE: Palmer, *Ceremonial Barges*, p.50.

75
St Lawrence from the Ironmongers' Company barge

1740
Wood, iron, 1430 × 980 × 600 mm (approx.)

The Worshipful Company of Ironmongers

The Ironmongers' Company was granted arms in 1455 and its first charter from Edward IV in 1463. One of the 'Great Twelve', the Company is tenth in order of precedence. The Ironmongers owned and hired a number of barges. Its records state, for example, that a barge was hired to escort Anne Boleyn from Greenwich to the Tower of London on the occasion of her coronation in 1533. This cost 33s 4d, with an additional 6d paid for cushions. In 1740, new stern carvings were commissioned for the barge and the figure of St Lawrence was produced at the same date. Lawrence, an early Christian martyr, was burned, or 'grilled', to death. He is often shown, as in this figure, carrying a gridiron, which provides a rather grisly connection with the Ironmongers' trade. [RB]

LITERATURE: Palmer, *Ceremonial Barges*, p.56.

76
St Peter from the Fishmongers' Company barge

1773
Gilded wood, 1450 × 830 x 550 mm

The Worshipful Company of Fishmongers

Simon the fisherman, later St Peter, is shown here with a radiant halo carrying the keys to the gates of Heaven in his right hand and the Holy Bible in his left. The 'prince of the Apostles', he was, with his brother Andrew, the first to join Jesus when they responded to the invitation 'Come with me, and I will make you fishers of men' (Matthew 4:19). St Peter is the patron saint of a number of other livery companies, but the connection to the Fishmongers is perhaps the most literal. [RB]

77
Ostrich from the Ironmongers' Company barge

1629
Wood, iron, 1120 × 470 × 740 mm (approx.)

The Worshipful Company of Ironmongers

The reason why the Ironmongers' Company carried an 'estridge', or ostrich, on its barge is partly found in ancient Rome. Pliny the Elder described the ostrich in his *Naturalis Historia*, noting that it could eat and digest anything. This belief was further exaggerated in the *Physiologus*, which proclaimed the giant bird's capacity to swallow iron and, more fancifully, hot coals. This notion persisted and was translated into heraldry, as seen in this seventeenth-century carving, where the ostrich is represented with a horseshoe in its mouth, symbolic of its iron-eating ability. The Company's coat of arms features salamanders, which were also believed to be able to withstand the heat of the forge. [RB]

78
Wine-bowl

1841
Wood and silver, 46 mm × 89 mm

The Worshipful Company of Goldsmiths

The Lord Mayor's procession of 1841 coincided with the birth of Queen Victoria's first child, Albert Edward. News of the royal birth reached the barge of the Goldsmiths' Company and this wooden bowl was used to drink a toast to the newborn prince. The bowl was preserved and later mounted in silver with an inscription: 'THIS WINE BOWL WAS SELECTED BY / John William Thomas, Goldsmith / UPON THE OCCASION OF FIRST DRINKING THE HEALTH OF ALBERT PRINCE OF WALES Nov. 9 1841 / on board the Barge of his Company. And mounted in remembrance of the since abolished ancient custom of accompanying / THE LORD MAYOR FROM LONDON TO WESTMINSTER'. [RB]

79 (below left)

Bargemaster's badge of the Haberdashers' Company

1689
Silver-gilt, mounted on oak as a snuffbox,
350 × 229 × 102 mm

The Worshipful Company of Haberdashers

80 (below right)

Bargemaster's badge of the Ironmongers' Company

c. 1760
RICHARD HARPER
Silver, mounted on walnut as a snuffbox,
200 × 150 × 90 mm

The Worshipful Company of Ironmongers

After the last Lord Mayor's river procession in 1856, the livery companies no longer needed to maintain or hire barges, ending some 400 years of tradition. Without a barge, there was no need for Company bargemasters and, therefore, no obvious use for the ceremonial arm badges associated with the office. Some badges were simply retained in Company vaults, but others were converted to different uses. The Merchant Taylors' badge (not illustrated) was mounted on an oak snuffbox, which bears the following 'verse' inscription inside:

> The lid of this box is the Barge
> Master's Badge
> Resplendent it shone on his Shoulder,
> But the barge was sold off, which made
> people cough,
> Perhaps they will sneeze at this ample
> Snuff Holder.

The last bargemaster of the Merchant Taylors was James Thomas, who held the position from 1826 to 1846, when the Company disposed of its barge. Thomas requested compensation for the loss of his situation. The Company minutes of 28 October 1846 record 'it was Resolved that upon his delivering up the Silver Badge worn by him as the Company's Barge Master he be allowed the sum of £10 per annum'. The Haberdashers' and Ironmongers' Companies also turned their badges into large table snuffboxes.

A number of livery company barges were sold to Oxford Colleges. Cambridge also purchased a number, but the attempt to tow them around the coast of East Anglia proved ill-fated: they foundered at sea. [RB]

LITERATURE: Fry and Tewson, *Illustrated Catalogue*, p. 23; Sayle, *Barges*, p. 62; Palmer, *Ceremonial Barges*, p. 150.

81

Sir Robert Carden

1866
JAMES EDGELL COLLINS (1819–95)
Oil on canvas, 1800 x 1440 mm (framed)

The Worshipful Company of Cutlers

Sir Robert Carden (1801–88) was a London-born banker who founded the City Bank in 1855. He was also MP for Gloucester (1857–59) and Barnstaple (1880–85), and Alderman for the City's Dowgate ward from 1849 to 1871. Carden became a rather unpopular Lord Mayor in 1857–58, in part because he tried to stop corruption. He also relinquished the City's long-held and jealously guarded rights of control over the Thames to the new Thames Conservancy Board in 1857, following a protracted legal wrangle with the government over the future development of the river. He was, therefore, the first Lord Mayor to abandon the traditional water procession in favour of the now familiar land-based pageant. [RB]

LITERATURE: *Oxford DNB*.

3

THE EIGHTEENTH-CENTURY RIVER

THE LATER HISTORY OF GREENWICH: A RIVER LANDSCAPE AND ARCHITECTURAL STATEMENT

JOHN BOLD

To see London you have to go up – a hill, a building, the London Eye – or down, to the river, which is central to its topography and to our understanding of its layout and history. This is what Canaletto did in order to capture in London an equivalent to the Bacino di San Marco in Venice. The Thames affords a wide, watery panorama which he exploited in views of St Paul's, Westminster, Whitehall, Chelsea and Greenwich. Now, we can do what countless landscape painters have done – go to the top of the hill in Greenwich Park and look towards St Paul's Cathedral, a protected view since 1937, or towards Docklands and Essex. The views remain dramatic, but they have changed, most apparently with the development of modern Docklands since the 1980s. The view south, however, across the river from Island Gardens remains recognisably the same as it was when depicted by Canaletto in the mid-eighteenth century, when the main phases of the building of the Royal Hospital for Seamen were coming to an end. There are two surviving views by Canaletto of Greenwich from the north. The first of these is datable to before 1746, when the artist travelled to England for the first time. It follows closely Jacques Rigaud's engraved prospect of 1736, copying his ships and boats and incorporating his topographical and architectural inaccuracies. The second, a substantially corrected version, although not without its own artful deceptions which indicate that the artist was depicting both what he saw on site and what he would have expected to see, is datable to around 1750, before Canaletto returned to Venice for eight months in the autumn of that year. [see cat. no. 86] This is a wonderful painting of a sublime architectural and landscape ensemble.

We may imagine Canaletto checking the view by standing on the wall which had been built to protect the Isle of Dogs, a tongue of reclaimed marshland, from flooding. Later viewers had the benefit of a platform. Other artists may well have relied on the work of previous engravers, not least because the design of the Hospital evolved over several years from the date of its foundation in 1694, during its subsequent laying out by Christopher Wren, and in the course of the building campaign itself. This was to last for over half a century, a timescale that encouraged speculation about the outcome. The public interest in the buildings created opportunities for commercial printmakers for whom the niceties of detail were not a priority.

They were countered on several occasions by the Governors of the emerging Hospital who ordered officially approved, accurate engravings in 1699, 1702, 1708 and 1711. The Governors feared that unsanctioned depictions, 'notoriously false and much to the discredit of that noble structure', would deter subscribers from contributing to a building campaign which was perennially short of funds until the allocation by Parliament of an annual grant in 1728, and then more substantially in 1735 through the granting of the rents and profits of the Derwentwater estate in Northumberland. The printmakers, both unauthorised and official, favoured the bird's-eye view from the north. This was not, however, the intended view when Island Gardens was later created at the southern tip of the Isle of Dogs. It was the vista from the Hospital rather than towards it which persuaded Sir Francis Baring, First Lord of the Admiralty, in 1849 to press the Commissioners of the Hospital to purchase the land for the gardens. Dr John Liddell, Medical Inspector to the Hospital, had argued for both vista and health in his report on the sanitary condition of the Hospital in 1848. His argument, however, that the acquisition of a short stretch of riverfront would be beneficial in reducing the pollution which was having a deleterious effect on the respiratory condition of the Hospital pensioners failed to sway the Commissioners who were, as ever, concerned with cost. Baring proved more persuasive:

> Greenwich Hospital is one of the finest Buildings of which we can boast. The erection of smoky Manufactory Chimnies directly opposite will materially affect the appearance of the Building – and I much fear when the thing is done and it is too late we shall be sorry that we have allowed the land to slip out of our control, and the public when they learn that there was an opportunity of securing it, *will cry out*.
>
> In order to make up my own opinion I went down to Greenwich, and … I came away entirely agreeing with … those who believe it will sadly affect the view … I cannot but think that it is very essential for the eye at least that some line of Trees or agreeable objects should close the Vista.
>
> As to the money question … you must recollect that the Foundation and Building is not done niggardly, and when a Palace is erected for such a purpose it is not improper that some consideration and expense should be incurred for appearance.[1]

The lease of Island Gardens was granted in 1852, remaining with the Hospital until 1895 when this 'little paradise' was opened to the public following its purchase by the London County Council.[2] This was primarily a local public since the Isle of Dogs was notoriously difficult to get into, or out of, until the completion of the Greenwich Foot Tunnel in 1902.

In 1710, Zacharias Conrad von Uffenbach, book collector and connoisseur, viewed Greenwich from the favoured perspective of the river. He found the buildings 'more elegantly and magnificently planned' than Chelsea Hospital, 'but it is not so easy to describe this building as to see it in the engravings there are of it'. He gave considerably more attention to the Royal Observatory, where the Astronomer Royal, John Flamsteed, 'received us with uncommon civility (which is in England most unusual)', showed 'a prodigious quantity of his written observations', pointed out 'astronomical phenomena' and assured them of a 'quite unprecedented eclipse' on 22 April 1715. From Flamsteed's observation platform his visitors enjoyed the 'charming prospect and the great traffic on the Thames. We had an excellent view because it was fair, clear weather, so that there was no coal-smoke or fog in the air'.[3] Sophie von la Roche came in 1786 by coach in heavy rain which 'to our joy' cleared enough to allow a view of the 'majestic pile' from afar, 'rising sheer above quantities of ships' masts'. Walking to the railings by the Thames, she 'gazed up and down this mighty river which is of such significance to the realm … pondered on the twelve thousand vessels employed by English commerce, the three hundred and fifty battleships which convey the wealth and character of the nation best of all'.[4] The river route was recommended in 1832 by the writer of 'Holiday Walks' in *The Penny Magazine*, who advised arrival by water rather than by land:

> the domes and colonnades of Greenwich will rise from the shore, and impress your mind with a magnificence of which the architecture of England presents few examples; – and you will feel an honest pride when you know that few of the great ones of the earth possess palaces to be compared with the splendour of this pile, which the gratitude of our nation has assigned as the retreat of its wounded and worn-out sailors.[5]

Louis Simond, an 'American in Regency England', unusually did not report on his mode of transport when he visited in 1810. But he noted the magnificence and cheerfulness of the Hospital, notwithstanding the 'tired and melancholy' aspect of the old sailors, 'warming themselves in the sun, or crawling

languidly along the magnificent colonnades or porticoes, of which the elegance and beauty makes a sad contrast with their crippled, infirm, and dependent old age'.[6] The Hospital had closed and the old men long gone by the time of Henry James's visit in 1877. He arrived by water on a grimy steamer:

> I find an irresistible charm in any sort of river-navigation, but I am rather at a loss how to speak of the little voyage from Westminster Bridge to Greenwich. It is in truth the most prosaic possible form of being afloat, and to be recommended rather to the enquiring than to the fastidious mind. It initiates you into the duskiness, the blackness, the crowdedness, the intensely commercial character of London. Few European cities have a finer river than the Thames, but none certainly has expended more ingenuity in producing an ugly river-front.

James was apparently unmoved by the 'great pompous buildings' of the former Hospital (by this time the Royal Naval College) but was pleased by the sight of the Observatory, since it brought back memories of childhood investigations in geography, and by the precipitous slopes which he had once imagined running down, but now, in his early thirties, was 'not even tempted to begin'.[7] James was evidently not the man to indulge in the popular frolic recorded in 1835 by Dickens during Greenwich Fair, namely:

> to drag young ladies up the steep hill which leads to the observatory, and then drag them down again, at the very top of their speed, greatly to the derangement of their curls and bonnet-caps, and much to the edification of lookers-on from below [8]

James was unusual in seeing pomposity where others had seen the magnificence famously deprecated by Dr Johnson. As Boswell recorded in 1763, 'he remarked that the structure of Greenwich hospital was too magnificent for a place of charity, and that its parts were too much detached, to make one great whole'.[9] However, a distinction should be drawn between luxury and magnificence. Magnificence can be defined as 'characterised by expenditure or munifence on a great scale', so it may be charitable to be magnificent when that magnificence is an indicator of a noble liberality. In his *Remarks on the Founding and Carrying on the Buildings of the Royal Hospital at Greenwich*, published in 1728, Nicholas Hawksmoor twice made the point that magnificence was part of the original brief from Queen Mary who had died in 1694. She had 'a great passion for Building' and desired that the

hospital should be built with 'great Magnificence and Order'. Her 'fixt Intention for Magnificence' had caused her to reject other sites for the Hospital since Greenwich was 'in the View of all the World', a 'noble Situation in the Sight of (the grand Emporium) *London*'. She required that the buildings should be 'capacious and durable', which as Hawksmoor reports, are absolutely necessary qualities in a public building, as well as 'regular and beautiful', which he notes 'cost nothing but the Care and Skill of the Architect'. This would be a building which in 'Strength, Beauty, and Convenience' would equal Les Invalides in Paris which, along with Wren's Chelsea Hospital, was a recurrent comparator in questions of architectural form, grandeur, provision for the men, conduct and costs.[10]

Wren gave his services to Greenwich Hospital free of charge. He produced a succession of designs and then laid out all the foundations between 1696 and 1701, so inhibiting future curtailment of the scheme: a wise precaution in a large building with uncertain financing. He would have preferred to have designed the Hospital as 'one great whole', as later required by Dr Johnson, with a central east–west domed range linking blocks to each side, framing a courtyard fronting the river. This would have followed the design proposed by John Webb in the 1660s for Charles II's new palace on the site which by 1672 was left with only one wing, the King Charles block, incomplete and boarded-up. This block, which according to Nicholas Hawksmoor was spared from demolition by Queen Mary, provided the starting point for Wren. He was enjoined to make the other side of the royal court 'answerable to it, in a proper Time'.[11] He also had to cope with a major constraint which was imposed by the terms of the royal bequest: Mary wished to retain the strip of land between the Queen's House and the river, giving her access to the house by water as well as by land. So Wren had to overcome the difficulty of creating a building without a centre, with the small-scale Queen's House terminating the view.

Wren retained responsibility as Surveyor until 1716 when he was succeeded by Sir John Vanbrugh. For many years, however, Wren's attendance had been infrequent since he was also engaged on St Paul's Cathedral and Hampton Court. In 1713, Hawksmoor and John James were given responsibility for drawing up contracts with the masons and preparing the account books. Hawksmoor, as Clerk of Works at Greenwich

since 1698 and Deputy Surveyor from 1705, had in fact been effectively in charge on site for most of the building campaign, making the designs for the Queen Anne building, for the wonderfully idiosyncratic façades of the King William building and for the superb detailing of the domes. Wren signed off the proposals in a manner now familiar in architectural practice in which the work of junior or associate architects may be approved by the head of the firm.

Vanbrugh, who died in 1726, presided over a period characterised by intermittent funding, and work in the early 1720s in particular was confined to the completion of parts begun rather than to new work. The opening of a new commission in 1727 and the approval by Parliament in 1728 of an annual grant of £10,000 gave renewed impetus to the completion of the Hospital. In the *Remarks* which complemented this initiative, Hawksmoor expressed his concern to ensure the proper completion of the building according to the original plans, indeed to go beyond them by providing an ambitious central chapel and handsome infirmary. In 1734, following the appointment in 1729 of the much-maligned Thomas Ripley over his head as 'our useless Surveyor', Hawksmoor complained that he had hoped Greenwich Hospital 'wou'd have been a publick Building, but it will sink into a deformed Barrac'.[12] His clerkship, by then nominal, was withdrawn in 1735 and he died the following year.

Ripley's contribution, the Queen Mary building, was assuredly less magnificent than anything conceived by Wren and Hawksmoor. He varied from the original design to create the extra accommodation required by the Governors at a time when there was a direct relationship between the number of pensioners and the Hospital's income. Ripley was pragmatic:

he created the Five-Foot Walk on the riverfront for the benefit of local residents; built the chapel (refitted by James Stuart and William Newton after a fire in 1779); and, most significantly, oversaw the completion of the main building programme. In doing so he was less biddable than the Governors perhaps expected, as well as more generous to the joint Clerks of Works, Hawksmoor and James, to whom payments had been suspended, paying them in 1734 out of his own pocket.

The siting of the Royal Hospital, and of the Tudor royal palace which preceded it, was of considerable significance at a time when river travel was of pre-eminent importance. The Royal Hospital, as Queen Mary had intended, was built on the site of the former Greenwich Palace at a point of maximum visibility, on one of the main routes into central London and beyond. Here at the palace, in the sixteenth and seventeenth centuries, extraordinary ambassadors had been greeted and bade farewell with appropriate ceremony. Here in 1697, Celia Fiennes reported seeing '100 saile of shipps pass by in a morning which is one of the finest sights that is'.[13] This was a public building on a prominent site with a very public and political message, expressing the strength and wealth of the state, the power and authority of the Royal Navy in

protecting worldwide national, commercial interests, and the benevolence of a grateful nation which looked after those sailors who had suffered and grown old in its service. Towards the end of his life, a sailor could sit on the immense terrace at Greenwich and contemplate the element that had brought him glory. As Louis Simond commented:

> whatever the feelings of the veterans may be on the subject, there cannot be any doubt as to the impression which this noble and comfortable establishment must make on the young seamen passing before it, going up and down the Thames.[14]

Finishing the Hospital buildings had been predicated upon precisely this belief. As Hawksmoor reported, the House of Commons had noted 'the indispensible Duty of those who have a just Sense of the great Importance of the Trade and Navigation of this Kingdom, to provide proper Encouragement for our Seamen'.[15] The Royal Navy, the largest and most expensive of the responsibilities of the state in the eighteenth century, recognised in Greenwich that it had a site commensurate with its status and worth. This perception continued throughout the years of both the Royal Hospital and the Royal Naval College. John Gwynn in 1766 argued for a *cordon sanitaire* around the buildings, calling for the demolition

of the 'great number of miserable houses, all of which should be immediately destroyed and not be permitted to deform and disgrace a work so truly magnificent'.[16]

The original grant of land for the Hospital had been less extensive than the founders wished: smaller than Chelsea, with a greater number of pensioners. The acquisition of more land to east and west was protracted but achieved to a limited extent in the 1750s, enabling the construction of gate lodges to each side, linked by a roadway. The subsequent increase in land ownership outside the walls of the institution enabled the building of Stuart's Infirmary (1764–68), Newton's Greenwich Hospital School (1783–84), and John Yenn's Civil Offices (1813–16). It was, however, the partnership of Edward Hawke Locker, Hospital Secretary from 1819, and Joseph Kay, Surveyor from 1823, which made the most profound impact upon the relationship between the Hospital and the town. The programme of improvements – clearing away extraneous buildings and walls, creating open space and regularising the approach to the Hospital – was said to have been in fulfilment of the original design. Kay's rebuilding of the town centre and market from 1827, and the creation of a ceremonial route to the Hospital gates, re-sited in their present position under the direction of Kay's successor Philip Hardwick, effected the final separation of town and institution. Shortly after the landscaping was completed, the Hospital closed in 1869, leaving the Royal Naval College from 1873 as the beneficiary of the programme of improvements.

The Royal Navy's keen sense of entitlement characterised its dealings with the Seamen's Hospital Society. Established in 1821, this was dedicated to the care of merchant seamen, using three hospital ships in succession, moored at Greenwich, where they served as a prominent advertisement for the mercantile service. When the Royal Hospital closed, the Society hoped to take over part of the Queen Anne building, thereby maintaining a riverside presence. This was rather too prominent for the Admiralty, which eventually agreed to the leasing of the former Hospital infirmary, which was set back from the riverfront and shortly to be further obscured by the Royal Naval College's Pepys Building. The Admiralty seems never to have been entirely comfortable with the presence of the mercantile service on the same site. It demanded the erection of railings on the unenclosed sides of the former infirmary and insisted on access being made only from the public streets to the south and west, rather than from the more convenient north side. Although there were occasional proposals for repossession of the building by the Royal Navy, the Dreadnought Seamen's Hospital continued in use until 1986.

The buildings of the former Royal Hospital School on the south side of Romney Road, which from the early nineteenth century had incorporated the Queen's House, were converted for the use of the National Maritime Museum, which opened in 1937. Public function continued also on the north side of the road: the former Hospital and College buildings, under the aegis of the Greenwich Foundation, are now occupied by the University of Greenwich and Trinity College of Music. These buildings, with the park to the south, have long been as well known through paintings and prints as they have been through direct experience. In his *Tour*, published in 1724–26, Defoe considered the buildings of Greenwich 'so well known, they need no particular description', preferring to consider the 'lustre of its inhabitants … a kind of collection of gentlemen … and of persons of quality and fashion'.[17] By this time Greenwich's attraction for the nobility had faded, following the removal of the royal court to Kensington and Hampton Court by William and Mary. It now became predominantly a town associated with the Navy, accommodating the families of seamen, soldiers and others still in service and business.

Fig. 15 Greenwich Palace and London from Greenwich Hill, pen, brown ink and wash, by Anthonis van den Wyngaerde, c.1544.

Ashmolean Museum, WA.C.LG.IV.8b.

Fig. 16 (overleaf) The Bellot Memorial at Greenwich Hospital, oil on canvas, by George Chambers, Jr, 1857.

National Maritime Museum, Greenwich Hospital Collection, BHC2393.

Greenwich Park, originally a royal domain with an appeal for the fashionable, was opened to guests from 1705 and to the public during holidays, becoming fully public in the 1830s. Following the introduction of river steamers in 1836 and the arrival of the world's first suburban railway line two years later, about 250,000 people were visiting Greenwich at holiday times. It was a resort for all, 'from the unwashed sweep, to the clean confectioner; the mealy baker, to the fan-tailed coalheaver'.[18] The Park had gained a reputation in the 1790s as 'a seminary of vice', haunted by 'loose women and disorderly men', an aspect it retained in part until the closure of the springtime fair, 'that old market of vice and debauchery', in 1857.[19]

The prospect towards central London from Greenwich Park was one of the earliest views in England from a high vantage point to be exploited by painters, since it offered the possibility of so much: the pleasures of landscape and sky, the river winding its way towards the City and St Paul's, architectural detail, shipping and incidental, often picturesque characters. As James Thorne observed in 1876: 'from the high and broken ground by the Observatory and One Tree Hill the distant views of London and the Thames, with its shipping, are of matchless beauty and interest'.[20] In the mid-sixteenth century Anthonis van den Wyngaerde produced outstandingly detailed views of Greenwich Palace looking north and south across the river (fig. 15). In Flemish school paintings of the early seventeenth century that were among the earliest painted prospects of London, we again see the old palace; then van Stalbemt and van Belcamp depict the royal party on the hill above the palace on the occasion of the recommencement of the construction of the half-built Queen's House for Henrietta Maria. These depictions are followed by the charting of the demolition of the old palace, the commencement of the building of the new one, the building of the Royal

Observatory, and the progress of the Royal Hospital and Royal Naval Asylum (later the Royal Hospital School) in views by Hendrik Danckerts, Johannes Vorsterman (fig. 14), Jan Griffier the Elder, Peter Tillemans and J.M.W. Turner. Pepys, a regular visitor on naval business, admired both Park and prospect. In 1662 he 'walked into the Parke, where the King hath planted trees and made steps in the hill up to the Castle [Duke Humphrey's Tower, later the site of the Royal Observatory], which is very magnificent'. Here again in 1665, 'the King and Duke are come by water this morn from Hampton Court … The King mightily pleased with his new buildings'. In 1669 Pepys commissioned paintings of four of the royal palaces from Danckerts, and in March 'I to the park, there to see the prospect of the hill to judge of Dancre's picture which he hath made thereof for me; and I do like it very well – and is a very pretty place'.[21]

Greenwich as an iconic site of national and maritime glory was reinforced by paintings of Nelson and his battles, displayed first in the 'Naval Gallery' in the Painted Hall from 1824 to 1936 and now in the National Maritime Museum, and also by paintings and engravings of the pensioners themselves. Thomas Davidson's 'England's Pride and Glory' of 1894 shows a mother and son looking at Lemuel Abbott's 'Nelson', the gaze of the boy being returned by the inspirational hero. Davidson's 'The Pensioner's Story' shows an heroic, peg-legged veteran outside the King Charles building, reminiscing to what appears to be three generations of a visiting family. Since the early eighteenth century the Hospital had been popular with visitors, with show wards – occupied by acceptably well-behaved and tidy pensioners – encouraging benevolence. Davidson's depiction appears the more remarkable for being dated 1883, fourteen years after the last of the pensioners had gone. In fact, depictions of pensioners had increased significantly in the years leading up to closure, as overall numbers declined: the *Illustrated London News* in 1865 provided especially detailed coverage. There was an element of commemoration in such depictions, both before and after the closure of the Hospital, as well as the celebration of naval power and the exemplary heroism of those who had served their country. The Bellot memorial, erected in 1855, is one of the two commemorative obelisks on the riverfront next to the Hospital informed by comparable notions of naval heroism.

The memorial was depicted two years later, with pensioners in attendance, by George Chambers junior (fig. 16). Bellot, a French naval lieutenant, died in the Arctic while conveying dispatches to Sir Edward Belcher who was searching for the lost explorer, Sir John Franklin. For Blanchard Jerrold in 1872 the Bellot memorial expressed 'the gratitude of a great maritime nation towards an intrepid foreign sailor, who put his life deliberately in peril, and who lost it, on a mission of help to an illustrious brother sailor'.[22] Nearby, the New Zealand war memorial commemorates the naval dead of the Maori Wars of 1863–64, which reduced Maori numbers by half.

The buildings of Greenwich have been both subject and backdrop in innumerable paintings and engravings from the early seventeenth century to the present day. Views from the top of Greenwich Hill, and to a lesser extent from the Isle of Dogs, have continued to be made but, in addition to these, many painters in the nineteenth and early twentieth centuries laid as much emphasis on the shipping as on the site. Taking a river-level viewpoint, they imparted an immediacy to paintings which, beyond their ostensible subject, were depictions of an imperial metropolis of wealth, power and modernity, paid for by trade and commerce, and protected by heroes. However,

modernity and prosperity came at a harsh price for many of the industrialised, coal- and gas-fired population. As Dr Liddell had feared:

> Fog everywhere … Fog up the river … fog down the river, where it rolls defiled among the tiers of shipping, and the waterside pollutions of a great (and dirty) city … Fog in the eyes and throats of ancient Greenwich pensioners, wheezing by the firesides of their wards.[23]

Fog-bound, smoky London is a less-depicted story, but although paintings and prints are partial in their disclosures, they contribute to a whole and those which celebrate Greenwich and the river on a clear day, as Canaletto's works did, tell us a great deal about the history and development of the place, and the attitudes that inform our modern understanding. Their contextualising of shipping, landscape and buildings may also serve to illustrate the remarks of the principal architect of Greenwich Hospital, Christopher Wren: 'Architecture has its political Use; publick Buildings being the Ornament of a Country; it establishes a Nation, draws People and Commerce; makes the People love their native Country, which Passion is the Original of all great Actions in a Common-wealth.'[24]

LORD NELSON'S PROCESSION BY WATER: THE RIVER THAMES AND LATE-GEORGIAN NAVAL SPECTACLE

TIMOTHY JENKS

Ceremonial, religious and even funerary uses of the River Thames can be traced to the period of prehistory. By the turn of the nineteenth century, the river was primarily a commercial artery sometimes punctuated by royal and civic spectacle. Perhaps the most fascinating such event occurred on 8 January 1806, when London witnessed Admiral Lord Nelson's funeral procession by water from Greenwich to Whitehall Stairs. Nelson's funerary pageant (which spanned five days, encompassing a lying-in-state, the procession by water and a procession from the Admiralty to St Paul's Cathedral) is an example of late-Georgian naval, royal and civic spectacle. In 1806, the London through which Nelson's body was processed was the imperial capital of a commercial and maritime nation at war. The river over which it travelled was not only an important source of Britain's maritime and commercial power, it was also, less obviously, a player in the performance of his funerary rites.

News of Nelson's death at Trafalgar on 21 October 1805 reached London in the early hours of 6 November. Expectations of a state funeral were immediate. Such a funeral was in the royal gift, and George III was pleased to grant it although he was not pleased to permit his eldest son, the Prince of Wales, to attend in an official capacity as Chief Mourner as the Prince wished. Interestingly, public expectations did not settle on the necessity of an extended procession on the Thames. The detailed suggestions made by the *Sun* newspaper, while alert to the interests of naval and maritime symbolism, made no mention of a procession by water. And when a procession by water was first announced, the plans were for a shorter procession from Greenwich only 'to the Tower, from which place the Funeral will proceed, in grand procession, to St Paul's Cathedral'.[1] The symbolic and ceremonial import of such a route should not be ignored. For, although it would have seen Nelson's body landed at the Tower (which was a royal palace), the cortège would have immediately entered the City of London.

Suggestions had just been made that Nelson's lying-in-state should to be at the Guildhall.[2] Had both plans gone forward, Nelson's funeral would have emphasised City associations at the expense of those royal and naval. The organisers of the funeral (the Prime Minister, William Pitt, and his minister, Lord Hawkesbury, in consultation with the King, and heralds)

clearly wished otherwise, and future announcements gave Whitehall Stairs as the landing point. This meant that the flotilla, instead of landing at the formal entry to the City of London, would enter the City by passing under London Bridge, and would proceed through the metropolis primarily by water. The route (which thus went under Blackfriars Bridge as well) permitted greater panoramic vistas and greater opportunities for spectatorship than the confined streets of the City. It also saw the body landed in the Whitehall precincts of royal government, and permitted a final stop at the Admiralty on the night before the funeral.

In the event, then, a decision for a substantial procession by water was made. Operating powerfully on late-Georgian minds at this point was the funeral of Edward Montagu, first Earl of Sandwich. Sandwich had gone down with his ship in battle during the Third Anglo-Dutch War in 1672. His body, later found floating in the Channel, was recognised only by his medals. There was an obvious parallel to Nelson, who also died wearing his orders and the funeral was used as an organisational precedent. Sandwich's body had been

> brought in a yacht to Deptford, and from thence conveyed, in a sumptuous barge, to Westminster, attended by the barges of the King, Duke of York, several of the Nobility, the Lord Mayor, and the different Companies of the City of London, equipped suitably to the melancholy occasion, with trumpets, and other music adapted to the solemnity; the Tower guns, and those at Whitehall, being discharged as the procession passed, and all the bells tolling.[3]

Responsibility for arranging a similar event fell to the heralds of the College of Arms, whose expertise extended particularly to matters of heraldic symbolism and precedence. According to the Windsor Herald, Francis Townsend, for Nelson's funeral, they were 'adopting as far as related to Water the precedent of that of Lord Sandwich in 1672 and the Land part of as far as Circumstances would permit was planned after that of Lord Chatham in 1778'.[4]

Precedence and place were highly symbolic, and regarded as widely significant, in the rank-conscious social hierarchy that was late-Georgian society. Attention to the order of procession underlines the degree to which organisers were interested in crafting an event laden with naval and maritime symbolism. Central here was the designation of Sir Peter Parker, the Admiral of the Fleet, as Chief Mourner, a position

that would have normally been taken by Nelson's heir (in this case, his newly ennobled brother William). This was done in order to propagate the reassuring notion that the Royal Navy itself was heir to Nelson's tactical genius. Naval associations were expounded throughout the entire funerary episode. The lying-in-state was held in the Painted Hall of Greenwich Hospital, the ceiling of which, by the artist Sir James Thornhill, powerfully asserted British maritime supremacy (fig. 17). A 'chosen band' of seamen from the *Victory* attended at the close of the lying-in-state, rowed the barges in the procession by water, and carried the colours in the procession to St Paul's. Forty-eight more of them (along with an equal number of Greenwich Pensioners, one for each year of Nelson's life) marched in the procession as well. By conscious design all of the assistant mourners were admirals, effectively ensuring that Nelson's family was displaced in favour of the Navy. The most successful effort to emphasise Nelson's naval associations came in the form of the specially designed funeral car. A modified representation of the *Victory*, it was the iconic image of the funeral. While funeral cars had been traditionally

used in heraldic funerals, this car, in its realistic modelling of Nelson's flagship, was designed to fuse heraldic decoration with a more popular contemporary style. It was a highly effective visual rendering of Nelson's naval career.

As pleasing as these innovations were, Nelson's funeral was not carried off without some controversy. As mentioned, the Prince of Wales announced his intention of serving as Chief Mourner, but was prevented from doing so by his father. Equally embarrassing was the effort made by the Lord Mayor of London to have prime place in the funerary proceedings. For a time this rendered unclear the Lord Mayor's position in the procession by water. Critics also raised the concern that the sailors of the *Victory* might not be prominent enough in the funerary spectacle.

Such ceremonial controversies were allowed to percolate, in part because of the long delay between Nelson's death at Trafalgar and the arrival of his body in the capital – a delay caused by the interaction of weather, wind, current and tide. The *Victory* had arrived at Spithead on 6 December 1805. After necessary repairs, it sailed for the Nore, waited four days at

Fig. 17 *Remains of Lord Viscount Nelson laying in state in the Painted Chamber at Greenwich Hospital,* coloured aquatint, by Charles Augustus Pugin, engraved by M. Merigot, published by James Cundee, London, 1 April 1806.
National Maritime Museum, PAH7322.

Dover in consideration of the tides, and arrived off Sheerness on 22 December. The next day, the body was shifted to the yacht *Chatham* for the voyage to Greenwich. Unfavourable winds, and allowances for the tides, meant that it did not arrive off Greenwich until 'about one o'clock' on 24 December and was not landed until after dark. At this point it was 'finally determined, that the procession by water shall take place on the 7th of next month', and soon after this was changed to 8 January.[5]

Thus, when the lying-in-state opened on 5 January 1806, it did so in an atmosphere of great anticipation. The essayist and poet Charles Lamb, writing to William Hazlitt, felt 'the whole town is in a fever … as unsettled as a young Lady the day before being married'. Lamb was not impressed by the prospect of what he called 'Great Aquatic bustle', but plenty of others were.[6] Advertisements were placed by those offering favourable positions from which to view the funerary procession and also by those desperately seeking them. Views of the procession by water were offered in private homes, riverside taverns and commercial premises 'fitted up for the occasion'.[7] Significant crowds of spectators were expected. Organisers attempted to facilitate them by closing 'all the avenues leading to the water-side, on the day of the procession by water … [in order] to prevent carriages from drawing down' and blocking the view.[8]

The 'Great Aquatic bustle' finally got underway at mid-day on 8 January, a Wednesday, at which time the tide was favourable for the voyage upriver. 'At an early hour … the road from town to Greenwich exhibited a numerous train of mourning coaches', carrying admirals, naval officers, officers of the College of Arms, the Lord Mayor and representatives of the several City companies. By noon all the participants had arrived, were mustered in the Painted Chamber, and at 12.30 the procession started out of the Painted Hall and down to the river.[9] Led by 500 Greenwich Pensioners who peeled off to form a line of guard, the funeral party marched through lanes created by lines of River Fencibles (a recent volunteer force created by the wartime Pittite state) and the Greenwich and Deptford Volunteers, then passed through the North Gate on to the causeway and into the barges. These barges, 'appropriately decorated for this solemn occasion' and escorted by the row- and gun-boats of the River Fencibles

and Harbour Marines, formed into the order of procession and proceeded, with the tide but against the wind, up the river to London (fig. 18).[10]

The order of the barges in the procession was determined by a joint interest in maintaining heraldic precedence and in presenting not only naval, but also the requisite maritime and *riverine* symbolism. While the protocols of aristocratic and military rank were to be observed on the water, the various authorities over the river were also to be recognised. Thus the procession opened and closed with the Harbour Masters. Partly this was related to the responsibility they had been given for marshalling the procession by water, but it is important to note they claimed that responsibility by virtue of being the authority responsible for vessels in the estuary and anchorages of the Thames. This authority ended at London Bridge, where the City of London assumed control of the river. Which is why, 'on passing London Bridge', the Harbour Masters were to surrender their place to the Water Bailiff, the City official responsible for regulating the river fishery under the authority of the Lord Mayor.[11] Immediately behind him, were the Company of Watermen. The chaplain and staff of the River Fencibles, followed by the officers and ten boats of Fencibles, came next.[12] Thus, the first four corporate places filled in the procession acknowledged groups with either commercial or military authority over the river. Their role was to escort the funeral party through their respective bailiwicks.

The funeral party itself rode on the four state barges – the first three covered in black cloth, the fourth, bearing the body, with black velvet. In the first, two captains present at Trafalgar, supported by lieutenants and accompanied by two pursuivants from the Herald's Office, carried the standard in the bow, and the guidon (heraldic flag), at the door-place. This pattern was generally repeated in the other barges. In the second, another pairing of two captains and lieutenants of Trafalgar carried Nelson's Banner of the Order of the Bath and the 'Great Banner'. Alongside them two heralds bore the ceremonial accoutrements of Nelson's aristocratic rank. Officers of the College of Arms had their places mandated by the offices they held – the selection of the individual naval officers in the barges was determined by their presence at Trafalgar, not by personal connection to Nelson. But in the third barge, which carried Nelson's coffin, connections to the *Victory* were

Fig.18 *Funeral Procession of the late Lord Viscount Nelson, from Greenwich to Whitehall on the 8th January, 1806*, coloured aquatint, by Augustus Charles Pugin, engraved by John Hill, published by James Cundee, London, 1 April 1806.

National Maritime Museum, PAH7323.

privileged. Six lieutenants of Nelson's flagship, each bearing a long pennant, or bannerol, travelled with the body and the senior herald who bore a 'Viscount's coronet upon a black velvet cushion'.[13] Use of the barge itself (which flew the Union flag, was festooned with black ostrich feathers, and surmounted with a large representation of a viscount's coronet) was another example of royal favour. Built under Charles II, it had strong associations with the ceremonial conveyance of royals. In 1761 the barge had been refurbished in order to land the future Queen Charlotte at Greenwich immediately prior to her wedding; in 1767 it landed the body of George III's brother, the Duke of York, after his death abroad. Being 'always used by His Majesty on reviewing the Fleets', it also had naval resonance.[14] The naval captains of the fourth barge were Thomas Hardy, bearing the 'Banner of Emblems', and Hon. Henry Blackwood, who bore the train of Admiral Sir Peter Parker, the Chief Mourner. The Windsor Herald and eighteen admirals, acting as assistant mourners and supporters, filled out the craft.

Immediately following the four state barges with their official mourners, was His Majesty's barge. Although this apparently contained the royal princes, that fact was not widely advertised, probably because the princes were attending in their private capacity only. The naval symbolism resumed in the next barge, that of the Lords Commissioners of the Admiralty. Following it was the ornate barge of the Lord Mayor and another, containing those liverymen honoured to have been elected to the Committee arranging affairs for Nelson's funeral. Immediately behind this powerful statement of civic pride, was a barge which returned attention to the specifically maritime contexts of the day. This was the City Committee for the Improving of the Navigation of the River Thames – a dual reminder, once again, of civic authority over the river and of the river's centrality to commercial concerns; next followed the barges of the eight City companies that participated in the procession. Not all companies were wealthy or had barges, so the participation of these individual companies was not symbolic in the particular sense, but ought to be read as a general tribute on the part of the imperial capital and port city.

As the flotilla moved up the river, tributes were paid from the banks, a fact that underlines the degree to which

contemporaries considered Nelson's funeral an interactive spectacle, laden with opportunities for calculated participation. Nelson's body was silently acknowledged by the vessels in the river, which lowered their ensigns to half-mast as the body passed. Contemporaries were struck by these salutes, seeing the implicit connection to the imperial commerce that Nelson and the Navy had protected. They were also impressed that what was ordinarily a very busy port had fallen silent for a day. 'Every ship and boat on the River, even to the smallest craft that could shew a flag, streamer, or other naval emblem, displayed it on the occasion'.[15] The tribute was paid, not just by the shipping in the river, but also by the wharfs, churches and private premises along the way. In places, this allowed for the private participation of persons and particular parties – frequently in a manner that indicated some preparation. One of the Fire Offices, which operated the *Lord Nelson* barge, displayed a 'portrait of the illustrious Hero at her bow'. Similarly 'a man in Fair-street, Rotherhithe, hoisted a large St George's Ensign, in a mourning position, on a staff outside his workshop'.[16] The sailors of the tender *Enterprise* were mustered on deck by their officer, Lieutenant Somerville, to give Nelson a salute and three 'spontaneous' cheers. Nearby, six barges filled with Colonel Hankey's regiment of City volunteers stood 'with arms reversed' while Nelson's body passed, 'and continued in that position till the procession was clear of the Tower'.[17] When the procession passed the Temple, it was the opportunity for the volunteer corps raised by the legal profession to take centre stage: 'The lawyers' corps did duty in the gardens, and preserved the most exact order. They reversed their arms as the body passed.'[18] Participation was a statement of loyalty and an assertion of status in the capital's wartime theatre of patriotism. And thus, groups that did *not* capitalise on the opportunity could find themselves censured. Hence the *Morning Chronicle*'s claim that 'It was remarked with surprise, that the Somerset-house Corps were not mustered on this occasion on the terrace'.[19] This was a pointed comment, since undoubtedly Somerset House was as inundated with advantaged spectators as the Temple. The latter's 'gardens were filled with spectators, and on the terrace were drawn up numerous carriages'.[20] Fine meals were apparently served (these had also drawn Charles Lamb's ire) and the Admiralty navigation barge, the *Crosby,* was moored in front of the

Templc. Normally stationed at Kew, it had been brought through Westminster Bridge for the first time, 'for the accommodation of such members of the Corporation (in deep mourning, and violet gowns) as were not actually engaged in the Procession'.[21] These liverymen ended up having an excellent view of the only mishap to strike the procession, when 'the barge struck the ground in passing the Temple'.[22]

Spectatorship at Nelson's funeral procession by water was participatory in some cases, privileged in others, but everywhere widespread. Crowds lined the river and bridges, and the 'decks, yards, rigging, and masts of the numerous ships on the river were all crowded with spectators'.[23] After a three-hour voyage against a persistent wind, the barges arrived at their destination, where 'the windows, as well as the streets, round Whitehall, were crowded with spectators'.[24] At this point, a chance intervention of the weather became one of the most affecting moments of the entire funeral. The voyage up the river had been windy, but apparently sunny – and it was a cold January day. However, as the funeral barge approached the stairs, the sun disappeared, the sky clouded over, and

'a tempestuous hail-storm succeeded until the body was landed, when it again cleared'. To contemporaries, the storm seemed 'to announce that the element on which he reaped his glorious laurels, was about to surrender with reluctance its immortal chicf!'[25] The coffin was brought ashore and marched by the funeral party to the Admiralty, where Nelson's body was to rest one final night. The City portion of the flotilla continued on to Palace Yard, where the Lord Mayor and liverymen disembarked and returned to the City by carriage. In what must have been a widely viewed, but not widely commented upon, coda to the event, all the boats and barges of the procession, save those of the City companies, 'returned in order with the tide down stream, firing minute guns the whole way; and, by six o'clock streets were quite clear of the populace'.[26]

From our perspective in the twenty-first century, Nelson's funeral procession by water seems a singular and remarkable event. Late-Georgian Londoners, of course, viewed it in a different context, in a different time. For them, the spectacle drew its power both from its singularity and from its familiarity.

Britons of this time were not unused to spectacle or to processions by water. George III, in fact, was particularly active in using royal ceremony to recognise the Navy. As early as 1781, when he took the royal, Admiralty and Navy barges on a visit to the fleet at the Nore, it was observed that 'His present Majesty, to his Honour, has paid more Visits to his Fleets, than any former British Monarch whatever'.[27] In 1794, he went to Portsmouth to bestow honours on Admiral Howe's victorious fleet after the 'Glorious First of June', repeating a visit of 1774. In 1797, after victories by Admirals Jervis and Duncan, a grand Naval Thanksgiving had been held at St Paul's. As a prelude to it, the King visited Duncan's victorious fleet at the Nore. An 'immense concourse of persons' on land and in boats on the water watched the Admiralty barge convey the royal party from Greenwich Stairs to the *Royal Charlotte* yacht, en route to the estuary.[28] Even more familiar than the royal barges used in Nelson's funeral were those of the City of London's livery companies, which were magnificent affairs, designed and decorated to display the pride, wealth and prestige of the company in question. They were not uncommon sights on the river, being regularly used in various official capacities. The popular mind would have most immediately associated them, though, with the Lord Mayor's Day.

This annual event saw the new Lord Mayor, accompanied by the livery companies, process down the river in order to take his magisterial oaths from the various courts at Whitehall. Given that this was the most regular ceremonial procession with which contemporaries were familiar, it is a useful comparative guide for understanding Nelson's funeral

procession and the criterion by which it was assessed. The Lord Mayor and his party embarked on their barges at 'Three Cranes', at 'the bottom of Queen-street'. They would land at Palace Yard, swearing oaths before the necessary courts at Westminster, and return to Blackfriars Bridge via the Thames.[29] During the river procession the City barges did not have exclusive run of the river. Contemporary accounts indicate that it was common practice for sundry boats of spectators and watermen to infiltrate the City procession. Similarly, in 1797, on its way to the planned naval review, the royal yacht was pursued down the Thames estuary by 'an immense number of Peter boats, Gravesend boats, Margate hoys, &c. Indeed so great was the number that they becalmed each other so much, that they could scarcely get on'.[30] Of course, both this royal departure and Lord Mayor's Day were spectacles of festivity, not solemnity. But the freedom with which non-participant watercraft impinged on such processions explains why contemporaries were so impressed with the order and regulation evidenced in Nelson's funeral procession (fig. 19).

When order was achieved in a river procession, Georgian observers found it pleasing. Achieving order, for Nelson's procession by water, presented a challenge. This was both because the procession was large (seventy-seven small boats and barges formed Nelson's funerary flotilla) and lengthy (from Greenwich to Whitehall, significantly longer than the Lord Mayor's Day processions). The marshalling of boats at Greenwich was a logistical challenge, overseen by the Harbour Masters and the commandant of the River Fencibles, and governed by a dense set of regulations that reveal a significant interest in maintaining the security and symmetry associated with 'order'.

The heart of the procession, of course, consisted of the seventeen state barges whose presence and precedence was determined by heraldic concerns. These barges, though, were escorted by the numerous row-boats and gun-boats of the River Fencibles and Harbour Marines, the military authority with direct responsibility for the estuary. While the presence of both groups had a symbolic importance, the scale of their participation in the procession was functional. Their primary role was 'to prevent any boats or vessels from intersecting the Line of Procession'. The Harbour Masters were similarly charged with responsibility for ensuring, prior to the assembling, that 'all obstacles likely to incommode or interrupt the Procession, are removed early in the morning'. Maintaining the purity of the processional line against intruders was thus a major concern, as was maintaining the regularity of the line itself. All the row-boats were numbered so they would serve as guides to the stationing, pacing and spacing of the barges, and also to ensure that the flotilla properly divided into the respective arches of London Bridge. To achieve the necessary funereal solemnity, the regulations closed with a final requirement: 'The Procession being slow and solemn, the rest on the oars must be long.'[31] In the event, these efforts paid off. 'A party of soldiers drilling on their parade, however, could not possibly have advanced in a more regular order' was the *Morning Chronicle*'s approving verdict.[32]

What else struck contemporaries as singular and impressive about this procession by water? As has been hinted above, the tributes paid to Nelson's body as it came up the river could not be separated from the significance of the stillness in which they occurred. The role of the Thames as both a means of transport *and* a place of work needs to be kept in mind. On an ordinary day, the early-nineteenth-century river would have been a bustling and busy place. The day of the procession by water it was 'very full of shipping'.[33] Nevertheless, 'all the ships that grace the port of London' saluted Nelson's remains and 'the people on board them preserved the most profound silence'.[34] Contemporaries were struck by the spectacle that was this complete cessation of ordinary river business: 'There was not a barge or heavy vessel

of any sort to be seen plying on the river, even the floating mill at Bankside was drawn close in shore to make room for the procession.'[35] Not all river traffic was involved in the commercial shipping of goods. By 1800 about 12,000 watermen worked the river ferrying passengers, along with lightermen, who transported smaller loads. They shared the river with barges frequently towed by haulers along tow-paths, and even fishermen, some 400 of whom worked the river between Deptford and London Bridge. And although the procession by water suspended their work for a day, many of these men likely participated in it. Uncounted watermen would have been present, not just as the official representatives of their company, but as individual members of the River Fencibles. This volunteer corps (whose members were immune from impressment) was formed from men who worked the river. Nelson's funerary procession, then, featured the (sometimes silent) participation of individuals, corporate bodies and watercraft with which Londoners would have been familiar. The aggregation of these familiar groups, in an exceptional circumstance, increased the sense that an active tribute was being paid to Nelson by the maritime, commercial and naval interests of Britain.

The funeral of Sir Winston Churchill 159 years later echoed Nelson's in appropriate ways. The obsequies for that 'Former Naval Person' also took place in January and they also featured a procession on the Thames. Perhaps the iconic image of Churchill's funeral was a naval one – that of the gun carriage carrying his casket being drawn towards St Paul's by a Royal Naval gun crew. His procession by water was a celebrated moment as well, but for reasons which illustrate both the changed nature of British military power and of modern spectatorship. The overwhelming majority of Britons viewed this event on live television and it was considered affecting largely because of the accompanying voice-over eulogy supplied by the former US President Eisenhower. And the air was rent on this occasion not by a hail-storm, but by RAF pilots conducting a fly-past salute. The motor launch of the Port of London Authority delivered Churchill's body from Tower Pier to Festival Hall Pier in fifteen minutes. Thus ended what *The Times* was pleased to call 'the first river procession of this sort since the funeral of Nelson'.[36]

GREENWICH: JAMES THORNHILL AND THE PAINTED HALL

The Royal Hospital for Seamen at Greenwich was founded in 1694, based on the models of the Chelsea Hospital and Les Invalides in Paris, and built on the site of the old Greenwich Palace. The unfinished King Charles block was remodelled by Sir Christopher Wren and his assistant Nicholas Hawksmoor and completed under the supervision of Sir John Vanbrugh .

Housed within the King William Court of the Royal Naval Hospital is the monumental Painted Hall, originally intended as the dining hall. Its painting was one of the first major projects undertaken by the English painter James Thornhill. It took so long to complete, however, that it was also to became his last. When the artist was given the commission to paint the Lower Hall in 1707, he was a relatively young painter, beginning to make a name for himself alongside his better-known rivals from the Continent. By the time his work at Greenwich was completed, nineteen years later, Sir James Thornhill had risen to become one of the most successful and most celebrated English painters of any age.

Thornhill devised an elaborate scheme that traced the recent royal history of the British Isles from the Glorious Revolution of 1688, but such was the timescale involved that the artist's plans changed with events. His drawings show how the final painted scheme emerged over several years, beginning with a glorification of the reign of William III and Mary II on the Lower Hall ceiling, and culminating on the west wall with a celebration of the recently installed Hanoverian dynasty. [RJ & SD]

82

Design for the Upper Hall ceiling of the Painted Hall, Greenwich

c. 1718
JAMES THORNHILL (1675/6–1734)
Pen and ink with wash, on paper,
287 × 328 mm

National Maritime Museum, PAH3350

This is a carefully worked design for the Upper Hall ceiling, close to the executed version. It centres on a circular portrait of Queen Anne and her consort, Prince George of Denmark. They are surrounded by an array of mythological and allegorical figures – most visibly Hercules, on the left, and Neptune, who offers the riches of the sea to the royal couple. [RJ]

83 (opposite above)

Design for the west wall of the Painted Hall, Greenwich

c.1718
JAMES THORNHILL
Pen and ink with wash, on paper,
260 × 347 mm
National Maritime Museum, PAH3348

Many of the details in this drawing appear in the final design of the west wall, including the principal group of figures, centred on George I, seated beside his eldest grandson, Prince Frederick. Though finished to Thornhill's design, much of the painting on the west wall was executed by the artist's assistants. [RJ]

84 (opposite below)

Design for the west section of the Lower Hall ceiling of the Painted Hall, Greenwich

c.1707
JAMES THORNHILL
Pen and ink on paper, 360 × 491 mm
National Maritime Museum, PAH4059

At the centre of this working drawing is a personification of the City of London, represented as a young woman holding a sword and a shield bearing the City's arms. She rests upon the shoulders of the River Thames (here in his familiar guise as an elderly man, or Father Thames) and the River Isis. The City, in turn, supports the Royal Navy, represented by the stern of a British warship, loosely sketched by the artist. It describes in some detail the west end of the Painted Hall ceiling, where Thornhill emphasises the interdependence of the Navy, the Thames and the kingdom's prosperity. [RJ]

85 (right)

Design for the Lower Hall ceiling of the Painted Hall, Greenwich

c.1707
JAMES THORNHILL
Pencil with pen and ink with wash, on paper,
517 × 234 mm
National Maritime Museum, PAH4060

This highly detailed drawing shows the overall scheme of the Lower Hall ceiling at Greenwich within a single view. The apotheosis of William and Mary is depicted within the central oval. This is flanked by two scenes of maritime triumph. It was probably made for the Hospital Commissioners' approval before work in the hall began. [RJ]

86

Greenwich Hospital from the north bank of the River Thames

1750–52
GIOVANNI ANTONIO CANAL,
known as CANALETTO (1697–1768)
Oil on canvas, 686 × 1067 mm

National Maritime Museum, Caird Collection, BHC 1827

Canaletto worked in England between 1746 and 1755 apart from eight months at home in Venice in 1750–51. He painted many Thames scenes while in London, imbuing the river with the light, colour and atmosphere that characterised the visual language of his famous Venetian views. He had in fact painted a similar view before he came to England, based on a perspective print published in Paris by Jacques Rigaud in 1736, well before the Hospital was completed in 1751. Despite some anomalies of architecture and vista, which are far from unusual in the artist's work, this view represents the great complex of buildings as finished, and it shows direct local knowledge. Canaletto would almost certainly have visited Greenwich to see Thornhill's Painted Hall.

The early provenance of the painting remains unclear. It may have been commissioned for Consul Smith in Venice, and stylistic evidence suggests it 'belongs to the years before Canaletto's temporary return [there] … when he retained something of the breadth in conception and treatment which mark his best Venetian work'. It is therefore possible that Canaletto delivered the finished painting during his home visit: by then, the Hospital was substantially complete, save for internal works. [RB & PVDM]

LITERATURE: Beddington (ed.), *Canaletto in England*, pp. 50–53.

HANDEL, THE WATER MUSIC AND ROYAL SPECTACLE

87 (opposite left)
Miniature of George I

1718
BERNARD LENS (1682–1740);
after SIR GODFREY KNELLER (1646–1723)
Watercolour on ivory, 72 × 62 mm

Victoria and Albert Museum, P.64-1987

George I (1660–1727), Elector of Hanover, ascended to the British throne in 1714 on the death of the childless Queen Anne. The new King greatly enjoyed music and regularly attended the opera and other musical events. He was particularly fond of the music of George Frederick Handel and went to performances of some seventeen of his operas.

Bernard Lens, the leading miniaturist in Britain from 1710 to 1740, copied this miniature of George I from a print, after a portrait by Sir Godfrey Kneller (the miniature is inscribed on the reverse with an exact transcription of the lettering on the print). Lens is credited with introducing the technique of painting miniatures on ivory, rather than on the traditional vellum, but this was probably the innovation of the Venetian artist Rosalba Carriera. Lens also painted copies of historical portraits for collectors. Both of these characteristics are in evidence here. [SD & JM]

LITERATURE: *Oxford DNB.*

88 (opposite right)
Miniature of George II

c. 1727
CHRISTIAN FRIEDRICH ZINCKE (c. 1684–1767);
after SIR GODFREY KNELLER
Enamel with ivory backing, 78 × 62 mm

Royal Collection, RCIN 421796

George II (1683–1760) came to the throne in 1727. During his reign, Britain fought in several Continental wars, including the War of Austrian Succession which began in 1740 and ended with the peace of Aix-La-Chapelle in 1748. This miniature of the King is based on Sir Godfrey Kneller's 1716 portrait of him as Prince of Wales, also in the Royal Collection. It shows the King wearing his coronation robes and the collar of the garter, with white lace steinkirk around his neck. The original was frequently reproduced in mezzotint and line, and reissued with minor alterations at the coronation in 1727. George, who usually hated sitting for painters, enjoyed Zincke's company, liked conversing with him in German, and admired his portraits. The King may also have appreciated Zincke's flexibility when it came to painterly realism: George asked him to paint Queen Caroline as if she were twenty-eight when, in fact, she was forty-nine, and the Queen urged Zincke to make the King look twenty-four years younger. [JM]

LITERATURE: Walker, *Eighteenth- and Early-Nineteenth-Century Miniatures*, p.19.

Music-making on the River Thames was a feature of London life throughout the eighteenth century. These musical spectacles ranged from intimate, personal affairs – such as the more modest, but still impressive, concerts put on by the Sharp family from their sailing barge, *Apollo*, at Fulham – to grand, state occasions in commemoration of events of great national importance. At this latter end of the scale were royal spectacles, often accompanied by dazzling firework displays. These could be enormous set-piece musical extravaganzas with specially commissioned music played by an army of musicians. Internationally renowned composers often wrote pieces for such occasions: two of George Frederick Handel's most famous works – 'Water Music' and 'Music for the Royal Fireworks' – were composed for performance on or near the Thames.

On a fine summer's evening in July 1717, a splendid court entertainment took place on the River Thames. The King and 'persons of quality' travelled in barges and boats up river from Whitehall to Chelsea accompanied by musicians, performing 'The Water Music' from a City barge. They disembarked at Chelsea where they had supper and heard another concert before returning at around two in the morning. The music was composed by Handel, the King's principal court composer. Friedrich Bonet, the Prussian Resident in London, attributed the organisation of the concert to Johann Adolf, Baron von Kielmansegg, George I's close aide. Bonet thought that it cost '£150 for the musicians alone' who 'played on all kinds of instruments, to wit trumpets, horns, hautboys [oboes], bassoons, German flutes, French flutes [recorders], violins and basses'. This occasion on the Thames was described in the *Daily Courant* of 19 July 1717:

> On Wednesday Evening [17 July], at about 8, the King took Water at Whitehall in an open Barge, wherein were also the Dutchess of Bolton, the Dutchess of Newcastle, the Countess of Godophin, Madam Kilmanseck, and the Earl of Orkney. And went up the River towards Chelsea. Many other Barges with Persons of Quality attended, and so great a Number of Boats, that the whole River in a manner was cover'd; a City Company's Barge was employ'd for the Musick, wherein were 50 Instruments of all sorts, who play'd all the Way from Lambeth (while the Barges drove with the Tide without Rowing, as far as Chelsea) the finest Symphonies, compos'd express for this Occasion, by Mr Hendel; which his Majesty liked so well, that he caus'd it to be plaid over three times in going and returning. At Eleven his majesty went a-shoar at Chelsea, where a Supper was prepar'd, and then there was another very fine Consort of Music; which lasted till 2; after which, his Majesty came again into his Barge, and return'd the same Way, the Musick continuing to play till he landed.

Handel's 'Music for the Royal Fireworks' was composed to coincide with a grand firework extravaganza to mark the signing of the Peace of Aix-la-Chapelle that brought to an end the long War of Austrian Succession in October 1748. Preliminary articles for peace were signed on 17 June 1748, and plans for a grand display of fireworks in London to mark the final treaty were in hand as early as the following day, with celebrations scheduled to take place in Green Park. Preparations were eventually brought to fruition in April 1749. The *General Advertiser* (22 April 1749) reported on the rehearsal for the music to accompany the display, which took place in the pleasure gardens at Vauxhall a week before the main event: 'Yesterday there was the brightest and most numerous Assembly ever known at Spring Gardens, Vauxhall, an audience of above 12,000 persons (tickets 2s 6d). So great a resort occasioned such a stoppage on London Bridge, that no carriage could pass for 3 hours.' At the firework display itself, over 10,000 rockets were shot into the sky, with *The Gentleman's Magazine* reporting that the whole event cost upwards of £8000 (although there is some suggestion that this is a misprint of £800). The event was directed by a group of Italian pyrotechnists specially brought over for the purpose. But, despite their necessarily ephemeral nature, firework displays also provided a stage for more enduring art forms, most notably 'a grand overture on warlike instruments' – Handel's famous 'Music for Royal Fireworks'. [JM]

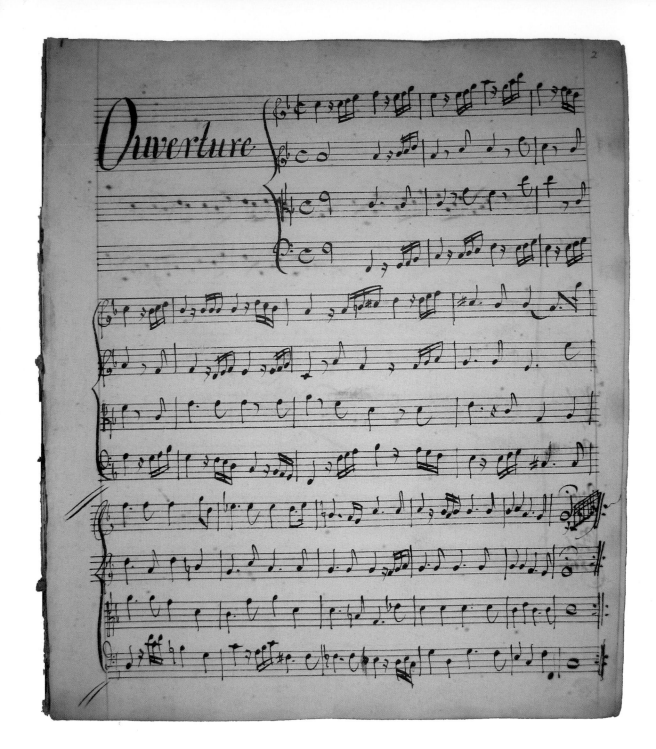

89
Score for Handel's 'Water Music'

c. 1718
Copy after GEORGE FREDERICK HANDEL
(1685–1759)
Manuscript, 290 × 250 mm (closed)

Library of The Royal Society of Musicians of Great
Britain, HWV348-350

George Frederick Handel was born in
Halle, Brandenburg. After spending time
in Hamburg and Italy, he went to Hanover
where he was appointed *Kapellmeister* at
the Elector's court in June 1710. However,
later that year he came to London,
remaining there during the opera seasons
and composing for the company based at
the Queen's Theatre in the Haymarket.
After the Elector's accession to the British
throne as George I, Handel based himself
permanently in London.

The 'Water Music' was performed on
the River Thames on 17 July 1717 before
George I and other guests. The complete
loss of the 1717 autograph of 'Water
Music' means that theories about the
original form and order of the movements
must remain speculative. But it is clear
that, as Christopher Hogwood suggests,
Handel was writing 'music on the water,
rather than about water'. This score
represents one of the earliest-known
copies. It is a full score in the hand of two
copyists, datable to before 1719. Although
'Water Music' circulated in manuscript
form soon after its first performance, it
was not published until 1733 and then
only in a partial and not wholly accurate
form. [SD & JM]

LITERATURE: Simon (ed.), *Handel*, p.255; Smith,
'The earliest editions of the Water Music', pp.269–87;
Hogwood, *Water Music*, pp.17–47.

90
Division viol

1698
Inscribed: 'Barak Norman / at the Baße Viol /
in St Paul's Ally / London Fecit / 1698'
BARAK NORMAN (1651–1724), London
Various woods, 1030 mm (length)

Royal Northern College of Music, V1

Musical spectacles required a wide variety
of instruments. Handel's composition for
'Water Music', for example, was originally
conceived for a massive ensemble of
instruments: three first trumpets, three
second trumpets, and three third
trumpets, and three pairs of kettledrums;
three first horns, three second horns,
three third horns; twelve first oboes, eight
second oboes, four third oboes; eight first
bassoons, four second bassoons, and
a double bassoon. In the end, it was
reported that a band of over one
hundred musicians played the piece.

  Viols of various sizes were a very
popular family of instruments in the
sixteenth and seventeenth centuries,
featuring in works by leading composers.
Unlike violins, which are tuned in fifths,
viols are normally tuned in fourths.
Although they remained in widespread
use in the eighteenth century, the
growing size of orchestras and concert
halls meant viols were increasing replaced
with instruments of the violin family,
which produced greater volume with a
more penetrating tone. Barak Norman
was one of the last celebrated makers of
the viol. [JM]

LITERATURE: Simon (ed.), *Handel*, pp. 108, 241.

91
Right- and left-handed orchestral horn and crooks

Mid-eighteenth century
JOHANN CHRISTOPH HOFMEISTER (*fl.* 1751–64),
London
Brass, 520 × 410 × 606mm

Bate Collection of Historical Instruments, University of
Oxford (on loan from the Lloyd-Baker Estate).

These instruments are associated with
members of the Sharp family, who were
famous for their riverine musical concerts.
The artist Johan Zoffany (1733–1810)
captured the unusual musical activity of
the family in a grand group portrait
commissioned in 1779 by William Sharp
(1729–1810). As the members of Sharp's
family had grown over the previous thirty
years, what had begun as a modest event
in the 1750s had become a musical
tradition: once a fortnight they assembled
in London for a Sunday concert that was
performed from their sailing barge on the
River Thames at Fulham.

  These orchestral horns are a true pair:
one left-handed and the other right-
handed. They were passed down through
the Lloyd-Baker family, the descendants of
the baby seated on her mother's lap in the
Zoffany painting. The instrument maker
Hofmeister, who sometimes anglicised his
name as 'Hofmaster', settled in London
before the mid-eighteenth century and
introduced a new type of orchestral horn,
built with detachable crooks. The great
advantage of this innovation was that
players could use the same instrument in
different keys, by merely changing the
couplers. [JM]

LITERATURE: Treadwell, *Johan Zoffany*, pp. 303–06;
Simon (ed.), *Handel*, p. 248.

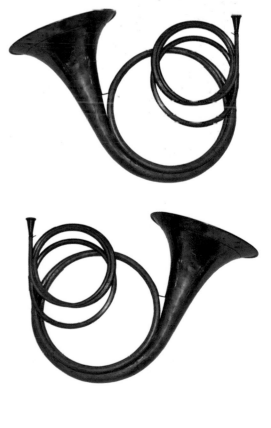

A VIEW *of the* FIRE-WORKES *and* ILLVMINATIONS, *at his* GRACE *the Duke of* RICHMOND'S *at* WHITE-H

Perform'd by the direction of Charles Frederick Esq.

Fix'd   Sun.

Regulated Piece of 5 Mutations.

Frutoni.

Vertical Wheel.

Spirah with Horisontal Wheel

Vertical Sun.

Battery of Marons.

Pots d'Aigretts with Fountains

N°1. *Pavillon beautifully illuminated.*
2. *The Duke of Richmonds House.*
3. *The Boats and Barges for the Aquatic Fire-workes.*
A. *His Majesty's Barge.*

Vue des FEUX d'ARTIFICE *et des* ILLUMINATIONS *donneés par Monseigneur le Duc de*
sur la TAMISE, *et vis a vis dé son Hotel, Lundi le* 15.*ieme* *de Ma*

on the River Thames, on Monday 15 May 1749.

Corded Mortars with Air Ballons

Do with Saucissons.

Flights of Sky Rocketts

Pots de Brin.

Water Rocketts.

Jatte d'eau.

Water Ballons
with 3 Stages of Lights

Vertical Illumination

MOND de LENOX et d'AUBIGNY,
9. Sous la direction de Mons. Frederick
a Londre.

N°. Le Pavillion magnifiquement
Illuminé.
2 L'Hotel de Monsig.r Le Duc de
Richmond.
3. Les Bateaux employes aux
Feux d'artifice
A. Barque de sa Majesté.

92
*A View of the Fire-workes and
Illuminations at his Grace
the Duke of Richmond's
at White-hall…*

1749
Hand-coloured etching, 425 × 560 mm
Victoria and Albert Museum, S.4218-2009

The Duke of Richmond's entertainment
on 15 May 1749 highlights the prevalence
of firework displays as part of public
celebrations in mid-eighteenth-century
London. His display was a direct result of
the Royal Fireworks at Green Park, which
had taken place a few weeks earlier to
celebrate the signing of the Peace of Aix-
la-Chapelle. When this was concluded at
midnight, the Duke acquired the fireworks
left over and used them for his own
celebration of the Peace. Advance
warning was given of the event so that
Londoners could watch the spectacle from
the Thames. According to Horace Walpole
(1717–97), the Duke 'took the pretence of
the Duke of Modena being here to give a
charming entertainment' in the private
gardens of his house at Whitehall. After a
concert was held, 'from boats on every
side were discharged water-rockets and
fires of all kinds; and then the wheels
which were ranged along the rails of the
terrace were played off; and the whole
concluded with the illumination of a
pavilion on the top of the slope, of two
pyramids on either side and the whole
length of the balustrade to the water'.
[JM]

LITERATURE: Cunningham, *Letters of Horace Walpole*,
vol. 2, pp.155–56.

PLEASURE GARDENS AT VAUXHALL AND RANELAGH

In the seventeenth century, a number of private gardens in London were opened to the public. Sir Samuel Morland (1625–95), for example, decided to allow the general public access to his suburban estate at Vauxhall, south of the River Thames. Initially, these gardens offered little more than the opportunity for relaxation in a bounded stretch of park and woodland. The gardens at Vauxhall were laid out in a series of straight paths and avenues, which enclosed a number of irregularly patterned 'wildernesses'. By the mid-eighteenth century, however, such 'pleasure gardens' had become fashionable places of entertainment and leisure, offering a range of divertissements for visitors. In addition to the Spring Gardens (as they became known) at Vauxhall, examples could be found at Ranelagh in Chelsea, at Mulberry Garden and New Wells in Clerkenwell, Cuper's Gardens in Southwark, and Marylebone Gardens, as well as at more disreputable places. Many of these gardens were located close to the Thames and river transportation was part of the experience. As *The Ambulator*, an eighteenth-century guide for visitors to London, put it in relation to Vauxhall: 'They are so commodiously situated near the Thames, that those who prefer going by water, can be brought within two hundred yards of this delightful place at a much easier expence [sic] than by land.'

Access to Vauxhall Gardens from the West End was by water, until the opening of Westminster Bridge in 1750 made travelling by road easier. On summer evenings, pleasure gardens were popular places for Londoners and visitors alike to go to experience the illuminations and other forms of entertainment offered there. Many contained large concert halls, or hosted promenade concerts. Music by Handel and other popular operatic composers was performed. More extravagant forms of entertainment, such as tightrope walkers, hot-air balloon ascents, or firework displays provided amusement. At Vauxhall in 1813, there was a fête to celebrate victory at the Battle of Vitoria, and in 1827 the Battle of Waterloo was re-enacted by a thousand soldiers.

Pleasure gardens drew all manner of people and attracted enormous crowds. One commentator remarked that Vauxhall had become 'the great resort of personages of the first rank'. But pleasure gardens also retained something of their earlier, more dubious, moral repute. Edward Gibbon wrote that Ranelagh was 'the most convenient place for courtships of every kind – the best market we have in England'. Notwithstanding this reputation for romantic assignations, James Boswell thought Vauxhall an 'excellent place of publick amusement'. On 14 April 1778, he wrote of his belief that the gardens there were 'peculiarly adapted to the taste of the English nation; there being a mixture of

In this exuberant and detailed evening scene, Rowlandson captures, in imaginary form, London society at play in the Vauxhall Gardens. The great vocalist Elizabeth Weichsel sings from the balcony with the orchestra behind and to the left. Beneath, in a supper box, are the famous author and lexicographer Dr Samuel Johnson, his friend and biographer James Boswell, and the author Oliver Goldsmith. They are accompanied by two women, one reputed to be Hester Thrale, later Viscountess Keith, a scholar and protégé of Johnson, whom he called 'Queeny'. A number of groups and individuals occupy the centre of the scene. The two women, arm in arm, are the Duchess of Devonshire and Lady Duncannon; the one-legged naval officer is probably Admiral Sir Thomas Pasley. Major Edward Topham, the journalist and playwright, stands in profile looking though an eyeglass. The elderly vicar staring at the Duchess from behind a tree may be William Jackson of the *Morning Post*, known as the 'Scrutineer', seeking out a story. Next to him, in Highland dress, is James Perry, the editor of the *Morning Chronicle*. To the right, the Prince of Wales, identified by his Garter star, whispers to the actress Mary 'Perdita' Robinson, with whom he had an affair, while her somewhat decrepit husband, Thomas, looks on. The rest of the scene is filled with merriment as people enjoy supper, music and other pleasures of a more carnal nature. [RB]

curious show, – gay exhibition, musick, vocal and instrumental, not too refined for the general ear; – for all of which only a shilling is paid'.

Music remained one of the pleasure gardens' most prominent attractions. At Vauxhall, the proprietor Jonathan Tyers (1702–67), hoped that the promotion of music would act as a counterweight to the less morally reputable activities, which often cast a pall over the gardens. The perceived power of music to calm the passions was specifically and overtly incorporated into the symbolic language of the gardens' decoration. Tyers also aimed to suppress vulgar noises in favour of pretty pastoral melodies and grander instrumental pieces written by the most distinguished composers of the day, including Thomas Arne, Johann Sebastian Bach and George Frederick Handel. [JM]

A View of the Canal, Chinese Building, Rotundo, &c. in RANELAGH GARDENS, with the MASQUERADE.

Vue du Canal, du Bâtiment, Chinois, de la Rotunda, &c. des JARDINS de RANELAGH un jour de MASQUARADE.

94

The interior of the Rotunda, Ranelagh Gardens

c.1751
GIOVANNI ANTONIO CANAL,
known as CANALETTO (1697–1768)
Oil on canvas, 517 × 770 mm

Compton Verney, CVCSC:0356.S

Ranelagh Gardens in Chelsea were laid out as a pleasure garden in 1741, opening the following year. The gardens occupied the site of Ranelagh House, built in 1688–89 by Richard Jones (1641–1712), the first Earl of Ranelagh, Paymaster General to the Forces and Treasurer of Chelsea Hospital. Ranelagh was considered more fashionable than its older rival Vauxhall Gardens; the entrance charge was two shillings and sixpence, compared to one shilling at Vauxhall.

The centrepiece of Ranelagh was a large rococo rotunda, designed by William Jones, a surveyor to the East India Company. Built entirely of wood, it had a raised stand for choir, orchestra and organ on one side, while the central architectural structure housed a large fireplace and chimney. The surrounding arcade contained two tiers of supper boxes comprising fifty-two in total. On 29 June 1/64, the nine-year-old Wolfgang Amadeus Mozart performed in this showpiece, which figured prominently in views of Ranelagh Gardens taken from the river.

Canaletto painted the interior of the Rotunda twice, for different patrons. This canvas was presumably commissioned as a pendant to 'The Grand Walk in Vauxhall Gardens, London' (c. 1751), which is also in the collection at Compton Verney in Warwickshire. The composition focuses on the central architectural feature of the Rotunda. [JM]

LITERATURE: Beddington (ed.), *Canaletto in England*, pp.117 19; Liversidge and Farrington (eds), *Canaletto & England*, p.91; Weinreb and Hibbert (eds), *London Encyclopaedia*, p.637.

95

A View of the Canal, Chinese Building, Rotunda &c in Ranelagh Gardens, with the Masquerade

1880 [1752]
After GIOVANNI ANTONIO CANAL, known as CANALETTO; engraved by CHARLES GRIGNION (c.1721–1810); originally published by ROBERT SAYER (1724/5–94), London
Etching and engraving, 262 × 402 mm

British Museum, 1880-1113,2450

The figures in the print are taking part in a masquerade ball. Formerly, this was a type of private, aristocratic entertainment, but its introduction to places such as Ranelagh brought it to a wider, middle-class audience. *The Ambulator* remarked that 'Ranelagh was not a place of very extraordinary note, till it was honoured with the famous masquerades: it was that brought it into vogue, and it has ever since retained the esteem and favour of the public'. All the participants at a masquerade had to be disguised or in fancy dress. Oriental costume was particularly favoured, making the backdrop of the Chinese House (erected in 1750) in this print particularly appropriate. Set in the late evening hours, music and lavish food and drink contributed to a festive and noisy atmosphere. Eating, drinking and gambling were 'unrestrained'. Ballrooms were often decorated with lights in order for participants to enjoy the festivities through the night. [JM]

LITERATURE: *The Ambulator*; Castle, *Masquerade and Civilization*, pp.24–26; Ribeiro, 'The exotic diversion', pp.3–13.

96

The Wapping landlady and the tars who are just come ashore

1741–42
FRANCIS HAYMAN (1707/8–76)
Oil on canvas, 991 × 1035 mm

Victoria and Albert Museum, P.29-1954

One of the innovations introduced by Jonathan Tyers was the installation of supper boxes, where patrons could dine in relative comfort at one remove from the noise and gaiety of general visitors. Soon after 1740, Francis Hayman was commissioned by Tyers to execute the series of supper-box paintings which were unveiled at Vauxhall some two years later. Hayman provided most of the subjects, which were rapidly executed by students and assistants in his studio. At a certain hour, all the paintings were let down at once, to offer some security to the companies at supper. Sophie von la Roche remarked that 'people can have morning breakfast or eat and drink during the evening; at the back of these boxes there is either a fresco painting or a mirror'. The theme of fiddling and drinking in a low Thames-side tavern, as depicted in this painting, was in many ways admirably suited to alcoves whose primary function was to provide a sheltered space in which the clientele could eat and drink, rather than galleries for viewing high-minded art. [JM]

LITERATURE: Allan, *Francis Hayman*, pp.107–08; Gowing, 'Hogarth, Hayman, and the Vauxhall Decorations', pp.4–19; Williams (ed), *Sophie in London*, p.280.

97
Admission tokens to Vauxhall Pleasure Gardens

Mid-eighteenth century
All by an unknown maker, possibly after a
design by WILLIAM HOGARTH (1697–1764)

(a) Top left: Inscribed on reverse:
'Mr Wm St Laurence'
Copper alloy, 41 x 35 mm

(b) Top right: Inscribed on reverse:
'Mr John Hinton 212'
Silver, 49 x 32 mm

(c) Centre: Gold, 42 x 40 mm

(d) Below left: Inscribed: on obverse:
'Blandius Orpheo'; on reverse:
'Sr Jon English Barnt 592'
Silver, 49 x 32 mm

(e) Below right: Inscribed: on obverse:
'Iocosæ Conveniunt Lyræ'; on reverse:
'Mr Tho Corner 726'
Silver, 44 x 34 mm

British Museum, J.3025, J.3032, MG.680–681,
MG.678

The Spring Garden or Gardens at Vauxhall
were the largest and most spectacular in
London. Jonathan Tyers took over the
lease in 1728, with the aim of developing
the gardens as a pleasure resort. He spent
considerable time and effort trying to
transform the gardens' reputation. A
shilling entrance fee was introduced in
1732, to exclude the inferior sort of
people without discouraging the lower
strata of the middling orders from visiting
and spending money on food and drink.
For regular and wealthy visitors, the
season-ticket was more economical. The
metal ticket changed in design or material
every season, and the name and number
of the ticket owner was generally
engraved on the back. Designs often
incorporated classical figures and
references. For example, token (c) depicts
Orpheus playing a lyre surrounded by
animals. The image of the ancient Greek
musician is almost certainly a reference to
the sculpture of Handel by Louis François
Roubiliac (1702–62), which stood in the
gardens. The statue of Handel also
appears in token (d), which belonged to
Sir John English. The Latin inscription on
the token is from Horace's *Odes* (book 1,
ode 24), where the poet refers to the
sweet music produced by Orpheus, the
classical figure with whom Handel was
compared in the iconography of the
Spring Gardens. The ticket belonging to
Thomas Corner, token (e), is decorated
with three cherubs playing a lyre, with
a tree and classical temple in the
background. The Latin inscription on the
obverse is also from Horace's *Odes* and
refers to the pleasing effects of music on
the senses. Token (b), belonging to John
Hinton, shows a seated woman who
probably represents Calliope, the Greek
Muse of Epic Poetry. Token (a) was issued
to William St Laurence, and depicts Arion
riding a dolphin and playing a lyre. Arion
was a classical figure known for his
musical inventions. [JM]

LITERATURE: Wroth, 'Tickets of Vauxhall Gardens',
pp.80, 83; Solkin, *Painting for Money*, p.110; Simon
(ed.), *Handel*, p.171.

98
Rural Beauty, or Vauxhal Garden

c. 1740
GEORGE BICKHAM (c. 1704–71), London
Engraving on paper, 390 × 230 mm
London Borough of Lambeth Archives, LP/14/581/65

This view of Vauxhall Gardens, with the
song sheet below, draws on the bucolic,
semi-rural experience offered to visitors
to the gardens. George Bickham was an
engraver and printseller who became one
of the most vibrant, energetic and
enigmatic figures in the London print
trade of his day. While he often courted
controversy in matters of piracy, obscenity
and political acceptability, he was also
one of the most talented political satirists
of the age. One of Bickham's first
ventures as an independent publisher was
The Musical Entertainer. Launched in
1737, it was a series of engraved song
sheets; this vignette of Vauxhall is part of
that oeuvre. [JM]

99
The Invitation to Mira, Requesting Her Company to Vauxhall Garden

1738
GEORGE BICKHAM; after HUBERT FRANÇOIS
GRAVELOT (1699–1773), London
Engraving on paper, 345 × 220 mm
London Borough of Lambeth Archives, LP/14/581/63

This song sheet is from the second volume
of George Bickham's *The Musical
Entertainer*. It was published in June 1738,
the month after the unveiling of Louis
François Roubiliac's statue of Handel in
the gardens and depicts the earliest
engraved view of the statue. The
sculpture appears in the headpiece, which
was designed by Hubert Gravelot, and
shows Handel in the guise of a classical
musician, presiding over an assembly of
dancers and putti. The music printed
below was written for the flute by
Thomas Gladwin, while the verses by John
Lockman are an invitation to Vauxhall:
'Come, Mira, Idol of ye Swains … To
Bowers where heav'n-born Flora reigns,
& Handel warbles Airs divine.' Both the
song sheet and statue from which it
draws its inspiration were enrolled in the
task of presenting Vauxhall as a place of
cultured and sophisticated entertainment.
[JM]

LITERATURE: Edelstein, *Vauxhall Gardens*, p. 39;
Simon (ed.), *Handel*, p. 170.

GEORGIAN KEW: FREDERICK AND GEORGE III

In 1729 the Prince of Wales, Frederick Lewis, the eldest son of George II and Queen Caroline, arrived in England from Hanover; around 1730 he took over the lease of the White House at Kew in Surrey, close to the Thames. William Kent immediately began redesigning the house in the latest Palladian style. The White House was conveniently situated adjacent to the Dutch House, where Frederick's sisters lived. Once the Prince married Princess Augusta of Saxe-Gotha in 1736, and especially after the birth of their first child in 1737, the White House became a favourite country retreat for their family. Avoiding court life because of Frederick's acrimonious relationship with his father, the royal couple sought to create a world at Kew for their eight children that was 'full of entertainment, learning and fun'. Frederick acquired some 50 acres of land to farm and began to lay out a botanic garden. After her husband's death at the age of forty-four, Augusta retained possession of the White House, and it continued to be one of her chief residences.

On his accession in 1760, their son George III took over the lease of the smaller but still substantial Dutch House next to Augusta's house at Kew. When she died, George and his wife, Queen Charlotte, moved into the White House and used the Dutch House as an overflow to accommodate their expanding family and households. Kew became their favoured summer residence. It combined the pleasure of the gardens and beneficial air of the country, yet was situated in relatively close proximity by river to Westminster and the seat of government. The landscape at Kew was shaped in part by Sir William Chambers, who was appointed architect to Augusta and architectural tutor to George in 1757. Chambers created an eclectic combination of buildings at Kew: the classically inspired temple of Bellona (1760), the Mosque (1761), the Pagoda (1761–62), and a rustic cottage, known as Queen Charlotte's Cottage (c. 1771), which was used as a teahouse. [SD]

100

Frederick, Prince of Wales and his sisters at Kew

1733
PHILIP MERCIER (1691–1760)
Oil on canvas, 451 × 578 mm

National Portrait Gallery, NPG 1556

In this small group portrait, or 'conversation piece', Philip Mercier shows Frederick in the grounds of the Dutch House at Kew playing the bass-viol with three of his younger sisters: Anne, Princess Royal, seated at a harpsichord, Princess Caroline playing a lute, and Princess Amelia reading a volume of Milton's poetry. The air of familial and musical harmony conveyed by Mercier's painting belies a much more difficult relationship between Frederick and his siblings, all of whom enjoyed a closer relationship with their father. Two other versions of the same painting are known and it is reasonable to conclude that all three were commissioned by Frederick as a gift to each of his sisters, in a gesture of rapprochement after years of discord. [RJ]

101
George III

c. 1781
THOMAS GAINSBOROUGH (1727–88)
Oil on canvas, 406 × 333 mm

Royal Collection, RCIN 400935

102
Queen Charlotte

c. 1781
THOMAS GAINSBOROUGH
Oil on canvas, 413 × 333 mm

Royal Collection, RCIN 400934

George III married Charlotte of
Mecklenburg-Strelitz in 1761. Although
they had not met before the wedding,
their marriage was happy since husband
and wife shared common interests in
science, art, theatre and music. With their
fifteen children, they presented a public
image of stable domesticity. Both portraits
are reduced versions of full-length
paintings of the King and Queen that
Gainsborough exhibited at the Royal
Academy in 1781. The close, head-and-
shoulder format, combined with
Gainsborough's distinctive, softening style
presents a far more intimate image of
monarchy than the imposing full-length
portraits from which they derive. Two
years later, the artist exhibited a group of
fifteen similar portraits, representing the
King and Queen alongside thirteen of
their children. [SD & RJ]

LITERATURE: *Oxford DNB;* Black, *George III,*
pp. 165–67.

103
Prince Frederick's barge

1731–32
Designed by WILLIAM KENT (c. 1686–1748);
built by JOHN HALL; carving by JAMES
RICHARDSON; gilding by PAUL PETIT (fl. 1724–57)
Painted wood, gilt, 2.59 × 19.63 × 2.29 m

National Maritime Museum, BAE0035;
on loan from Her Majesty The Queen
[not displayed in the exhibition]

This royal barge was built for Frederick, Prince of Wales (1707–51). The new barge was used on its first day in the water to take Frederick, his mother Queen Caroline and his five sisters from Chelsea Hospital to Somerset House to observe the cleaning of the royal pictures. The party was attended by two other barges: one carrying officers and ladies; a 'Set of Musick', i.e. musicians, in the other. After Frederick's death in 1751, it was regularly employed by monarchs as the principal royal barge until 1849, when last used by Prince Albert to open the Coal Exchange in London.

The clinker-built barge was constructed by John Hall at his yard on the south bank of the Thames opposite Whitehall. The design was commissioned from William Kent, who was then working on the interiors of Lord Burlington's villa at Chiswick; the barge employs many of the same architectural motifs. The intricately carved decoration was interpreted and executed by James Richardson, who had replaced Grinling Gibbons as master carver to the Crown in 1721. Paul Petit then gilded the scheme in twenty-four-carat gold. The magnificent result was, of course, complemented by the twenty-four liveried oarsmen, who wore silver badges by the prominent Huguenot goldsmith Paul Jacques de Lamerie (1688–1751). [RB]

LITERATURE: Norton, *State barges*, pp. 16–20.

QUEEN CHARLOTTE, THE CHILDREN AND DOMESTIC LIFE

Queen Charlotte took a personal interest in her children's upbringing. Before they were set up in their own establishments, the royal children were educated largely at Kew: the boys learned about farming as well as mathematics, history, natural philosophy and literature; the daughters received a thorough education in scholarly and artistic subjects. Kew was also the scene of a family tragedy. In May 1783, George III's youngest and favourite son, Octavius, died there shortly after being inoculated against smallpox. Although a beloved family retreat, in later years George III's unmarried daughters came to view their life at Kew as overly restrictive.

One of the last times that Kew was used for a family occasion was the double royal wedding in July 1818 of William, Duke of Clarence (the future William IV) to Adelaide of Saxe-Meiningen, and of Edward, Duke of Kent (father of Queen Victoria) to Princess Victoria of Saxe-Coburg-Saalfeld, who were married there in the presence of Queen Charlotte, then too ill to travel. Charlotte died at Kew in November that year. [AM]

104
Miniature of Lady Charlotte Finch

c. 1802
PRINCESS ELIZABETH (1770–1840);
after HENRY EDRIDGE (1768–1821)
Watercolour on ivory, 100 × 80 mm
Royal Collection, RCIN 420972

When Horace Walpole met the fifteen-year-old Lady Charlotte, second daughter of the first Earl of Pomfret, in Florence, he described her as 'the cleverest girl in the world'. Six years later, in 1746, she married William Finch (1691–1766), second son of the seventh Earl of Winchilsea. On the birth of the Prince of Wales, the future George IV, Lady Charlotte (1725–1813) was appointed royal governess. For the next thirty years she was responsible for the early education of both the princes and princesses: the boys until they were set up with their own households and tutors, and the girls until they reached the age of twenty-one. Lady Charlotte shared a keen interest in educational theories and practices with the Queen, which was revealed in their thoughtful and warm correspondence on the subject. The original portrait, from which this version is copied, was painted by the miniaturist Henry Edridge around 1802. It is likely that the present copy – an example of the highly accomplished work of Princess Elizabeth – was made around the same time. The Princess enjoyed a considerable reputation as a royal artist. As well as painting miniatures, she was also a skilled painter in oils and a talented interior designer. [AM & RJ]

LITERATURE: Roberts & Lloyd, *George III and Queen Charlotte*, pp.84–85.

105

Prince Adolphus later Duke of Cambridge, with Princess Mary and Princess Sophia

1778
BENJAMIN WEST (1738–1820)
Oil on canvas, 2426 × 1499 mm

Royal Collection, RCIN 405406

The American-born Benjamin West's full-length portrait of the (then) three youngest children of George III and Queen Charlotte, was painted for the King's Closet at St James's Palace, but shows the children in the gardens at Kew. At the centre is the infant Princess Sophia (1777–1848), born the previous November, supported by her two nearest siblings, Adolphus (1774–1850) and Mary (1776–1837), and attended by two dogs. The view of the palace gardens in the background encompasses the lake and Great Pagoda, a ten-storey tower designed in imitation of a Chinese pagoda by the architect William Chambers and erected in 1762. Chinese-derived design remained popular throughout the eighteenth century, but Chambers was one of only a few practitioners with first-hand experience, having made several visits to Canton during the 1740s. West exhibited this painting at the Royal Academy in 1780. [RJ]

106
Egg boiler

1803–04
JOHN EDWARDS III, London
Engraved with ciphers of George III and his
five youngest daughters
Silver-gilt, 360 × 210 × 120 mm

Royal Collection, RCIN 49122

This egg boiler was presented to George
III on his sixty-sixth birthday in 1804 by his
five youngest daughters: Augusta,
Elizabeth, Mary, Sophia and Amelia. An
account of the morning rituals of the
royal family, included in *The Public and
Private Life of King George the Third*,
published in 1821, describes their
breakfast at Windsor. After divine service,
'the king, instead of proceeding to his
own apartment, and breakfasting alone,
now takes that meal with the queen and
the five princesses … the breakfast does
not occupy half an hour'. The egg boiler,
complete with egg timer, would have
been used by the King at the table. The
eggs were held in place by means of an
internal frame and the water was kept
boiling by a spirit lamp beneath. [AM]

LITERATURE: Roberts & Lloyd, *George III and Queen
Charlotte*, pp. 332–33.

107
Tea-kettle and stand with
cipher of Queen Charlotte

1761–63
Struck with hallmarks for 1761–62 (tea-kettle)
and 1762–63 (stand)
THOMAS HEMING (*fl.*1745–73), London
Silver-gilt with fruitwood handle,
375 × 165 × 250 mm

Royal Collection, RCIN 49128

108
Teacup and saucer

c. 1780
Worcester
Porcelain, cup, 48 × 86 mm;
saucer, 107 mm (diameter)

Royal Collection RCIN 73111.a–b

This teacup is believed to have
belonged to Queen Charlotte; the
kettle was a private commission.
Tea drinking was a fixture of Queen
Charlotte's daily routine at court and tea
was taken during evening entertainments,
made by Charlotte and 'carried … about
to the Ladies by the King'. At Kew, Queen
Charlotte's Cottage was a rustic retreat
used by the royal family for informal teas
and picnics. Charlotte even attempted to
grow her own tea in the gardens. The
central motif on the saucer is an urn
inscribed 'KEW', making it probable that
these items were used in the cottage
as part of the family teas. [AM]

LITERATURE: Roberts & Lloyd, *George III and Queen
Charlotte*, pp. 309, 330.

SCIENCE: KEW AS AN ENLIGHTENMENT VILLA

109

Silver microscope made for George III

c. 1763
GEORGE ADAMS (c. 1709–72)
Silver, steel, 532 × 280 × 205 mm
Museum of the History of Science, 35086

This is one of two almost identical silver microscopes known to have been made for the royal family around 1763. The other, in the Science Museum, remained with the family and is thought to have been owned by the Prince of Wales, later George IV. This one, acquired by the collector Frank Crisp from the collection at Kew, was probably made for George III. The instrument is based on the 'Universal Double Microscope' design published by George Adams, consisting of a simple microscope on one side and a compound system on the other. It is, however, much more highly decorated, with architectural features, including urns and a fluted Corinthian column, putti and allegorical figures. There are two specimen stages, with mirrors to aid illumination set beneath each. There is a micrometer on the compound tube, an ornate, articulated arm that supports a lens at the top of the column, and two figures support the decorated body tube. This is an instrument designed to say more about the maker and the owner than to facilitate practical scientific study, although it was capable of making precise measurements. Adams was showing off both his skills as a maker and the importance of his patrons, while George III was able to demonstrate both his taste and his patronage of the sciences. Adams's pride is made clear by the fact that he displayed the instrument in his Fleet Street shop before it was presented to the King. [RH]

LITERATURE: Whipple, 'An Old catalogue and What it tells us', p.516; online catalogue of the Museum of the History of Science, Oxford www.mhs.ox.ac.uk/collections; Morton and Wess, *Public and Private Science*, p.484.

Caroline of Brandenburg-Ansbach, Consort to George II, initiated the link between the monarchy and the newly fashionable natural philosophy. Her view of science, and its support of religion, was developed through close acquaintance with Gottfried Leibniz.

Caroline's son, Prince Frederick, likewise took an interest in scientific learning. He appointed John Theophilus Desaguliers, a well-known lecturer in experimental philosophy, as his chaplain. At the White House in Kew, Desaguliers set up instruments and a planetarium and lectured, reputedly daily, to the Prince. Whether his son, the future George III, benefited from this expertise is not clear, although from 1755 he was tutored by John Stuart, the third Earl of Bute, and attended lectures by Desaguliers's student, Stephen Demainbray. George was evidently influenced by this and, almost immediately upon becoming King in 1760, he commissioned the respected instrument-maker George Adams to make apparatus to demonstrate pneumatics and mechanics. Anecdotal evidence suggests that George III and Queen Charlotte made use of these instruments over the next decade for personal interest and education, as well as to provide entertainment for guests and to display their taste and knowledge.

George's continued interest in the scientific world was evidenced by a number of interventions. He provided support for the lecturer–demonstrator James Ferguson, the astronomer William Herschel and the clockmaker John Harrison, as well as the Trigonometrical Survey and the Royal Society's expedition to observe the transit of Venus in 1769. The rare event of the transit prompted George to build, equip and staff an observatory at Kew in order to observe it himself. Designed by William Chambers, with Demainbray appointed as superintendent, the observatory was ready for the King to make his observation on 3 June. There is little evidence of the King's further use of the observatory, although he did take part in the testing of Harrison's sea watch, H5, there. By and large, however, Demainbray seems to have been content to enjoy his sinecure, making some observations of the weather, checking the clocks that provided time for Parliament and perhaps giving a few lectures.

The observatory at Kew and George III's remarkable collection of scientific instruments are testament to the respect that members of the royal family accorded natural philosophy. The estates at Kew and Richmond were retreats from London in which the monarch and his family could indulge and display their taste for learning. Astronomy and mechanics were just two facets; Kew and its gardens also reveal architecture, botany, horticulture, geography, music and the arts to be essential elements in the Hanoverian idea of Enlightenment learning. [RH]

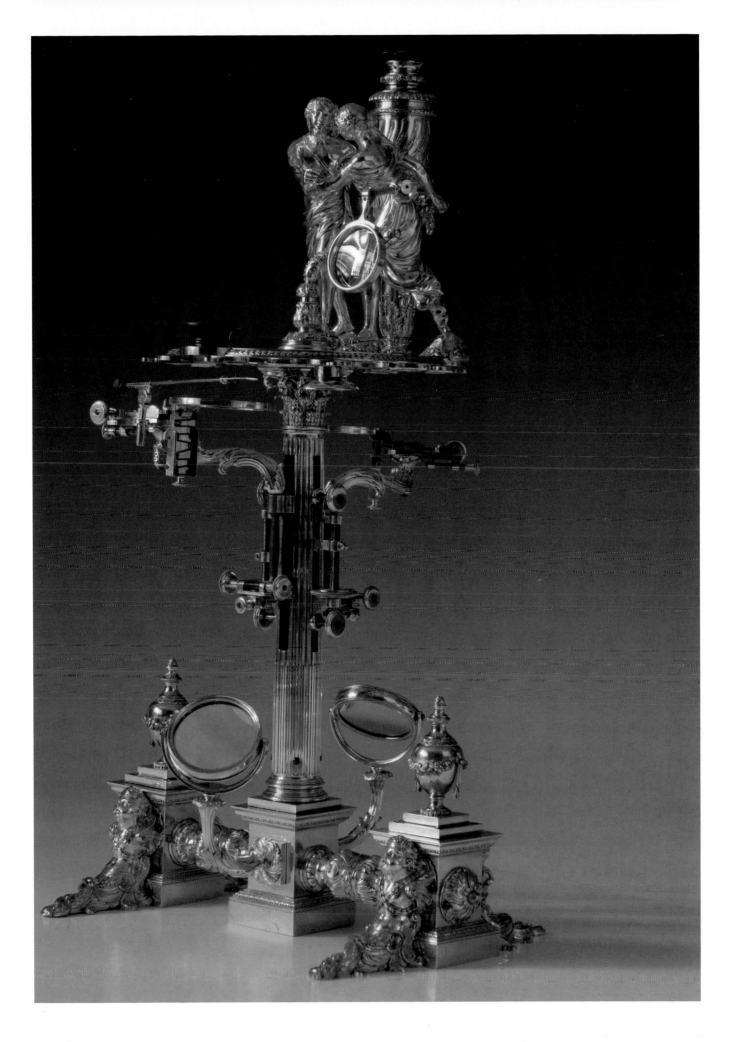

155

110
Telescope used by George III at Kew

1768–69
THOMAS SHORT (*fl.* 1748–88), London
Brass, glass, speculum metal,
413 × 902 × 223 mm

Armagh Observatory, IA1.11

This telescope, with a 6-inch mirror and 2-foot focal length, was used by George III at Kew Observatory to observe the 1769 transit of Venus. There is a focusing mechanism on the side of the tube and the angle of the telescope can be altered with the adjustable arm fixed to the pillar base and eye-end. The accessories include a solar filter.

The maker, Thomas Short, was brother to the much more famous and fashionable telescope-maker James Short (1710–68). The telescope is marked with a serial number, 2/1371 24, which continues the series begun by James. This suggests that the order for the instrument was given to the elder Short but undertaken, or completed, by Thomas when he came down to London on his brother's death in June 1768. Prior to this, Thomas Short had been an optician and instrument-maker based in Leith, near Edinburgh. [RH]

LITERATURE: Mollan, *Irish National Inventory*, pp. 19–20; Andrews, 'Cyclopaedia of Telescope Makers', p. 99.

111
Globe electrical machine

c. 1760
Attributed to GEORGE ADAMS (*c.* 1709–72)
Glass, brass, steel, sheepskin, wood,
410 × 343 × 335 mm

Science Museum, 1927-1186

The purpose of this instrument is to generate static electricity. It consists of a glass globe that can be rotated by turning the handle, via gearing enclosed within the brass box. A brass cup on a steel support holds a piece of sheepskin against the globe and the action generates static electricity. The instrument can be clamped to a table or stand: the one shown here is not contemporary. Although not signed by Adams, the instrument is similar in design, material and details to others by him. Stephen Demainbray, the young George's tutor, used an instrument of this type when lecturing. [RH]

LITERATURE: Morton & Wess, *Public and Private Science*, p. 506.

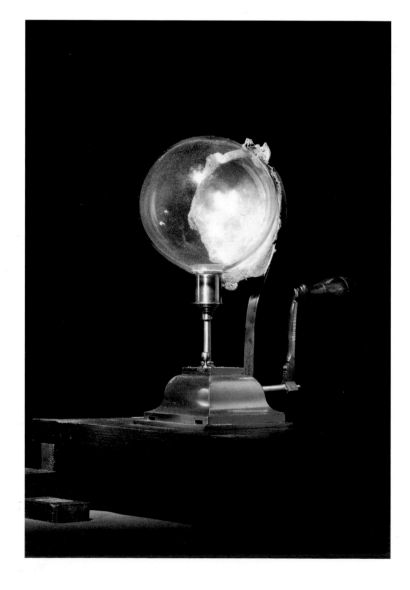

112
George III's astronomical clock

1768
CHRISTOPHER PINCHBECK (1709/10–83)
and others, London
Tortoiseshell, wood, gilt bronze, silver, brass,
enamel, 778 mm (height) × 514 mm
(diameter)
Royal Collection, RCIN 2821

Made for George III, and partly to his
design, this is one of the most complex
and finely constructed astronomical clocks
of the period. Undoubtedly influenced by
the slightly earlier clock of very similar
design by Eardley Norton of about 1765
(also in the Royal Collection), this version
is larger and of even higher quality. The
technical design and practical construction
were carried out by the clockmakers John
Monk and John Merigeot, under
Pinchbeck's supervision, with additional
case design contributed by the King's
architect, Sir William Chambers. The clock
has dials on all four sides. The principal
one indicates time of day on a twenty-
four-hour dial, showing apparent solar
time (i.e. 'sundial time') and mean time
(i.e. clock time), including sunrise and
sunset, and local times in a number of
different countries across the globe. A
second dial has a vertical orrery showing
the relative positions of the six known
planets of the solar system. There is also a
bimetallic thermometer dial, marked from
twenty-five up to eighty-five (presumably
representing the Fahrenheit scale). The
third side has lunar indications, including
a globe moon showing the moon's phase
and a central twenty-four-hour dial
enabling high tides to be determined at
forty-three different ports (mostly British)
and showing their tidal establishments.
The fourth dial incorporates a large
celestial planisphere as well as providing
a full calendar. Although this particular
clock was made for use at Buckingham
House, its multi-purpose complexity
perfectly represents the King's keen
interest in science and innovation, which
was so assiduously cultivated at Kew. [JB]

THE MADNESS OF KING GEORGE: KEW AS A ROYAL ASYLUM

In 1788, George III was struck down by a mysterious illness. He suffered a savage bilious attack at Windsor Castle on 17 October; barely a week later, his speech became rambling and incoherent. This was soon compounded by other physical problems, including rheumatic pain and lameness, and before long he had problems with sight, hearing and memory. On 5 November, George became delirious and, two days later, it became common knowledge that he was seriously ill. As a result, his doctors decided the best place for him was Kew, where he could have relative privacy. He stayed at the White House and the members of his household took up residence in the Dutch House, now known as Kew Palace.

The omens for George's recovery were not particularly promising: he was fifty when he suffered this attack and his father had died at forty-four. Six of George's siblings had also died before the age of fifty. The nature of the King's illness has been the subject of much debate among historians; some have suggested that he was suffering from the effects of the arsenic used in his wig. However, it is now recognised that he was probably the victim of the genetic disorder porphyria: its most telling symptom is the purple urine from which the modern medical name derives. At the time, the King's illness was most commonly described as an ague or insanity, and hopes for his return to health appeared forlorn. By February 1789, however, there were signs of recovery. Celebration balls and thanksgiving services were held across the country in subsequent months. Although George's symptoms of insanity passed on this occasion, they foreshadowed the periodic bouts of illness that would plague the King for the rest of his days. The mental confusion, apparent madness and outbursts of frustrated rage continued to cause personal anguish for his family, and political difficulties for his ministers. George's illness, however, has inspired some of the strongest modern interest in the King, most notably expressed in Alan Bennett's play *The Madness of George III* (1991) and the subsequent film adaptation in 1994, directed by Nicholas Hytner and starring Nigel Hawthorne. [JM & SD]

113

Fan made to celebrate George III's recovery in 1789

PRINCESS ELIZABETH (1770–1840)
Inscribed on border of leather leaf: 'Health is restored to one and Happiness to Millions'
Ivory and leather, 260 mm (guard length)

Royal Collection, RCIN 25087

George III's restoration to health after his first illness was marked by celebrations around the country and the widespread production of commemorative items, including a number of painted fans. The novelist Fanny Burney (1752–1840), one of Queen Charlotte's retinue, recorded attending a celebratory event at which the Queen presented her with a fan ornamented with the same words as are inscribed here. Several identical versions of this fan were presented to guests at parties to celebrate the King's recuperation. The dark blue and white colouring of this fan suggests that it may have been presented at the 'Gala', held at Windsor Castle on the evening of 1 May 1789. According to the *Annual Register*, the 228 guests were invited by the Princess Royal and the Queen, and 'the dresses were the Windsor uniform … The gown was white tiffany, with a garter blue body'. A scrap of paper inscribed during the lifetime of Queen Victoria (who received this fan as a Golden Jubilee gift from Lady Holland), indicates that it was made by George III's third daughter, Princess Elizabeth. While it is unlikely that Princess Elizabeth painted hundreds of similar fans, she may have produced this one as a prototype to be replicated by others. [JM]

LITERATURE: Roberts, *Royal Artists*, pp.82–83; Roberts, Sutcliffe & Mayor, *Unfolding Pictures*, pp.88–89; Roberts & Lloyd (eds), *George III and Queen Charlotte*, pp.80–81.

114
Gold medallion commissioned by Queen Charlotte to celebrate the recovery of George III

1789
Inscribed: 'REGI · AMATO · REDVCI / MART · X / MDCCLXXXIX and VIVAT / G III R'
Gold and enamel, 35 mm (diameter)
Royal Collection, RCIN 65800

A grateful government, spared the prospect of a regency under the rather wayward Prince of Wales, ensured that Parliament presented addresses of congratulation to the King on 10 March, the date inscribed on this enamelled gold medallion. This medal is much rarer than many other commemorative items produced in celebration of the King's recovery because it appears to have been commissioned by Queen Charlotte herself. The inclusion of a loop and ring suggests that the medals were intended to be worn by the courtiers to whom the Queen presented them. Fanny Burney, who served as the Queen's Second Keeper of the Robes from 1786 to 1791, recorded in her diary that Lord Harcourt 'showed me a new medallion, just presented him by the Queen, with a Latin inscription in honour of the King's recovery'. [JM]

LITERATURE: Brown, 'Queen Charlotte's Medal', pp. 183–84; Roberts & Lloyd (eds), *George III and Queen Charlotte*, p. 366.

115
Medal commemorating the recovery of George III

1789
Metal, 33 mm (diameter)
British Museum, M.4970

Dr Francis Willis (1718–1807), whose image appears on this medal, was brought in as George III's doctor in December 1788, when the King was displaying alarming signs of dementia. The King's usual physicians were unable to find a cure and, as a last resort, the Earl and Countess of Harcourt recommended Willis who had treated Lady Harcourt's mother. Then aged seventy, Willis had considerable experience of treating mental illness, having run a private lunatic asylum for over a decade. Willis insisted on exclusive medical control, thereby alienating the King's regular physicians. Furthermore, his methods were highly unconventional. Believing madness was essentially a product of over-excitation, he relied on enforced calm – including the use of a gag, straitjacket and a restraining chair – to produce results. By February 1789, the King had largely recovered. This was very probably a spontaneous recovery from a bout of porphyria and had little to do with Willis's therapies. Nevertheless, Willis was quick to claim the credit and had a token struck bearing his likeness, with an inscription on the reverse: 'Britons rejoice. Your King's Restored. 1789'. In gratitude, Parliament granted Willis an annual pension of £1000 but George III suffered recurring bouts of illness until his death. [JM]

LITERATURE: *Oxford DNB*; Black, *George III*, pp. 278–80; Macalpine and Hunter, *George III and the Mad-business*, *passim*.

116
Dessert service commissioned to commemorate George III's recovery in 1789

Made by SÈVRES, France, 1789

Plate inscribed: 'Huzza the King is Well!'
Porcelain, 241 mm (diameter)

Plate inscribed: 'God save the King'
Porcelain, 241 mm (diameter)

Plate with profile portrait
Porcelain, 240 mm (diameter)

Three preserve pots and stand
Porcelain, 208 × 231 × 205 mm

Royal Collection, RCIN 95588.2, 15, 22; RCIN 95605

The King's recovery provided the impetus for the production of medals, porcelain and other commemoratives that tapped into the public mood of celebration and thanksgiving. The pieces of this service were specially commissioned from the Sèvres factory outside Paris, which produced the finest and most technically accomplished of all eighteenth-century porcelain. The dessert service comprises over a hundred pieces in total. It is decorated with portrait medallions of the King, the crowned cursive initial 'G' encircled by a laurel wreath, and various inscriptions including 'Huzza the King is Well!' and 'God save the King'.

The fact that the service was commissioned from the French King's porcelain factory may account for the grisaille profile on the dessert plates resembling that of Louis XVI more closely than George III. The service was commissioned by the Spanish ambassador, the Marquis del Campo, who also celebrated the King's recovery by holding a grand gala in the Rotunda at Ranelagh Gardens on 2 June 1789. The Marquis presented the dessert service to Lord and Lady Harcourt in 1796. [JM]

LITERATURE: De Bellaigue, 'Huzza the King is Well!', pp.325–31; Roberts & Lloyd (eds), *George III and Queen Charlotte*, pp.315–16.

117
George III during his last illness

1827
JOSEPH LEE (1780–1859);
after JOHN JACKSON (1778–1831)
Inscribed on the counter-enamel: 'His Majesty
George the 3rd / from the Original sketch by
John Jackson, Esq. R.A. / Joseph Lee Pinxt /
London 1827'
Enamel on copper, 222 × 172 mm

Royal Collection, RCIN 421492

George III suffered from recurring attacks of porphyria after his recuperation in 1789, but his relapse at the end of 1810 proved permanent and resulted in the total breakdown of his health. Blind, deaf and deluded, he no longer recognised his family and took solace in imaginary conversations. For the remainder of his life the King remained in seclusion at Windsor, often subjected to the same degrading system of restraint imposed in 1789. He died of pneumonia on the evening of 29 January 1820 in his room overlooking the North Terrace at Windsor.

The Prince of Wales, who had acted as Prince Regent for the previous nine years, then succeeded him as George IV. This portrait, one of the last images of George III, depicts a blind and bearded old man far removed from the grandeur of his early reign. Majesty and monarchy are subverted by delusion and decayed reason. Joseph Lee turned to painting at about the age of thirty after an unsuccessful start in business. He was probably self-taught, studying the work of Christian Friedrich Zincke. [SD & JM]

LITERATURE: Black, *George III*, pp.409–10.

118
The Castellated Palace, Kew

c. 1817
WILLIAM INNES POCOCK (1783–1836)
Watercolour on paper, 129 × 411 mm

Royal Collection, RL 17948

The Castellated Palace was built on the site of a number of old buildings on the riverside at Kew, a few hundred yards up river from the Dutch House and overlooking the village of Brentford. Work on this new building began in 1801 and George III intended it to be the main royal residence at Richmond and Kew. The vast building employed various technical innovations, such as cast-iron supports, and proved very expensive. Allocated £40,000 in 1800, the costs had risen to

£100,000 by 1806, and some estimates suggest that they had reached £500,000 by 1811. It stood as a monument to George III's 'building mania'.

Upon his assumption of the regency, the Prince of Wales abandoned the project and left the building in the state that is shown in this watercolour. Demolition was finally ordered in 1827. Materials from the palace were reused in Buckingham Palace and Windsor Castle, both of which were then being

redeveloped. Like some of George III's architectural projects at Windsor, the Castellated Palace is a poignant reminder of the King's last physical decline. Its demolition also symbolised the removal of the royal court from Kew to Buckingham Palace in central London. [JM]

LITERATURE: Cloake, *Palaces and Parks*, pp.142–46; Roberts & Lloyd (eds), *George III and Queen Charlotte*, pp.132–33; Watkin, *The Architect King, passim*.

LORD NELSON'S FUNERAL, 1806

119
The immortality of Nelson

1807
BENJAMIN WEST (1738–1820)
Oil on canvas, 908 × 762 mm

National Maritime Museum, Greenwich Hospital
Collection, BHC2905

Originally conceived as the central
'altarpiece' of a sculptural wall
monument, this smaller version of
Nelson's apotheosis employs the whole
breadth of neo-classical allegory to
celebrate his heroism and sacrifice at
Trafalgar on 21 October 1805. Clad in a
white shroud with the blood of his fatal
wound just visible, the lifeless body of
Nelson is lifted by Neptune out of the
waves into the receiving arms of
Britannia. He is surrounded by numerous
references to his victories; nereids, putti
and a winged figure of Victory mourn
his death. Benjamin West exhibited the
painting at the Royal Academy in 1807.
It was engraved as the frontispiece for
the first major biography of Nelson,
published in 1809. [JGM]

LITERATURE: Lincoln (ed.), *Nelson and Napoleon*,
no. 303.

A great river procession marked the funeral of Horatio, Viscount Nelson, killed at the Battle of Trafalgar on 21 October 1805. Knowledge of his famous victory over the combined French and Spanish fleets took some time to reach London. Entrusted to Lieutenant John Richards Lapenotière, commanding officer of HMS *Pickle*, dispatches were delivered to the Admiralty early in the morning of 6 November. Rushed into print by every newspaper, accounts of the battle and of Nelson's death then sped across the nation. The public reaction was an immediate and extraordinary synthesis of jubilation and grief, expressed through theatrical performances, ballads, loyal addresses, pictures, commemorative objects and mourning tokens. Relief that Napoleon's apparently inexorable advance had been checked at sea struggled with the loss of a figure whose status as a national hero had already been secured by the Battles of the Nile (1798) and Copenhagen (1801).

This potent mixture of triumph, sacrifice and popular feeling demanded appropriate symbolic acknowledgment from those in authority. Moreover, the government was keen to exploit Trafalgar for domestic political ends, promoting national unity and bolstering public support for the war. For all of these reasons, Nelson's funeral became an occasion of unparalleled spectacle and magnificence. While the patched and battered HMS *Victory* was still at sea, carrying the Admiral's body back to England, the King gave his approval for a state funeral. The College of Heralds immediately set to work adapting the ancient monarchical and aristocratic precedents of this ritual, and tense negotiations were conducted between the government and the Lord Mayor of London. It was decided that Nelson's body would lie in state at the Royal Hospital, Greenwich, before being carried upriver in a vast waterborne cortège to Whitehall Stairs. After resting at the Admiralty for one night, a specially designed funeral car would then transport the coffin through the streets to St Paul's Cathedral for the service and interment in the crypt. In the event, vast crowds gathered to pay their respects, lining the banks of the Thames and the route to the cathedral in their tens of thousands. Nelson's final journey bound together the capital, the Royal Navy, the people and the river, and bathed them all in the patriotic sentiments he had come to personify. [QC]

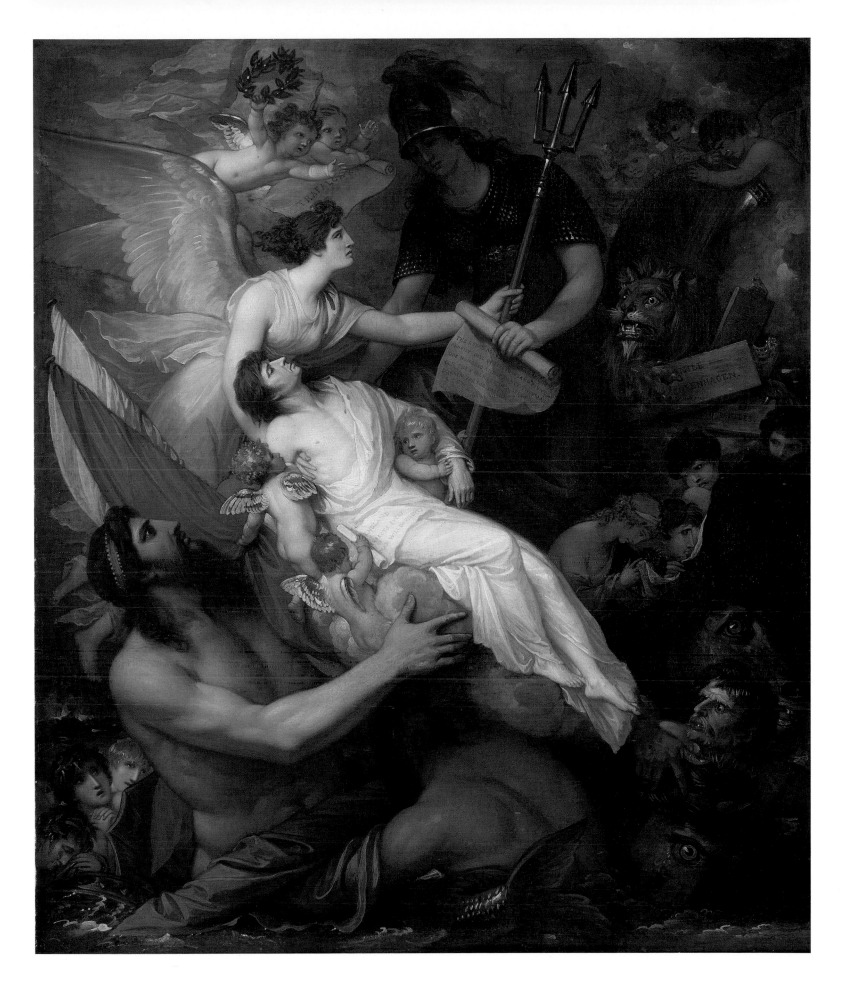

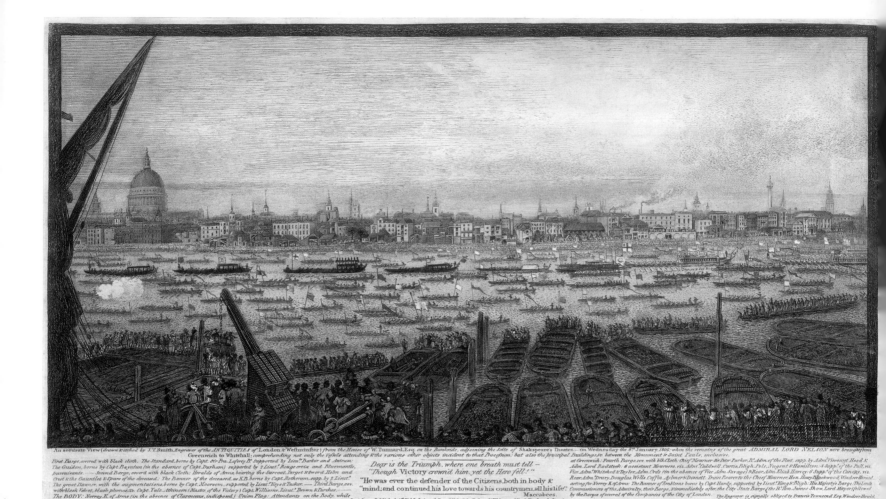

An accurate View (drawn & etched by J.T.Smith, Engraver of the ANTIQUITIES of London & Westminster) from the House of W.Turnard, Esq. on the Bankside, adjoining the Scite of Shakspeare's Theatre – on Wednesday the 8th January 1806; when the remains of the great ADMIRAL LORD NELSON were brought from Greenwich to Whitehall; comprehending not only the Vehicle attending & the various other objects incident to that Procession, but also the principal Buildings, &c. between the Monument & Saint Paul's, inclusive.

Dear is the Triumph, where one breath must tell –
"Though Victory crowd'd him, yet the Hero fell!"

"He was ever the defender of the Citizens, both in body &
"mind; and continued his love towards his countrymen, all his life".
Maccabees.

London: Published 15th Feb.r 1806, and Republished by Robert Wilkinson, No.125, Fenchurch Street.

120

An accurate View … of the Antiquities of London & Westminster … on Wednesday the 8th January 1806; when the remains of the great Admiral Lord Nelson were brought from Greenwich to Whitehall…

15 February 1806
Engraved by and after JOHN THOMAS
SMITH (1766–1833); published by
ROBERT WILKINSON, London
Hand-coloured etching, 280 × 462 mm

National Maritime Museum, PAG6706

First published on 15 February 1806, this etching shows the great spectacle of Vice-Admiral Lord Nelson's funeral procession as it made its gradual progress from the Royal Hospital in Greenwich to Whitehall. The perspective chosen by the artist, John Thomas Smith, directs the viewer from the south bank of the Thames towards a section of river and skyline defined by St Paul's Cathedral on the left and the Monument on the right. The stage this creates is then dominated by the flotilla of small craft. Nelson's coffin was carried by a state barge with black plumes, which appears third from the left. It, in turn, was followed by the various barges of City livery companies. This image is made still

more noteworthy by its portrayal of the thickets of onlookers who gathered to watch the procession pass. Commentators who more usually viewed the behaviour of 'the crowd' with apprehension were also struck by the quiet and dignified manner in which this event was marked by the London public. [QC]

LITERATURE: Lincoln (ed.), *Nelson and Napoleon*, no.293.

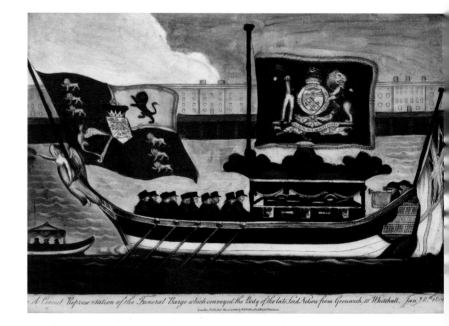

A Correct Representation of the Funeral Barge which conveyed the Body of the late Lord Nelson from Greenwich to Whitehall, Jan.y 8th 1806.

123
Two mourning rings commemorating Nelson

1805

(a) Below left:
Inscribed (inside the bezel):
'Lost to his country 21 Octr 1805 Aged 47'
JOHN SALTER, London
Gold, enamel, 20 mm (diameter)

National Maritime Museum, Nelson-Ward Collection, JEW0167

(b) Below right:
Inscribed: 'Gloriously fell on 21st Oct. 1805 in the action with the combined fleets of France and Spain'
JOHN SALTER, London
Gold, enamel, 19 mm (diameter)

National Maritime Museum, JEW0163

These are two of at least fifty-eight gold mourning rings made to commemorate the death of Vice-Admiral Lord Nelson and distributed by Nelson's executors for recipients to wear on the occasion of the funeral. The design shows a viscount's and a duke's coronet, beneath which can be seen the initials 'NB' (for 'Nelson' and 'Bronte'), and the word 'Trafalgar'. All of these devices are set against a black enamel ground, with further details of the coronets picked out in red and white enamel. The hoop of the ring is inscribed with Nelson's Latin motto.

The ring (a) belonged to Thomas Bolton (1786–1835), Nelson's nephew and later the second Earl Nelson, and was among thirty-one presented to the Admiral's relations. Family tradition maintains that Thomas Bolton lost the ring the day after the funeral, and that it was found by a gardener forty years later. The bezel of this ring opens up to reveal a lock of plaited hair held under glass.

The ring (b) belonged to the naval officer and Arctic explorer Sir John Franklin (1786–1847), who served as a signal midshipman on board HMS *Bellerophon* at the Battle of Trafalgar. He attended Nelson's state funeral, though his name does not appear on the list of those who received mourning rings sent out by the Admiral's executors. [QC]

LITERATURE: Prentice, *The Authentic Nelson*, pp. 173–4; George A. Goulty, 'Nelson's Memorial Rings', *passim*.

121 (left)
A Correct Representation of the Funeral Barge which conveyed the Body of the Late Lord Nelson from Greenwich to Whitehall, Jany. 8th 1806

1 March 1806
W.B. WALKER, London
Transfer print on glass, 302 × 401 × 23 mm
National Maritime Museum, GGG0526

Published in London on 1 March 1806 by W.B. Walker, this image is a rather fanciful portrayal of Charles II's royal barge, which was lent by George III to carry Lord Nelson's coffin upstream from the Royal Hospital, Greenwich, to Whitehall Stairs. Adorned with black funeral plumes, the barge is shown flying the royal standard and the white ensign. The third flag bears Nelson's coat of arms and his Latin motto: *Palmam Qui Meruit Ferat* ('Let him bear the palm who has deserved it'). Two heralds are shown positioned at the stern of the vessel, with the oarsmen seated on their benches forward of the canopied enclosure containing Nelson's body. Although not apparent in this rather simplified image, five lieutenants from HMS *Victory* accompanied the coffin on its journey up the River Thames: John Pasco, Edward Williams, Andrew King, John Yule and George Browne. The Master of Nelson's flagship, Thomas Atkinson, was also present. [QC]

122 (above)
Flag flown on the Apothecaries' barge at the funeral procession of Lord Nelson

c. 1797
Painted silk
The Worshipful Society of Apothecaries of London

Ordered from the boat-builder Charles Cowndell in 1764, the Society of Apothecaries' barge was one of a number of City livery company craft that participated in Nelson's funeral procession. This flag is one of those flown from the barge on 8 January 1806. The Company has a further three flags and two long banners: all are believed to have been purchased in 1797. The silk flag is painted with the Company's coat of arms, which shows Apollo, the inventor of physic, with a bow and arrow supplanting a serpent and supported by two unicorns. The crest is a rhinoceros, representing the contemporary belief that its powdered horn had valuable medicinal properties. The motto, *Opiferque per orben dicor* ('I am called throughout the world the bringer of aid') is from Ovid's *Metamorphoses*. The Society of Apothecaries had its origins with the Company of Pepperers, but was incorporated as a livery company by royal charter in December 1617. [OC & RB]

LITERATURE: Palmer, *Ceremonial Barges*, pp. 134–35.

4

THE WORKING RIVER AND ITS VICTORIAN TRANSFORMATION

THE TRANSFORMATION OF THE THAMES IN THE NINETEENTH CENTURY

GLORIA CLIFTON

The River Thames played a vital role in the life of London. At the start of the nineteenth century it was at once a major thoroughfare, an increasingly congested port, a source of domestic water and a receptacle for the drainage of the city. Wharfs and factories crowded along the river banks. Congestion on the river and in the port was intensified by the growing size and prosperity of the capital. Trade had grown during the preceding century, so that the total value of London's imports and exports more than trebled. The population reached about a million at the beginning of the nineteenth century, with a consequent increase in river traffic. The greater numbers of people generated more waste, part of which found its way into the Thames because most of the existing sewers ran north or south into the river. Some of the problems were already being tackled in the eighteenth century, with the building of additional bridges across the river and the first moves towards the construction of new enclosed docks for trading vessels and cargo handling. But it was during the nineteenth century that a significant transformation was achieved in both the appearance of the riverside and in the water quality of the Thames. One reason why more improvements were finally achieved was that for the first time London had a local authority with the power to carry out public works for the whole of the built-up area of London. This was the Metropolitan Board of Works, created by Act of Parliament in 1855. It was indirectly elected by the London parishes and City Corporation, and was replaced in 1888–89 by the directly elected London County Council (LCC), which continued the improvement work.

London's townscape was changed significantly by the construction of new bridges across the Thames in the nineteenth century. They also eased movement around the city, reducing congestion on the existing bridges and cutting the detour which often had to be made to reach a bridge and get to the opposite bank, especially for goods. People frequently used one of the small boats operated by Thames watermen to cross the river, and the watermen were vocal opponents of new river crossings, which reduced their trade. This was one reason why earlier attempts to build more bridges had often failed.

The oldest and most famous bridge was London Bridge, which had existed in one form or another since Roman times.

The bridge in use at the start of the nineteenth century had first been built in the late twelfth century, though it had been extensively repaired and altered. In particular, the houses and shops that once used to line the bridge had been removed between 1758 and 1762. At the same time the stone arches were strengthened and the two central spans were replaced by a single larger one, to make it easier to navigate the bridge. Despite these measures, the old bridge was in a poor state and too narrow for the volume of traffic using it by the late eighteenth century. The City Corporation, which was responsible for the bridge, decided that it would have to be completely rebuilt. A new design was drawn up by the well-known civil engineer, John Rennie, but unfortunately he died before it could be built, so the work was carried out by his son of the same name. The new bridge was accorded the honour of a royal opening on 1 August 1831 by William IV and Queen Adelaide. By the mid-twentieth century, the bridge was no longer fit for purpose and it was finally replaced by the present structure in 1972. Rennie's bridge was sold and shipped to the United States: it can now be seen at Lake Havasu City in Arizona.

The early nineteenth century also saw the construction of a number of completely new bridges, providing additional crossings. One, at Vauxhall, was the first iron bridge to be built over the Thames and was opened in 1816. It was originally named Regent's Bridge in honour of the Prince Regent, the future George IV. It was a toll bridge owned by the Vauxhall Bridge Company. John Rennie also designed the Southwark and Waterloo Bridges. The latter was opened by the Prince Regent in 1817 on the second anniversary of the battle of Waterloo. Further new crossings followed in the second half of the century, including the suspension bridges, Chelsea in 1858 and Lambeth in 1862, which replaced the old horse ferry. A rather different design was used for the new Albert Bridge, a little further west, which was opened in 1873 and named in honour of the late Prince Consort. It was a cantilever bridge by Roland Mason Ordish.

Most of the bridges over the Thames were originally built and owned by private companies which charged tolls for using them, the only exceptions being London and Westminster Bridges. The City Corporation, which controlled the ancient square mile of the original medieval City, was responsible for

London and later Blackfriars Bridges. Blackfriars had originally been a toll bridge, but it was bought out by the government and made free in 1785. It was rebuilt in the 1860s to the designs of Joseph Cubitt (d. 1872) and opened by Queen Victoria in 1869. Westminster Bridge was maintained by central government through the Office of Works, and was rebuilt between 1854 and 1862. In 1877 the Metropolitan Board of Works obtained an Act of Parliament, enabling it to acquire bridges across the Thames and free them from the remaining tolls. In May 1879, Albert, Battersea, Chelsea, Lambeth and Vauxhall Bridges were formally declared free of tolls by the Prince and Princess of Wales, who celebrated the event by driving in their carriage across all the bridges, one after the other. The footbridge at Richmond lock was the last bridge in the London area to charge tolls, finally becoming free in 1894. The Board also made repairs and improvements to a number of the bridges, including strengthening Albert Bridge, rebuilding Putney and Hammersmith Bridges, and beginning work on a new Battersea Bridge, all to the designs of their engineer, Sir Joseph William Bazalgette (1819–91). The LCC continued the work of improving the existing bridges, including reconstructing Vauxhall Bridge in 1895–1906 so that it could accommodate tramlines.

Until the late nineteenth century London Bridge remained the final Thames bridge before the open sea, but the expansion of the East End created a demand for a crossing further downstream. There were objections, however, to any bridge which would hinder the passage of cargo vessels on the river, so the first attempt to provide a crossing was a tunnel. This was initiated in 1805 at Rotherhithe by the Cornish engineer Robert Vazie and worked on by Richard Trevithick. Technical difficulties and serious flooding overwhelmed the project and it was abandoned before completion. Marc Isambard Brunel returned to the idea of a

tunnel in the 1820s. He devised the first tunnelling shield to try to overcome the problem of inundation, but it was not until 1843 that work was completed. It had been hoped to build access ramps for vehicles, but there was never enough money and it remained a foot tunnel (fig.20) until it was taken over by the East London Railway for their new line in the 1860s.

The demand for a vehicle crossing below London Bridge remained and eventually a select committee of the House of Commons reported in favour of two such crossings, with the result that the City Corporation built Tower Bridge and the new LCC constructed the Blackwall Tunnel. Both of these overcame the problem of maintaining access for ships, Tower Bridge being the only lifting bridge in London. The final design of Tower Bridge was partly the result of government insistence that it should be in keeping with the neighbouring Tower of London.

Another new feature of the nineteenth century Thames was the railway bridge. The first railway to be built in the capital was the London to Greenwich line in 1836, but this terminated at London Bridge Station, just to the south of the river. It was not until 1859 that the first railway bridge across the Thames within central London was completed, enabling the London, Brighton and South Coast Railway to take trains to a terminus north of the river at Victoria Station. Blackfriars Railway Bridge followed in 1864, designed by Joseph Cubitt for the London, Chatham and Dover Railway. Also completed in 1864 was Charing Cross Railway Bridge. This used the piers of Isambard Kingdom Brunel's Hungerford Bridge, a suspension bridge for pedestrians which had been opened in 1845 to provide access for Hungerford market. But the market was not a commercial success and the land was acquired by the South Eastern Railway Company to build Charing Cross Station. The chains of Brunel's bridge were sold and used for his Clifton Suspension Bridge in Bristol. The South Eastern

THE LONDON BATHING SEASON.

"COME, MY DEAR!—COME TO ITS OLD THAMES, AND HAVE A NICE BATH!"

Railway obtained an Act of Parliament allowing it to build a station at Cannon Street. This involved building a railway bridge, known as Alexandra Bridge, which was designed by the Company's consulting engineer, Sir John Hawkshaw (1811–91), and opened in 1866. Further railway bridges were built at Battersea, Putney, Barnes and Kew.

Meanwhile, the increasing congestion in the port of London at the end of the eighteenth century caused delays to trade and provided many opportunities for the theft of valuable cargoes. The first groups of merchants to succeed in obtaining improvements were those engaged in the sugar trade with the West Indies. In 1799, they secured an Act of Parliament to create the West India Dock Company, which set about constructing enclosed docks with proper warehousing across the Isle of Dogs. They began operating in 1802, though further extensions and improvements were to follow.

This venture was soon followed by other enclosed dock schemes: the London Docks at Wapping opened in 1805 and the first part of the Surrey Commercial Docks, on the south bank, came into operation in 1807. The London Docks specialised in brandy, wine, rice and tobacco. The docks on the south bank between the Lower Pool and Limehouse reach were developed piecemeal by a number of companies and incorporated the old Howland Great Dock of 1697, which had been for ship repair rather than for cargo handling. Timber was the major import handled at the Surrey Docks.

The East India Company already had a dock at Blackwall, but this was only for ship repair and refitting. In the first decade of the nineteenth century it too developed plans to expand the existing facilities and convert them for cargo handling. The old Brunswick Dock was enlarged and used for exports, while a new larger dock was constructed to the north to handle the Company's imports.

The engineer John Rennie, who designed a number of London's bridges, also had a major role in the construction of

Fig.21 'The London Bathing Season',
Punch, 18 June 1858.

National Maritime Museum, L4686-3.

the new enclosed docks along the Thames in the early nineteenth century. He was consultant for the West India Docks, working with the engineer for the scheme, William Jessop, and also for the London Docks. He was also appointed joint engineer with Ralph Walker for the East India Docks.

A further phase of dock development occurred in the 1820s, with the construction of St Katharine's Dock, under the supervision of Thomas Telford. This was much closer to the City than the other enclosed docks, being just below the Tower of London, and aroused considerable criticism because of the number of existing buildings that had to be destroyed and the fact that over 11,000 people had to be moved to alternative housing. The dock was completed in 1828 and there was then a lull in dock building until the second half of the century, when another spate of construction further downstream created the Royal Victoria (1855), the Millwall (1868) and the Royal Albert Docks (1880). Also, between 1850 and 1860, there was a further extension of the docks on the Surrey side of the river, with the creation of the Albion Dock. All of these schemes were accompanied by the building of warehouses and locks, which did much to change the view of the river banks.

However, the most striking change to the appearance of the London river frontage in the nineteenth century came with the building of the Victoria, Albert and Chelsea Embankments in the 1860s and 1870s by the Metropolitan Board of Works. Before these developments, wide mud banks lined both sides of the river at low tide. These not only looked unsightly but, given the polluted state of the river, caused a very offensive smell in warm weather. The stench was particularly bad in the hot summer of 1858, which became known as the 'Great Stink'. The idea of embanking the Thames had been discussed before but there was strong opposition from the owners of wharfs and riverside land, so it was not until the 1860s that it was possible to win enough support for the idea. The fact that the Houses of Parliament were right next to the river, and that the bad smell in hot weather permeated the rooms used by the Members, doubtless helped to concentrate their minds on the need to improve the situation. As *The Times* put it:

Parliament was all but compelled to legislate upon the great London nuisance by the force of sheer stench. The intense heat had driven our legislators from those portions of their building which overlook the river. A few members, indeed, bent upon investigating the matter to its very depth, ventured into the library, but they were instantaneously driven to retreat, each man with a handkerchief to his nose.[1]

The necessary legislation for an embankment on the north side of the river between Blackfriars and Westminster was passed in 1862 and the Metropolitan Board of Works instructed Joseph Bazalgette to draw up the necessary plans. Funding for the work was to come from the duties on coal and wine entering London. The completion of the embankment was delayed by the subsequent agreement that a new underground railway should be constructed beneath it. This was originally entirely a commercial venture, but is now part of the London Underground network. Much of the reclaimed land along the new embankment was laid out as public gardens, providing a welcome green space. The formal opening ceremony for the Victoria Embankment was carried out on 13 July 1870 by the Prince of Wales, on behalf of the Queen.

Meanwhile, the Metropolitan Board of Works obtained Acts of Parliament empowering it to create an embankment on the south side of the Thames, to be called the Albert Embankment, and another at Chelsea. Again Bazalgette was instructed to draw up the plans and oversaw the work. The Albert Embankment was opened fairly quietly on 24 November 1869 by the Chairman of the Board of Works, John Thwaites, so as not to outshine the main event, which was to be the royal opening of the more extensive Victoria Embankment in the following year. Instead of the small boat yards which had previously lined the south bank of the river, new buildings for St Thomas's Hospital were erected on the reclaimed land next to Westminster Bridge, completely transforming the view from the Palace of Westminster. The series of improvements was finally completed with the royal opening of the Chelsea Embankment in May 1874 by Queen Victoria's second son and his wife, the Duke and Duchess of Edinburgh.

The embankments not only enhanced the appearance of the riverside, but also improved the flow of water, carried new highways and footpaths and helped to prevent the flooding of

Lambeth and Chelsea, which had been a frequent problem in the past. Indeed, improving the flood defences had been one of the principal aims behind the creation of the Albert and Chelsea Embankments. The work had all been carried out by private contractors, closely supervised by assistant engineers and clerks of works employed by the Metropolitan Board of Works. It had been a massive undertaking and left the river frontage with new granite-faced walls, which gave the heart of the capital a much more imposing appearance. Even the lamp-posts for the gas lighting along the embankments were specially designed, with entwined dolphins supporting the columns.

The construction of the Thames embankments was the most visible part of a series of public works designed to improve the state of the river within London. The polluted condition of the Thames had become an acknowledged national disgrace by the mid-nineteenth century. It even inspired the magazine *Punch* to produce a rhyme as well as many cartoons (figs 21 and 22), the first verse of which went as follows:

> Filthy river, filthy river,
> Foul from London to the Nore,
> What art thou but one vast gutter,
> One tremendous common shore? [2]

It was not only the satirical press like *Punch* which campaigned about the state of the river, but also influential newspapers such as *The Times*. The problem had worsened noticeably during the early nineteenth century for a number of reasons; one was the huge growth in the population of London, from just under a million at the first census in 1801, to almost two million in 1841. More people meant more waste. London had a system of sewers and drains that were originally intended simply to carry away rainwater and which flowed directly into the Thames all the way along the river banks. They were managed by a series of eight separate Commissions of Sewers, each with their own systems and sizes of drains, with the result that improvements by one commission could cause bursts and flooding in the neighbouring area. Many houses just had cess pools and in poorer parts of London, where serious overcrowding was increasing, they tended to overflow into the street drains or contaminate local wells. In the wealthier areas householders were increasingly connecting domestic waste

systems directly into the sewers, while the volume to be removed was being rapidly increased by the spread of the water closet. All of this effluent went into the Thames along with waste from industrial premises along the river, creating the problems exemplified by the Great Stink. It was mainly the smell that concerned contemporaries, not only because it was unpleasant, but because it was widely believed at the time that the bad air itself caused disease: the so-called 'miasmic theory'. Typhoid fever was extremely common, especially in the poorer areas, and from 1831 onwards there were periodic outbreaks of cholera, but it was not until the late nineteenth century that the role of sewage-contaminated water in spreading disease was fully understood.

Serious attempts to improve matters began in the 1840s with the creation of a unified Metropolitan Commission of Sewers for the whole of London outside the square mile of the ancient City. It succeeded in carrying out a proper survey of the entire system for the first time, but focused on removing cess pools and improving house drainage, rather than on the state of the Thames. Six different sets of Commissioners were appointed, but their work was hampered by disagreements over the best system of drainage and over difficulties in financing the work.

The opinion grew that a representative body of some kind should oversee the spending of the large sums of public money necessary for a new drainage system for London. This led to the creation of the Metropolitan Board of Works, which began work at the start of 1856. It appointed Joseph Bazalgette as its engineer; he had held the same office in the later years of the Metropolitan Commission of Sewers. The Act setting up the Board required that sewage should be prevented from entering the Thames 'in or near to the Metropolis', so Bazalgette set about designing a system of intercepting sewers parallel with the river, that would cut off the old sewers, taking their contents well to the east of the City and discharging them into the river on the ebb tide, so that noxious matter would be taken out to sea. [3] Similar plans had been discussed by the Metropolitan Commissions, but Bazalgette put together ideas from a number of proposals and combined them into a workable whole. Even more important, he proved to have the managerial ability and drive to see the whole massive project through to completion. There were some delays at the start,

PUNCH, OR THE LONDON CHARIVARI, July 10, 1858.

THE "SILENT HIGHWAY"-MAN.

"Your MONEY or your LIFE!"

because of disagreements with the government's first Commissioner of Works, who was supposed to approve the Board's plans, but the Great Stink of 1858 forced Parliament to rethink and a new Act was passed that summer, giving the Board full powers to create the system it considered best and to raise the necessary funds by borrowing. The principal sewers were completed by 1865, including the northern low-level sewer which was combined with the building of the Victoria Embankment. The whole new main drainage system cost some £4.6 million, a huge sum for the time.

At first, raw sewage went into the Thames from outfalls at Barking to the north and Erith to the south, which caused complaints from local inhabitants. Further doubts about the wisdom of this practice were raised in 1878, when an excursion boat run by the London Steamboat Company, called the *Princess Alice*, sank after a collision with a collier, the *Bywell Castle*. Over 600 people died, some trapped in the sunken boat, but the enquiry into the disaster concluded that pollution from

the sewer outfalls contributed to the deaths of those who were thrown into the water. Eventually, after an investigation by a Royal Commission, which reported in 1884, the Board was forced to build treatment works at the outfalls. As a result of the Board's efforts, the condition of the river was vastly improved and, in recognition of his contribution, Joseph Bazalgette was knighted in 1874, just after the completion of the embankments.

Thanks to the innovative and visionary work of British civil engineers, the Thames had changed enormously by the end of the nineteenth century. Embankments, bridges, tunnels and docks made the appearance of the late-Victorian river very different to that of a century earlier. The transformation was achieved by the need to improve communications, to maintain the efficiency of the world's greatest port, and to safeguard the health of the vast and growing population of the metropolis, which had become the largest city on Earth.

THE WATERMEN

Before the mid-eighteenth century, a good 'taxi service' across the Thames was essential because only one bridge spanned the river in London until Westminster Bridge was completed in 1750. Barges were also needed to take passengers up and downstream since road transport was slow and often uncomfortable. The royal family, the livery companies and some wealthy individuals owned river barges, but ordinary men and women had to hire boats for transportation. To ensure that skilled and honest boatmen manned these vessels, an Act of Parliament was passed in 1555, founding a company to regulate the apprenticeships of the Thames boatmen and to fix fares. In 1566 another Act of Parliament was passed, which was designed to put an end to the 'divers[e] and many misfortunes and mischances' that were caused by 'evil and ignorant persons who robbed and spoiled their [passengers'] goods … and also drowned them'. The Watermen's Company, therefore, was established to protect customers and prevent malpractice; in 1585 it received a royal coat of arms from Elizabeth I. From 1696, each waterman had to have his boat numbered, carry his licence and display the fare-list – a system similar to the one that exists for London's black cabs today.

The watermen usually operated in small boats, called wherries, swift, sharp-bowed vessels that could carry up to five passengers. They plied their trade at official hiring stops, known as stairs, many of them named after waterside taverns; the 'stairs' were often, quite literally, a number of steps leading down to a jetty where the boats were moored. Watermen were only allowed to carry passengers with a reasonable amount of luggage; cargo was left to lightermen who unloaded goods from ships (making them lighter) and carried them to the quayside in their barges with large holds. In 1700 the lightermen, who had been members of the Woodmongers' Company, joined the Watermen.

Watermen in the service of the monarch were required to row barges on ceremonial occasions and to provide transport between the royal palaces situated along the Thames. They were employed when required by two royal bargemasters, who were salaried officials. The first mention of watermen in the service of the monarch relates to King John travelling by river to Runnymede to confirm the final draft of Magna Carta in June 1215. Edward VII halved the original number of forty-eight. Today twenty-four royal watermen are retained in a purely ceremonial role and the posts are still filled by licensed Thames watermen. They take part in any state occasion on the Thames and act as footmen on royal carriages. At the state opening of Parliament, the Queen's bargemaster and four royal watermen guard the crown and regalia as they travel to and from Buckingham Palace and Westminster. [SD & BT]

124
A Thames waterman's licence badge

c. 1824
Sheffield plate (silver on copper) with a ferrous metal backing, 120 × 118 mm
National Maritime Museum, PLT0255

To find work on the Thames, the watermen had to serve an apprenticeship and gain the Freedom of the Company. Freemen wore arm badges, known as brassards, showing their licence numbers; these were sewn on their coats. This example is embossed at the top with the arms of the City of London, consisting of the cross of St George with a sword in the first quarter representing the martyrdom of St Paul, and inscribed 'FREE WATERMAN'. The arms at the base are those of the Watermen's Company, depicting a shield bearing a skiff and crossed oars supported by dolphins. The Company motto – 'AT COMMAND OF OUR SUPERIORS' – is inscribed on the ribbon below. Badge number 6363 was worn by Henry Scarlett of Edward Street, Limehouse, East London, who was apprenticed to Thomas Platt in 1814 and became a Free Waterman in 1824. [BT]

125
Model of Greenwich waterman's skiff

c. 1950
Wood, cotton, brass, 145 × 795 × 225 mm,
scale 1:8

National Maritime Museum, SLR1450

A skiff is a small, open wooden boat for
carrying people. It may be rowed with two
oars, one on each side of the boat, or it
can be sculled with a single oar over the
back. Smaller and much lighter than
wherries, skiffs were also used in the many
races and regattas held on the Thames,
which allowed watermen to demonstrate
their stamina and prowess. [RB]

126
Coloured porcelain figure of a Thames waterman

c. 1753–55
Bow Porcelain Factory, London
Porcelain, 200 × 145 × 85 mm

Victoria and Albert Museum, C.80-1938

This soft-paste porcelain figure depicts
a Thames waterman. He is shown
wearing a yellow coat with a pink lining,
black breeches, a pink-lined black cap
and lavender neckerchief. He stands on
a white mound base and is supported
by a tree stump. The brassard on his
outstretched arm is painted with the
fouled anchor badge of the Admiralty.
Self-employed watermen wore a
characteristic dress similar to this.
Watermen employed by livery companies,
the Crown or as firemen by insurance
companies were provided with a uniform.
On particularly grand occasions they
might even be dressed in theatrical
costume. [BT]

Scullers. Oars. Oars—

127
The Miseries of London ... being assailed by a group of watermen ...

1816
Inscribed: 'Scullers, Oars, Oars'
THOMAS ROWLANDSON (1757–1827)
Pen and ink with graphite and watercolour,
292 × 240 mm

National Maritime Museum, PAF5935

Published as part of a series by Rudolph
Ackermann, Rowlandson's *Miseries of
London* featured a capital beset with
traffic congestion and street brawls.
The location of Rowlandson's drawing,
as indicated in the published print, is
Wapping Old Stairs. Several brash and
forceful watermen harass a potential
fare as she makes her way down to the
river laden with wine bottles from
a neighbouring tavern. Complaints
about bad language and disorderly
behaviour were common. In *An apologie
for watermen*, 'the water-poet', John
Taylor (1578–1653), a Thames waterman,
writer and adventurer, wrote:

> Some may replie to my apologie
> How they in plying are unmannerly
> And one from tother hale, and pull
> and teare,
> And raile and brawle, and curse, and
> ban and swear;
> In this I'll[l] not defend them with excuses,
> I alwa[y]s did and doe hate those abuses.

At the time that Rowlandson produced his
caricature, the situation was much the
same except that watermen were now
losing trade: former passengers were
using the new bridges built upstream
from the pool of London. [BT]

LITERATURE: Humpherus, *History of the Origin and
Progress of the Company of Watermen and
Lightermen*, pp.269–70.

128
The Watermen's Company beadle's hat and truncheons

Nineteenth century
Textiles, painted wood

The Company of Watermen and Lightermen of the
River Thames

Watermen had a reputation as a
somewhat rough-and-ready breed of men.
The Watermen's Company, as the
regulatory authority, therefore had to
impose a degree of discipline on its
freemen. In 1761, for example, a fine of 2s
6d was imposed for verbal offences, the
proceeds providing welfare for Company
families. Watermen did, however, have
many causes for complaint including ice in
the Thames, impressment into the Royal
Navy, or cut-throat competition. The latter
was the greatest threat as the increase in
carriages and the building of bridges
reduced their business significantly.
Similarly, the enclosed docks eventually
lessened the need for lightermen. [RB]

129
Oar mace of the Sheriff of Middlesex

1832
Inscribed: 'William Levy, Officer to the Sheriff of Middlesex 1832'
Silver, steel, 194 mm (length)

The Worshipful Company of Goldsmiths

This mace bears the royal arms, those of the City of London and an anchor; concealed inside the mace is a steel file. Through a charter of Henry I, the livery of the City gained the right to elect two sheriffs for London and Middlesex. They had wide-ranging judicial powers and it is thought the hidden file relates to their right to search cargoes on the Thames, enabling them to open sacks and bags to check the contents. Sheriffs are still elected today and attend to the justices at the Central Criminal Court of the Old Bailey. [RB]

130
William Timms, bargemaster

1838
(ELIZABETH) EMMA SOYER (1813–42)
Oil on canvas, 749 × 622 mm

Duke of Northumberland

William Timms, a native of Isleworth, was a waterman to three dukes of Northumberland and a royal waterman to three monarchs: George III, George IV and William IV. He is shown here in his royal livery at the age of ninety-five.

Emma Soyer (née Jones) was a London-born portrait painter. A precocious child, she studied art under the instruction of the Flemish painter François Simoneau, who married her mother in 1820. She exhibited at the Royal Academy aged ten. Emma married Alexis Benoît Soyer, the celebrated chef of the Reform Club, in 1837. By the time of her untimely death, she had produced some 403 pictures. [RB]

131
Royal waterman's uniform

1910–52
Woollen textiles, breeches,
912 × 455 mm; coat, 850 × 530 mm

National Maritime Museum, UNI1361–63; lent by Her Majesty The Queen

The uniform of a royal waterman still consists of a red wool coat and breeches with red stockings and a black cap and shoes. The coat has a blue wool lining and gilt buttons with a distinctive gathered skirt. The body of the garment closes at the front and a panel is buttoned over the central opening. It carries a gilt-metal badge displaying the royal arms flanked by the initials of the monarch, in this case 'GR' (either George V or VI), with the Crown above. [BT]

THE DOGGETT'S COAT AND BADGE RACE

132
Thomas Doggett

c. 1691
THOMAS MURRAY (1663–1735)
Oil on canvas, 1920 × 1220 mm

The Company of Watermen and Lightermen
of the River Thames

Thomas Doggett (c. 1670–1721) was 'a clever actor, endowed by nature with a mirthful physiognomy'. He was also a fervent Whig supporter and established a river race, with a prize of an orange-red coat and silver badge, to mark the first anniversary of the Hanoverian succession. The race was no mere one-off. It was advertised, thus, in the *Daily Courant* (1 August 1716):

> This being the Day of His Majesty's happy Accession to the Throne, there will be given by Mr Doggett an Orange Colour Livery, with a Badge representing Liberty, to be Rowed for by six Watermen, that are out of their Time within the year past. They are to Row from London Bridge to Chelsea, and will be continued Annually upon the same Day for ever. They are to start exactly at 4 a Clock.

In this portrait, Doggett is probably shown in one of his most celebrated roles: that of Nincompoop in *Love for Money* by Thomas D'Urfey (c. 1653–1723). [RB]

Legend has it that, one night after a play, the Dublin-born actor and theatre manager Thomas Doggett was waiting by a set of stairs for a waterman to row him across the river to his lodgings. The weather being bad and the tide very strong, Doggett could not find a freeman to accept his fare until, at last, one young waterman agreed to take him. Doggett later discovered that the young waterman was just out of his apprenticeship. It was supposedly to express appreciation of the strong waterman that Doggett set up a rowing match for six watermen who were in the first year out of their apprenticeships. It is far more likely, however, that Doggett, a staunch Whig, founded the race to celebrate the anniversary of the accession of the House of Hanover to the British throne.

The race was to cover a distance just short of five miles between the old Swan Tavern at London Bridge and the new Swan Tavern at Chelsea. Exactly when the first race took place is not entirely certain: most probably it started in 1715; it definitely took place on 1 August 1716. Thanks to Doggett's marriage to a 'gentlewoman of £20,000 fortune', he had the resources to endow the race 'for ever', and his will established an endowment for an annual race. He died in September 1721 and is buried at St John's Church, Eltham. The Doggett Race still takes place annually in August. [SD & BT]

133
Doggett's coat and badge

1886
Badge made in Sheffield
Woollen textiles, silver;
cap, 95 × 240 × 220 mm;
breeches, 765 × 463 mm;
coat, 850 × 570 mm

National Maritime Museum, UNI0495–97, PLT0273

The scarlet coat, cap (not shown) and breeches were won in 1886 by Henry Cole of Deptford (1865–1943). The silver arm badge bears the white horse of Hanover and a scroll inscribed 'LIBERTY'. [BT]

134
The first winner of the Doggett's Coat and Badge Race

1715
PETER MONAMY (1681–1749)
Oil on canvas, 810 × 1065 mm

The Company of Watermen and Lightermen of the River Thames

During the early eighteenth century, it was not uncommon for watermen to row for prizes or to settle a wager. Most probably held on 1 August 1715, the first Doggett Race covered the four miles and seven furlongs between London Bridge and Chelsea. The name of the first winner is not known, although this painting is believed to depict him in his boat. The race has continued to this day. Since Doggett's death, it has been organised by the Fishmongers' Company. Nine races were held in 1947 to allow watermen who had served during the Second World War to row for their respective year. This means that there is an unbroken record of races. It is unfortunate, however, that there is not a complete list of winners. [RB]

LITERATURE: Cook, *Thomas Doggett*, p.28.

WATERMEN'S RACES AND REGATTAS

Races and regattas have long been held all along the Thames. Some competitions were held annually and still continue today; others, like the *'Dreadnought* Race' had a shorter history. The Gravesend Regatta is one of the oldest competitions, dating to at least 1698; it became very popular in the mid-nineteenth century. Fishermen competed in sailing boats and the watermen raced in rowing boats.

Prizes could be lucrative. In 1801, the winner of the apprentices' rowing match at the Blackwall Regatta was awarded 'a new wherry, eighteen guineas'. The winner in 1846 of the apprentices' race at Gravesend was similarly awarded a fully equipped waterman's boat, which would have set him up for life. However, more usually, decorated backboards were the prizes for apprentices' races. Backboards were seat rests usually placed at the back of the boat, but the prize backboards were highly decorated and designed for display. Those participating in the apprentices' race needed to train hard and traditionally the winner gave his backboard to his coach.

[SD]

135 (above)

Backboard, Greenwich Regatta

1852
Painted mahogany, 419 × 1473 mm

National Maritime Museum, EQA0035

This mahogany backboard, painted with the City of London arms, was a prize awarded for the Greenwich Regatta competition held on 26 July 1852. It was won by John Griffiths of Greenwich, who later served in the Royal Navy as a gunner's mate, boatswain and then as a boatman in the coastguard. He left the service in 1871 and returned to Greenwich, working in his latter years as a lighterman. [BT]

136 (below)

Backboard, Greenwich Annual Town Regatta

1888
Painted mahogany, 483 × 1384 mm

National Maritime Museum, EQA0033

This backboard was awarded to S. J. Hayes as a prize at the Greenwich annual town regatta of 1888. Traditionally the backboard was presented to the winner's coach, but it must have been kept by Hayes himself as it was presented to the National Maritime Museum by his descendants. The backboard is decorated with a view of Greenwich Hospital from the Isle of Dogs, flanked by banners and with cherubs holding garlands of flowers. The name of the chairman of the organising committee is prominent: Edward Spencer Stidolph was an engineer who was active in the Greenwich Conservative Club and in local sport. [BT]

137
Greenwich Watermen's Apprentices' Annual Regatta, winner's coat and badge

1874
Woollen textiles, silver

The Company of Watermen and Lightermen of the River Thames

The first Greenwich Regatta was held in 1785. During its history there was at least one fatality and the outcome of some of the races was disputed. This coat and badge were won by John McPherson, born in Rotherhithe in 1852 at the seventeenth regatta. He was bound apprentice on 14 March 1871 to George Child Peek and made a freeman of the Watermen's Company five years later. Afterwards he worked as a lighterman and docker. The red jacket has a gathered skirt, black velvet sleeve caps and trimmings. The buttons are silver-plated. The silver badge has London hallmarks and is embossed with the arms of the Company of Watermen and Lightermen. [BT]

138
Robbins's coat and badge

1851
Badge made by FIRMAN, London
Woollen textiles, silver

The Company of Watermen and Lightermen of the River Thames

Prince Albert (1819–61) presented this coat and badge to George Robbins (c.1830–91) at the Great Exhibition of 1851 for winning a rowing race from London Bridge to Chelsea. Robbins lived all his life in Bermondsey. At the time of the race he was apprenticed to his father Joseph, a licensed waterman. George's son and grandson were also freemen of the Watermen's and Lightermen's Company and were employed as inspectors of the tide boards, measuring the height of the river. The coat is made of sage-green wool with dark burgundy velvet collar, cuffs and sleeve caps. The badge is silver, embossed with the V&A monogram, the royal arms and the date 1851. [BT]

139
Seamen's Hospital Society, first *Dreadnought* coat and badge

1930
Coat made by HOBSON & SONS, London;
badge made by MAPPIN & WEBB, London
Woollen textiles, silver

The Company of Watermen and Lightermen of the River Thames

This coat and badge was the prize of a short-lived rowing race which took place between 1930 and 1934. It was named after HMS *Dreadnought*, a hulk which had been the original home of the Seamen's Hospital. The Society was founded in 1821 to provide medical services for the merchant marine and fishing communities. The first race was won by John Richard Edward Burberry (b.1908) during his apprenticeship. The coat is a long navy blue jacket trimmed with gold lace. The badge is embossed with a foul anchor over crossed oars, displaying the initials of the Seamen's Hospital Society. [BT]

140
Wandsworth coat and badge

1908
Coat made by JOSEPH CHARLES CHILD,
Wandsworth; badge made in Birmingham
Woollen textiles, silver

*The Company of Watermen and Lightermen of the
River Thames*

The Wandsworth Race was run on three
occasions. The coat was designed and
made by a local tailor. It is of exceptionally
high quality, trimmed with dark green
velvet and silver lace. The badge is
enamelled with the Borough of
Wandsworth coat of arms, which was
granted in 1901. George Robert Luck
(1885–1970) of Erith won the race in 1908.
He became a freeman of the Watermen's
and Lightermen's Company the following
year. [BT]

SWAN-UPPING

Until the nineteenth century, young mute swans were highly valued as food and served to great acclaim at feasts and banquets. Traditionally, unmarked swans on the River Thames belonged to the monarch, who could also grant the right of ownership to others. Some aristocratic families, institutions and guilds were given these rights, which they maintained and asserted through the annual ceremony of 'swan-upping'. Dating back to the twelfth century and controlled by the Crown, swan-upping involved rounding up the season's new cygnets on the Thames between London and Henley and cutting unique marks of ownership into their bills. Some of the swans were released back on to the Thames to maintain a breeding stock, while others were taken to be fattened for the table.

Today, only two of the City's livery companies, the Vintners and the Dyers, maintain their right to own swans alongside Her Majesty The Queen. Swan-upping, thought to take its name from the customary cry of 'All up!' on sighting a brood of cygnets, continues to take place every July. The Vintners', Dyers' and royal swan uppers take to the water in traditional wooden skiffs dressed in their fine livery. Over five days they cover 79 miles of the river between Sunbury in Surrey and Abingdon in Oxfordshire. As swans are no longer eaten, swan-upping is now an important annual census for conservation and welfare purposes. This involves counting, weighing and checking the young birds for injury before ringing them, instead of marking the bill, according to ownership. [KM]

141
Mute swan

700 × 1067 × 510 mm (cased)

The Worshipful Company of Dyers

Mute swans (*Cygnus olor*) may have been introduced to England by Richard I (1157–99), although their presence on British waterways possibly goes back much further. The grey feathers on parts of this swan's body and the less-pronounced knob at the base of its bill identify it as a juvenile bird. Swan-upping traditionally takes place in late July when the cygnets still have their grey downy plumage and are not yet able to fly. Catching birds is a difficult and dangerous job that involves corralling them into a group using the swan uppers' skiffs and then hooking them from the water with a swan crook. The swans are taken ashore for examination and a ring is placed around one of their legs. This specimen is displayed at the Dyers' Hall and is carried in procession during the Company's annual Swan Feast in November. The Company no longer eats swan at the feast; turkey is usually served instead. [KM]

LITERATURE: Ticehurst, *The Mute Swan, passim.*

142 (left)

The Dyers' Company swan-upping banner

Textiles, 850 × 850 mm
The Worshipful Company of Dyers

During swan-upping, banners are flown from the stern of the six rowing skiffs to identify them. Two skiffs fly this 'Dyers Royalty' flag and two fly the 'Vintners Royalty' flag (a similar design with a scarlet background). The royal skiffs fly two flags: a crown and royal cipher on a white background from the stern, and a smaller flag depicting a swan and crown on a red background at the bow. As the skiffs pass Windsor Castle, the swan uppers stand to attention and salute 'Her Majesty The Queen, Seigneur of Swans'. [KM]

143 (below)

Register of the Gylde Haule of Windesore

Seventeenth-century copy
ELIAS ASHMOLE (1617–92)
Manuscript, 340 × 450 × 15 mm (open)
Bodleian Library, Oxford, Ashmol. MS., No. 826, fols 138–9b

This manuscript records the distinctive beak marks used by those who had the right to own swans on the Thames. It is a copy made by the antiquary Elias Ashmole from the earliest-known Thames swan roll, a late-fifteenth to early-sixteenth-century vellum roll in the custody of the mayor and bailiffs of the area. Once the ownership of young swans had been established by the monarch's swan warden these marks were cut into the surface of the bird's beak or bill with a sharp knife. More than 900 different swan marks are known to have existed. Some were complex, based on the owner's initials or coat of arms, while others consisted of simple nicks, notches or cuts. At this time, severe punishments existed for those who were caught falsely marking swans, stealing birds or their eggs, or unlawfully carrying a swan crook. Swan-upping was upheld by many families and institutions as a symbol of status and privilege but, as the importance of swan as a food began to diminish and domestic poultry became more popular, few people retained the right beyond the mid-nineteenth century. [KM]

LITERATURE: Ticehurst, *The Mute Swan*, passim.

144
Photograph album compiled by Richard Turk

1924–42

River and Rowing Museum, 2005.3

Living alongside the Thames at Cookham, the Turk family's close links to the river as boat builders, bargemasters and watermen go back centuries. Since the early twentieth century, several members of the family have been swan-upping officers. Richard Turk was swan marker and bargemaster to the Vintners' Company between 1904 and 1960 when he compiled this album of personal photographs and swan-upping memorabilia. Turk's photographs give a candid view of swan-upping by someone at the very centre of the ceremony. He was succeeded by his son Michael, also a Queen's Waterman, who held the post until 1978. [KM]

145
Vintners' Company swan marker's coat

1972

J. DEGE & SONS LTD, London
Woollen textiles

The Company of Watermen and Lightermen of the River Thames

The legal right to own swans on the Thames may well have been bestowed on the Vintners' Company by the charter granted by Edward IV in 1473, although the earliest written evidence dates to 1509. During the ceremony, swan uppers wear different coloured uniforms: the royal swan uppers wear scarlet, the Dyers' navy blue and the Vintners' white and blue. The swan marker wears a blazer-style jacket and peaked cap crowned by a swan feather. This jacket belonged to Vintners' swan marker Michael Turk (b. 1936). Traditionally it was the swan marker who cut the nicks into the beak of the bird: two for the Vintners and one for the Dyers. Royal birds stopped being marked in the nineteenth century at the request of Princess Alexandra, who was concerned that it caused them unnecessary pain and distress. [KM]

146 (top left)
Vintners' Company swan warden's badge

Seventeenth century
Silver, 62 × 65 × 28 mm

The Worshipful Company of Vintners

147 (below right)
Swan upper's badge

1794

FRANCIS THURKLE (fl. 1773–c. 1795), London
Silver, 67 x 57 mm

The Worshipful Company of Vintners

148 (below left)
Bargemaster's gorget

1789–90

HESTER BATEMAN (d. 1794), London
Silver, 200 × 250 × 115 mm

The Worshipful Company of Vintners

These badges are worn by swan officers of the Vintners' Company at the annual swan-upping ceremony and Swan Feast. The model swan is worn suspended from a ribbon around the neck of the swan warden who since the early sixteenth century has supervised swan-upping and organised the Court's visit to watch the ceremony. The collar-shaped gorget is worn by the bargemaster in charge of the skiff, together with a silver arm badge. Smaller shield-shaped badges are worn by the swan uppers who catch and restrain the birds. The bargemaster's and swan upper's badges are chased with the arms of the Company depicting three tuns, or barrels, used to transport wine. [KM]

LITERATURE: Lee, *Catalogue of plate*, pp. 100, 104.

149 (top right)
Vintners' Company bargemaster's badge

1716–17

RICHARD BAYLEY (fl. 1708–48), London
Silver, 242 × 202 mm

Worshipful Company of Vintners

This badge, also worn during swan-upping, was made by order of the court of the Vintners' Company in response to a petition from James Richardson, the bargemaster, for new livery. The Company's arms of a chevron and three tuns are shown surmounted by the figure of St Martin of Tours (316–97) dividing his cloak with a beggar. Martin, the Company's patron saint, has been linked to the Vintners since at least the fifteenth century, but the association is almost certainly much older and related to the establishment of the early guild in the ward of Vintry near the church of St Martin. [RB]

LITERATURE: Lee, *Catalogue of plate*, pp. 18, 100.

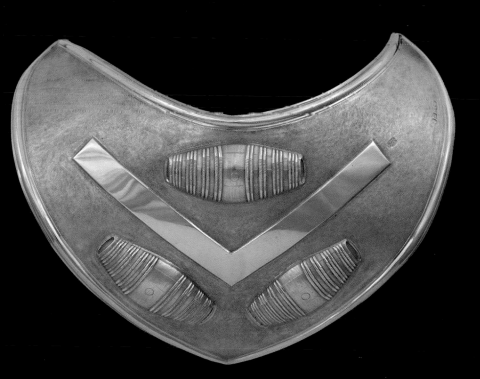

THE NEW LONDON BRIDGE, 1831

The role of the River Thames and the geography of London changed fundamentally, and with increasing speed, from the middle of the eighteenth century onwards. For centuries, London Bridge had been the only Thames crossing with any proximity to the centre of commerce. In 1721 a petition to Parliament called for a bridge to be built at Westminster. This reflected the increased traffic to the area, but raised concerns within the City and Corporation of London about a threat to their monopoly on trade. The Company of Watermen was particularly anxious about the impact of bridges on its business, and it had successfully opposed any building schemes during the previous century. Despite this, the Act authorising the construction of Westminster Bridge was passed in 1736.

Keeping pace with the growing city, and its increasing wealth and population, the beginning of the nineteenth century saw a series of new bridges, notably the Waterloo, Southwark and New London Bridges, all of them designed by the civil engineer John Rennie. Each one was seen as modernising the city and as a triumph of science and engineering, especially because of the difficulties in building on the unsteady ground of the tidal river. The New London Bridge, which replaced the medieval structure, was a particularly potent symbol. On the occasion of laying the foundation stone, in 1825, the Lord Mayor, John Garratt, spoke of 'the increased commerce of the country, and the rapid strides made by the Sciences in this Kingdom', which rendered the old bridge inadequate and the new one both possible and desirable. Its building, he said was 'a great national enterprise', but it was one that highlighted the central role of the capital city.

Many further bridges followed, some – such as Blackfriars and Charing Cross – reflecting the growth of the railways. They were generally funded by private companies, but their openings were, nonetheless, opportunities for civic and national celebration. Many were opened by members of the royal family, with appropriate ceremony and speech-making on the triumph and wider meaning of each project. The designers and engineers were celebrated for their achievements and some bridges, most obviously Tower Bridge, became symbols of the city itself. Although there was, inevitably, an effect on river traffic and the livelihoods of watermen, these crossings allowed the growth of London and its suburbs, especially to the south of the river, creating the modern city with which we are now familiar. [RH]

150
Model of the pile-driver invented by James Vauloué

1739
JAMES FERGUSON (1710–76)
Wood, metal, 515 x 345 x 175 mm
Science Museum, 1903–2 (Woodcroft bequest)

151
A Perspective View of the Engine now made use of for Driving the Piles of the New Bridge at Westminster

[1739]
Designed by JAMES VAULOUÉ; drawn by
HENRI FRANÇOIS GRAVELOT (1699–1773);
engraved by WILLIAM HENRY TOMS (d.c.1750);
printed for CARINGTON BOWLES (1724–93),
London
Engraving on paper, 470 × 380 mm (framed)
Science Museum, 1899-177

Vauloué's pile-driver was used in the construction of Westminster Bridge between 1739 and 1750. James Vauloué, a watchmaker, invented the machine in about 1737 and was rewarded with £150 by the Westminster Bridge Committee, and the Royal Society of London's 1738 Copley Medal. Pile-drivers consist, essentially, of a large hammer that can be dropped in order to drive the iron-tipped beams that act as foundations for buildings and bridges into soft ground. They relied on various methods of raising the hammer, but the one invented by Vauloué used three horses harnessed to a capstan. This turned a winding drum attached to a follower that lifted the hammer with tongs. A fly, geared to this system, prevented the sudden loss of tension when the hammer fell. In 1815, Charles Hutton called this pile-driver the 'commonest type', its great advantage being its efficiency: 'this machine will drive the greatest number of piles in the least time, and with the fewest labourers'.

This model, made by the celebrated instrument-maker, writer and lecturer in natural philosophy, James Ferguson, appears to represent a version for smaller spaces that used men rather than horses to drive the machine. There are many models of Vauloué's pile-driver from this period, including one in the George III Collection, now principally at the Science Museum. They were used during lectures to demonstrate basic mechanical principles, and in celebration of the engineering achievement of Westminster Bridge's construction. The engraved perspective view of the pile-driver has a detailed key to the working parts and a depiction of the three horses required to drive the machine. A detailed list of 'References' describes the various parts of the diagram and the working of the machine. [RH]

LITERATURE: Hutton, *Philosophical and Mathematical Dictionary*, vol. 2, p.187; Morton and Wess, *Public and Private Science*, pp.106–09, 149.

152
The building of Westminster Bridge

1749
Samuel Scott (1701/2–72)
Oil on canvas, 813 × 1498 mm

Bank of England, 0589

Until the completion of Westminster Bridge, designed by the Swiss architect Charles Labelye and built between 1739 and 1750, the nearest bridge to London Bridge was in Kingston. The new bridge's arrival was, therefore, a significant event, representing the rapid growth of the city. Samuel Scott made many sketches of the bridge, at various stages of its construction, and painted it several times. This version was painted for Sir Edward Littleton. The view shows four of the eventual fifteen arches, and a pile-driver preparing further foundations. Westminster Bridge suffered badly from sinking foundations during construction, and took much longer to be completed than was anticipated. The view here appears to depict its appearance about May 1742, and is taken from the Surrey side of the river, looking towards Westminster Abbey. The Abbey, though, looks somewhat unfamiliar, with a slightly distorted perspective and only one of the western towers, designed by Nicholas Hawksmoor, completed. [RH]

LITERATURE: *Oxford DNB*; Preston, *London and the Thames*.

153
John Rennie, the Elder

c. 1810
SIR HENRY RAEBURN (1756–1823)
Oil on canvas, 740 × 620 mm

Institution of Civil Engineers, GR0054

John Rennie (1761–1821) was an engineer who made his name working for James Watt and Matthew Boulton as a millwright, and also looking after their London business interests. He moved into civil engineering after 1790, when appointed surveyor to the Kennet and Avon Canal. He focused on river navigation improvements and dockyards, and was much in demand in assessing and reporting on the schemes of others. His greatest legacy, however, was as a bridge-builder, most famously in London, with the Waterloo, Southwark and New London Bridges. The first is considered his masterpiece and the last, designed with his sons George and John, was built posthumously. Rennie was well respected as a 'philosophical' engineer, and was elected Fellow of the Royal Society in 1798. He declined the knighthood offered to him by the Prince Regent, who, with the Duke of Wellington, opened Waterloo Bridge in 1817. There is another portrait of Rennie by Raeburn at the Scottish National Portrait Gallery. This version was presented to the Institution of Civil Engineers by John Rennie the Younger when he was President in 1845–48. [RH]

LITERATURE: *Oxford DNB*.

154
Invitation to the laying of the foundation stone of the New London Bridge

1825
London Bridge Committee;
printed by PERKINS, London
Engraving on paper, 95 × 30 mm

Science Museum, 1982-257

This invitation, numbered 977, admits the bearer 'to witness the ceremony of laying the first stone of the New London Bridge' on 15 June 1825. Across the top is an engraved illustration of the proposed bridge, and the invitation is signed by Henry Woodthrope Jr, who was Town Clerk and Clerk of the London Bridge Committee. The ceremony included a procession with several bands. Among the dignitaries who attended were John Garratt (the Lord Mayor), the Duke of York, John Rennie the Younger (who had taken over the role of engineer on the project after the death of his father), Sir Humphry Davy (President of the Royal Society), a large number of aldermen and the Great Officers of State. The first stone, of Aberdeen granite, was laid at the west end of the first pier from the Surrey shore about 40 feet below low-water mark. Tickets were, apparently, in great demand, although there were some 1600 available. [RH]

LITERATURE: Thomson, *Chronicles of London Bridge*, p.640.

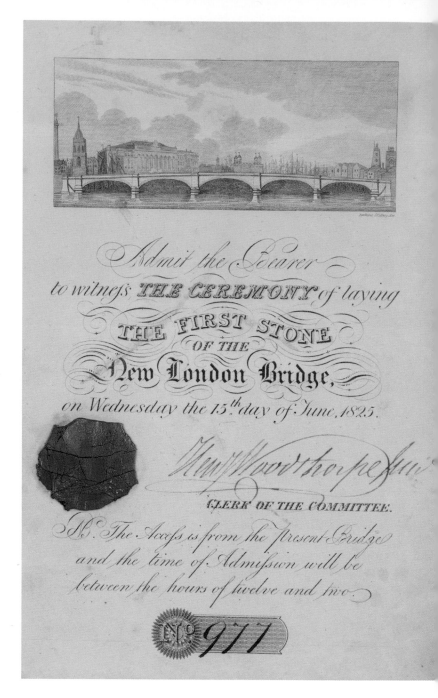

155

Laying the foundation stone of New London Bridge

1825
RICHARD DIGHTON (1795–1880)
Watercolour on paper, 440 × 550 mm

London Metropolitan Archives, q6888848

This watercolour shows the Lord Mayor holding the golden, or silver-gilt, trowel used to spread mortar on the foundation stone of the New London Bridge. Opposite him is Frederick, Duke of York (1763–1827). It is possible that George IV (1762–1830) declined to attend the ceremony because his relationship with the Corporation of London had become fraught owing to the support some City officials had given to George's estranged wife, Caroline of Brunswick (1768–1821), in her claim to the title of Queen Consort.

The ceremony took place in a coffer-dam, an area on the riverbed from which water had been pumped out by steam engine. Access was through a covered, wooden bridge leading from an opening in the old bridge. For the ceremony, this area was covered with an awning, decorated with flags and opened to ticketed spectators who were allowed either on to the platform or the surrounding galleries. Just before the moment depicted in this image, the Lord Mayor had deposited a bottle containing several coins, a glass plate and brass plaque, both inscribed to mark the occasion, inside the stone. The stone was afterwards lowered down and secured by masons, the job of checking the level again falling to Garratt. The day ended with separate City and royal dinners at the Mansion House and Carlton Place respectively.

The artist, Richard Dighton, is better known for his caricature etchings of contemporary Londoners. This crowded watercolour is full of individual portraits and depictions of London society. [RH]

LITERATURE: Thomson, *Chronicles of London Bridge*, pp.635-66.

156
Medal commemorating the opening of London Bridge

1831
Brass, gilt metal, 28mm (diameter)

British Museum, M.6089

The opening of the New London Bridge was a major public event. Numerous commemoratives were produced to celebrate the occasion. This medal is typical of a number that were struck; it records both the laying of the foundation stone and the royal opening. The reverse details the physical dimensions of the bridge. [RB]

157
The royal procession at the opening of London Bridge

c.1831
GEORGE JONES (1786–1869)
Oil on canvas (with sketch key, pen and ink on paper), 1690 x 1510 (framed)

Sir John Soane's Museum

This painting (right), with its contemporary key (below), marks the procession headed by William IV and Queen Adelaide for the opening of the New London Bridge on 1 August 1831, a date that marked the anniversary of the accession of the House of Hanover. The scene shows numerous figures, some identifiable and others representative of London's population, including several children in the right foreground. In the background is the marquee in which the celebrations took place and on the right are the Monument and tower of St Magnus the Martyr. According to the *Gentleman's Magazine* (August 1831), the King had commanded that the procession should be by water, 'with the double view of benefiting the men employed on the river, and of enabling the greatest possible number of his loyal subjects to witness the spectacle'. The procession began at the water gate of Somerset House at three in the afternoon and was accompanied by bands, the firing of cannon, 'shouts and huzzahs, [and] the waving of hats and handkerchiefs' which were 'kept up without intermission along the whole line on the river, and the shores at both sides'. The barges did not approach the bridge until nearly four in the afternoon. The painting depicts the royal party on the bridge. Upon entering the pavilion, they sat down to a banquet with toasts, the national anthem and speeches. The King, who had earlier been presented with a gold medal, was also given a gold cup and responded with reference to 'the great work which has been accomplished by the citizens of London'. He then proposed a toast to the 'source from whence with vast improvement sprung, "The trade and commerce of the city of London"'. [RH]

ROYAL PROCESSION
ON THE OPENING OF LONDON BRIDGE
WITH THE ARRANGEMENTS OF THE ENTERTAINMENT.----MONDAY, AUG. 1, 1831.

Thursday the London Bridge Committee assembled at Guildhall, for the purpose of making arrangements for the first of August, the day on which his Majesty is to open the New Bridge. Directions had been previously given by the Committee, to cover a considerable part of the road—lowly awning, and the workmen were rapidly advancing in the necessary operations, when the Chairman and several Members of the Corporation went, at three o'clock, to judge of the probable effect of the plan upon which the ceremony is to be conducted.

The Royal tent is to be pitched at the London side of the Bridge, near to the place on which Fishmonger's Hall stood, and will command an unobstructed view of the whole line of road to the Southwark side. The Royal table will be laid for about twenty persons. On the left of it, extending to one of the entrances from Thames street, will be laid two tables for the noble persons who will accompany their Majesties. One of these tables will be laid for 68, the other for 76 individuals. A large space will be left open at the right of the Royal tent, it being the intention of their Majesties to disembark at the Grand Wharf on the right of the Bridge; and the Committee having appointed that the procession shall go forward from that spot the moment their Majesties land. A double row of tables will be ranged, on each side of the wide space through which the procession is to pass, for the accommodation of the other visitors, who are to be admitted, if we may judge from the present appearance of the arrangements, to the number of 1,560. The awning, which is to be placed over the long table, will extend to the length of about 400 feet; there are to be three roofs to the large awning, so that the company will be as effectually secured against bad weather as if they were to be shut up in the Guildhall, which the art of man could never make worthy of a comparison with the scene which will be presented on the 1st of August on London Bridge, the river, and in the surrounding neighbourhood. Flags and colours, with emblems and devises, will wave above the heads of the company, and cannon will be fired at intervals. Bands of music will, in various parts of the arena, perform during the ceremony, and every thing that can contribute to render the spectacle delightful to the public will be done, at least so far as the Committee may be able to satisfy the public curiosity. The works on the Bridge are superintended by Mr. Montague, the Clerk of the Works.

The Lord Mayor has given up the authority over the river for the day of the ceremony to Sir Byam Martin, and the arrangements on the water are to be under the direction of Mr. George Ledwell Taylor, the Surveyor to the Navy. Their Majesties are to go on board the Royal Barge at Somerset House at three o'clock in the after-

noon, and the procession on the Thames is to be as follows :—First advances the Trinity barge, next the Victualling Board barge, and then follow in order the Navy Board barge, the Treasurer of the Navy's barge, the Board of Ordnance barge, the the Admiralty barge, the Lords of the Treasury barge, the Royal barge, the Royal Family's barge, the barge of the Lords and others in attendance upon his Majesty.

From Somerset House to London bridge barges splendidly decorated will be moored on each side of the river, and between the barges so moored, room will be left for the small boats, so that immense numbers of persons will be enabled to see the water procession, which, it is expected, will be infinitely more grand, as it will be infinitely more extensive than the procession on the bridge. The barges of all the Companies will be ranged near the bridge, splendidly decorated. The river will, during the whole ceremony, present the most brilliant exhibition. Not a vessel or boat will be seen to move in the line of procession, with the exception of those which are to perform the procession itself. In the barges moored along the line of procession, seats are to be fixed one above another for the accommodation of the public.

Barriers are to be fixed at Fish-street-hill, at Little East-cheap, Gracechurch-street, in Cannon-street, in Mile's-lane, and in Upper Thames-street.

The Thames Police are to take their station on the river to prevent accidents. It has not yet been determined in what dress the Corporation are to receive their Majesties, but it is supposed that the Lord Mayor and Aldermen will appear in their robes, and the Members of the Court of Common Council in their gowns.

Much as had been expected from the splendid preparations at Guildhall, it is impossible that the spectacle could, if the entertainment had taken place, been at all comparable to that which will be displayed on the 1st of August.

⊚⊚⊚⊚⊚

The Landing of
ROYAL WILLIAM and ADELAIDE at London Bridge.

HORSE to horse, and man to man,
  To London City leads the van,
To welcome on a glorious plan,
  The Queen and Royal William.

  Chorus.

Welcome WILLIAM from the Thames,
On all our hearts you have just claims,

And joyfully we'll bless those names
Of Adelaide and William.

His very presence hope instils,
And drives afar the thought of ills.
True courage every bosom fills,
        Welcome William, &c.

Behold him leave the subject tide,
And Adelaide around his side,
He opens London Bridge with pride,
All cry, Live Royal William.
        Welcome William, &c.

The thistle, shamrock, and the rose,
The brilliant flags above disclose,
And sounds of cannon interpose,
To honour Royal William.
        Welcome Williaml &c.

This Bridge, upon a strong built form,
Will weather many a wintry storm,
Coeval with that great Reform,
Brought on by Royal William.
        Welcome William, &c.

Peace and joy attend his way,
Justice marks his Sovereign sway,
He's dearest friend, in truth, is Grey,
Hurrah for Royal William.
        Welcome William, &c.

Commerce hails this happy day,
Keels shall cut the watery way,
Trade once more be brisk and gay,
Hurrah for Royal William.
        Welcome William, &c.

Breathes there a degenerate son,
Who would not to his standard run,
The battle of Reform is won,
And that by Royal William.
        Welcome William, &c.

The father of his people he,
Lord of the isles and every sea,
Then let us toast with heartfelt glee,
The Queen and Royal William.
        Welcome William, &c.

London Bridge is opened wide,
The Citszens may shout with pride,
" Often may we from the tide."
Welcome Royal William.
        Welcome William, &c.

King of a nation without stain,
Our rights he'll manfully maintain,
Supreme upon the land and main,
Long life to Royal William.

  Chorus.

Welcome, Welcome, from the Thames,
Every tongue the praise proclaims,
Of those beloved and honoured names,
Queen Adelaide and William.

New London Bridge and King William for ever !

Our King has gone forth, unto every
        one dear;
And dear is the Queen, who in all her just
        ways,
Demands from her people attention and
        praise.

  Chorus.

Heart of Oak is our King,
  Long may he preside,
To reign and command
  On the land and the tide.

Father THAMES to the monarch his Trident
        resigns,
And COMMERCE with him obedience combines ;
With the hearts of his subjects the NAIDS
        agree,
To hail him the Lord of the land and the sea.

We see London Bridge a proud structure
        expand,
Connecting a portion of this happy land;
The King gives the word, there is no toll to
        pay,
And blest are the people upon this happy
        day.

Chorus.—Heart of Oak is our King, &c.

The thunder of cannon resounds through
        the skies,
And God save the King in a thousand tones
        rise ;
As over the Bridge, he moves on with his
        Queen,
A happier sight has old England ne'er seen.
For the good of the nation the Sovereign
        attends,
With his people he mixes, and thus he
        makes friends ;
No feasting he wants, and would rather
        endure
A fast, and give every thing to the poor.

London Bridge now will stand on a solid
        foundation,
Reflecting both honour and pride on the
        nation ;
And Reformers who pass it, will say with
        three cheers,
It's strength's in the people and not in the
        Peers.

Chorus.—Heart of Oak is our King, &c.

. Catnach, Printer, 2, Monmouth-Court, 7 Dials.

158

Royal Procession on the Opening of London Bridge

1831
Published by JAMES CATNACH (1792–1841),
London
Print and wood engraving on paper,
483 × 352 mm

British Museum, 1874-0411-62

The opening of the New London Bridge
was an event with significant public
interest. This broadsheet has a lively hand-
coloured wood engraving that shows the
new bridge decorated with flags. The
events of the day are shown, with the
barge procession, the pavilion in which
the ceremony took place, and a hot-air
balloon above. The riverbanks and nearby
buildings are crowded with spectators.
The text includes a description of the day's
entertainments and two songs, entitled
'The Landing of Royal William and
Adelaide at London Bridge' and 'New
London Bridge and King William for
ever!'. The hot-air balloon belonged to
Charles Green (1785–1870), a celebrated
aeronaut who had made his first ascent
from Green Park ten years earlier in
celebration of the coronation of George
IV. He made some 500 ascents after this,
and constructed the balloon used at
Vauxhall Gardens in 1836. [RH]

LITERATURE: *Oxford DNB.*

159

Cutlery set made from the
remains of Old London Bridge

1832–33
JOHN WEISS (d. 1843), London
Iron, wood, 427 x 490 x 347 (open)

Museum of London, 38.139

This fine set of knives, with carving knife
and fork, was made from wood from the
Old London Bridge. The handles have
engraved and repoussé decoration,
including silver caps with the crest
of the City of London and shields that
commemorate the first stone bridge,
with the date 1176. This example was
made for the family of the wealthy
London merchant and financier Nathan
Mayer Rothschild (1777–1836), but other
similar sets were manufactured, as were a
large number of souvenirs made from – or
claimed to be made from – materials from
the demolished bridge. The maker, John
Weiss, an Austrian immigrant who arrived
in London in 1787, was a Master Cutler,
surgical instrument-maker and 'Razor-
Maker to the King' under William IV. He
also made steel razors from the iron of the
old bridge, likewise marked with shields.
He held the view 'that steel seemed to be
much improved when it
had become rusty in the earth' and had,
therefore, 'purchased, as soon as an
opportunity offered, all the iron,
amounting to fifteen tons, with which the
piles of London Bridge had been shod'.
John Weiss and Son continue to produce
surgical instruments today. [RH]

LITERATURE: T.J.H., 'The improvement of the quality of
iron and steel', pp.75–77.

THE THAMES TUNNEL

The early nineteenth century saw interest in connecting the banks of the Thames by tunnelling beneath the river, a project which had the obvious advantage of not disrupting shipping. Several attempts were made around the turn of the century, including a tunnel between Rotherhithe and Wapping which would link the expanding docks that lined the shores of the Thames. This scheme had the support of the Duke of Wellington, but progress was frustrated by difficulties in tunnelling through soft ground. Marc Isambard Brunel's solution was his recently patented tunnelling shield, designed to provide support in the tunnel before permanent reinforcement could be introduced. He received the backing of private investors who formed the Thames Tunnel Company in 1824 and appointed Brunel as Chief Engineer. The first brick was laid at the Rotherhithe shaft on 2 March 1825. This was to be the first tunnel ever constructed under a navigable river anywhere in the world.

The project took a great deal of time, however, because of the difficult ground, several floods and mounting costs. The expense proved enormous: when funds ran out in 1828, after a significant flood, work was suspended for seven years, only being restarted with a government loan of £247,000. Throughout the project, Brunel worked closely with his son, Isambard Kingdom Brunel. His young grandson, Henry Marc, later a consulting engineer for Tower Bridge, was the first person to pass through the tunnel in 1841. It was completed and opened to pedestrians, with some ceremony, on 25 March 1843.

There had been great popular interest in the project, its progress and setbacks throughout the period of construction. This was sustained by Brunel and the Thames Tunnel Company with the production of informative souvenir booklets and engravings. Visits could be made to the shield itself, to see work underway, and I. K. Brunel organised the stunt of holding a dinner inside the tunnel in 1827, in order to emphasise its safety. After opening, it continued to be a popular attraction, and accounts, images and souvenirs of this 'eighth wonder of the world' proliferated, especially with the first of the annual fêtes, or fancy fairs, held within the tunnel in April 1843, which attracted over 66,000 visitors. The tunnel received the further boost of a visit by Queen Victoria and Prince Albert on 26 July 1843. This attention to London's East End by the more fashionable members of society was an unusual and noteworthy occurrence. The promotion was necessary as the heavily indebted enterprise made use of public money. Celebrated though it was, the tunnel never became the thoroughfare for horses and carts originally intended. It remained pedestrian-only until it became part of the East London Railway in the 1860s. It is still in use today. [RH]

160
Sir Marc Isambard Brunel

c. 1835
SAMUEL DRUMMOND (1765–1844)
Oil on canvas, 1270 × 1016 mm
National Portrait Gallery, NPG 89

Sir Marc Isambard Brunel (1769–1849), was born in Normandy and trained in hydrography in Rouen, but left Revolutionary France for America in 1793 and settled in Britain in 1799. His best-known achievement, the Thames Tunnel, is depicted to the right, based on a painting by Thomas Bury. This image, an idealised vision of what the completed tunnel would look like, was much reproduced as an engraving and in souvenir booklets advertising the scheme. On the table are objects representing other aspects of Brunel's work as an engineer and man of science: a miner's safety lamp, a cotton-winding machine and a model of a lighthouse. The portrait was painted before the tunnel was completed, although Brunel was already celebrated for the ambitious project. The artist, Samuel Drummond, was a prolific portrait and history painter who exhibited regularly at the Royal Academy. [RH]

LITERATURE: *Oxford DNB.*

Thames Tunnel

Thames Tunnel.

March the 10th 1842.

The day I again met your
dear Grand Mama after a
Separation of Six years
viz in 1799

My dear Sophia Hawes

Your dear Grand-Mama wishes me to give you the circumstance which led me to think of a Plan for making Tunnels

After the attempts which had been made at Gravesend and at Rotherhithe, between the years 1799 and 1807, had so completely failed that I conceived all further exertions on that subject quite fruitless, most particularly after the Report of two eminent Engineers to whom 58 plans had been refered, in 1809.

However, about the year 1812, being then employed in the Dock Yard at Chatham, where I had directed the construction of a Tunnel, I happened to see before me a piece of condemned Timber, a portion of the Keel of a Ship, wherein the Sea-worm, the Teredos navalis, (Navium calamitas) had made many erosions, even near the water edge, I went on a little way towards my Tunnel, I then said to myself these little things have made little Tunnels, So might we, by adopting some corresponding means of protection — we might soon cross the Medway, a great desideratum, it has always been!

Having studied the question in various ways, from the round form, with a Shield a head, I at last, settled on the plan of a number of Cells (viz 36) or 12 Frames divided into three Stories each, Thus 36 Excavators or Miners can be equally protected, One half in cutting out the ground and the other half, viz 18, in advancing the Frames and Securing them by means of powerful Screws. In the meantime a certain number of Bricklayers construct the Double arch, in Brick and Roman Cement as it seen above

Thus by the Agency of the Shield, the Tunnel has been made under the Thames, and connected with both Shores on a range exceeding 1200 feet

The area of the Excavation being 875 feet

and five Irruptions of the River have been overcome

Your affectionate
Grand father.

Mc. J. C. Brunel

161

Letter from M.I.Brunel to Sophia Hawes

10 March 1842
MARC ISAMBARD BRUNEL (1769–1849)
Ink on paper
National Maritime Museum, AGC/1/45

This letter, dated 10 March 1842, is written by Marc Isambard Brunel to his granddaughter Sophia on Thames Tunnel Company notepaper. An engraved section of the tunnel under a bustling river appears at the top. The letter, written once the tunnel was completed, was sent because 'your dear Grand-Mama wishes me to give you the circumstance which led me to think of a Plan for making Tunnels'. Brunel explains that when working on a tunnel at Chatham, he noticed 'a piece of condensed Timber, a portion of the Keel

of a Ship, wherein the sea-worm … the *Teredos navalis*, (*Navium calamitas*) had made many erosions'. Observing the worms closely, he thought of devising a tunnelling shield. This development allowed thirty-six men to work simultaneously, half excavating and the others working to advance the frame itself, while bricklayers shored up the tunnel behind. This account of the shield's invention links Brunel's work to observation and the natural world in a way that would have appealed to contemporary men of science. Brunel had told this story at least as far back as 1831 to the Royal Academy of Sciences in Rouen and it is interesting that he and his wife were concerned that it be taught to their granddaughter. It became a popular, and typical, account of a 'eureka moment'. [RH]

LITERATURE: Clements, *Marc Isambard Brunel*, passim.

162

The Tunnel !!! or another Bubble Burst!

1827
CHARLES WILLIAMS (*fl.* 1801–30); engraved by
SAMUEL KNIGHT (*fl.* 1805–40), London
Etching on paper, 250 × 370 mm
London Metropolitan Archives, p5432075

Responding to flooding in the Thames Tunnel building works, this satirical print highlights fears about the safety of the tunnel and of investments in the company. Pedestrians flee from a torrent of water gushing in from the roof, and the satirical verse beneath has Father Thames taking Brunel to task for the disturbance of his 'bed' as he 'destroys the

great projector's frame'. The tunnel, and especially Brunel's shield, had been presented by those supporting the project as a means of conquering nature, but the flood of May 1827 demonstrated how problematic it remained. While those who financed the project were seduced by its novelty and daring, they were, nonetheless, anxious about their investment. Father Thames warns that they and Brunel should not 'count their chicks before they'r hatched'. The decision by the government to refinance the project in 1835 met with severe criticism from some MPs and *The Times* as an investment that was, at best, precarious.
[RH]

LITERATURE: Pike, '"The greatest wonder of the world"', p.345.

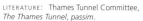

163
Longitudinal Section of the Thames Tunnel

1844
THOMAS RUMBALL (1824–1902)
Hand-coloured print, 608 × 3246 mm

Royal Collection, RCIN 1046869

This depiction of a lengthy section of the tunnel was presented to Prince Albert, who had lent his support to Brunel when times got difficult during the Thames Tunnel project. It has been suggested that the Prince Consort encouraged Queen Victoria to knight Brunel in 1841. He clearly wished to appear supportive by visiting the tunnel and other projects by the Brunels, such as the Clifton Suspension Bridge and the Royal Albert Bridge in Cornwall, which he opened in 1859. Albert was a patron of the Society of Arts and the Royal Institution of Great Britain, and he closely identified himself with the world of scientific learning and great engineering and improvement projects. He was later directly involved with a bridge project, the Albert Bridge in Windsor, and was said to have contributed to its design. Thomas Rumball was a member of the Institution of Civil Engineers and later worked as a railway engineer in Portugal, Spain and Argentina. A scale across the bottom shows the progress of the tunnelling over time. [RH]

164
Commemorative trowel

1825
Inscribed: 'THE THAMES TUNNEL COMPANY INCORPORATED 24 June 1824', 'THE FIRST STONE OF THE TUNNEL Was Laid WITH THIS TROWEL on The 2d March 1825 By WILLIAM SMITH ESQR M.P. CHAIRMAN OF THE COMPANY', with a crest
Silver, 323 × 86 × 27 mm

Science Museum, 2000-2

This trowel was used by William Smith MP, Chairman of the Thames Tunnel Company, to lay the first stone on 2 March 1825. Engraved on the underside is an image by Silvester & Co. of the double tunnel beneath the Thames whose surface is crowded with ships while pedestrians, riders and carriages pass sedately through the tunnel. This image was to be much reproduced in the coming years, especially in the publicity materials of the Thames Tunnel Company, although it was eighteen years before the tunnel opened.

Smith's speech on this occasion emphasised the novelty of the techniques that would be used in the project. He linked it directly with the wider aim of improving the lot of mankind, the growth of learned societies and new discoveries in industry, engineering and chemistry. After the speech, he used this silver trowel to spread cement on the foundation stone, which had been filled with an engraved plate and coins, and directed its lowering and levelling. He then drank to its success and was answered with cheers from the many spectators, a peal of church bells and a band playing 'God Save The King' and 'Rule Britannia'. [RH]

LITERATURE: Thames Tunnel Committee, *The Thames Tunnel*, passim.

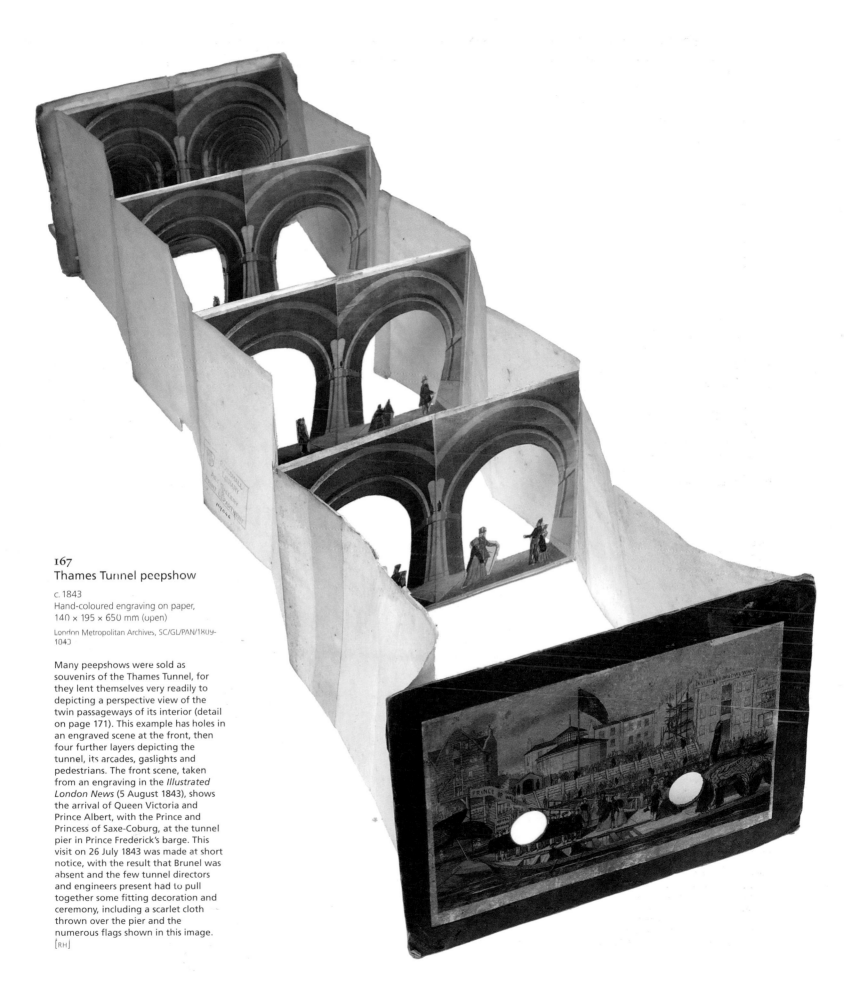

167
Thames Tunnel peepshow

c. 1843
Hand-coloured engraving on paper,
140 × 195 × 650 mm (open)

London Metropolitan Archives, SC/GL/PAN/1809-1843

Many peepshows were sold as souvenirs of the Thames Tunnel, for they lent themselves very readily to depicting a perspective view of the twin passageways of its interior (detail on page 171). This example has holes in an engraved scene at the front, then four further layers depicting the tunnel, its arcades, gaslights and pedestrians. The front scene, taken from an engraving in the *Illustrated London News* (5 August 1843), shows the arrival of Queen Victoria and Prince Albert, with the Prince and Princess of Saxe-Coburg, at the tunnel pier in Prince Frederick's barge. This visit on 26 July 1843 was made at short notice, with the result that Brunel was absent and the few tunnel directors and engineers present had to pull together some fitting decoration and ceremony, including a scarlet cloth thrown over the pier and the numerous flags shown in this image.
[RH]

168
Surveying level

c. 1830
ABRAHAM ABRAHAM (*fl.* 1817–50), Liverpool
Wood, metal, 120 × 490 × 100 mm
(without tripod)

National Maritime Museum, NAV1433

It is believed that this surveying level and
tripod belonged to either Marc Isambard
Brunel or to his son, Isambard Kingdom
Brunel, and that it was used during the
construction of the Thames Tunnel. Its
purpose was to determine differences in
height, or elevation, presumably in this
instance to ensure the tunnel itself was
level. Along with a measuring tape and
theodolite, it formed an essential part of
the surveyor's basic tools. The maker,
A. Abraham, was an optician and
mathematical instrument maker with a
shop in Lord Street, Liverpool, from 1817.
In 1841 he briefly joined forces with John
Benjamin Dancer, who subsequently went
on to make his own reputation. [RH]

169
Crushed tankard

c. 1843
Inscribed: 'Spread Eagle/ Rotherhithe'
Pewter (and earth), 115 mm × 100 mm

London Transport Museum, 2006/7718

This crushed tankard was found inside the
Thames Tunnel as work was carried out in
2006 to incorporate it into the London
Overground line. The 'Spread Eagle/
Rotherhithe' was the nearest public house
to the entrance of the tunnel works on
the south bank of the river. This still exists,
on Rotherhithe Street, now renamed 'The
Mayflower', after the ship that sailed from
Rotherhithe to Southampton, and on to
New England, in 1620. [RH]

170
Commemorative medal

1843
Silver-gilt and white metal,
25 mm (diameter)

London Transport Museum, 2009/6999, 7000

171
Flask

Mid-nineteenth century
Salt-glazed stoneware,
250 × 180 × 140 mm

Fitzwilliam Museum, C.1217-1928

172
Souvenir mug

Mid-nineteenth century
Inscribed below this view: '1,200 feet long,
76 feet below high water mark, was 8 years
building & cost £446,000. Opened the 25th
day of March, 1843'
Lead-glazed Staffordshire earthenware,
transfer-printed in underglaze black,
95 × 98 mm

Victoria and Albert Museum, 3641-1901

Large numbers of souvenirs were made
to celebrate the Thames Tunnel, many of
which could be bought from stalls within
the tunnel itself. The mug, with a foliated
loop handle, has on one side a portrait of
Marc Isambard Brunel, and on the other a
view from the Rotherhithe entrance to the
tunnel, after an engraving by T.H. Ellis.
The more roughly made gin flask is
moulded on one side to depict the
Wapping entrance. [RH]

THE PALACE OF WESTMINSTER

173
Sir Charles Barry, RA

c. 1836
HENRY WILLIAM PICKERSGILL (1782–1875)
Oil on canvas, 1448 × 1118 mm
Palace of Westminster Art Collection, WOA 2729

Charles Barry (1795–1860) was born, perhaps prophetically, within sight of the old Palace of Westminster at 2 Bridge Street. In the 1820s, his architectural career included designs for a number of churches, which deepened his interest in the Gothic style that eventually became his trademark. Barry was, however, eclectic in his practice and also produced plans in the Italianate and Greek revival styles. The 1830s saw him rise to public acclaim following his success in the competition to rebuild the Travellers' clubhouse in Pall Mall 1829, culminating in his winning design for the new Houses of Parliament in 1836. The building of Barry's Palace of Westminster proved an all-consuming and exhausting enterprise, which absorbed his time for more than two decades and cost him many of his private architectural commissions. The very considerable strain of seeing through the great project and negotiating with the many bodies involved in the planning, construction, decoration and inevitable alteration of the Palace undoubtedly shortened Barry's life: he died suddenly of a heart attack on 12 May 1860. The iconic and instantly recognisable Palace of Westminster remains his lasting legacy.
[RB]

LITERATURE: *Oxford DNB*.

Standing on the north bank of the Thames, the Palace of Westminster had been the principal residence of English kings from the reign of Edward the Confessor until 1512. Henry III was the King who left the greatest mark on the Palace, by making it the centre of royal government and building splendidly decorated private apartments. From his reign onwards, parliaments also met in the Palace, regularly convening in the King's bedchamber, known as the 'Painted Chamber', or in the adjacent Queen's chamber, sometimes called the White Chamber. When the two houses sat separately after 1341, the Lords assembled in the Queen's chamber (until 1801) but the Commons had no fixed abode until 1547 when Edward VI gave them the permanent use of St Stephen's Chapel in the Palace.

Like other palaces, Westminster was susceptible to fire and was badly damaged or partially destroyed several times. After a fire in 1263, Henry III carried out substantial rebuilding and refurbishments, but the fire of 1512 gutted the residential apartments, and Henry VIII abandoned the Palace for Whitehall. The surviving buildings were used for governmental and administrative business, housing the Exchequer and Court of Chancery for example; Parliament also continued to sit there. A third major fire was the most devastating of all. At six o'clock in the evening of 16 October 1834, fire broke out beneath the House of Lords. It rapidly took hold and swiftly spread through the fabric of the Palace. The following day *The Times* reported:

> The conflagration, viewed from the river, was spectacularly grand and impressive. On the first view of it from the water, it appeared as if nothing could save Westminster Hall from the fury of the flames. There was an immense pillar of bright clear fire springing up behind it, and a cloud of white, yet dazzling smoke, careering above it, through which, as it was parted by the wind, you could occasionally see the lantern and pinnacles, by which the building is ornamented.

Contemporary reactions to the destruction of the Palace were mixed: while some mourned the loss of their Parliament's home, others welcomed the unexpected opportunity to build a new, modern legislature that that would be better suited to a nation reaching the height of its imperial and international power.

The first issue to be decided was where precisely to build the new Houses of Parliament. William IV, never very fond of Buckingham Palace, immediately offered this recently refurbished residence to the nation as a potentially suitable site. Charing Cross and Green Park, among a host of others, were also mooted as possible alternative locations to Westminster; but historic ties to the old riverside location proved too strong. The second issue was what the new legislature should look like, and a furious debate

174

The burning of the Houses of Parliament, 16 October 1834

c. 1835
Attributed to DAVID ROBERTS (1796–1864)
Oil on canvas, 380 × 625 mm

Palace of Westminster Art Collection, WOA 2806

The burning of the Houses of Parliament was the largest fire in the capital since the Great Fire of London in 1666. An unusually low tide hindered efforts to control the blaze, and much was lost before great jets of water from a river steamer could be directed towards the Palace. Despite the prodigious effort, both Houses of Parliament and the bulk of the rambling complex were either completely gutted or badly damaged. The sudden destruction of such an iconic landmark immediately became a popular subject among painters, most of whom recorded the view from across the river (the south bank was busy with artists and sightseers for days after the fire). Unlike most artists, however, David Roberts depicts the morning after the flames had taken hold, as teams of firemen begin to control the blaze and reveal the smouldering carcass of St Stephen's Chapel (then used as the chamber of the House of Commons).
[RB & RJ]

raged over the architectural style of the building, which was to be the greatest and most prestigious project of the nineteenth century. The survival of Westminster Hall and the proximity of the Abbey suggested a Gothic design. But there was considerable support for a more classical approach, creating a 'senate house' to encapsulate the building's legislative functions and signify the progress of representative government over more feudal institutions. However, advocates of the Gothic revival argued that neo-classicism was pagan and derived, as Augustus Pugin put it, from 'nations whose climate, religion, government, and manners were totally dissimilar to our own'. Neo-classicism was associated with the architecture of Revolutionary France and the Napoleonic Empire, both alien to Britain's sense of national identity. Unsurprisingly then, a Commons select committee, appointed in March 1835, reported that the new building would be in the 'national' style, which was considered to be Gothic or Elizabethan. In June, it announced an architectural competition to which anyone could submit an anonymous entry that met this criterion. Out of the ninety-seven entries, Charles Barry's Perpendicular Gothic design was picked as the winner. [SD & RB]

175
Westminster Bridge, London

c. 1747

GIOVANNI ANTONIO CANAL, known as
CANALETTO (1697–1768)
Pen and ink with grey wash over graphite,
227 × 484 mm

Royal Collection, RL 7558

This elaborate drawing captures a view of
Westminster Bridge with a number of
barges and smaller river craft busily
passing through its arches. The old palace
complex, with Westminster Hall and the
Abbey, appears on the right. Westminster
Palace was, in fact, an extraordinary and
jumbled accretion of buildings, which had
developed over many centuries. Its lack of
architectural uniformity mirrored the
heterogeneity of its use. The fire of 1834
swept away almost all of these buildings.

   The drawing is one of several
depicting Westminster and its bridge
made by Canaletto for Consul Joseph
Smith (1673/4–1770), the artist's patron in
Venice, who introduced him to many
English grand tourists. A number of these
in turn were to become Canaletto's clients
during his stay in London between 1747
and 1755 and were also involved in the
prestigious civic building project of
Westminster Bridge. The drawing,
though, predates the completion of the
bridge by about three years and
anticipates its final appearance. [JGM & RB]

176 (opposite above)
East front showing the Queen's entrance from the river

c. 1836

SIR CHARLES BARRY (1795–1860)
Graphite and wash on paper,
380 x 546 mm (framed)

Palace of Westminster Art Collection, WOA 4690

Between 24 August and 1 December
1835 submissions were invited for the
architectural competition that would
determine the character of the new
Palace of Westminster. Each of the ninety-
seven entries was identified with a symbol
to maintain anonymity and avoid any
preferential treatment by the judges, who
were all amateurs rather than
professional architects. Charles Barry's
winning scheme bore the symbol of a
portcullis. The original design for the
Palace included grand water gates to the
north at the Clock Tower and to the south
at the Victoria Tower, allowing Parliament
to be reached from the Thames. In the
final built version, a terrace replaced the
gates: the Palace, with its imposing river
façade, could not be approached from the
Thames, an extraordinary shift from
earlier centuries and an indication of its
declining importance as a stage for
national ceremony. Nevertheless, river
access proved vital during the
construction of the Houses of Parliament:
coffer-dams held back the Thames to
allow work on the massive river frontage
and vast quantities of materials were
delivered by barge to the site. Spectators
watched the progress of Barry's 'great
work' from Westminster Bridge. [RB]

LITERATURE: Jones, *The Great Palace*, ch. 5; Riding
and Riding (eds), *The Houses of Parliament*, pp.99–
111, 113–35.

177 (opposite below)
Perspective Elevation of the River Front

1840

H. JONES; after THOMAS HOPPER
(1776–1856), London
Lithograph, 610 x 889 mm (framed)

Palace of Westminster Art Collection, WOA 1659

This lithograph, an elevation from
Thomas Hopper's unsuccessful
competition entry, also shows a proposed
new palace accessible from a central
water gate, which forms part of a grand
embankment along the riverside. Hopper
was a successful architect, but failed to
win any of the great commissions for
major public buildings in the late-
Georgian and early-Victorian period.
Following Barry's victory, he became a
strident and determined critic of the
Westminster competition judges and
published works at his own expense
outlining his various objections. He was
also thwarted in his efforts to design the
Nelson memorial in Trafalgar Square.
Hopper's practice mainly consisted of
country house commissions. His finest
work, adopting a picturesque Norman
style, was probably Penrhyn Castle in
Caernarvonshire, 1822–37, built for
George Dawkins-Pennant. [RB]

LITERATURE: *Oxford DNB*

178
Augustus Welby Northmore Pugin

1845
JOHN ROGERS HERBERT (1810–90)
Oil on canvas, 900 × 700 mm

Palace of Westminster Art Collection, WOA 2586

A.W.N. Pugin (1812–52) was just twenty-three years old when he assisted Barry in the designs for the new Palace of Westminster. The coat of arms, richly decorated wallpaper (one of Pugin's own designs), and even the colour scheme of this half-length portrait reflect Pugin's design ethos, which identified the Gothic Revival as a morally just, inherently British style that looked back to the nation's pre-Reformation past. The medievalising design of the portrait even extends to the frame, which was designed by Pugin and made by his long-time collaborator, John G. Crace (1809–89). Like the painting, the frame also incorporates the sitter's arms, bearing a martlet, with the motto *en avant*, 'onwards'.

As well as being a fellow champion of the Gothic revival, the artist John Rogers Herbert had known Pugin since childhood and the two remained firm friends, both converting to Catholicism as adults. Here the artist represents his friend at a drawing table, in a pose that may have been intended to recall Hans Holbein the Younger's portrait of the Catholic martyr Sir Thomas More (Frick Collection, New York). Herbert's painting was reproduced as a lithograph by James Henry Lynch (d. 1868) in 1853, the year after Pugin's death. [RJ]

LITERATURE: *Oxford DNB.*

179
Chair for the Palace of Westminster

c. 1847
Designed by A.W.N. PUGIN (1812–52)
Carved mahogany with later red leather upholstery, 1003 × 451 × 457 mm

Palace of Westminster, POW 04387

180
Encaustic floor tiles

1847–50
Designed by A.W.N. PUGIN;
made by MINTON & COMPANY, Stoke-on-Trent
Earthenware with coloured clay inlay, 115–230 mm square

Palace of Westminster

The interiors of the new Palace of Westminster were an extraordinary statement of Pugin's all-encompassing decorative vision. Ornamentation covers every surface to create an exuberant Gothic fantasy, drawing on his understanding of the medieval past. Pugin lavished painstaking attention on every minute detail of the scheme. His x-frame chairs, for example, were possibly based on a seventeenth-century continental pattern book: a similar design appears in a Dutch publication of 1642. The carvings and construction of these chairs comply with Pugin's beliefs that design must be honest in its use of materials and embellishment. The nail heads were intended to emulate the Gothic style. Those shown here, in the Royal Gallery, are covered in red material indicating the Lords' precinct of the Palace; green denotes the Commons.

The tiling scheme for the floor of the new Palace was equally elaborate. Also designed by Pugin, it was undertaken by the Stoke-based ceramics firm of Minton & Company. In this case, Pugin used more complex colour combinations instead of the traditional and relatively simple scheme of brown and buff. While the designs are based on well-known medieval motifs, Pugin created much more complicated patterns incorporating mottoes and heraldry. The challenging use of multiple and intricately arranged colours pushed the Minton factory to new feats of technical achievement.
[AM, JM & RB]

181
Wallpaper design

1848
Designed by A.W.N. PUGIN
Red, blue, black and yellow body colours on red paper, 585 × 533 mm

Victoria and Albert Museum, D.719-1908

Pugin was an ardent design reformer and felt strongly that the flat surfaces of walls should be decorated with flat patterns. He believed that popular paper designs that used perspective to create the illusion of depth were both inappropriate and morally dubious. He designed nearly all the furnishings and decorative fittings for Westminster, including more than a hundred different wallpapers. This design features the crowned portcullis, Tudor rose motifs, and the 'VR' for Victoria Regina. Although many of Pugin's designs were felt to be overly ecclesiastical in their content, these papers were deemed particularly appropriate for the official, government spaces of Westminster. The finished paper was produced by Samuel Scott and supplied by the firm of John G. Crace & Son. [AM]

CHOLERA, THE 'GREAT STINK' AND THE NEW EMBANKMENTS

The filthy state of the River Thames was a growing problem by the early nineteenth century. An invention which in other ways was a great benefit – the water closet, or flushing toilet – caused a rapid deterioration in the quality of the river water. The reason was that the sewers, originally intended to carry away rainwater, ran downhill directly into the Thames in the heart of London. As more household drains were connected to the sewers, the problem worsened. The process was further intensified by the rapid growth of London: the population doubled from just under a million in 1801 to nearly two million only forty years later, and continued to expand throughout the Victorian period.

In hot summers the stench from the river was overpowering. It was particularly bad in 1858, when it became known as the 'Great Stink'. Not only was the bad state of the Thames unpleasant, it also helped to spread illness, as many households' drinking water came from the river. The waterborne disease cholera first struck London in 1832. At the time, the cause was unknown, and many doctors thought the bad smell itself led to illness: the so-called 'miasmic theory'. The increasing use of microscopes by nineteenth-century doctors and scientists led to the discovery of bacteria. In 1854 the Italian Filippo Pacini, Professor of Anatomy at the University of Florence, discovered cholera bacilli, but it was not until the experiments of the German physician, Robert Koch in the 1880s, that it was widely accepted that bacteria and similar organisms could cause disease.

The widespread belief in the miasmic theory of disease also meant that the pioneering work of Dr John Snow in London was largely ignored. During an outbreak of cholera in the Soho district of the city in 1854 he became convinced, from studying where victims lived, that the cause was contaminated water from the Broad Street pump. He persuaded the local authorities to remove the handle of the pump so residents could not use it and the epidemic subsided. But critics argued that the disease was waning anyway and it took another thirty years for the waterborne theory to be accepted.

In the end, the improvement of the River Thames came about not through the efforts of doctors but through the work of engineers. The belief that bad smells caused disease meant the stink had to be removed. Several Commissions of Sewers were appointed in London in the 1840s to grapple with the problem. They failed to make much headway largely because of arguments between the engineers and supporters of the civil servant in charge of the General Board of Health, Edwin Chadwick, about the correct shape and size of drains. To end the stalemate a new body elected by the London parishes was created, called the Metropolitan Board of Works. It began work at the

182
Compound microscope

c. 1853
ANDREW ROSS (*fl.* 1830–59), London
Brass, glass, 500 × 220 mm
Museum of the History of Science, 10700

The microscope was invented in the Netherlands around 1600, and at first it was mostly used by naturalists to study plants and insects. It was not until the nineteenth century that its use became widespread in medicine. Microscopes allowed doctors and scientists to observe that river or sewer water contained many micro-organisms which were invisible to the naked eye. [GC]

183
Monster Soup commonly called Thames Water being a correct representation of that precious stuff doled out to us!

1828
WILLIAM HEATH (1794/5–1840);
published by THOMAS McLEAN, London
Coloured etching, 220 × 340 mm
Wellcome Collection, 12079i

The print shows an elegantly dressed lady and the sample of Thames water which she is viewing through a microscope. She is so horrified by what she sees that she drops her cup of tea. The title of the engraving is 'Microcosm dedicated to the London Water Companies. Brought forth all monstrous, all prodigious things, hydras and organs, and chimeras dire.' Microscopy was capturing the imagination of a wide section of the population, with London opticians producing reasonably priced versions for use at home or by students. Heath's print uses the widespread knowledge that all kinds of strange organisms could be seen when river water was examined through a microscope in order to criticise the water companies. [GC]

beginning of 1856, appointing as chief engineer Sir Joseph William Bazalgette, who had also worked for the Commissioners of Sewers. He refined earlier plans for a series of intercepting sewers, which would prevent the contents of the old drains from entering the Thames in the centre of London and instead discharge the sewage into the river on the ebb tide, well to the east of the city. Again delays were caused by arguments between the new Board and central government, but the Great Stink of 1858 prompted Parliament to pass a law giving the Board full powers; Bazalgette's new system was built, being largely complete by 1870. The result was a major improvement in the state of the Thames, contributing much to the health of Londoners. [GC]

184

Salus populi suprema lex

1832

GEORGE CRUIKSHANK (1792–1878); published by
S. [SAMUEL] KNIGHT (fl. 1805–40), London
Coloured etching, 164 × 239 mm (image)

British Museum, 1862-1217.517

In the early nineteenth century there was widespread anxiety about the poor quality of the water supply available to many Londoners and its potentially harmful effects. A Royal Commission on London Water Supply in 1828 had recommended improvements. The five companies supplying the north bank looked for purer sources than the Thames and installed filter beds, but the Southwark Company continued to supply river water. When cholera reached London in 1831, anxiety about threats to health from Thames water and its smell were intensified, even if the exact mechanisms were not understood. These fears are fully expressed in this print. The satirical 'Royal Address' depicts John Edwards-Vaughan (1772–1833), Welsh politician and owner of Southwark waterworks, as 'Water-King of Southwark'. He is dressed as an ancient Welsh chieftain and crowned with a chamber pot. Part of the rhyme below contains a graphic description of the composition of the water supplied by Edwards's company:

> … small living creatures, and large
> ones deceas'd,
> The liquefied bodies of man and of beast,
> Sluic'd with sauce from the sewers, in all
> quite a feast …

The ironical Latin heading *Salus populi suprema lex* translates as 'the safety of the public is the supreme law'. [GC]

ROYAL ADDRESS

OF

CADWALLADER ᴀᴘ-TUDOR ᴀᴘ-EDWARDS ᴀᴘ-VAUGHAN,

WATER-KING OF SOUTHWARK,

SOVEREIGN OF THE SCENTED STREAMS,—AUTOCRAT OF ALL THE SLUSHES,—RAINING PRINCE OF THE GOLDEN SHOWERS,
PROTECTOR OF THE CONFEDERATION OF THE (U)RHINE,—APPROPRIATOR OF THE DIET OF WORMS,
PALATINE OF THE LOWER ISSUES,—MAR-GRAVE OF OFFALS,—LORD OF THE STRAY OILS,—AGITATOR-IN-CHIEF OF THE INTESTINAL CANALS,
NIGHT-CHAIR-MAN OF THE BOARD OF FLUX-IONS,—LORD OF THE MAN-URE OF SHETLAND,—WARDEN OF THE SINK PORTS,
RECEIVER GENERAL AND DISTRIBUTOR OF SEWERS,—GRAND CROSS OF THE MOST MUDDY ORDURE OF THE *BATH*,
AND REPRESENTATIVE IN THE IMPERIAL PARLIAMENT FOR *WELLS*,

TO HIS SUBJECTS OF THE BOROUGH.

My People of Southwark! your Monarch addresses you,
And deigns to declare, that with pride he possesses you,
Yet shudders to hear of the shocking excesses you
    Project in the cause of Reform :
Reformation by Land, he is told, will not quiet you,
But a Water-Reform, both in Washing and Diet, you
Insist on effecting, or kick up a riot you
    Will—and a terrible storm ! (1.)

As your King, I demand—What the deuce can the matter be ?
What can the meaning of all this loud clatter be !
What would ye insinuate can in the Wat*er* be,
    Except what it ought to contain ?
Such as small living creatures, and large ones deceas'd,
The liquefied bodies of man and of beast,
Sluic'd with sauce from the sewers, in all quite a feast,
    And yet you presume to complain !

Oh ! how could you dream there was any thing vicious
In matter putrescent, or excrementitious,
Or refuse of gas-works, that poisons the fishes,
    Which rot in the water you drink !
Nay ! chop me no logic, nor say that it follows
That a man must be poison'd if poison he swallows,
As sure as a sow must be daub'd when she wallows
    In the mire of a puddle or sink.

For a wholesomer fluid can't be, to my thinking,
Since it serves you at once both for eating and drinking :
Then gobble it down, my good Folk ! without shrinking.
    Why es-chew what has chew'd been before ?
Your minds first of prejudice nobly divesting,
That 'tis good for weak stomachs you'll own is past question, (2.)
Having already gone through a course of digestion,
    In whole or in part—less or more.

Just between Southwark Bridge, and its New London brother,
Three Crane Wharf on one side, Horse Shoe Alley on t'other,
You may scent out THE SPOT—there is not such another—
    (Should such vain curiosity seize you)
Where I pump up the stream all your wants to supply ;
No other you get but what drops from the sky,
And if it won't suit you, you needs must go dry :
    I despair to make water to please you.

For the use of your *Hospitals* look at my liquor !
Oh, pray do not fancy it makes the sick sicker,
Though in *brewing* arises a scum that is thicker
    Than if meat had been boiled in the copper ; (3.)
And though in the *bath*, when prescribed for your good,
If diseased in your bowels, your nerves, or your blood,
You find yourself stuck in a mass of my mud,
    For your health it is all very proper.

The dolts of the City conceive it a virtue,
To transfer from their dwellings all things that are dirty,
To the great Common Sewers—a hundred and thirty,—
    And plump in my Wet the muck souses ;
And should they be touched with the Sunderland gripes,
The balmy effects of their stomachs and tripes
Are infallibly destined to roll through the pipes
    By which I replenish your houses.

Then why with alarm do you tremble and gape,
Since should you not wholly the *Morbus* escape,
You'll have it, no doubt, in a modified shape
    If thus *second-hand* you can catch it ;
And some lucky night there may come a great fire,
Which, in cases of pest, is a grand purifier :
You need have no fear it too soon should expire,
    Without water sufficient to match it. (4.)

King WILLIAM and I are of different opinions !
I oppose all Reform within both our dominions,
And should THE BILL pass, I shall weep without onions,
    And loathe even leeks in my sorrow.
Then let not Reform, though she daily grows stronger,
Decree that no borough shall rot any longer ;
Still buy putrefaction of me, the old monger,
    And there yet shall be one ROTTEN BOROUGH.

Your thirsts, my brave People ! still venture to quench,
To boil all your victuals, your skins all to drench,
With my liquid Corruptions—regardless of stench,
    And every unnameable thing :
At defects so innoxious continue to wink,
And without further stir for my Wet give your chink,
For the more that you stir it, the more it will stink :—
    And so ends the Speech of your King !

*Exit " in all the Majesty of Mud," Groom of
the Stool bearing his train, grand flourish of
wind-instruments ; Privy Councillors and Courtiers chaunting—*

Ho ! ho ! with his water, pray why should you differ ?
You never had friend that would stick to you stiffer :
    Like clay it will handle,
    And taste like a candle,
    And smell like the snuff ;
    'Tis exquisite stuff !
And so long as it sells his honesty seen :
Should it *lie on his hands*, they would never be clean.

PUBLISHED BY S. KNIGHT, SWEETING'S ALLEY.—(Price 6d. plain, 1s. coloured.)

218 THE WORKING RIVER AND ITS VICTORIAN TRANSFORMATION

MAP I.

SCALE 30 INCHES TO A MILE.

C. F. Cheffins, Lith. Southampton B^{gs} London.

185

On the Mode of Communication of Cholera, 2nd edition

1855
JOHN SNOW (1813–1858);
published by JOHN CHURCHILL, London
Printed book, 232 × 255 × 70 (open)

Wellcome Collection, WC2621855567

Dr John Snow was one of the great pioneers of both anaesthetics and epidemiology. He first encountered cholera as an apprentice surgeon and apothecary in the area around Newcastle-upon-Tyne in 1831. His theory that cholera was a waterborne disease was originally published in his book, *On the Mode of Communication of Cholera* in 1849, but attracted little attention. The outbreak of cholera in Soho in 1854, when over 500

people died in ten days, gave him the opportunity to make a statistical survey of the disease. One survey showed that the majority of victims drew their water from the Broad Street pump. Another statistical study of cholera in South London showed that households supplied by the Vauxhall and Southwark Water Company, which drew its water from the Thames in the immediate neighbourhood, were eight or nine times more likely to succumb to the

disease than households whose supplies came from the Lambeth Water Company. They drew water from Thames Ditton, well away from the parts of the river into which the London sewers discharged. These results were presented in the second edition of Snow's book. However, he was not able to prove exactly how cholera spread and many doctors remained sceptical of his theories. [GC]

186
Handbill issued by the parish of St James in Westminster

1853
Printed paper
City of Westminster Archives Centre, WCA 00044

In the Victorian era, parish authorities were responsible for the relief of the poor and their resources were strained by serious epidemics, which left orphans to be supported and heads of households unable to work. Therefore, they took an increasing interest in the prevention of disease. Although the exact means by which sickness spread was not fully understood, the link between dirt and disease was well established. Not surprisingly, the handbill issued by the Parish of St James Westminster in 1853, when cholera was once more threatening London, emphasises the need for cleanliness. It also recommends drinking moderate amounts of 'sound Beer'. This was certainly good advice, given the unwholesome state of much of the London water supply at the time. Not only did many water companies draw supplies from the polluted River Thames, but the alternative sources, from public wells and pumps, were often contaminated by the overflowing cess pools of the many houses without a connection to the sewers. [GC]

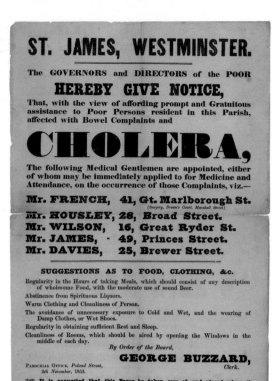

187
Appendix to Report of the Committee for Scientific Inquiries in relation to the cholera epidemic of 1854

1855
Published by GEORGE E. EYRE and WILLIAM SPOTTISWOODE, London for Her Majesty's Stationery Office
Printed book, 242 × 296 × 110 mm (open)
Wellcome Collection, M9300

The General Board of Health was created in 1848 and reorganised in 1854 at the height of the cholera epidemic. Its President, Sir Benjamin Hall (1802–67), was determined to investigate the causes of the disease. He set up a Medical Council to advise the Board, which in turn ordered the scientific enquiries detailed in this report, which was presented to Parliament. The investigations were carried out by a committee of five, including Dr John Snow. They analysed the statistics of the disease, studied the nature of the air and water in the vicinity of the most serious outbreaks and evaluated the various remedies that had been tried. They consulted a wide range of experts, including James Glaisher (1809–1903) of the Royal Observatory, Greenwich, a pioneer of meteorology, on the possible influence of the weather. They also had microscopical studies made of the contents of water supplies and sewers, which contained careful drawings of the various micro-organisms they observed. These were included in an appendix to their report. However, the state of knowledge at the time did not enable them to make a direct causal link between microbes and disease. [GC]

188
Medal to commemorate the thanksgiving service at St Paul's for the Prince's recovery from typhoid fever

1872
JOSEPH SHEPHERD and ALFRED BENJAMIN WYON (1837–84)
Copper alloy, 77 mm (diameter)
British Museum, M.9044 / MB4p285.2928

During a visit to Londesborough Lodge, North Yorkshire, in the winter of 1871 Albert Edward, Prince of Wales (1841–1910), the eldest son of Queen Victoria and heir to the throne, became ill with typhoid fever. This was the same disease that was thought to have caused the death of his father, Prince Albert, ten years earlier. Like cholera, typhoid could be spread by contaminated water and there were frequent outbreaks in the poorer parts of London and other cities. At Londesborough the outbreak was blamed on bad drains. Fortunately, the Prince of Wales made a full recovery from the disease and a number of public celebrations were organised to express the widespread public relief that he had been spared. One was a Thanksgiving Service at St Paul's Cathedral in the City of London, for which this special commemorative medal was struck. [GC]

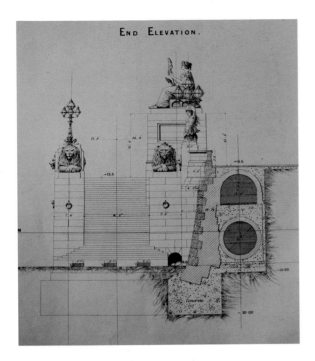

END ELEVATION.

189
Contract drawings for the Thames Embankment

Mid-nineteenth century
JOSEPH BAZALGETTE (1819–91)
Printed book, 540 × 670 × 60 (closed)

Institution of Civil Engineers, B862BAZTEM

The plans for the embankment of the River Thames, involving a series of surveys, were drawn up by Bazalgette and his staff at the Metropolitan Board of Works. The plans shown are for the embankment on the Middlesex side of the river, later called the Victoria Embankment in honour of the Queen. This was the most complex part of the scheme, since it had to be combined with the commercial undertaking to build the first underground railway in London, the Metropolitan Railway. Another novel feature was the construction of an extra tunnel to house gas and water pipes, so that utility companies would not have to dig up the roadway when repairs were needed. The construction was carried out by a number of independent contractors, who submitted competitive tenders for building a section of the system. Their work was supervised by three district engineers employed by the Board, supported by teams of clerks of works. One of the assistant engineers, John Grant, carried out pioneering experiments on Portland cement to ensure that it could be mixed to a consistent quality for constructing the foundations of the embankments. These were then faced with granite.

The Victoria Embankment was opened on 13 July 1870 by the Prince and Princess of Wales. Bazalgette was knighted once the final section of the Embankment had been opened in 1874 by the Duke and Duchess of Edinburgh, Queen Victoria's second son and his wife. After his death, a memorial to Bazalgette was built into the wall of the Victoria Embankment near Hungerford Bridge, where it can still be seen. [GC]

190
Sir Joseph William Bazalgette

1878
ALESSANDRO OSSANI (fl. 1857–88)
Oil on canvas, 900 × 700 mm

Institution of Civil Engineers, GR0109

Joseph William Bazalgette (1819–91) was the civil engineer who finally gave London an effective drainage system. His other major contribution to the improvement of the city was the construction of embankments on both sides of the River Thames: the Victoria and Chelsea Embankments to the north and the Albert Embankment to the south. A trained and experienced engineer, Bazalgette joined the Metropolitan Commission of Sewers as assistant surveyor in 1849. When the Commission was replaced by the Metropolitan Board of Works in 1856 he became their Chief Engineer with responsibility for drawing up detailed plans for a new main drainage system for London to prevent sewage entering the River Thames within the built-up area. Once the plans had been agreed he had to implement a vast programme of works right across London. This involved building a series of intercepting sewers parallel to the Thames, three to the north and two to the south of the river, totalling 82 miles in length. Some 165 miles of existing sewers were also enlarged or repaired. Four large pumping stations were built to raise sewage from the lower levels of the system, with outfalls into the Thames at Barking Creek on the north bank and Crossness Point to the south. The northern low-level sewer was combined with the building of the Victoria Embankment and the Metropolitan underground railway. [GC]

LITERATURE: Oxford DNB.

VIEW OF THE NORTH BANK OF THE THAMES FROM WESTMINSTER BRIDGE TO LONDON BRIDGE

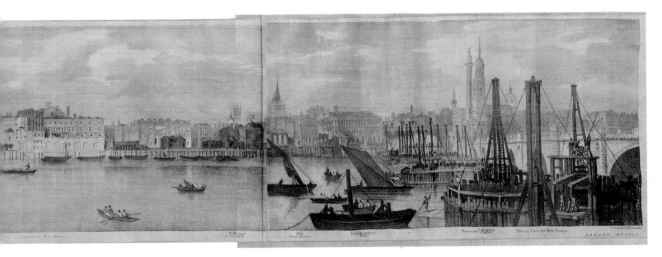

191
Prospectus of a proposed improvement on the Banks of the River Thames

3 February 1825
Printed by C. HULLMANDEL; after T. M. BAYNES and T. DIGHTON; published by HURST & ROBINSON, London
Lithograph, 254 × 4884 mm

Royal Collection, RCIN 817056

One reason why the Thames gave off such a bad smell in summer was that, at low tide, wide mud banks were exposed to the heat. Several plans had been proposed for building solid wharfs or embankments on either side of the river to reduce the extent of the marshy ground and mud banks and to speed up the flow of water. As early as the seventeenth century, Sir Christopher Wren had advocated embanking the Thames as part of the rebuilding after the Great Fire of London, but it had never been carried out. By the beginning of the

nineteenth century there was also a sense that the appearance of the existing river frontage was not in keeping with the growing importance of the imperial capital. In 1824 a proposal for a new quay along the northern bank from Charing Cross to Blackfriars was put forward by Frederick Trench (c.1777–1859), an army officer who had become a Member of Parliament. He introduced a bill in Parliament in 1825 to authorise building a Thames quay according to his plan, but was defeated by those who owned land and

warehouses along the river bank. This panorama, depicting the impact of the improvments, was published in support of his scheme. Another attempt was made in 1844, when a Royal Commission was set up on the subject of embanking the Thames. However, the strength of competing commercial interests and the absence of any local authority with responsibility for all public works over the whole of the London area at that time, made it impossible to implement any major scheme. [GC]

192
Metroplitan Board of Works.
Deptford Pumping Station

1 March 1860
Hand-coloured print
London Metropolitan Archives, MBW/2505, plate 5

193
Invitation to the formal opening
of Crossness Pumping Station

1865
Lithograph, 255 × 147 mm
Science Museum, 1983-1188

Bazalgette's scheme for the southern outfall sewer comprised pumping stations at Deptford and, further east, at Crossness. The Crossness station was opened on 4 April 1865 by the Prince of Wales, the future Edward VII. It marked the completion of the main phase of the drainage works, except for the northern low level sewer which was delayed by the construction of the Metropolitan Railway and the Victoria Embankment. The Prince travelled by boat down the Thames from Westminster to Crossness and formally started the four great steam engines which drove the pumps. The engines were named, perhaps a little incongruously, after senior members of the royal family: Victoria, Prince Consort, Albert Edward and Alexandra.

The event was attended by many influential figures, from the Archbishop of Canterbury and Bishop of London, members of both Houses of Parliament, to representatives of the City Corporation and the Metropolitan Board of Works. Joseph W. Bazalgette gave a speech explaining the principles of the main drainage system, and the formalities ended with a luncheon in one of the buildings designed to be a maintenance workshop for the plant. *The Times* commented, 'Contrary to the general rule, which makes an engine house a disfigurement to the surrounding country, this at Crossness Point is a perfect shrine of machinery'. The station was elaborately decorated in the prevailing neo-Gothic style. [GC]

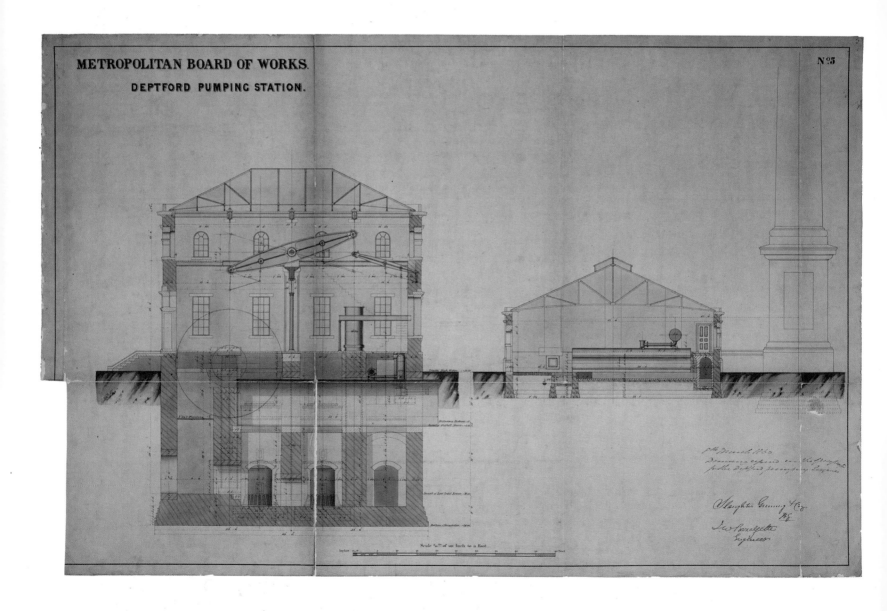

METROPOLITAN BOARD OF WORKS.
DEPTFORD PUMPING STATION.

Nº5

SOUTHERN PUMPING ESTABLISHMENT
AT CROSSNESS.
(14 MILES BELOW LONDON BRIDGE)

THE METROPOLITAN MAIN DRAINAGE WORKS,

will be opened at Crossness on the 4th day of April 1865.

BY

HIS ROYAL HIGHNESS THE PRINCE OF WALES

MEMBERS OF THE METROPOLITAN BOARD OF WORKS
JOHN THWAITES, ESQ. CHAIRMAN

Adams, B. H. Esq.	Hall, J. O. Esq.	Peckett, George, Esq.
Beven, Thomas, Esq.	Harris, Charles Esq.	Pew, James, Esq.
Bidgood, Henry, Esq.	Healcy, F. Esq.	Phillips, John, S Esq.
Brooker, James, Esq.	Hudson, George, Esq.	Richardson, G. B. Esq.
Brushfield, Thos. Esq.	Judkins, B. L. Esq.	Roche, C. M. Esq.
Carpmael, W. Esq.	Lammin, W. H. Esq.	Samuda, J. D'A. Esq.
Collinson, E. Esq.	Le Breton, P. H. Esq.	Saunders, J. E. Esq.
Crellin, Philip, Esq.	Legg, Cyrus, Esq.	Savage, John, Esq.
Dalton, W. H. Esq.	Long, Jeremiah, Esq.	Shepherd, Edward, Esq.
D'Iffanger, Thos. Esq.	Lyon, Major W.	Tanner, J. J. Esq.
Dixon, Benjamin, Esq.	McDonnell, D. Esq.	Taylor, Hy. Lowman, Esq.
Doulton, Fred. Esq. M.P.	Miller, T. J. Esq. M.P.	Taylor, Robert, Esq.
Evans, B. Esq.	Moreland, Joseph, Esq.	Taylor, Silas, Esq.
Finnis, Thos. Q. Esq. Aldern.	Newton, W. Esq.	Tite, William, Esq. M.P.
Freeman, Robert, Esq.	Nicholay, John Augustn. Es.	Westerton, Charles, Esq.

J. W. BAZALGETTE, ESQ. ENGINEER IN CHIEF.
THOS. LOVICK ESQ. ASSISTANT ENGINEER.
JOHN GRANT ESQ. .... Do.
EDMUND COOPER ESQ. .... Do.

Area drained on the North & South sides of the Thames	*117½ Square Miles.*
Daily discharge of Sewage	*14,000,000 Cub. Ft*
Area of Reservoirs (together)	*16 Acres*
Engine Power	*2380 H.P.*
Length of Main Drainage Sewers	*82 Miles*
Main drainage works commenced	*31st Jany. 1859.*

JOHN POLLARD ESQ. CLERK OF THE BOARD.

194
The Embankment

1874
JOHN O'CONNOR (1830–89)
Oil on canvas, 905 × 1435 mm

This scene is more often associated with
the Venetian artist Canaletto, who
painted the same view of the Thames
from the terrace of (old) Somerset House
in the late 1740s (Royal Collection RCIN
400504). In the foreground is a well-to-do
young woman with a child and a baby in a
perambulator, looking over the balustrade
of Somerset House at a passing company
of Guards. The most striking difference
between O'Connor's painting and the
view Canaletto recorded around 125 years
earlier concerns the industrial nature of
the city and the changing architecture of
the Thames itself, with the addition of the
new Blackfriars Bridge (first opened 1769,
rebuilt 1869) and the Embankment.
Bazalgette's massive undertaking
significantly narrowed the Thames in
central London, leaving the previously
riverside Somerset House, with its water
gate, marooned on the bank.

John O'Connor began his artistic career
as a scene painter, first in Belfast then in
London's Drury Lane and Haymarket
theatres, later specialising in views of
London and other cities. He exhibited
regularly at the Royal Academy and
enjoyed the patronage of the royal family,
for whom he recorded a number of visits
and pageants, including Queen Victoria's
Golden Jubilee service at Westminster
Abbey in 1887. In 1854, he exhibited a
diorama of Queen Victoria's first visit to
Ireland in 1849. [RJ]

5
ROYAL YACHTS AND THE NAVY

THE VISIT OF GEORGE IV TO SCOTLAND, AUGUST 1822

GEORGE R. DALGLEISH

Fig.23 *The embarkation of his most Gracious Majesty George the Fourth at Greenwich, August 10th, 1822 for Scotland*, aquatint engraving, by Robert Havell, Jr, London, August 1822.

National Maritime Museum, PAD6656.

At about twenty minutes before four o'clock on the afternoon of Saturday 10 August 1822, a most extraordinary and flamboyant flotilla set sail from the riverside steps of the Royal Hospital, Greenwich (fig.23). So began the 'One and Twenty Daft Days' of the 'King's Jaunt', the royal visit of George IV to Scotland.

When George disembarked on the quayside of Leith some five days later, he was the first reigning British monarch to set foot on Scottish soil since Charles II in 1650–51. Indeed, the only time a prince of the House of Hanover had visited the country was when William, Duke of Cumberland, had suppressed the last Jacobite Rebellion in 1745–46 with a brutality that earned him the title 'Butcher'. The 1822 visit was intended to build bridges between George IV and his Scottish subjects and to improve the image of the Crown, which had been badly tarnished by his recent and rather messy attempted divorce from Queen Caroline. The event was stage-managed by Sir Walter Scott, who very deliberately set a 'Highland' tone. Clan chiefs were encouraged to attend official engagements with a 'tail' of clansmen retainers, all bedecked in kilts and tartan. It was undoubtedly an important event in both the monarchy's developing relationship with its northern kingdom, and in defining the changing visions of Scotland's own identity. It also exhibited much of the hypocrisy of the period. While Scott and his friend David Stewart of Garth established the Edinburgh-based Celtic Society (which included both Highland chiefs and lowland gentry) to promote Highland culture, they were roundly condemned by the highly volatile Alasdair Ranaldson MacDonell of Glengarry for not being pure-bred Gaels. He established his own Society of True Highlanders and continually sought to up-stage Scott throughout the visit. The reality of the situation, however, was that many of the chieftains, members of either Society, struggled to find enough clansmen to man their tails because of their enthusiastic policy of 'clearing' these self-same highlanders off their ancestral lands. Individuals such as Glengarry himself, but also the Duke of Sutherland, were to the forefront of this policy. The bitter irony of this situation was not lost on several critical commentators at the time, but the lasting legacy of the royal visit undoubtedly helped to cement a vision of Scotland that was romantically Highland.

Headed by the King's own royal yacht, the *Royal George*, a squadron of ships, ceremonial barges, tenders and steamships had been assembling on the Thames for some days in readiness for the royal departure. These vessels included the sumptuous barges of several of the City's livery companies headed by that of the Lord Mayor. A huge number of spectators turned out to see off the King, lining the route from Carlton House to the Royal Hospital. The latter had been chosen as the embarkation point by the King himself 'because of the peculiar convenience which it afforded … [and] from the desire he had to pay a deserved compliment to an institution combining in itself so many claims on public gratitude'.[1] So great was this assembly that 'the oldest inhabitants of Greenwich scarcely recollected on any occasion, not excepting that of the memorable and melancholy spectacle of Lord Nelson lying in state, to have witnessed so extraordinary an influx of strangers'.[2]

After numerous false starts and delays, the King arrived at the Hospital just after three o'clock in the afternoon, descended the water steps to his barge and was rowed out to the *Royal George*. This elegant vessel, the same one that had conveyed him on his visit to Ireland the previous year, was built in 1817 at Deptford. She acquitted herself particularly well on the rather stormy Irish voyage, where she not only shipped scarcely any water but also showed she could out-sail almost any of the accompanying men-of-war. Unfortunately, even this splendid vessel could not sail against the wind, and she was towed down river by the steam packet *Comet*. She was followed by the colourful armada of smaller craft, many of which accompanied the royal yacht as far as Gravesend. The royal flotilla proceeded northwards at a leisurely pace, the King's ship either going under her own sail or being towed alternately by the steamers *Comet* or *James Watt*. Most of the King's household, including his state carriages, horses and a 'sumptuous throne' for use in the Palace of Holyroodhouse, had been dispatched from London a few days earlier and were ready for him when he finally arrived in his northern capital.[3]

After the success of the royal visit to Ireland in 1821, it was hoped that the King's unpopularity in Scotland could be in some small part mitigated by a similar excursion northward. His treatment of his estranged wife, Caroline, that unlikely figurehead of the reform cause, rankled particularly with

many Scottish Whigs and radicals; indeed her defence against George's attempts to divorce her in 1820 was led by the Edinburgh lawyer and leading Whig, Henry Brougham. George had also caused resentment by his dissolute, spendthrift ways and in particular by the lavish spending on his coronation in July 1821, at a time when many were destitute because of the decline in the economy. The recent 'Radical War' in Scotland had been brutally crushed by a nervous government. Partly as a response to all this, Sir Walter Scott, who had first met the then Prince Regent in 1815 and who was the first baronet created by George when he became King in 1820, convinced him to visit Scotland in the guise of a new 'Bonnie Prince Charlie', a true descendent of Scotland's ancient royal lineage. It was to be a time of rehabilitation and reconciliation, healing the old Stuart/Hanoverian wounds, and winning the Scots' affections away from radical reform. More importantly, in the eyes of the government ministers, including Lords Liverpool and Castlereagh, George had to be prevented at all costs from attending the forthcoming Congress of Verona. They did not want him to meddle in the delicate and finely balanced diplomatic negotiations nor to pick up any more ideas from, or be outmanoeuvred by, the wily absolutists Tsar Alexander or Prince Metternich. The proposed visit to Edinburgh was therefore a timely distraction. George,

however, prevaricated and by the time he finally agreed, only some four weeks' official notice was given to the Scottish establishment, including the Provost and magistrates of Edinburgh. Despite this, all was made ready in time and a huge number of people turned out to welcome the King when the *Royal George* finally sailed into the Firth of Forth and dropped anchor in Leith Roads on Wednesday 14 August.

Unfortunately, the weather was so wet (a not uncommon experience in the Firth of Forth) that the waiting crowds had to curb their excitement, as the King stayed on board ship until the next day. The King's comment when Scott arrived alongside to make arrangements prior to landing displays his esteem for both the man and his role in the forthcoming pageantry: 'What! Sir Walter Scott? – The man in Scotland I most wish to see! Let him come up.'[4] By this date Scott was an internationally acclaimed poet, author and dramatist of unparalleled popularity and was 'truly the catalyst, inspirer and first begetter of the whole extravaganza'.[5] He was the impresario who, aided by the theatrical expertise of Daniel Terry and William Murray (the actor–manager of the Theatre Royal in Edinburgh) and by the redoubtable Colonel David Stewart of Garth, the recently acknowledged expert on all matters Highland, created a series of ceremonies for which there was no real historical precedent. Sir Walter's anonymously and swiftly published pamphlet *Hints addressed to the Inhabitants of Edinburgh and others in prospect of His Majesty's Visit, by an Old Citizen* was the essential handbook for both the order of service and for the standards of deportment and fashionable dress that was expected of His Majesty's loyal Scottish subjects. He can be argued to have 'invented a picturesque identity for his country which fully satisfied national pride'.[6]

The 'Celtified Pageantry' (so called by his own son-in-law, John Gibson Lockhart) that Scott created for the visit was to be centred around several major public set-piece events. The first of these actually took place before the King even arrived in Scotland.[7] On Monday 12 August (coincidentally the King's birthday), the Honours of Scotland – the ancient Royal Regalia consisting of the Crown, Sword and Sceptre – were taken from their normal abode in the Crown Room of Edinburgh Castle to the Palace of Holyroodhouse, where the King would preside at some of the other state functions. The Honours were placed in the care of Sir Alexander Keith, the Knight Marischal, and guarded by detachments of the 77th Regiment of Foot, a squadron of the Midlothian Yeomanry and, perhaps most spectacularly, a guard of Highlanders fully dressed and equipped in 'traditional' style, with pipes playing and banners flying. In the vanguard of this group was Clan Gregor, headed

by Sir Evan MacGregor of MacGregor, armed with a silver basket-hilted broadsword, which family tradition asserted had been carried by his ancestor when serving in Bonnie Prince Charlie's Jacobite army in 1745–46.[8] Once at Holyroodhouse, the Honours were officially received by Sir Patrick Walker, Usher of the White Rod. This outrageously vain man was spectacularly attired in a jacket and mantle of crimson and white satin that he had last worn, somewhat contentiously, at the coronation of the King just over a year before. This entire episode was of particular significance, given that the ancient Honours had only recently been 'rediscovered' in their bricked-up resting place in the castle, where they had been consigned as part of the conditions of the Treaty of Union between Scotland and England in 1707. This unearthing had been at the behest of Sir Walter Scott, who in 1818 had persuaded George, then Prince Regent, to authorise a commission to find them. Their ceremonial presence during the visit was undoubtedly part of Scott's plan to 'authenticate' George's position as King of Scots.

The next formal event was the landing at the quay of Leith. This scene was captured by a troop of artists, including J.M.W. Turner, William Collins, Robert Dighton and Alexander Carse, who had assembled in Edinburgh to record the details of the jaunt for posterity. Alexander Carse produced what was undoubtedly the largest of the canvases. At over 11-feet long, it shows George IV setting foot on Scottish soil for the first time. However, perhaps the most fascinating pictorial record of the event is the tiniest: the engraved vignette produced by William Home Lizars for inclusion on the one-guinea banknotes (fig.24) of the Leith Banking Company (a bank that included Sir Walter Scott as one of its account holders). Lizars also produced a number of larger-scale engravings to illustrate the detailed contemporary account of the visit by Robert Mudie. All the images of the events emphasise the sheer scale of the crowds that turned out to catch a glimpse of the monarch. It has been estimated that over 300,000 people were packed into Edinburgh and Leith: some three times the total population of the city at the time. They lined the entire route from the quay, up Leith Walk to Picardy Place, where a theatrical set of town gates had been erected, to effect a ceremonial presentation of the Keys of the City by the Lord Provost. The huge procession carried on to

Princes Street and, by way of Calton Hill, to the Palace of Holyroodhouse, where the King was shown the newly installed Honours. He was not to stay in the palace of his ancestors, it being deemed unfit for royal habitation, having been called 'the most depressing, the most irresistibly sepulchral … of all the royal residences in Europe'.[9] This verdict by *Blackwood's Magazine* was undoubtedly somewhat harsh, particularly as Holyrood had been considered suitable enough to accommodate the exiled French royal family a few years before. During the entire visit George resided at nearby Dalkeith Palace, as a guest of the young Duke of Buccleuch.

The King actually appeared in public relatively few times during his fifteen-day stay in Scotland. These brief public shows included a formal levee at Holyroodhouse on Saturday 17 August where some 2000 noblemen and gentlemen 'kissed hands' with their King.[10] At the equally formal Dressing Room in the palace on the following Tuesday, the King did the kissing, 'bussing' the cheeks of over 550 ladies in a mere 75 minutes.[11] Perhaps the most spectacular events, and certainly those where the King was most visible to his subjects, were the grand procession from Holyroodhouse to Edinburgh Castle on 22 August and the royal review of over 3000 volunteer cavalrymen on Portobello Sands the following day.

The latter prompts the thought that while much has been made of the show of 'Highland dress' during the visit, this should be seen in the context of the general preponderance of military or quasi-military uniforms on display in Edinburgh in August 1822. The city was full of officers and men from regular regiments such as the 2nd Dragoons (Scots Greys), the 77th, 13th and 66th of Foot, over and above the even more elaborate and sumptuous rig of the numerous Yeomanry units. Add to this the legal and civil uniforms on show, and the overall impression must have been of a brilliantly colourful military tattoo.

Military uniform had a tremendous influence on gentlemen's tailoring and fashion of the day. This love affair with military style possibly owed much to the high regard in which both the Navy and army were held for their parts in the still-recent final victory over Napoleon. Equally, in the more immediate past, it was the military, aided and abetted by the amateur Yeomanry culled mainly from the ranks of the land-owning classes, that had put down the radical uprisings across the country, from Peterloo to Bonnymuir. The so-called Radical War in Scotland – that doomed attempt by some political activists to gain a measure of representation and reform – had been cruelly suppressed only some two years before the visit. It is perhaps no coincidence that those with so much to lose in a radical revolution chose to dress in a style culled from the very military that had helped suppress any revolt and thus protect their property and possessions.

The kilt and tartan had survived the proscription after the last Jacobite Rebellion mainly by being adopted by Highland units within the army; the feared 'rebel savages' of the '45 had swiftly become the loyal storm troops of empire. It was through the medium of military uniform that Highland dress had become transformed into civilian national costume by the late eighteenth or early nineteenth century. Some less well-off young bucks even bought second-hand officers' uniforms to wear when showing off in public and it was said in 1819 that Highland regimental dress was 'universally looked upon as holy-day uniform of all the writers' clerks in Edinburgh'.[12]

The rage for Highland dress in 1822 should perhaps be seen as simply one element of a generally uniformed pageantry rather than a specifically 'plaided panorama'.[13] Indeed, Scott's first reference to what the populace should wear for the visit does not mention tartan at all, but rather states: 'all gentlemen to appear in a uniform costume, viz. Blue Coat, White Waistcoat, and White of Nankeen Pantaloons. The ancient national cognisance of St Andrew's Cross, white upon blue ground, is also to be universally worn by way of a cockade'.[14] It is not until he deals with the Highland Ball to be thrown by the nobility on the evening of 23 August, that Scott indicates the obligatory wearing of Highland dress.[15] It was, of course, this injunction that was taken up with such gusto by many of those involved in the visit and it is the resultant image that defines it, for better or worse. Scott's own son-in-law, while agreeing that the visit had been a great success for the King, had some doubts about its taste: 'Whether all the arrangements which Sir Walter dictated or enforced were conceived in the most accurate taste is a different question'.[16]

Perhaps the most spectacular (or ridiculous, depending on one's view) scene of the entire visit, was the King regaled from head to foot in full Highland dress. George had undoubtedly listened to Sir Walter's promptings and set out to show himself to his people as a new 'Jacobite' King, the 'descendent of a long line of Scottish kings' resplendent in the aforementioned 'garb of old Gaul'.[17] The King, in fact, appeared in Highland dress only once during the visit, at the short levee held at Holyroodhouse on Saturday 17 August. Much has been made of him wearing pink tights to disguise his swollen legs; these were more accurately described as 'buff coloured trousers like flesh to imitate his Royal knees'.[18] The sight undoubtedly polarised opinions at the time. Visually, this was nowhere more obvious than in the merciless caricatures by Thomas Rowlandson and others of the King and his crony Sir William Curtis as fat, gluttonous lechers in over-short kilts at one end of the spectrum, with the equally fictitious formal, dignified deportment of the King in Sir David Wilkie's full-length portrait, completed some seven years after the visit, at the other (fig. 25). Contemporary descriptions also varied, depending on the persuasion of the commentator. Robert Mudie's rather sycophantic account asserted that 'In compliment to the country, his Majesty appeared in complete Highland costume, made of Royal Stewart tartan, which displayed his manly and graceful figure to great advantage', although he hints that the King may not have been without some self-awareness when he noted that 'His Majesty on coming out of his dressing room at Dalkeith house, arrayed in the Highland garb, was observed to look down at his kilt and heard to say "I cannot help smiling at myself"'.[19] Others were far less complimentary both of the King's outfit itself or the use of Highland imagery in general. James Stuart of Dunearn famously and pointedly opined 'Sir Walter has ridiculously made us appear a nation of Highlanders, and the bagpipe and the tartan was the order of the day'.[20] Another dissenting voice came from closer to Scott's Border homeland. Gilbert Elliot, second Earl of Minto, was no fan of Scott's or the King's politics or of the 'Celtification' of the event: 'The Pageantry in general was good & the effect very striking in the fine scenery of Edinr.; but there was an absurd affectation of Highland display as if all the Scotts [sic] were highlanders.'[21] Clearly Sir Walter's attempts at reconciliation between Highland and Lowland, Jacobite and Hanoverian, Tory and Whig had not won over everyone.

Regardless of the debate about how the King *looked* in his Highland dress, there is no doubting the magnificence of the outfit itself. Costing the small (or even medium) fortune of £1354 18s (equivalent to over £110,000 today), it comprised 'Two complete Highland dresses, including coat, kilt, hose, bonnet, etc of the royal Stuart tartan … The finer suit was intended for the drawing-room to be held, the other for the levees'.[22] The receipted bill still survives and shows that no fewer than '61 yards of Royal Sattin Plaid, 31 yards Royal Plaid Velvit and 17½ yards Royal Plaid Casemere' went into the making of the King's ample outfits. He was also supplied with a gold-mounted white goatskin sporran, a powder horn, a dirk and a fine basket-hilted broadsword. The entire ensemble was topped off with a truly magnificent gold 'Head Ornament' set with diamonds, rubies, pearls and emeralds – this alone cost £375.[23] It is perhaps worth remembering, however, that the King's appearance in Highland dress in 1822 was not the first time he had been so dressed. As far back as 1789, the then Prince of Wales wore complete Highland dress to a 'Mrs Sturt's masquerade'. The sett of the Royal outfit was on this occasion what would now be described as Black Watch, the muted government pattern, whereas in 1822, George wore the bright red sett which was to become known as Royal Stewart.[24]

The widely held misconception that the 1822 visit 'invented' Highland dress as the national costume of Scotland is clearly nonsense. However, there is no doubt that it did an enormous amount to popularise it both nationally and internationally, incidentally providing a huge sales boost to manufacturers, and contributing to the demand-driven urge to codify family tartan setts so beloved of tourists and locals alike today.

After the levee, the King never appeared in Highland dress again. He was probably shocked by adverse public reaction to the ridiculous sight of his even-more corpulent crony and erstwhile Lord Mayor of London, Sir William Curtis, squeezing himself into an equally elaborate confection. Even at the Peers', or Grand Highland, Ball on the evening of 23 August, George wore a field-marshal's uniform, when all around him were in variations of Highland dress. The King only stayed for a short while and did not attempt any of the dances, although he did watch others with evident delight. Miss Mary Grant of Rothiemurchus suggested that the reason for the royal inactivity was that George had injured his foot 'by

Fig. 25 George IV, oil on canvas, by Sir David Wilkie, 1829.
Royal Collection, RCIN 401206.

the awkwardness of a would-be Celt who in making his bow at the levee to kiss the King's hand dropped his pistols on His Majesty's great toe'.[25]

The other grand events, such as the Lord Provost's banquet in Parliament Hall, the Grand Procession to Edinburgh Castle to return the Honours, and Sunday worship at the High Kirk of St Giles went off with no obvious mishaps. The visit drew to a close with a trip to the palatial seat of the Earl of Hopetoun for lunch, before setting sail from nearby Port Edgar. Family tradition records that before he sat down to sup a bowl of turtle soup, the King washed his hands in an exquisite silver basin and ewer which had belonged to the Hopetoun family since it was made in Edinburgh in 1706–07. They were thereafter used at the baptism of succeeding earls. It was also during this final engagement that the King conferred knighthoods on the artist Henry Raeburn (who only enjoyed his elevated status for a matter of months before his death on 8 July 1823), and Adam Ferguson. One of the oldest friends and a close neighbour of Sir Walter Scott, Ferguson had previously been made Keeper of the Regalia and his knighthood was undoubtedly a mark of respect for both men.

The royal party took its leave of Hopetoun and boarded the *Royal George*. Again she was towed by the steamship *James Watt* and surrounded by a host of smaller vessels as she sailed down the Firth of Forth, followed by the echoing sound of salutes from guns on board warships and from shore batteries on both sides of the Firth. The royal squadron took just three days on the southward journey, arriving back at the Royal Hospital in Greenwich on Sunday 1 September. Yet again, a large crowd had assembled to welcome George back from the now less-unknown north. 'The people on both shores cheered and his Majesty, taking off his hat, bowed to all sides, and appeared truly delighted with his reception.'[26] The King's Jaunt was over, but what were its results?

Before the King prepared to leave Scotland on 29 August, the entire visit had already been generally deemed a great success. Even the *Scotsman* newspaper, a Whig organ normally at odds with the Tory establishment, rather grudgingly agreed that 'None can deny that his majesty's visit was an act of kindness and condescension on his part', although it was less sure about any lasting benefits. 'As a mere piece of ceremonial and of state pageantry, the state visit was

well enough; but to suppose it will lead to any important political consequence, evinces an extreme degree of silliness and credulity.'[27] There is no doubt, however, that the 1822 'Jaunt' set the pattern for future royal visits, from the production of vast numbers of royal souvenirs (varying in quality from exquisite to execrable) to a standardised programme of ceremonial processions, visits and involvement of Scottish institutions, such as the Church. Victoria was the next monarch to visit Scotland and eventually the presence of the royal family in this country became an annual event. Perhaps more importantly, however, whether one approves of it or not, George IV's visit in 1822 set in train the development of an *idea* of Scotland and, as John Prebble puts it 'a picturesque national identity where none had been wholly satisfying since the Union'.[28] This was to have a lasting impact on both the growing tourist industry and, for good or ill, on the national psyche itself.

THE KING'S SHIPS AND DOCKYARDS

Yachting has been the called the sport of kings. It was introduced to England by Charles II and taken up enthusiastically by most succeeding monarchs until the reign of George V. Between 1661 and 1663 five new royal yachts were built to designs by Peter and Christopher Pett and Thomas Shish, namely the *Anne*, *Katherine*, *Charles*, *Jemmy* and *Henrietta*. John Evelyn tells of a yachting race on 1 October 1661 between Charles II in the *Katherine* and his brother James in the *Anne* for a wager of £100. As Charles's reign progressed, however, the royal yachts were used less for fun and came to serve with the Royal Navy.

During the second half of the seventeenth century, the Royal Navy emerged as a professional force, distinct from the merchant marine, with technologically advanced warships that could compete with European rivals. Charles II and James II shared a deep and genuine interest in all aspects of maritime activity. Both men understood that a monarch's prestige was reflected in his great ships, and recognised that England's commercial interests depended on having a strong fleet. Despite setbacks – notably when the Dutch mounted a surprise raid up the River Medway in 1667, sinking or burning seven English warships and towing away the *Royal Charles* as a prize – the Royal Navy during the reigns of Charles and James grew in size and became more professionally administered. A substantial naval building programme took place despite a shortage of funds; Articles of War on board ships established a disciplinary code at sea; some formal arrangements were introduced for training young officers; and the Navy Board introduced reforms that allowed it to manage its responsibilities with a reasonable degree of probity and efficiency.

After the Glorious Revolution in 1688, the Royal Navy continued to grow in size and became more effective in warfare. By the accession of George I, it was twice the size of the Dutch navy and about 60 per cent larger than the French. The number of ships was not reduced greatly during peacetime because its force could be usefully employed to support Britain's mercantile interests.

To service the Navy, dockyards greatly expanded and improved their facilities. The dockyards at Chatham, Deptford and Woolwich made use of their geographical advantages in this respect, namely proximity to the Admiralty and Navy Board and easy access to the most important shipbuilding community in the country. Dockyards were powerful manifestations of the state and, therefore, of royal power. These yards were the administrative centres that propagated British maritime mastery. They were increasingly at the cutting edge of technological innovation. When, in 1698, Peter the Great of Russia

195
Peter Pett and the *Sovereign of the Seas*

c. 1645–50
SIR PETER LELY (1618–80)
Oil on canvas, 1395 × 1560 mm
National Maritime Museum, Caird Collection, BHC2949

Peter Pett (1610–c. 1672) was an English Master Shipwright and, from 1647 to 1667, Commissioner at Chatham Dockyard. Although he sided with Parliament during the Civil War, he continued in business at the Restoration. However, in June 1667, he was blamed for the insufficient protection of the British fleet at Chatham, and disgraced after saving his own property before the King's during the Dutch attack on the Medway. Pett is shown here with the stern view of the *Sovereign of the Seas*, which he had built at Woolwich in 1637 to the designs of his father, Phineas. In size and armament, the *Sovereign of the Seas* eclipsed all earlier warships. It was the first 100-gun ship of the Royal Navy heralding a new generation of larger, more heavily armed ships. It was also the last of a kind: its lavish decoration was never surpassed.

Lely's painting alludes to the ship's dazzling quality, since Charles I insisted that only black and gilt be used as colours. The ornately carved stern and the guns are carefully delineated, detailing the iconographic scheme for the ship's decorations. Together, these allegorical references promoted Charles's claim to sovereignty of the seas and naval might as both a deterrent and an instrument of peace. [JD & RJ]

LITERATURE: Callender, *The Portrait of Peter Pett and the* Sovereign of the Seas, *passim*.

visited Deptford and learnt about seamanship and shipbuilding, the Tsar was knowingly visiting the most technologically advanced yard in the world. Dockyards were thus vital to British naval supremacy, creating a naval force that would protect and extend the maritime commerce of Britain and its growing empire. In this, sense the dockyards were 'gateways to the world'. The expeditions of Cook, Frobisher, Vancouver and Parry, for example, all left from Deptford Dockyard.

The dockyards on the Thames also took on symbolic roles as arenas where royal status was celebrated. The launching of ships by royalty was co-ordinated as a public spectacle, and attended by all levels of society. Into the eighteenth and nineteenth centuries, this symbolic role became less overtly 'royal' and increasingly 'national' as ship launches became a focus for patriotic fervour. [SD & JD]

196
James, Duke of York

1672–73
HENRI GASCAR (1635–1701)
Oil on canvas, 2286 × 1625 mm

National Maritime Museum, Greenwich Hospital Collection, BHC2797

This vibrantly coloured full-length portrait shows James, Duke of York, in the role of Mars, the Roman god of war. The Duke's mythological guise and the plate armour at his feet make an exaggerated claim for the sitter's military prowess, while also inviting comparisons with the theatrical court culture of the earlier Stuart monarchs. James was Lord High Admiral from 1660 to 1673, during the reign of his elder brother, Charles II. Accordingly, James stands with the English fleet in the background, and his flagship *Royal Prince* of 100 guns prominent in the scene. The Duke was in personal command of the fleet at the victory over the Dutch off Lowestoft in 1665, and again at the Battle of Solebay in 1672, an event this portrait may have been commissioned to commemorate. Solebay was the last occasion in which a member of the British royal family personally commanded a fleet in action. An experienced and brave soldier by land and sea, James was a diligent admiral and showed a keen interest in the administration of the Navy. He encouraged Samuel Pepys as Secretary of the Navy Board and later of the Admiralty, becoming his most important patron (other than Charles II himself) after the death of Pepys's cousin, the Earl of Sandwich in 1672. [JD & RJ]

197

Carved Stuart coat of arms from the *Royal Charles*

c. 1664

Painted pine, 2770 × 3780 × 1200 mm

Rijksmuseum, NG-MC-239

The *Royal Charles* was an 80-gun ship of the line, built by Peter Pett at Woolwich Dockyard. Launched in 1655 as the *Naseby*, her original name commemorated the battle in which Oliver Cromwell decisively defeated the Royalist army under Charles I in 1645, during the English Civil War. At the Restoration, she was flagship of the fleet sent to bring Charles II home from Holland to England, when her figurehead of Oliver Cromwell was symbolically removed. Edward Barlow, a young English sailor, was serving in the ship and recorded the events surrounding the Restoration. When Charles was proclaimed King on board 'every man in the ship had a pint of wine given him to drink His Majesty's

health'. The ship was ordered to Holland to convey the King to 'his crown and kingdom' and was 'made as fine as possible … flying three silk flags'. Upon seeing the King for the first time, Barlow recorded:

> All the men in the ship gave a great and loud shout, many of them hurling their caps or hats into the sea as a token of their joy to see His Majesty. That done, and he coming aboard, we fired above seventy pieces of cannon, three times, one after another … And all the admirals having fired then began all the rest of the fleet to fire, they firing all together, which made such a rattling in the sky as though it had been a great storm or tempest of thunder and rain.

Shortly before departing for England, the King renamed his new flagship the *Royal Charles*. On 25 May 1660, the King's fleet arrived off Dover. The advent of the King was announced by a peal of ordnance 'which made the very hills and

Dover cliffs to sound the echo with the like harmony, as though they were all glad to bear him up and have the happiness to welcome home the true sovereign, King Charles II, for whom the land had so long grieved'.

The *Royal Charles* subsequently saw much action during the Second Dutch War (1665–67) – the Battle of Lowestoft, the Four Days Battle and the St James's Day Fight – serving at each with distinction. However, in June 1667, a Dutch force under Michiel de Ruyter (1607–76) made an audacious raid into the Medway; it seized the *Royal Charles*, which had only 32 guns mounted, from her moorings off Chatham and took her home in glory as a prize. This triumph of arms, signalling the ability of the Dutch navy to strike at the heart of England's maritime infrastructure, was widely celebrated in art. Ludolf Backhuysen (1631–1708) was one artist who responded to the anti-English sentiment that prevailed in the Dutch Republic during the conflict. He

immortalised the de Ruyter victory in a large oil painting showing the *Royal Charles*, now wearing the Republic's tricolour, being carried into Dutch waters.

Since ships were the largest and most visible manifestations of state and monarchical power, the naming (or re-naming) was of undeniable significance, providing a source of pride in times of victory and of humiliation in defeat or loss. As a political scandal, the 'Medway Raid' was therefore made even worse by the seizure of a flagship so emblematic of the restored Stuart monarchy.

This coat of arms was retained as a trophy when the ship was broken up in 1673. It still holds a special place in Dutch naval history and its loan to the *Royal River* exhibition, 345 years after the celebrated (or notorious) Medway Raid of 1667, is the first time it has ever left the Netherlands since then.

[JD, JM & PVDM]

LITERATURE: Lubbock (ed.), *Barlow's Journal*, vol. 1 pp. 42–45; Gaschke (ed.), *Turmoil and Tranquillity*, p. 19; Laird Clowes, *The Royal Navy*, vol. 2, pp. 291–93.

198
Rosewater dish and porringer

1668
Inscribed: 'At the launching of His Majesty's ship The Royal Charles the 5th of April 1668. Built at Deptford by Mr Ionas Shish, His Majesty's Master Shipwright there. Burthen 1258 tunns, Men 700, Guns, 96'
Silver, rosewater dish, 380 mm (diameter); porringer, 220 × 190 mm
The Honourable Society of Lincoln's Inn, ID 35/46

This dish and porringer were presented to Charles II at the launching of the *Charles* at Deptford Dockyard in 1668. Designed to carry 96 guns, the *Charles* was the first great ship to be built during the reign of Charles II. It was completed by Jonas Shish, following the death of Christopher Pett shortly before the launch. The ship replaced the *Royal Charles*, the flagship that had been captured by the Dutch the previous year. As Pepys recorded at its launch 'God send her better luck than the former!' Officially named *Charles the Second*, the ship's 'Royal' prefix was presumably an acknowledgement of the King's presence at the launch. [JD & SD]

199
The Duke of York's coat of arms

c. 1665–73
Wood, 1055 × 150 × 740 mm (framed)

National Maritime Museum, ZBA3082

This coat of arms probably comes from the cabin of the *Anne*, the yacht that belonged to the Duke of York, later James II. Named after his first wife, the *Anne* was built in 1661 at Woolwich specifically for the Duke by Christopher Pett, the younger brother of Commissioner Peter Pett. The royal arms with the label for the second son are surrounded by a royal crown, placed on an Admiralty anchor, recognising the Duke of York's position as Lord High Admiral, and tying ideas of monarchy to the sea. The medals of the coat of arms are inscribed with references to the Duke of York, and *GENVS ANTIQVVM*, a reference to Virgil's *Aeneid* that evokes the idea of ancient lineage. The royal yachts were built for speed, but always sumptuously fitted with special decorative carving and gilt. Costing £1815, the *Anne* was 52-feet long, of 100-tons burden, and displayed typically intricate decoration, not least in this coat of arms. [JD]

LITERATURE: Gavin, *Royal Yachts*, pp.51–56; Naish, *Royal Yachts*, p.2.

200
Coat of arms of William III

Late seventeenth century
Painted wood, 610 × 700 × 100 mm

National Maritime Museum, HRA0014

This coat of arms was a fixture at the Commissioner's Office at Deptford Dockyard, latterly the Superintendent's Office. Deptford was a bastion not just of political and naval administration, but also of royal power. The Commissioner was the senior official at the yard, holding an important political position. As such, the carving of this exquisite coat of arms in his offices tells us much about the growing importance of the Royal Navy. The coat of arms was made during the reign of William III (1688–1702). The Dutch-born King did little to change the royal arms, adding only an escutcheon of Nassau, a golden lion rampant on a blue field, seen at the centre. [JD]

201

A List of all the Ships and Vessells of His Majesties Royal Navy, with their Rates, Numbers of Men and Guns in Peace and War

1714/15
ADMIRALTY OFFICE
Paper and ink, 235 × 185 × 15 mm

Royal Collection, RCIN 1081229

George, Elector of Hanover, was crowned King of Great Britain on 20 October 1714. This list was drawn up for him in December 1714 and January 1715 in an attempt to comprehend fully the size and quality of his primary military arm. The Admiralty was happy to oblige, partly for its own administrative purposes, but also as an opportunity to demonstrate the power and importance of the Navy. This was a politically charged issue, with rival proponents of naval force and Continental armies at loggerheads. Despite the Duke of Marlborough's recent conquests in Europe, British national interests were tethered to the Royal Navy, which prevented invasion, protected trade and, thus, advanced national wealth. Widespread concerns over permanent standing armies made the Navy more politically acceptable to a nation that still remembered Oliver Cromwell with unease. George would have taken comfort from what he read in this list, which details a navy with numerous first- and second-rate ships, capable of operations in home and foreign waters.
[JD]

202

Model of a royal yacht

c. 1690
Wood, brass, mica, gilt,
1035 × 1280 × 400 mm, scale 1:32

National Maritime Museum, SLR0378

This full-hull Navy Board model of a late-Stuart sailing yacht is similar in design to royal yachts of the period, although it has not proved possible to identify the exact vessel it represents. The model shows the highly decorated, gilded stern carvings and figurehead typical of the period. It was re-rigged in the 1930s, when the sails were added. [RB]

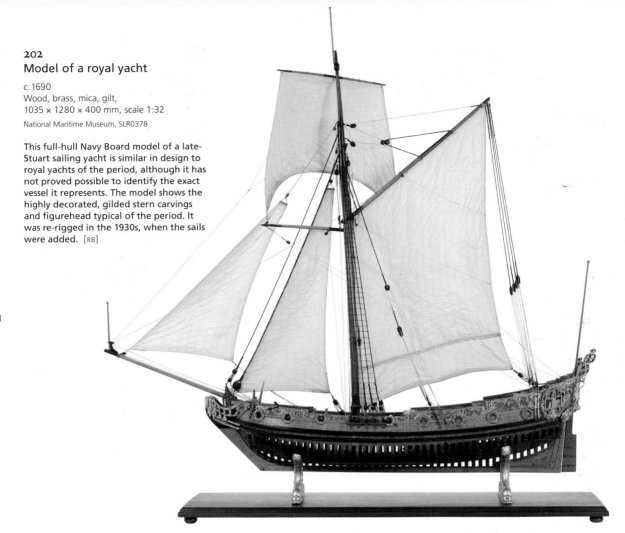

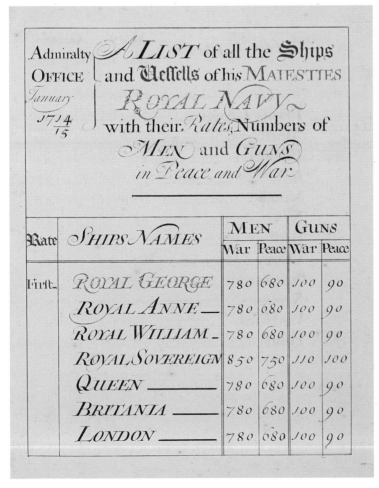

Admiralty Office	A LIST of all the Ships and Vessells of his MAJESTIES ROYAL NAVY with their Rates, Numbers of MEN and GUNS in Peace and War			
January 1714/15				

Rate	SHIPS NAMES	MEN		GUNS	
		War	Peace	War	Peace
First	ROYAL GEORGE	780	680	100	90
	ROYAL ANNE	780	680	100	90
	ROYAL WILLIAM	780	680	100	90
	ROYAL SOVEREIGN	850	750	110	100
	QUEEN	780	680	100	90
	BRITANIA	780	680	100	90
	LONDON	780	680	100	90

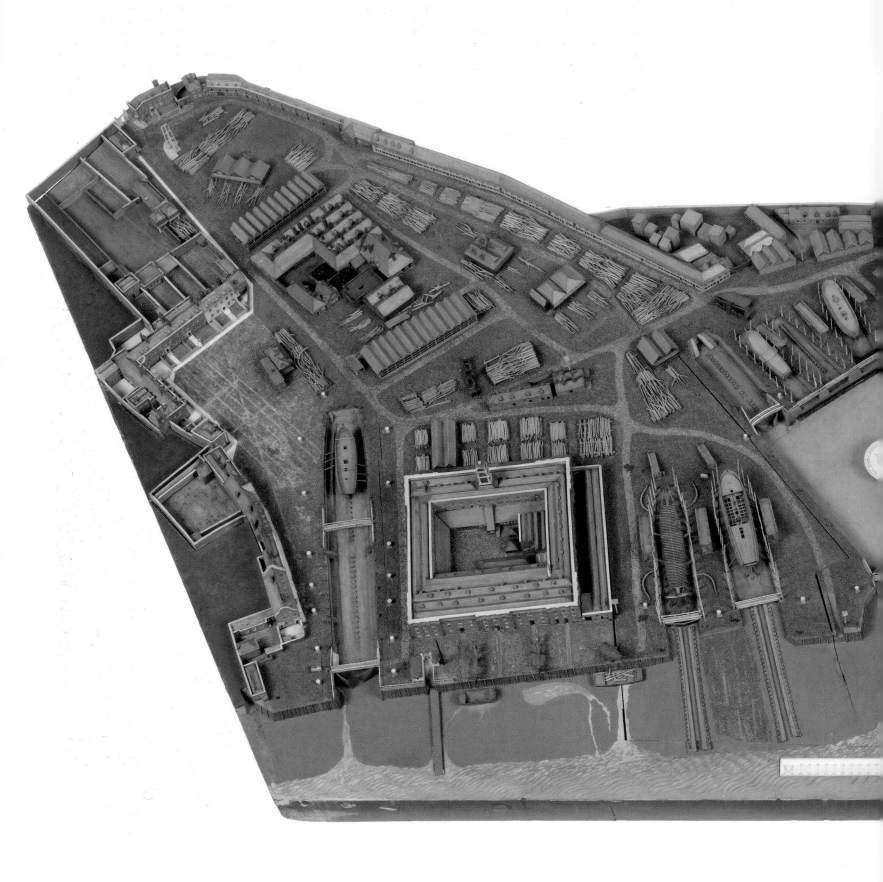

203
Model of the Royal Dockyard at Deptford

c. 1774
Made by THOMAS ROBERTS (shipwright)
and WILLIAM REED (joiner)
Wood, paper and metal,
170 × 1628 × 915 mm, scale 1:576

National Maritime Museum, SLR2906

Deptford was the fourth largest of the royal dockyards by the 1770s and the headquarters of the naval transport service. This model gives a good impression of its scale and extent, allowing the viewer to imagine the hive of activity there. It was one of six models of the royal dockyards commissioned by the Admiralty under the fourth Earl of Sandwich between 1772 and 1774. They were all presented to George III in an attempt to raise the King's awareness of, and interest in, the Royal Navy. The model clearly illustrates the process of shipbuilding with

barges carrying unprocessed timber, still in the round, being unloaded by cranes. This was then sent to the various areas of the yard for seasoning, sawing, drying and storage, prior to use in the construction of the hull of a warship. The key stages of shipbuilding are shown across the model, ranging from a keel on the blocks, a hull in frame and, finally, a fully planked hull on a slipway and in a dock. As well as the construction and fit-out of the hull, the masting and rigging were also undertaken by dockyard workers. The masts were delivered by river aboard specially

designed ships, unloaded and floated in through channels at high tide and then stored underwater in the mast ponds for seasoning. Two large sheets of mica have been used to simulate the water in the ponds on the right-hand side of the model. On the left-hand side are various buildings, including the living accommodation of the Master Shipwright and dockyard officers complete with walled gardens. [SS]

LITERATURE: Graves, *George III's Miniature Dockyards, passim*; Lavery and Stephens, *Ship Models*, p.155.

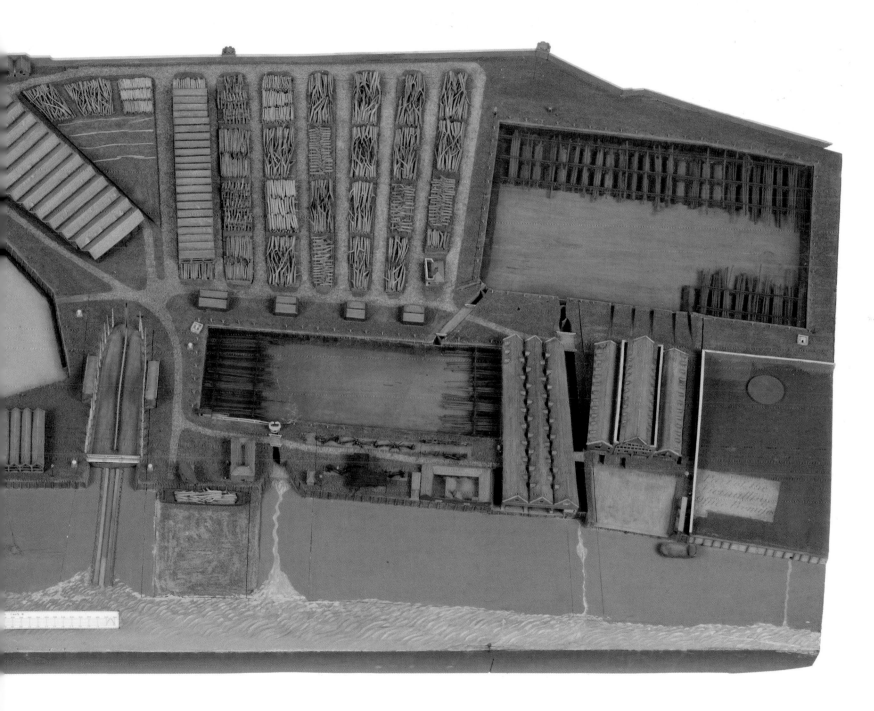

204
Admiral of the Fleet's baton presented to HRH William Henry, Duke of Clarence, 1821

Inscribed around the base of the baton: 'From His Majesty GEORGE IV King of the United Kingdom OF GREAT BRITAIN & IRELAND TO FIRST ADMIRAL OF THE FLEET, His Royal Highness WILLIAM HENRY, Duke of Clarence K.G. 1821.'
JOHN NORTHAM (for Rundell, Bridge & Rundell), London
Gold, velvet, 525 × 45 mm

National Maritime Museum, PLT0025

William Henry, the third son of George III, entered the Royal Navy at the age of thirteen, joining the *Prince George* as a midshipman in 1779. However, he soon showed his incapacity for high command at sea and his naval career largely came to an end when he was created the Duke of Clarence in 1790. His role as Admiral in 1798 was largely titular; he was never given command during the French Revolutionary and Napoleonic Wars. In 1811 he was appointed to the honorary position of Admiral of the Fleet and in 1827 to the more active office of Lord High Admiral, a post last occupied in the previous century. In this position William had repeated conflicts with his Council and he was eventually dismissed in 1828. For most of his reign William IV was nicknamed the 'Sailor King'.

This baton dates from his time as Admiral of the Fleet. The body of the baton was covered with blue velvet, of which only the black backing has survived. Small gold lions are mounted on the velvet in four straight lines. Batons of Admirals of the Fleet were the same in appearance as those for Field Marshals, the latter being covered in red rather than blue velvet. However, only four Admiral of the Fleet batons were ever made, and these were presented by the sovereign on special occasions as a personal honour. [JD]

205
Figurehead from the Royal Yacht *Royal Charlotte*

1824
Painted wood, 2159 × 1118 × 1295 mm

National Maritime Museum, FHD0097

While the exuberant carved decoration of the Stuart royal yachts gave way to a slightly more subdued look in the Georgian period, the figurehead remained as a richly decorated component that signalled the importance of these vessels. The figureheads of two royal yachts are preserved in the collections of the National Maritime Museum. That of the *Royal George* (1817) shows George III wearing a laurel wreath in the guise of a Roman emperor with two kneeling African supporters on either side. His wife, Queen Charlotte, is depicted here in the exceptionally fine figurehead of the *Royal Charlotte*, launched at Woolwich in 1824. She is shown as a young woman wearing a crown and carrying an orb and sceptre with attendant cherubs; to her right is the Hanoverian coat of arms with the Union flag to the left. The *Royal Charlotte* was seldom used and broken up only eight years after its launch. [RB]

GEORGE IV'S VISIT TO SCOTLAND, 1822

In August 1822, George IV left London by royal yacht on a three-week progress to Edinburgh. While all royal visits involved a certain pomp and ceremony, this particular tour was markedly different. The affair, a quasi-military Highland fantasy, was meticulously stage-managed by Sir Walter Scott. In many respects, the 'King's Jaunt' was the first 'modern' royal visit, containing a series of 'set-piece' events, designed both to allow the King to be seen by the public and to present him as the central figure in the spectacle of monarchy. While the image of the monarchy has certainly changed since the somewhat turbulent reign of George IV, the format of royal engagements continues to reflect the pattern set by the extraordinary Scottish visit of 1822. [RB]

206 (far left)
Bust of George IV

1826–27
SIR FRANCIS LEGGATT CHANTREY (1781–1841)
Marble, 813 × 635 mm
National Maritime Museum, Caird Collection, SCU0024

Chantrey's bust of George IV (1762–1830) was commissioned by the Duke of Devonshire in 1821. It was exhibited at the Royal Academy the following year and became an immediate success, with many requests for copies. The bust was also used by William Wyon as the profile portrait for new coinage. This example, the eleventh copy, was completed in 1827 at a cost of 200 guineas; it was presented by the King to Frederick Robinson, the Chancellor of the Exchequer. [RB]

LITERATURE: *Oxford DNB*; 'The Chantrey ledger', pp. 166, 207.

207 (left)
Bust of Sir Walter Scott

1841
Studio of SIR FRANCIS LEGGATT CHANTREY
Marble, 762 mm (height)
National Portrait Gallery, NPG 993

Chantrey became the most celebrated British sculptor of the early nineteenth century. His bust of Sir Walter Scott, (1771–1832) commissioned in 1820, was one of his most popular. Chantrey liked to observe his sitters informally, and requested that Scott 'should breakfast with me, always before sittings, and never come alone, nor bring more than three friends, and they should all be good talkers'. Scott warmed to Chantrey, describing him as 'a right good John Bull, blunt and honest and open without any of the nonsensical affectation so common amongst artists'. This bust is a late copy delivered after Chantrey's death; the original is at Abbottsford, Scott's ruinously expensive Scottish home near Melrose. [RB]

LITERATURE: *Oxford DNB*; 'The Chantrey ledger', pp. 136–37.

208
Embarkation of George IV for Scotland

1822
ROBERT HAVELL (*fl.* 1808–37)
Watercolour on paper, 241 × 374 mm

Royal Collection, RL 20268

On 10 August 1822, the King departed for Scotland on board the *Royal George*. Huge crowds gathered at Greenwich, pressed against the Hospital railings and along the riverfront, to witness the event, but so vast was the assemblage that few caught a glimpse of the King or even the yacht. Havell's watercolour captures the scene, showing the scale of the crowd. City barges attended the yacht, as did the steamers *Comet* and *James Watt*, which were to tow the *Royal George* out to sea.

The King was greeted enthusiastically with cheers. There was, however, some misunderstanding over the time of departure and George IV, eschewing a 'collation' in the Hospital, immediately proceeded to the water gate to board the royal barge. This was potentially a tricky manoeuvre for the rather portly monarch, but all went well as *The Times* reported (12 August):

> The royal barge was admirably manned, and the precision with which she was pulled, there being 14 oars, was at once imposing and surprising. Her head was run over the lowest step, and the King was thus enabled to step into her with the utmost ease.

Regal dignity intact, the voyage to Scotland began. [RB]

LITERATURE: Prebble, *The King's Jaunt*, pp. 159–63.

209
Glass reputedly used at a banquet to celebrate the visit of George IV to Scotland

1822
Engraved with a crown and wreath of thistles
LEITH GLASS WORKS
Glass, 120 × 95 mm

National Museums Scotland, H.MEN 35

The civic banquet held in the Great Hall of Parliament House in the Old Town of Edinburgh was an extravagant affair. Three hundred guests attended: all men. A vast and varied amount of food and drink was served: turtle and grouse soups, stewed carp and venison, roast grouse and chicken, sole, veal, pigeon pâté, vol-au-vents, hams, haggis, hodge-podge and sheep's head. The King ate delicately and drank Moselle wine, champagne and claret. He retired before the last of the forty-seven toasts was drunk from glasses especially made for the event. [RB]

LITERATURE: Prebble, *The King's Jaunt*, pp. 314–16.

210 (right)
£5 banknote
c. 1822
LEITH BANKING COMPANY
Printed paper
National Museums Scotland, H.OIA 69

211 (see fig. 24 / page 232)
One Guinea banknote
1825
LEITH BANKING COMPANY
Printed paper, 139 × 113 mm
National Museums Scotland, H.OIA 68

212 (centre)
Dish with bust of George IV
c. 1822
Earthenware, 160 × 140 mm
National Museums Scotland, A.1889.141

213 (below)
Figurine of George IV
1822
RATHBONE'S POTTERY, Portobello, Midlothian
Earthenware, 152 × 105 × 55 mm
National Museums Scotland, H.1993.3

214 (below right)
Jug depicting the Genius of Scotland presenting the Scottish crown to George IV
c. 1822
Earthenware, 140 × 95 mm
National Museums Scotland, H.1938.500

Such was the popular impact of George IV's visit to Scotland that commemorative wares abounded. The King was depicted on hastily produced ceramics, some of which bore very little, if any, resemblance to the monarch. Banknotes showed George's arrival at Leith, an event marred by poor weather but marked by enormous crowds of people who displayed genuine enthusiasm. [RB]

215
Tartan suit made for George IV's visit to Scotland
c. 1822
Suit owned by Donald Munro Ross
Woollen textiles, 1000 × 640 mm
National Museums Scotland, H.1992.1829.3

The wearing of tartan by members of Scottish society presented to the King at a number of specifically 'Highland' events was an essential component of Sir Walter Scott's vision for the visit. Highlander and lowlander alike were to be clad in plaid, building upon a gradual revival of tartan in the early nineteenth century, which now received an astonishing boost. This continued during Victoria's reign: annual trips to Balmoral put Scotland firmly on the royal map. [RB]

THE ARRIVAL OF A ROYAL BRIDE

216

The landing of H.R.H. the Princess Alexandra at Gravesend

1864
HENRY NELSON O'NEIL (1817–80)
Oil on canvas, 1321 × 2134 mm
National Portrait Gallery, NPG 5487

O'Neil's painting shows the royal couple on the festively decorated Terrace Pier at Gravesend processing towards the viewer. Princess Alexandra, travelling to Britain on the royal yacht *Victoria and Albert II*, was greeted by a large welcoming committee, including the Mayor of Gravesend and several girls dressed in white and red, scattering flowers. Albert and Alexandra were accompanied by members of the Danish royal family. The artist, who also included himself in the picture, took the principal figures from life studies and, in case of the Danish royal family, from photographs. The painting was exhibited at the Royal Academy in 1864. A much smaller version exists in the National Maritime Museum's collection. [JGM]

Princess Alexandra of Denmark (1844–1925), the eldest daughter of the heir to the Danish throne, became the bride of Albert Edward, Prince of Wales (1841–1910) in 1864. The marriage was largely engineered by Albert's sister, Victoria, the Crown Princess of Prussia, who thought Alexandra 'outrageously beautiful' and introduced the couple to each other at Speyer in The Palatinate in September 1861. Albert proposed the following year. Queen Victoria had initially considered the Danish match to be unsuitable for her heir, but she was soon won over by the Princess's charm and beauty.

A few months after she accepted Albert's proposal, Alexandra travelled to England for the wedding. She embarked on the royal yacht *Victoria and Albert II* at Flushing, and found her cabin filled with roses sent by her husband-to-be. Escorted by two warships, the royal yacht arrived at Margate on 6 March 1863, where Alexandra accepted an address of welcome from the Mayor and Corporation and received the admirals and captains of the Royal Navy. The next morning the yacht landed at Gravesend, where Alexandra was met by the Prince of Wales. Their marriage took place on 10 March but in St George's Chapel, Windsor, not in London, because the Court was still in full mourning for the Prince Consort who had died in December 1861. Nonetheless, crowds had the opportunity to see the royal couple when a carriage procession rode through London. They spent their honeymoon at Osborne House on the Isle of Wight.

The marriage was a success, despite Prince Albert's extra-marital affairs. Princess Alexandra bore six children, and the couple spent time together at their homes in Sandringham and London. They also travelled together on royal cruises. However, a bout of rheumatic fever contracted while Alexandra was pregnant with her third child brought on a deafness inherited from her mother and resulted in the Princess's withdrawal from the lively social scene she had previously enjoyed. Consequently the royal couple came increasingly to lead separate lives. [SD]

217
Panorama of Princess Alexandra's Arrival and Public Entry into London

1863
Coloured print on paper, 19 sheets, each sheet 120 × 140 mm

London Metropolitan Archives, 18973630

The arrival of a royal bride was a popular event, and Alexandra proved to be a popular figure. This panorama of Princess Alexandra's arrival at Gravesend and procession into London was one of the many souvenirs available to commemorate the occasion. The nineteen panels of the panorama follow the royal couple into London and to the wedding ceremony at Windsor. Although Alexandra arrived in England by sea, she travelled to London by royal train. [AM]

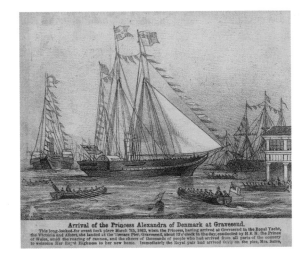

Arrival of the Princess Alexandra of Denmark at Gravesend.

Presentation of a Bouquet of Flowers by the Mayoress of Gravesend.

218
A Welcome to Her Royal Highness the Princess of Wales

1863
ALFRED, LORD TENNYSON (1809–92);
illustrated by OWEN JONES (1809–74)
Pinhead grain cloth binding, colour lithographs, 300 × 220 mm

Royal Collection, RCIN 1054596

Upon her arrival at Gravesend and at her official entry into London, Alexandra was ceremonially presented with a number of illuminated addresses by local dignitaries. This 'Ode of Welcome' was composed by Poet Laureate, Alfred, Lord Tennyson, and illustrated by Owen Jones. One of the most influential designers and architects of his age, Jones was a pioneer in the chromolithograph process used to illustrate this address. *The Times* published the ode on 10 March 1863, the day of the royal wedding. It begins: 'Sea-kings' daughter from over the sea, Alexandra!/ Saxon and Norman and Dane are we,/ But all of us Danes our welcome of thee, Alexandra!' [AM]

219
Bonnet worn by Princess Alexandra on her arrival in England

1863
Lace and artificial roses

Royal Collection, RCIN 71913

An account in *The Times* (9 March 1863) of the Princess's official arrival noted that, at first, she was dressed entirely in white, which gave her a very young and girlish appearance. Before disembarking, she changed her clothing and 'now wore a mauve-coloured silk with a richly embroidered violet velvet mantle'. Her lilac mantle was of Irish poplin, the colour indicating half-mourning for Albert, the Prince Consort. She also wore this bonnet, trimmed with roses, which she had made herself. Alexandra was raised in a relatively modest environment, and she and her sister Dagmar, later Empress Maria Feodrovna of Russia, regularly made their own bonnets and clothing. [AM]

220
Badge of the Order of Victoria and Albert (First Class)

Cameo by T. SAULINI, 1862–63;
mount by R. & S. GARRARD, 1864
White on brown sardonyx, silver-gilt, enamel, diamonds, rubies, emeralds, and silk, 85 × 44 mm

Royal Collection, RCIN 441446

An award of merit for noble ladies, the Royal Order of Victoria and Albert was created by Queen Victoria in 1862. It was limited to forty-five holders, including the Queen, at any one time. The first-class order, of which this is an example, was only for female members of the British royal family; it features a sardonyx cameo set with precious stones and suspended from a white moiré ribbon. Alexandra was appointed to the order the day before her marriage, and wore this badge on the sleeve of her wedding dress. No further awards of the order were made after Queen Victoria's death, although it has never been formally abolished [AM]

LITERATURE: Werlich, *Orders and Decorations*, p. 154.

221
Princess Alexandra in her Wedding Dress

1863
DAVID MOSSMAN (1825–1901)
Hand-coloured photograph, 158 × 129 mm

Royal Collection, RCIN 420284

This hand-tinted photograph shows Alexandra in her wedding dress which, like Queen Victoria's, was made of Honiton lace. The flounces were embellished with national symbols: the rose, shamrock and thistle. The dress was adorned with artificial orange blossom and the bridal bouquet had real orange blossoms, white roses, orchids and sprigs of myrtle tied with Honiton lace. According to *The Times*, 'it is … Her Majesty's desire to have myrtle plants raised and kept in the gardens at Osborne from each of the bridal bouquets of the Royal family in remembrance of these auspicious events'. Osborne myrtle continues to be used in royal wedding bouquets. [AM]

222 (opposite, left)

Artificial orange blossom from the bridal wreath of Princess Alexandra

1863
Wax and paper, 75 × 64 mm

Royal Collection, RCIN 54331.a

Alexandra's crown and wedding dress were festooned with artificial orange blossom. The orange flower was a symbol of betrothal made popular by Victoria, who wore a wreath of real orange blossom in her hair and on her dress at her wedding in February 1840. Alexandra and the Prince of Wales were married on 10 March at St George's Chapel, Windsor Castle. As Victoria was in full mourning for her husband, Prince Albert, she witnessed the wedding from the Katherine of Aragon closet in the Castle. Victoria preserved this sprig of orange blossom from the bridal wreath in this envelope, on which she wrote the inscription: 'From Alix's P of Wales Bridal Wreath March 10th/63'.
[AM]

223 (opposite, centre and right)

Wedding favours

1863
Textiles

Royal Collection, RCIN 55807; RCIN 55851

These rosettes were produced to commemorate the wedding of Princess Alexandra and Prince Albert Edward. Combining the Danish flag and the Prince of Wales's feathers, with official portraits of Alexandra and Albert Edward, the favours were produced in red and white – the colours of Denmark – and were worn by onlookers in London and Windsor. An account in *The Times* of Alexandra's arrival at Gravesend, official entry into London and subsequent journey to Windsor also notes that women 'were elegantly dressed and wearing red and white "favours"'.
[AM]

224 (opposite, below)

Princess Alexandra's ivory brisé Danish fan

1863
I.G. SCHWARTZ & SON, with carving by CHRISTIAN CARL PETERS (1822–99)
Ivory, 254 mm (guard length)

Royal Collection, RCIN 25033

The excitement generated by the royal wedding was such that, to mark the wedding day, communities in Britain and Denmark took up collections for gifts for the bride. The ladies of Leeds gave her a diamond bracelet, while those of Edinburgh offered a Celtic brooch. A group of Danish ladies presented Alexandra with this ivory brisé fan, decorated with a conjoined double 'A' cipher for Albert and Alexandra. The pin is set with Alexandra's birthstone, a turquoise, which is also a symbol of true love. Christian Carl Peters was a prominent Danish sculptor. [AM]

225

London Bridge on the night of the marriage of the Prince and Princess of Wales

1863
WILLIAM HOLMAN HUNT (1827–1910)
Oil on canvas, 650 × 980 mm

Ashmolean Museum, A268

Observed from a slightly raised viewpoint, the painting depicts the huge, noisy crowd celebrating the marriage of Prince Albert and Princess Alexandra of Denmark as it pushes across London Bridge into the foreground. The sense of elation and excitement can be picked up from the carefully studied faces of the people moving along the pavement, spilling over the sides and on to the balustrades of the bridge and holding on to the flagpoles, which fly the Danish colours.

While the flags increase the diagonal thrust of the composition, Hunt has also revelled in the pictorial contrast and drama created by the effects of both artificial and natural light. The artist had been present at the celebrations on 10 March 1863 taking sketches; he has included images of himself and friends in the painting. Hunt also designed the frame, which displays elements from the Danish and the British royal arms. [JGM]

FLOATING PALACES OF STATE: THE VICTORIAN AND EDWARDIAN ROYAL YACHTS

226
Model of HMY *Victoria and Albert II*

c. 1855
Painted wood, brass, metal, glass,
430 × 2240 × 440 mm, scale 1:48

National Maritime Museum, SLR0882

This contemporary builder's style model of HMY *Victoria and Albert II* was probably made by the Surveyor's Department of the Royal Navy for discussion with and presentation to Queen Victoria and Prince Albert. It is highly detailed and was put on display in the South Kensington Museum from 1865. It is complete with a full set of boats including the royal barge just forward of the paddle box on the port side, and a pair of the newly invented lifeboats, fitted with internal buoyancy, and located aft off the paddle boxes on either side. On deck is the large dining saloon, which is just forward of the ornate double steering wheel at the stern. Forward of the bridge are a number of smaller skylights for the accommodation below as well as tea houses for taking refreshments on deck. Measuring 300 feet in length by 40 feet in the beam, it had a displacement tonnage of 2479 and was capable of 14¾ knots service speed. During its first voyage in 1855, and on many subsequent occasions, the yacht proved to be a good sea boat that Queen Victoria used extensively. After a major refit in 1868, the royal yacht continued in service until 1901; it was broken up in 1904. [SS]

LITERATURE: Gavin, *Royal Yachts*, pp.129–43, 151; Lavery and Stephens, *Ship models*, p.216.

Queen Victoria and Prince Albert both enjoyed yachting and they cruised every summer along some part of the English coast and occasionally further afield. The royal cruise was not simply for their private entertainment and health, but an integral part of court life and a form of royal progress. At every British port they visited, the royal couple would be greeted by crowds, and the Mayor and Corporation would come aboard to present a loyal address. Their first yacht was a sailing ship, the *Royal George* (1817), but the *Victoria and Albert* (renamed *Osborne* in 1855) – built at Pembroke Dock and launched in 1843 – was the first powered by steam. The *Victoria and Albert II*, also a paddle steamer, was launched twelve years later and remained the Queen's principal yacht for nearly half a century.

Queen Victoria had resisted change as she was used to the familiar surroundings of her beloved *Victoria and Albert II*, now well over forty years old. It proved difficult to persuade the elderly Queen to consider a new yacht, but the notion that the monarch of the world's pre-eminent maritime power should be conveyed to royal engagements in an antiquated paddle steamer became indefensible when the large, lavishly appointed *Standart* entered service for the Tsar of Russia in 1896. Finally swayed, the Queen wrote to her Prime Minister, Lord Salisbury, '*Victoria & Albert [II]* is no longer in accord with our dignity as the head of a great maritime State, and is the subject of continuous comment among our relations on the Continent'. The *Victoria and Albert III* was launched on 9 May 1899, but the Queen never set foot on board. In December 1900, Victoria crossed to Cowes for the last time and she died at Osborne House on 22 January 1901. Her body was brought back to Southsea on the *Alberta* before being conveyed to London by train.

Throughout the reign of Edward VII the royal yacht would usually go on a Mediterranean cruise in spring. The royal party would make for Corfu or Athens where Queen Alexandra would meet her brother King George of the Hellenes. In the summer, the yacht took the Queen to Christiania (now Oslo) so that she could visit her daughter, the Queen of Norway, and then go on to Copenhagen where she would see her Danish relations.

[SD & JG]

227
Launching casket for HMY
Victoria and Albert II

1855
Wood, silver, 80 × 250 × 145 mm
National Maritime Museum, OBJ0228

Launched at Pembroke Dockyard on
16 January 1855 by Lady Milford,
Victoria and Albert II was built a hundred
feet longer than her predecessor to
accommodate the growing size of the
Queen's family. The new yacht was to be
called *Windsor Castle*, but her name was
changed to *Victoria and Albert* at her
launch with the old yacht of the same
name being renamed *Osborne*. The new
yacht's construction was suspended by the
Crimean War and the urgent need for
more small naval ships to be supplied
for the Baltic campaign.

Before it became fashionable to
launch ships by breaking a bottle of
champagne over their bows, the ceremony
consisted of severing a rope that
symbolically held the vessel fast on the
slipway. The chisel and mallet used for this
purpose were contained in a launching
casket and frequently, as in the zebra
wood example here, contained
information about the vessel itself. [JG]

228
Albert Edward, Prince of Wales's uniform on HMY *Victoria and Albert I*

1846
White cotton-duck with blue-jean collar and cuffs, and metal buttons

National Maritime Museum, UNI0293–94

This outfit launched the fashion for children's sailor-suits. The Queen recorded in her diary the first time her son, Albert Edward, Prince of Wales, wore it: 'Bertie put on his sailor's dress, which was beautifully made by the man on board who makes for our sailors. When he appeared, the officers and sailors, who were all assembled on deck to see him, cheered, and seemed delighted.' This entry was included in *Leaves from the Journal of Our Life in the Highlands* (1868), a popular published version of Victoria's diary, which had a section about life on board the royal yacht. [AM]

229
The young Albert Edward, Prince of Wales, in sailor-suit

1846
FRANZ XAVER WINTERHALTER (1805–73)
Oil on canvas, 1273 × 883 mm

Royal Collection, RCIN 404873

The sailor-suit commissioned by Queen Victoria for her eldest son was intended as a surprise for his father, Prince Albert. It was such a success that this portrait was commissioned from Winterhalter, a German artist who first visited Britain in 1842. He became one of the royal couple's favourite painters, creating about 120 works for them. His images of the royal family are some of the best known and sustained their popularity through reproduction in books, in the press and as commemorative pieces. He also painted the aristocratic and royal families of Europe, was court painter to King Louis-Philippe of France and later to the family of Napoleon III. [AM]

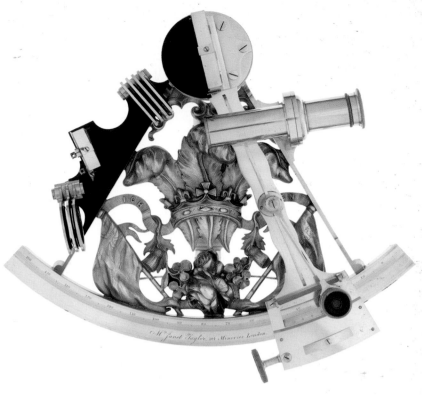

230
Quintant

c. 1850
Inscribed on the limb: 'Mrs. Janet Taylor, 104 Minories London'
JANET TAYLOR (1804–70), London
Silver, gold, ivory, glass, 152 × 170 × 85 mm

National Maritime Museum, NAV1135

When displayed at the Great Exhibition of 1851, this exuberantly atypical navigating instrument was described simply as a 'sextant for measuring angular distances between heavenly bodies'. The Exhibition jury noted, however, that it seemed 'intended for show rather than use'. The costly but impractical materials confirm this and exaggerate the decorative treatment, in which the frame has become the Prince of Wales's crest and is adorned with a British ensign, the Royal Standard and thistles, roses, shamrock and a daffodil to symbolise Scotland, England, Ireland and Wales. Its maker, Janet Taylor, was similarly exceptional – a precociously talented mathematical prodigy who ran a navigation school and warehouse near the Tower of London – and clearly had an eye for the higher prize of royal patronage. Not long after the Great Exhibition, she presented the instrument to Albert Edward, Prince of Wales, then a boy of about eleven. [RD]

LITERATURE: Croucher, 'An Exceptional Woman of Science', *passim*; Croucher and Croucher, 'Mrs Janet Taylor's "Mariner's Calculator"', p.252.

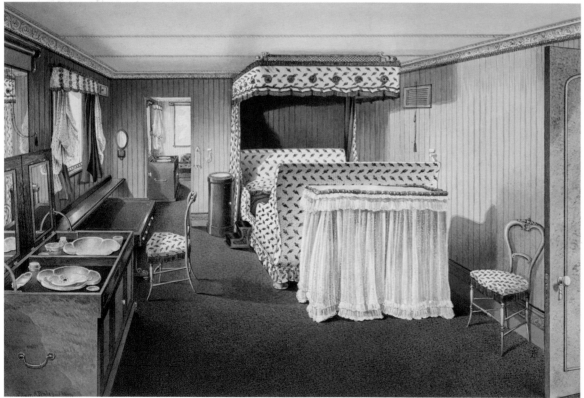

231
The dining saloon on HMY *Victoria and Albert II*

1864
EDWIN AARON PENLEY (*fl.* 1844–90)
Watercolour, 262 × 545 mm

Royal Collection, RL20293

232
The Queen's bedroom on HMY *Victoria and Albert II*

1864
EDWIN AARON PENLEY
Watercolour, 246 × 356 mm

Royal Collection, RL20296

Prince Albert designed the interiors of *Victoria and Albert II* himself, seeking to use new technologies wherever possible. The floors were covered with linoleum and laid with Brussels carpets in red and black when the Queen was on board. Although relatively simple in style, the interiors were very spacious. The dining room was one of the largest on the yacht, measuring 24 by 17 feet. It could comfortably seat eighteen guests. The chairs were mahogany, covered with leather. In this painting, the table is shown laid for eight, and on the sofa on the left is the red box containing official papers.

The Queen's bedroom was fitted with mahogany furnishings and an upholstered and canopied bed. These watercolours by Penley were done after the death of Prince Albert from suspected typhoid. They were intended as a memento of the time he and Victoria had spent together on the royal yacht. The artist's uncle was, at the time, giving drawing lessons to Prince Arthur, which may be why Penley was given the commission for the paintings of the interiors. [AM]

LITERATURE: Millar, *Victorian Watercolours and Drawings in the Collections of Her Majesty The Queen*, vol. 2, pp.688–89; Gavin, *Royal Yachts*, pp.129–34.

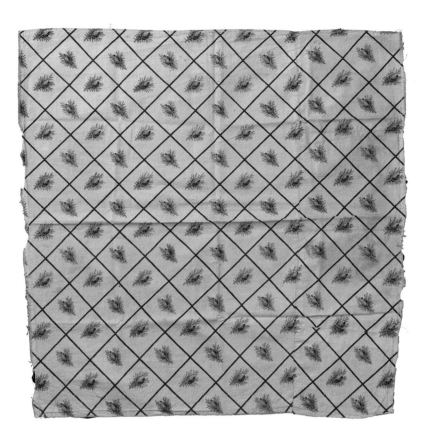

233
Panel of rosebud pattern chintz

1855
MILES & EDWARDS, Bannister Hall Factory,
Preston
Glazed cotton, 490 × 480 mm

National Maritime Museum, TXT0122

Prince Albert personally chose the
furnishing fabric for *Victoria and Albert II*.
Chintz was used as both an upholstery
fabric, specifically in the Queen's
bedroom, and to line the walls in the
drawing room and corridor. Albert
preferred to use relatively plain and
practical fabrics, such as muslin and
chintz. The latter was particularly popular
as changing technologies meant that it
could be brightly printed and, as it was
glazed, it would be hardwearing. [AM]

234
Stern carvings from HMY *Victoria and Albert III*

1899
Wood, various sizes

National Maritime Museum, FHD0130.1–111

Victoria and Albert III was 80 feet longer
than her predecessor, over twice the
displacement and her engines were more
than four times as powerful. She was built
of steel and clad in teak to maintain
a constant temperature within. The
standard of fitting-out was extremely
high, a fact reflected in her total cost of
£512,034. The yacht was commissioned on
23 July 1901; by the outbreak of war in
1914, she had become a highly visible
symbol of British maritime prowess,
making over sixty overseas voyages.
George V used her for the Silver Jubilee
Review of the Fleet in 1935, and she
attended George VI's Coronation Review
two years later. Her refit following the
end of the Second World War included
new cabins for Princess Elizabeth and
Princess Margaret. But the yacht was
never used again and, in October 1951,
the Admiralty announced the building of
a new royal yacht. *Victoria and Albert III*
was broken up at Portsmouth in 1954.
Much of her furniture and many of her
fittings were salvaged and installed in
Buckingham Palace and in the new
royal yacht, *Britannia*. [JG]

LITERATURE: Gavin, *Royal Yachts*, pp. 155–92.

235

The Prince of Wales's Royal Standard from HMY *Victoria and Albert III*

1908
LANE AND NEAVE, London
Silk, 3861 × 7696 mm

National Maritime Museum, AAA0800

The standard is machine-sewn and painted on the right side. It is marked with a maker's name and date. The Prince of Wales in 1908 was the future George V. This standard was flown on the *Victoria and Albert III*. It bears the modern royal arms: the first and fourth quarters show England as represented by three lions passant, the second quarter is Scotland,

symbolised by a lion rampant, and the third quarter contains the harp of Ireland. The white label, or strip, placed across the top of the standard is used for the family of the sovereign, with three points denoting children and five points for grandchildren. That of the Prince of Wales is plain, those of other family members are charged with various devices. [BT]

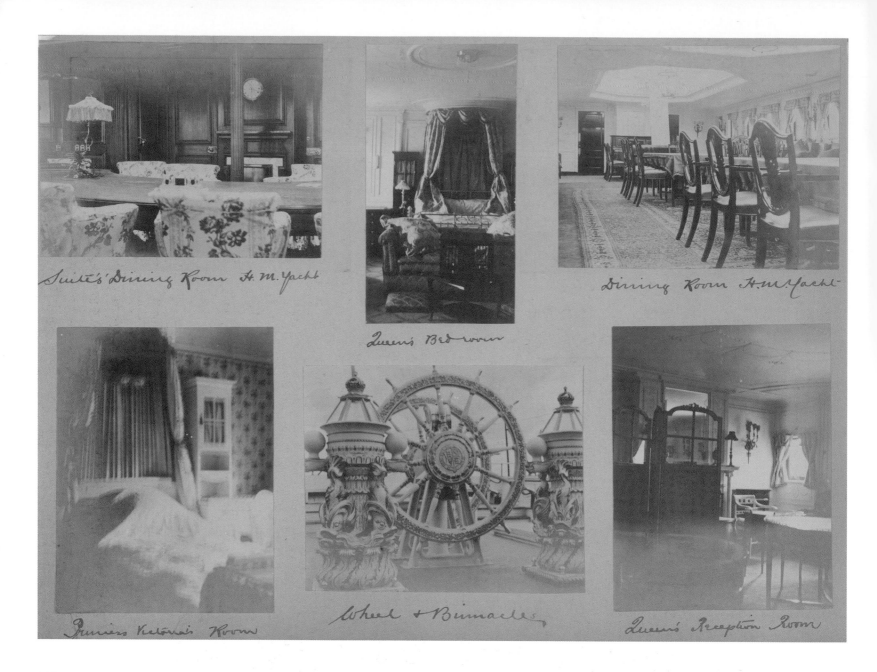

Suite's Dining Room H. M. Yacht

Queen's Bedroom

Dining Room H.M.Yacht

Princess Victoria's Room

Wheel + Binnacles

Queen's Reception Room

236
Photographs of HMY
Victoria and Albert III

Photograph album of LIEUTENANT JOSEPH
HENRY HILL IRELAND, c. 1899–1902 (above)
250 × 336 mm (closed)

National Maritime Museum, X1999.004

Photograph album of SUB-LIEUTENANT
E.W.E. FELLOWS, c. 1909–20 (opposite)
280 × 750 mm (open)

National Maritime Museum, ALB1094

The photographs by Lieutenant Ireland
show HMY *Victoria and Albert III* around
the time of her commissioning on 23 July
1901. They include the bedrooms originally
intended for Queen Victoria and a lady-
in-waiting, the bridge, the magnificent
double steering wheel and binnacles.

The photographs by Sub-Lieutenant
Fellows show how widely travelled the
yacht was in the years before the First
World War. The photographs were taken
in 1909 when the yacht's itinerary consisted

of a spring cruise, Cowes Week and an
autumn cruise, with a review of the fleet
by the King on 2 August accompanied by
Tsar Nicolas of Russia. The photographs
shown here are of the yacht in Christiania
(Oslo) with members of the British and
Norwegian royal families. The two families
were related through the marriage of
Princess Maud (1869–1938), the youngest
daughter of Edward VII and Queen
Alexandra, to Haakon VII of Norway
(1872–1957). [JG]

Prince Olaf   Princess Victoria   100

Princess Victoria   Prince Olaf   101

Princess Victoria
Prince Olaf   102

Christiania

Roy. Yacht Virian   Miss Knyvett   Hon. Charlotte Knollys   Mty. of Maurice   Queen Alexandra   Prince Olaf   Queen Maud   Princess Victoria   Oct. 1905

Commodore Palmer

237
Binnacle and compass from HMY *Victoria and Albert III*

c. 1817 and 1899
Compass by KELVIN AND JAMES WHITE, Glasgow
Wood, copper, 1510 × 1000 × 670 mm

National Maritime Museum, NAV0352

When the HMY *Victoria and Albert III* was removed from the Navy List in 1954 after over half a century of service, it was seen as the end of an era. For 110 years, three yachts of that name had faithfully served four monarchs and there was a general feeling throughout the nation that the new *Britannia* was uncompromisingly modern and the embodiment of the 'new Elizabethan age'. The *Illustrated London News* (9 October 1954) carried an article entitled 'The end of an old Royal Yacht: stripping H.M.Y. Victoria and Albert'. It specifically mentions, among other treasures re-allocated to various institutions, that the Merchant Taylors' Company was to receive the silver ship's bell, which it had originally presented to the V&A at the beginning of the century.

A binnacle is a casing which supports and protects a ship's compass. The elaborately carved example here is one of an identical pair, originally installed in HMY *Royal George* that had been launched in 1817. Named after the Prince Regent, not George III, the yacht was the epitome of his flamboyant and expensive taste. Queen Victoria used the *Royal George* only once, to visit Scotland in 1842, before a new steam yacht was commissioned. Thereafter the binnacles were transferred to, and used on, successive yachts. This one was last used on HMY *Victoria and Albert III*, housing a compass made by the firm of Kelvin and James White, to patent no. 7376, taken out by Sir William Thomson, later Lord Kelvin. The twin to this binnacle was installed on the veranda deck of HMY *Britannia* in 1953 and fitted with a repeater from the yacht's gyro-compass. The ship's wheel follows the same decorative scheme as the binnacle and other wheelhouse fittings for the yacht.
[JG]

238
Electrical appliances from HMY *Victoria and Albert III*

1910–11
Fire (centre); kettle, engraved with the cipher of George V; coffee percolator; curling tong warmer; cigar lighter; saucepan; switch; kettle, engraved with the cipher of Edward VII (items left to right)
Fire: copper, glass; other items: silver, Bakelite, various sizes

Royal Naval Museum, 1994.129.1–8

Despite initial reservations, in the nine years of his reign, Edward VII made extensive use of HMY *Victoria and Albert III*, visiting many ports both at home and on the Continent. The combination of speed, elegance and comfort was exploited to the full by the King and Queen Alexandra. The yacht was seen frequently during Cowes Week where she had her own moorings. The accommodation for guests, comprising fourteen cabins, was luxurious but not ostentatious and there were an additional seven cabins for maids

and valets. The yacht generated its own power supply and the very latest electrical gadgets were available for the convenience of the royal party and its guests. Electric heaters kept cabins warm and cosy, with the teak cladding of the hull providing good insulation. Queen Alexandra continued regularly to use the yacht after the King's death in 1910, which included her annual excursions to Copenhagen and her last cruise to the Mediterranean in the spring of 1911. [JG]

239

Chinaware used on the royal yachts

Edward VII inherited no fewer than five royal yachts from Queen Victoria. But whereas the Queen had, in her later years, used them as a fleet of comfortable and largely private homes, the King loved entertaining. He was an amiable, albeit a highly demanding, host and standards for His Majesty were as high on HMY *Victoria and Albert III* and the smaller, elderly, royal yachts *Osborne II* and *Alberta* as they were in any of the royal residencies ashore. Large dinner parties consisting of around a dozen courses accompanied by an equally impressive wine list were frequently held in the *V&A*. Gentlemen would be attired in white tie and tails, and wearing their decorations, while ladies were adorned with, according to one commentator, 'every rock in the book'. Among the thirty or so servants was an Arab boy whose sole job was to provide the King with his favourite coffee. Though the furnishings changed very little during George V's reign, on his accession the yacht was naturally supplied with additional china and porcelain bearing His Majesty's cipher. [JG]

(a)

Coffee pot

c. 1891
COALPORT PORCELAIN WORKS, Shropshire
Porcelain, 215 × 225 × 160 mm

National Maritime Museum, AAA5384

This floral coffee pot was used by Queen Victoria on the royal yacht *Alberta*. It was part of a service purchased from J. Whitman of Cowes on the Isle of Wight. [RB]

(b)

Tureen with lid and stand

Early twentieth century
ROYAL CROWN DERBY PORCELAIN COMPANY
Porcelain, various sizes

National Maritime Museum, AAA5413

This white and gilt dinner service was first used by Edward VII on *Victoria and Albert III*, with a similar set employed on HMY *Alberta*. As with other services, it was added to by subsequent monarchs: George V in 1911 and George VI in 1939. [RB]

(c)

Coffee cup and saucer and sugar-bowl

Early twentieth century
MINTON, Stoke-upon-Trent; W.T. COPELAND
& SONS, Stoke-upon-Trent
Porcelain, various sizes

National Maritime Museum, AAA5412, 5418–19

This dessert service, originally from the Minton factory, was used by Edward VII on HMY *Osborne*. It is decorated with royal ciphers and gilt rope twists on a green reserve. When George V acceded to the throne in 1910, the set was supplemented with new pieces, bearing his cipher 'GRV', purchased from the London retailer G.T. Goode & Sons. [RB]

240
Glassware used on the Royal Yacht *Alberta*

1891–1901
Glass, various sizes

National Maritime Museum, GGG0245–46, 0248–49, 0253, 0256, 0258, 0271

Most of the items here are known to have been used in HMY *Alberta*, a paddle yacht, launched in 1863. The decision to build the yacht with paddle wheels rather than a propeller was taken largely because the former method of propulsion would be far more stable. A lack of motion was particularly important for Queen Victoria who could take several days to recover from a rough passage. Stability was especially important on occasions of formality and dignity, such as the great naval review at Spithead on a squally day in July 1867 where one of the guests in the *Alberta* was the Sultan of Turkey. He was a poor sailor, but received the Order of the Garter from Her Majesty at sea; the ceremony was followed by luncheon for sixteen in the deck saloon.

The glasses here are all elegant but substantial, with goblet-like bowls and heavy feet; while the decanters are tall, they have a low centre of gravity and thick bases. [JG]

A MODERN ROYAL PROGRESS TO GREENWICH, 1937

On 27 April 1937, George VI, Queen Elizabeth and the eleven-year-old Princess Elizabeth boarded the motor barge of the Commander-in-Chief of the Nore at Westminster Pier. Their destination was Greenwich and the opening of the new National Maritime Museum. The royal barge was escorted by four torpedo boats and led by a Port of London Authority launch. As *The Times* reported the following day:

> The Thames has had little of pageantry in its recent history, and until yesterday there had not been since 1919 anything in the nature of a Royal progress along London's river. The people of London enjoyed the occasion. It was impressive rather than picturesque. Many people who looked on at yesterday's procession remembered the grand old Royal barge, with its long scarlet oars. It had given place to the severely practical barge of a modern navy. With the change there had gone a great deal of the picturesqueness of river pageantry, but the swift relentless machine that had come on the scene was impressive in its efficiency and wonderful movement. Of the thousands of persons who looked across Westminster Bridge and over the embankment parapets, few seemed able to realise that the King and his escort were out of sight in a few seconds. The modern age of mechanical transport seemed to have intruded into the traditions of Thames pageantry unheralded and with startling suddenness.

A route down the Thames was cleared of shipping, with riverside buildings and moored vessels bedecked in flags and bunting in the April sunshine; the progress was marked by cheers, sirens and large crowds. For the young Princess Elizabeth, the visit to Greenwich was a birthday treat; it was also her first official engagement.

[RB]

241

H.M. King George VI: Address at the Opening of the National Maritime Museum

27 April 1937
Signed: 'George R.I.'
Typescript in leather-bound folder

National Maritime Museum, HSR/V/12

The King gave a short, formal address in the Neptune Hall of the Museum, standing on a dias in front of one of the large Battle of Solebay tapestries from Hampton Court Palace:

> My early life was spent in the Royal Navy and I am glad that the opening of the Museum should be one of the first ceremonies of my Reign. But for the enterprise, the courage and the character of our seamen, the British Commonwealth of Nations would never have come into existence. The qualities of Drake, Nelson and Franklin are as necessary today as ever in the past, and it is well that we should recall the exploits of men such as these, so that the part which our seamen have played in our history may never be forgotten.

Having declared the Museum open, the King and the royal party, which included Queen Mary, toured the galleries before returning to Buckingham Palace by motor car. [RB]

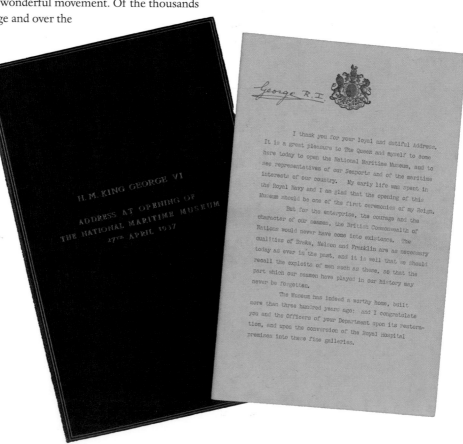

242
Medal commemorating the coronation of George VI and the opening of the National Maritime Museum

1937
SPINK & SON, London
Silver, 57 mm (diameter)

National Maritime Museum, MEC2109

The obverse of this medal shows the King and Queen in profile, both crowned and wearing their coronation robes. The reverse features the Queen's House at Greenwich. A number of commemorative medals were struck to mark the coronation and the opening of the Museum, and in this case both. After the difficulties and considerable strain of the abdication crisis, there was great relief that the coronation was such a huge and popular success. [RB]

243
George VI's full dress uniform of Admiral of the Fleet

1937
Woollen textiles and other materials
Royal Collection, RCIN 104595

Prince Albert, later George VI (1895–1952), embarked on his naval training at Osborne and Dartmouth between 1909 and 1912. He served in HMS *Collingwood* and HMS *Malaya* during the First World War, seeing action at Jutland in 1916. He also trained as a pilot in the fledgling Royal Naval Air Service, becoming one of the first officers of the newly instituted RAF in April 1918. As Duke of York, he concentrated on royal duties. He acceded to the throne upon the abdication of his brother in December 1936. The opening of the National Maritime Museum on 27 April 1937 was one of the first public engagements of the new King. George VI was crowned at Westminster Abbey just over two weeks later on 12 May, the date originally set for the coronation of Edward VIII.

On the uniform are displayed the Sash, Badge and Star of the *Légion d'Honneur*, the Star of the Order of the Garter, the Star of the Order of the Bath, a Sovereign's Badge of the Order of the Bath, the Royal Victorian Chain, and the King's medals. [RB]

THE COMMONWEALTH TOUR, 1953–54

244

No. 2 ratings uniform worn on HMY *Britannia*

1954–97
Woollen and cotton textiles
National Maritime Museum, ZBA0579–82

The crew of *Britannia* consisted of a commander, usually an admiral, twenty officers and 220 yachtsmen. For 'yachtsmen', life was rather different from their fellow seamen in the Royal Navy. They were chosen to meet the highest possible standards of professional service and duty that were required to maintain the yacht in pristine condition. [RB]

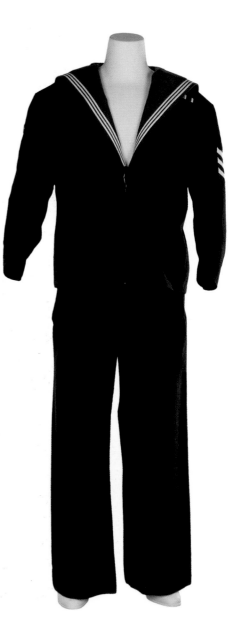

For the new Queen, Elizabeth II, 1953 was a momentous year. On 2 June she was crowned; earlier, on 24 March, her grandmother Queen Mary had died; and on 24 November Elizabeth and her husband, Prince Philip, set off without their children on a six-month Commonwealth tour. A grand royal tour overseas had been in the planning for six years, but the time seemed particularly opportune for a visit to countries of the former British Empire as the Queen had just become 'Head of the Commonwealth' under the Royal Titles Act (3 April 1953). This tour remains the longest of her reign; the royal party visited thirteen countries and covered 43,618 miles – 10,000 by plane, 900 by car, 2500 by rail and the rest by sea. Because HMY *Britannia* was not yet ready, the sea voyages were taken on the ocean liner, the *Gothic*; however, the new yacht *Britannia* met the Queen and Prince Philip at Tobruk in North Africa. On board were Prince Charles and Princess Anne, and the reunited royal family completed the last stage of the journey together, arriving back at London on 15 May 1954 to a grand welcome. Crowds lined the banks of the Thames to see the Queen's return, and a red and white banner was hung from Tower Bridge bearing the words 'Welcome home'. *Britannia* progressed down the Thames to Westminster to the sound of a forty-one-gun salute fired from the Tower of London. At Westminster crowds waving flags greeted the Queen.

The Commonwealth Tour was prominently covered in the British press, newsreels, radio and television. Later in 1954, a film made in colour by British Movietime News was released under the title *Flight of the White Heron*. Its narrative was structured around several traditional themes: constitutional monarchy (the Queen is shown opening parliaments in New Zealand, Australia and Ceylon); her position as head of the Church of England (the royal couple attended church services wherever they went); and the involvement of Commonwealth countries in the Second World War. [SD]

This bowl and stand was presented to
Queen Elizabeth II in Ceylon during her
Commonwealth tour of 1953–54 by
officers of the Department of Agriculture
during a visit to the Royal Botanic Gardens
at Peradeniya. The embossed and chased
silver bowl, supported by elephants, has a
fluted rim and five ivory panels incised in
red with scenes of the gardens. [RB]

NORMAN WILKINSON

246
HMY *Britannia* arriving at Greenwich, 15 May 1954

1954
NORMAN WILKINSON (1878–1971)
Oil on canvas, 762 × 1016 mm

National Maritime Museum, BHC3751,
©Norman Wilkinson Estate

The return of the royal party to London in the new royal yacht *Britannia* provided a fitting climax to their epic Commonwealth tour. Mooring briefly at Greenwich, as so many yachts had done in the past, *Britannia* took on board Queen Elizabeth The Queen Mother and Princess Margaret, before proceeding upstream to a tumultuous welcome. The Queen had been away for six months and the scale and enthusiasm of the reception made it clear that Britain was glad its new monarch was 'home'.

Norman Wilkinson was a prolific marine painter and graphic artist. This painting of the royal yacht at Greenwich was purchased by the Museum in 1954. He also depicted *Britannia* passing under Tower Bridge, a painting now in the Royal Collection. [RB]

ENGLAND'S RIVER: THE THAMES AS A NATIONAL RIVER

JONATHAN SCHNEER

The Thames is unique. Although its meaning has shifted according to time and circumstance, it is inextricably linked to England's sense of itself. No other river can make a similar claim. Either it runs through a nation so large that there can be no national river, or it runs through more than one nation, or it serves as a border between nations. Much of England's history, however, has unfolded on the Thames or within sight of it. As a result: 'The Thames is within us', T.S. Eliot once remarked. 'It is the golden thread of our nation's history', claimed Winston Churchill.[1] It is, in fact, England's river.

During the first century BC the Thames served as a border between rival Belgic tribes. It provided a defensible contour. In the year AD 52, the Belgic King, Caratacus, lined up his soldiers on the north bank of the river, near present-day London Bridge, to face the invading Romans. He thought the water would block or at least impede them. It did not. They came, crossed and conquered.

Nevertheless, the military importance of the river was evident to England's new rulers. They constructed an enormous, brooding fortress at Reculver, overlooking and guarding the estuary. It was 200-yards long and 190-yards wide; its walls were nine-and-a-half-feet thick. The point was never to let invading armies enter the river at all. After the collapse of Roman rule they did enter, however. At one point or another Saxon Angles and Jutes, Viking Danes and Norwegians, all sailed up the river from the estuary, seeking booty or dominion. It had become the pathway to London, now England's largest, richest and busiest port. It was an arrow, albeit a twisty, looping one, aimed at the heart of the nation.

Unsurprisingly, the Norman conquerors of England built additional defences along the river, for example a fortress, west of the great city, upon a bluff that dominated the surrounding countryside – but we have long since ceased to think of Windsor Castle as a military fortress. They built a great tower commanding the immediate approach to the city from the east as well. This Tower of London would come to play its own part in English and riverine history and myth. Later still, Henry VIII built a great military fortress further east, at Tilbury. These imposing structures, modified and embellished over the centuries, were originally meant, in part, to guard the approaches to London.

Still the enemy continued to come, or tried to, or planned to. In 1588, when Phillip II of Spain sent an Armada to win England for the Roman Catholic faith, England blockaded the river with a line of ships. In 1667 the Dutch broke the chain meant to block them in, turned and, bearing fire and sword, penetrated as far as Gravesend. In 1797, amazingly, it was the turn of mutinous British sailors; they had established a 'floating republic' among His Majesty's ships stationed at the Nore near the estuary, and were balanced there upon the knife-edge of revolution. They sent a longboat upriver to Dartford where four additional ships of the line were anchored, hoping to persuade their crews to join the mutiny. As the longboat passed the fort at Tilbury, soldiers within opened fire. Fearing the worst, many Londoners took flight.

As late as the twentieth century the river retained military significance. Before the Second World War, military planners anticipating a German invasion lined the north bank of the river with concrete bunkers commanding a field of fire. Many of them are still there. And during the war, German pilots, much like their Saxon forebears, except at high altitude, traced the river's course from the estuary all the way to the docks and wharfs of East London, where they dropped their bombs and incendiaries. Josef Goebbels, the Nazi Minister of Propaganda, released a photograph meant to depict the imminent defeat of England. It shows the River Thames and London Docks at the mercy and beneath the wings of a Heinkell III (fig.26). (It is now notorious that Goebbels doctored the image, superimposing the aircraft over an aerial photo taken before 1939 when there had been no cover protecting the north terrace of Millwall Football Club's ground.)

So the Thames is a national river in part because it winds right through the most important and perilous moments in English history. Think of the Roman invasion and think of Caratacus and his troops on the banks of the Thames; think of Saxons and Vikings riding the tide up to London; recall Elizabethan England confronting the Spanish Armada and think of the warrior Queen addressing her troops at Tilbury, promising 'to live or die' with them. Think of the Battle of Britain and it is hard not to remember the firestorm unleashed upon the docks and wharfs in East London, and the dogfights carried on 10,000 feet above the winding ribbon of water. At this supremely perilous moment in England's

Fig.26 Heinkel 111 superimposed on a pre-war photograph of the Thames and the London docks.
Imperial War Museum, P20492.

history, Goebbels had tried to conscript the river, to make it stand for all England, laid waste by the aircraft of triumphant Germany.

The Thames winds through English history in a less dramatic fashion as well. Josef Goebbels was not original in thinking that the Thames symbolised all England. Long before he tried it, personages much less objectionable had conscripted the river for their own less-odious purposes. Henry VIII planned for his bride Anne Boleyn to be crowned Queen at Westminster Abbey on 1 June 1533. She travelled there over a few days by stages, and first of all by water, from Greenwich to the Tower of London (an ill-omened destination for her, had she but known it). Henry chose the water route for a purpose.

Early on the sunny afternoon of 29 May, Anne came down to the river from the palace at Greenwich where there waited for her fifty barges of the London livery companies, decorated with flags, banners and bunting draped with gold foil, packed with musicians and cannon. The Lord Mayor's barge was hung with cloth of gold and silver. It displayed thirty-six shields showing the coats of arms of the Tudors and the Boleyns. Many smaller vessels also awaited the Queen-to-be. Accompanied by the most important and sumptuously attired ladies of the Court, Anne, who was even more splendidly garbed than they in a dress of cloth of gold, boarded her own magnificently decorated barge. Additional barges drew up to serve other courtiers. Still more came for the King, his guard, royal trumpets and minstrels. Eventually more than 300 vessels made the journey upstream into the sun, past a long line of anchored sea-going ships that saluted with firing cannon. And when they reached the Tower, the gunners there 'loosed their ordnance', creating a thunderous welcome.

In this instance the Thames provided a flowing stage upon which Henry VIII declared to the world that he would wed whom he chose, whatever the opposition. He had conscripted the river to express his, and accordingly his country's, defiant anti-Catholicism. He had orchestrated a pageant, a spectacle and an unmistakably bold statement. The waterway served as his instrument as well as his stage; he played upon it with great skill.

And he set an example: in 1662, Charles II, only recently restored as England's monarch after decades of civil war, planned to travel downstream from Hampton Court to Whitehall with his bride, Catherine of Braganza. He too wished to make a statement: that his people welcomed the restoration of the House of Stuart, and that the days of the Republic and Protectorate were over. Someone from his court contacted the Lord Mayor of London. The latter then issued the following exhortation to the City's great livery companies: the King 'expects such demonstracion of affection from this Cittie as [previously] hath bin vsual upon so greate & solemne occasione'.[2] The City jumped to obey; indeed it outdid itself in its attempt to please His Majesty.

According to the great seventeenth-century diarist John Evelyn, *Aqua Triumphalis*, as the extravaganza was termed, was

> the most magnificent Triumph ever floted on the Thames, considering the innumerable number of boats & Vessels, dressd, and adornd with all imaginable Pomp: but above all the Thrones, Arches, Pageants & other representations, stately barges of the Lord Major & Companies, with various Inventions, musique, & Peales of Ordnance both from the vessels and shore.[3]

According to another account 10,000 boats had come out, so that the river all but disappeared from view, except for a narrow channel in the middle left open for the King, whose own barge was hung with crimson damask and bore a canopy of cloth of gold supported by Corinthian pillars, themselves wreathed with ribbons and garlands of flowers.

Somewhere 'between Chelsey and Pox-hall' (presumably Vauxhall), as the King's barge glided past them, Thames watermen, who earned their living ferrying passengers along the river, declared their loyalty to the King, just as he had intended they should. They sang in three parts: 'Let sadness flie Boyes, flie; The King and Queen draw nigh.' Further downriver seamen threw 'themselves into severall Antik postures and dances' to honor the royal couple. And then an

Fig.27 *The fair on the Thames, Feby 4 1814*, aquatint engraving, by Luke Clennell, London, 1 May 1814.

National Maritime Museum, PAH9908.

actor portraying Isis, 'Lady of the Western Meadowes and Wife to Tham', addressed them: 'Divinest pair! … Isis (to meet your unmatch'd loves) kisses your Sacred feet.'[4] The actor stood for the river, which stood for the nation. Even Henry VIII had not required such obsequious protestations of submission as this.

The Thames could be conscripted by the common people as well as by royalty; for example, on the recurring occasions when the river froze and all London walked out upon the now stilled and glassy stream (fig.27). Then Thames watermen, unable to ply their ferrying trade, would turn their boats into sleighs and pull people over the ice. Faced with competition from hackney coachmen who drove their horses onto the frozen river, they would erect tents that were often nothing more than blankets draped over crossed oars, but with a fire inside and a vent for smoke, and from these primitive shops they would sell food and drink. London traders would erect more elaborate booths and stalls, and soon entire streets would appear in which nearly anything could be purchased: all kinds of food and drink, both hot and cold, plus 'Earthen Wares, Brass, Copper, Tinn and Iron, Toys and Trifles'. Barbers set up shop; so did whoremasters. Printers brought out their presses. All sorts of entertainments might take place: fireworks, games, gambling, races and rides.

These 'frost fairs' no longer occur, not because of global warming, but because the old London Bridge no longer stands. Before 1831, however, if it grew cold enough, chunks of ice floating downstream might lodge against its nineteen narrow arches, impeding and eventually stopping the tide. Then the river above the bridge came to rest; it stood still, like a great lake; and it might freeze.

The best-chronicled frost fair began in mid-December 1683 and lasted until the second week of February in 1684. 'People

of all quallityes and ages as has hardly ever been seene before' appeared upon the river.[5] Upon the King (the same Charles II who had been honoured by the City of London in 1662) and his royal family, upon men and women with money in their pockets and a little time on their hands, upon enterprising traders with something to sell, the frozen Thames acted as a magnet. Even those entirely without money headed for the river, where at least they could warm themselves in watermen's tents alongside fires mulling wine, heating water for hot chocolate and coffee, roasting meats, and baking pies, gingerbread and pancakes: 'The prentices starv'd at home, for want of coals, / To catch them a heat do flock thither in shoals.'[6] Once warmed, they could emerge to gawk at the hawkers, costermongers, skaters, bowlers, fiddlers, men on stilts, sword swallowers, fire-eaters; at the sliding chairs 'and other devices such as were made of sailing Boats, Charriots and Carrow-Whimbles'. In 1683 a butcher roasted an entire ox upon the glassy river; a showman displayed a menagerie of 'pleasant monkey[s]'; a fox was set loose for the King and companions to hunt. So many 'whimsies on the frozen ice', wrote one poet, 'make some believe the Thames a paradice'.[7]

Not everyone viewed it this way, however. During frost fairs people of all stations crowded together in unaccustomed and dangerous proximity. This worried more than a few. Something of the French charivari, the ritualised carnival when rich and poor exchanged places if only for a day, appeared upon London's river. Democracy had conscripted the Thames, to turn the world upside down.

> … the country squire
> does stand and admire
> At the wondrous conjunction of water and fire;
> Straight comes an arch wag, a young son of a whore,
> And lays the squire's head where his heels were before.[8]

Frost fairs encouraged freedom and licence. They were the opposite of the festivals manufactured by royalty, when a representative of the nation declared that he would kiss His Majesty's feet. Here the atmosphere contained a hint of menace, of class antagonism, the possibility of 'rough music', as it has been termed. Frost fairs reversed nature. Water had ceased to flow and turned hard; men could walk upon it; they could burn hot coals upon it.

> Paradise and hell themselves exchanged places.
> Call fire a Pleasure henceforth, not Doom!
> A fever is become a Wish. We sit,
> And think fall'n angels have one Benefit.[9]

Frost fairs were not simple festivals if they encouraged sympathy for the devil. They were charivaris in the most profound sense. Charivaris writ large.

Like all charivaris, they did not last. Frost fairs disappeared when the weather warmed and nature righted itself, when water flowed, fish swam and boats sailed. Then the natural order, including the social order, reappeared. For an instant, however, frost fairs might offer something unique: a freeze-frame vision of the larger society, including all classes and stations. At these moments the Thames, like glass, had become a mirror to reflect England as it really was. The last frost fair took place in 1814. Already the country's greatest artist had realised that his depictions of life along the Thames also might reflect all England, for better or for worse.

Joseph Mallord William Turner (1775–1851) spent the year 1805 exploring the river, sometimes tramping, usually sailing in a small boat with a little cook-stove and retractable awning to protect him from the elements. He closely and sympathetically observed the men and women who worked near or on the water, recording his impressions in sketchbooks, on canvases and on wooden panels. He did not idealise the scene: some of his sketches depict hungry, weary or disputatious people.

In the main, however, his watercolours of that year are about light on the river, and the sky, clouds and rainbows above it, and the effects of weather upon it. Man-made objects nestle comfortably in the landscape or against the riverbank. Boats float easily over the stream. Usually his men and women, even when they are working, exist in harmony with land and riverscape.

The vision was personal in the sense that Turner portrayed the Thames Valley as the antithesis of London and the Royal Academy, where politicking and intrigue, of which he was heartily sick, prevailed. But the vision was larger, because in 1805 Britain expected yet another invasion, French

this time, under the leadership of Napoleon Bonaparte. In his watercolours, Turner was picturing what he believed needed and deserved defending. In his mind the river and surrounding countryside stood for the national virtues and verities, for England's essential character, indeed for the nation itself.

Forty years later, approaching the end of his career, Turner surpassed himself in depicting all England in yet another painting in which the Thames plays an essential part. This masterpiece he exhibited in 1844 under the title 'Rain, Steam and Speed – The Great Western Railway' (fig. 28). In the painting, a locomotive hurtles forward towards the viewer, over a broad flat bridge resting upon a great arch surmounting the River Thames at Maidenhead. It emerges from a windswept, rain-swept, sun-swept sky that is yellow, white and grey. The landscape behind is indistinct, but we can make out to the left the graceful old bridge still used by pedestrians and horse-drawn wagons, which the pitilessly straight and massive railway bridge has rendered obsolete. To the right is a ploughman bathed in light and on the river itself a small boat, with a figure under an umbrella. He seems to be fishing or sketching. It must be Turner as he had been in 1805. And we know, although it is now covered by accretions of dust and dirt, that Turner added to this scene a hare scampering for its life just in front of the demonic engine. It cannot possibly outrun the mighty machine. It is doomed.

In this single work of art, Turner captured the great transformation wrought upon England by the Industrial Revolution. The human-scaled, slow-paced, nature-determined life on the Thames as he had known it in 1805, and as he recalls it in this canvas, cannot survive the rushing, fiery, unstoppable, inscrutable steam-powered juggernaut that hurtles toward the viewer. He presents this juxtaposition not as tragedy or elegy but as fact. And when we try to imagine England in 1844 we cannot do better than to think of Turner's great painting of a mighty locomotive vaulting the Thames, recalling English life as it once had been and as it now had become.

Finally we turn to another great English artist in whose work the Thames looms large. William Morris (1834–96) owned a house near the Thames in London at Hammersmith and a second home, deeply loved, upriver on one of its westernmost reaches at Kelmscott. The Thames wound through his life, and dreams, and work. His love for it and the surrounding countryside shaped his red-green vision of England's future, his understanding of what England some day might be.

Morris first came to love the Thames when he went up to Oxford in 1856, where it remained largely untouched by the process Turner had depicted so brilliantly twelve years earlier and some thirty miles downstream. Morris would love the river and the land through which it ran all his life: field and forest alike, the golden Cotswold villages along its banks, the arched little bridges that crossed it, the men and women who worked on or near it. This was the Thames that Turner too had loved.

As with Turner in 1805, the river wound through some of Morris's most beautiful art, in his case poetry. To walk or lie in the meadows by the river on a summer's day was as close to heaven as Morris could conceive:

> In this sweet field high raised above the Thames
> Beneath the trenched hill of Sinodun
> Amidst sweet dreams of disembodied names
> Abide the setting of the August sun.
> Here where this long ridge tells of days now done;
> This moveless wave wherewith the meadow heaves
> Beneath its clover and its barley-sheaves.
>
> …
>
> Rest here awhile, not yet the eve is still,
> The bees are wandering yet, and you may hear,
> The barley mowers on the trenched hill.
> The sheep-bells, and the restless changing weir,
> All little sounds made musical and clear
> Beneath the sky that burning August gives,
> While yet the thought of glorious summer lives.[10]

It need not be summer. The house at Kelmscott, which stood almost within sight of the narrowing stream, delighted him equally. He loved nothing better than returning to it from London on a winter night:

> The wind's on the wold
> And the night is a-cold
> And Thames runs chill
> Twixt mead and hill
> But kind and dear
> Is the old house here,
> And my heart is warm
> Midst winter's harm.
> Rest, then and rest,
> And think of the best.[11]

But he could not think only 'of the best', even when he was at Kelmscott. Morris was as aware of the great transformation as Turner had been. Perhaps it affected him more deeply. He could see that the land was being degraded, the river polluted, and the working population exploited. Even the agricultural labourers of Kelmscott village suffered: 'spindle-legged back-bowed men and haggard, hollow-eyed women', whose labour was drudgery because it was involuntary and ill paid. They 'wore down the soil … with their heavy hopeless feet from day to day and season to season and year to year'.[12]

Morris became a socialist. But for him the co-operative commonwealth meant humankind co-operating not simply with one another, but with the land too: nourishing and replenishing it as well as taking from it. In his famous utopian novel, *News from Nowhere* (first published in 1890, forty years after Turner's death), Morris imagines all England as the earthly paradise he had discerned already and fervently hoped to preserve, in the uppermost reaches of the Thames Valley. The river winds through this book, as through Morris's life, and through his vision of the better England to be.

The plan of the book is simple and well known. William Guest (clearly William Morris) awakens one morning in Hammersmith to find himself magically transported into the future. A great change has taken place. 'How clear the water is', he notices when he approaches the riverbank, and plunges in. How quiet is the morning, how different the prospect: 'The soap works with their smoke-vomiting chimneys' have gone, 'the engineer's works gone; the lead-works gone; and no sound of riveting and hammering'. Hammersmith Bridge has been replaced by an idealised version of old London Bridge, with 'stone arches, splendidly solid and as graceful as they were strong; high enough also to let ordinary river traffic through easily', and with quaint and fanciful little shops and houses upon it.

Guest emerges from the water refreshed, as Morris longed to be. He quickly makes friends and discusses with them various aspects of 'the great change' (it occurred in 1952, Guest learns). He falls in love with Ellen, tanned, grey-eyed, tawny-haired, lithe, a 'good fairy' possessing 'a wild beauty'. Together they journey up the river to Kelmscott. They dine at Hampton Court, whose great hall is open to all. They stop at Eton where anyone may learn from its resident scholars. Windsor Castle

has become a combination apartment building and museum. The woods beneath the Cliveden escarpment, which Morris once had judged prissy and 'gamekeeperish', now were wild and beautiful, as they were always meant to be, 'though the trees were clearly well seen to'.[13]

Once Morris had bidden readers to 'Suppose the haymakers were friends working for friends on land which was theirs, as many as were needed, with leisure and hope ahead of them instead of hopeless toil and anxiety'.[14] In *Nowhere* this has become their condition. As he and Ellen travel slowly up the river the men and women they see take pride and pleasure in their work; they are clean-limbed, happy, frank, curious and generous. Moreover the entire riverside, from London to Kelmscott is beautiful and sweet, a 150-mile-long garden made for the pleasure and livelihood of all. The two travellers glide past villages in which no signs of poverty or shabbiness are present, and the buildings are handsome, simple and

functional. They arrive at a great house at Kelmscott unchanged since 1890, because there, at least, no change was necessary. 'Oh me! Oh me!' cries Ellen, giving voice to William Morris's deepest feeling. 'How I love the earth, and the seasons, and the weather, and all things that deal with it, and all that grows out of it – as this [house] has done!'[15]

Then William Guest remembers the haggard, gaunt and dreary agricultural workers of his own day. He half expects them to appear. In a sense they do, for Guest's time in *Nowhere* is drawing to an end. He will awaken to find himself back in the dismal Hammersmith of 1890 soon enough. Still Morris had seen it, the new and better England, and he had shown it to us. It is a country viewed from and characterised by a gleaming, sweet river. Like so many before him, William Morris too had conscripted the Thames. England's river would show us what England can be.

CONTRIBUTORS

Essay authors

Ian Archer is fellow and tutor in modern history at Keble College, Oxford. His research and publications focus on the history of early modern London.

John Bold is senior lecturer in architecture at the University of Westminster. He is the author of *Greenwich: An Architectural History of the Royal Hospital for Seamen and the Queen's House* (2000).

Gloria Clifton is curator emeritus at the National Maritime Museum and formerly head of the Royal Observatory, Greenwich. Her research interests include the Metropolitan Board of Works and, more recently, the history of British instrument makers.

George R. Dalgleish is principal curator of Scottish history at National Museums Scotland in Edinburgh. He has published widely on Scottish ceramics, glass and silver.

Timothy Jenks is associate professor of history at East Carolina University in Greenville, North Carolina. He specialises in eighteenth-century British history and is the author of *Naval Engagements: Patriotism, Cultural Politics, and the Royal Navy, 1793–1815* (2006).

Sarah Monks is lecturer in European art at the University of East Anglia. Her research focuses on art, the sea and empire.

Julie Sanders is professor of English literature and drama at the University of Nottingham. She has edited a number of critical editions of seventeenth-century dramatists; her latest book is *The Cultural Geography of Early Modern Drama, 1620–1650* (2011).

Jonathan Schneer is professor of modern British history at Georgia Institute of Technology in Atlanta. He has published widely on British history and that of London more specifically, including *The Thames: England's River* (2005).

David Starkey is a leading expert on the royal history of Britain and especially of Tudor England. He is the author of numerous books, including, most recently, *Henry: Virtuous Prince* (2008) and *Crown and Country: A History of England Through the Monarchy* (2010). Dr Starkey appears regularly on television, the radio and in the press, presenting major history series and commenting on current affairs.

Simon Thurley is an architectural historian and the chief executive of English Heritage. Among his publications are studies of Somerset House and of the palaces of Hampton Court and Whitehall.

Catalogue contributors

Susan Doran is senior research fellow in history at Jesus College, Oxford. She is the author and editor of many books on the Tudor period, covering religion, foreign policy, marriage and the lives of Henry VIII, Mary Tudor and Elizabeth I. [SD]

Jenny Gaschke-Massey is curator of fine art at Bristol Museum and Art Gallery. Until 2011, she was art curator at the National Maritime Museum. She is editor of *Turmoil and Tranquility: The Sea Through the Eyes of Dutch and Flemish Masters, 1550–1700* (2008). [JGM]

The staff of the National Maritime Museum, Greenwich wrote all the other entries.

Jonathan Betts is senior curator of horology. [JB]

Robert Blyth is curator of imperial and maritime history. [RB]

Gloria Clifton is curator emeritus. [GC]

Quintin Colville is curator of naval history. [QC]

James Davey is curator of naval history. [JD]

Richard Dunn is senior curator of the history of navigation. [RD]

John Graves is curator of ship history. [JG]

Rebekah Higgitt is curator of the history of science and technology. [RH]

Richard Johns is curator of prints and drawings. [RJ]

Margarette Lincoln is deputy director of the National Maritime Museum. [ML]

John McAleer is curator of imperial and maritime history. [JM]

Kris Martin is curator of exhibitions. [KM]

Amy Miller is curator of decorative arts. [AM]

Simon Stevens is curator of ship models. [SS]

Barbara Tomlinson is curator of antiquities. [BT]

Pieter van der Merwe is general editor of the National Maritime Museum. [PVDM]

NOTES

David Starkey
[pp.10–17]

1 Thomas, *Great Chronicle of London*, p.315.

2 *Ibid.*, p.316.

3 *Ibid.*, p.312.

4 Leland, *Collectanea*, vol.4, pp.202, 218, 250.

5 Griffiths, *Reign of King Henry VI*, pp.488–89; Smith (ed.), *Coronation of Elizabeth Wydeville*, p.7.

6 Leland, *Collectanea*, vol.4, p.218; Hall, *Union of the Two Noble and Illustre Famelies*, pp.798–99.

7 Wriothesley, *Chronicle of England*, vol.1, p.44.

8 *Ibid.*, pp.111–12.

9 *Ibid.*, pp.121–24, 143; Starkey, *Six Wives*, p.716.

10 Nichols (ed.), *Progresses and Public Processions*, vol.1, pp.69–72; vol.2, pp.538–39.

11 *Oxford DNB*.

Simon Thurley
[pp.20–25]

1 D'Aulnoy, *Memoirs of the Court of England*, p.311.

Sarah Monks
[pp.26–32]

1 Tytler, *Life of Henry the Eighth*, p.331, closely based on Holinshed, *Third Volume of Chronicles*, p.930.

2 Carley, 'John Leland's *Cygnea cantio*', pp.225–41.

3 Bjorvand, '*Prothalamion*', pp.561–62.

4 Shrank, *Writing the Nation*, p.97.

5 Drayton, third eclogue, in *Idea: The Shepherd's Garland*. See Nichols, *Progresses and Public Processions*, vol.3, p.63; Elton, *Michael Drayton*, passim.

6 Drayton, 'To the River Ankor', *Idea's Mirror*.

7 Drayton, *Poly-Olbion*.

8 Spenser, *The Faerie Queene* (1596), book III, canto XI, *Complete Works in Verse and Prose of Edmund Spenser*, available online at www.luminarium.org/renascence-editions/fqintro.html.

9 Weston-Lewis, 'Orazio Gentileschi's Two Versions of *The Finding of Moses* Reassessed', p.29.

10 Longstaffe-Gowan, 'Brazen Proclamations', pp.54–55; Ogilby and Morgan, *London &c. Actually Survey'd*, where the fountain first appears in outline. See Faber, *Caius Gabriel Cibber*, p.48.

11 Sheppard (ed.), *Survey of London*, vols 33 and 34: St Anne's, Soho, pp.27–36, 42–51, available online at http://www.british-history.ac.uk/report.aspx?compid=41024.

12 Chamberlayne, *Second Parte of The Present State of England*, pp.303–04.

13 Hatton, *New View of London*, vol.2, p.789.

14 Pasquin, *Memoirs of the Royal Academicians*, p.83.

15 Esdaile, 'Bacon's *George III*', p.168.

16 Potts, 'Picturing the Modern Metropolis', pp.28–56.

17 Cordulack, 'Victorian Caricature and Classicism', pp.535–83.

18 Lyles (ed.), *Constable*, pp.184–89.

19 Bronkhurst, *William Holman Hunt*, vol.1, p.200.

20 Nead, *Victorian Babylon*, pp.18–59.

Julie Sanders
[pp.33–37]

1 Samuel Daniel, 'Tethys' Festival', in Lindley (ed.) *Court Masques*, line 2, pp.62–63.

2 *Ibid.*, line 169.

3 Carnegie, 'Galley-foists', p.53, citing the chronicler Edward Hall.

4 Dr Meddus to the Reverend Joseph Mead, 17 June 1625, in Birch (ed.), *Court and Times of Charles I*, vol.1, pp.29–30.

5 *A True Discourse*, sig. E2v; Birch (ed.), *Court and Times of Charles I*, vol.1, p.30.

6 Dr Meddus to the Reverend Joseph Mead, 17 June 1625, in Birch (ed.), *Court and Times of Charles I*, vol.1, pp.29–30.

7 Tatham, *Aqua Triumphalis*, sig. D2r.

8 Shirley, *A Contention for Honour and Riches*, sig. B4v. For a discussion of the same passage, see Hill, *Pageantry and Power*, p.180.

9 Richard Brome, *The Sparagus Garden*, edited by Julie Sanders in *The Complete Works of Richard Brome Online,* general ed. Richard Cave, http://hrionline.ac.uk/brome/.

10 Heywood, *A True Description.*

11 National Library of Wales, Aberystwyth, MS 53086, fol. 12r; Britland, *Drama at the Courts of Henrietta Maria*, p.225.

Ian W. Archer
[pp.80–85]

1 Burton, *Historical Remarques*, p.71.

2 Dekker, *London's Tempe*, sig. B1.

3 Pepys, *Diary*, vol.1, p.277; vol.4, p.356.

4 Leathersellers' Company, Liber Curtes 1, p.56.

5 British Library, Cotton MS, Julius B XII, fols 34v–35r.

6 Dillon, *Performance and Spectacle in Hall's Chronicle*, p.142.

7 London Metropolitan Archives, MS 169692/2, fol.222r, cited by Hill, *Pageantry and Power*, p.157.

8 *Calendar of State Papers Venetian*, XV, p.159.

9 Dekker, *Troia Nova Triumphans*, sig. D1v.

10 Goldsmiths' Company Register H, p.43, cited by Lancashire, *London Civic Theatre*, p.150.

11 Nichols (ed.), *Diary of Henry Machyn*, p.96.

12 Munday, *Chruso-Thriambos*, sig. A3v.

13 Middleton, *Triumphs of Truth*, sig. B1r.

14 Munday, *Triumphs of the Golden Fleece*, not paginated.

15 Munday, *Metropolis Coronata*, sig. A4.

16 London Metropolitan Archives, MS 16969/2, fols 222r, 243v, cited by Hill, *Pageantry and Power*, p.181.

17 Sayle, *Barges of the Merchant Taylors' Company*, p.9.

18 Whittet, 'Barges of the Society of Apothecaries', p.5.

19 Dillon, *Performance and Spectacle*, p.141.

20 Drapers' Company, Bachelors' accounts, fol.88, cited by Hill, *Pageantry and Power*, pp.156–57.

21 Sayle, *Barges of the Merchant Taylors' Company*, p.11.

22 *Ibid.*, pp.24–25.

23 Whittet, 'Barges of the Society of Apothecaries', p.8.

John Bold
[pp.114–20]

1 Porter (ed.), *Survey of London*, vol.44: *Poplar, Blackwall and the Isle of Dogs*, pp.518–19.

2 *Ibid.*, p.522.

3 Quarrell and Mare (eds), *London in 1710*, pp.20–26.

4 Williams (ed.), *Sophie in London*, pp.250–53.

5 *The Penny Magazine*, 9 June 1832.

6 Hibbert (ed.), *Louis Simond*, pp.51–52.

7 James, *Portraits of Places*, pp.219–22.

8 Dickens, *Sketches by Boz*, p.138.

9 Boswell, *Life of Samuel Johnson*, p.284.

10 Hawksmoor, *Remarks*, pp.8, 13, 21–22.

11 *Ibid.*, p.13.

12 Webb, 'The Letters and Drawings of Nicholas Hawksmoor', pp.145, 153.

13 Morris (ed.), *Journeys of Celia Fiennes*, p.131.

14 Hibbert (ed.), *Louis Simond*, p.52.

15 Hawksmoor, *Remarks*, p.24.

16 Gwynn, *London and Westminster Improved*, pp.118–19.

17 Defoe, *A Tour through the Whole Island of Great Britain*, pp.94–95.

18 Bold, *Greenwich*, pp.24–25.

19 *Ibid.*; Crook and Port, *History of the King's Works*, p.328.

20 Thorne, *Handbook*, p.259.

21 Pepys, *Diary*, vol.3, p.63; vol.6, p.169; vol.9, p.485.

22 Jerrold, *London*, p.xxv.

23 Dickens, *Bleak House*, p.1.

24 Soo, *Wren's 'Tracts' on Architecture*, p.153.

Timothy Jenks
[pp.121–27]

1 *The Times*, 15 November 1805.

2 *Sun*, 14 November 1805.

3 *The Times*, 17 December 1805. See also *Naval Chronicle*, 15 (1806) pp.33–34.

4 College of Arms, London, Funeral of Viscount Nelson MSS, fols 87–105.

5 *The Times*, 25 December 1805; *The Times*, 30 December 1805.

6 Charles Lamb to William Hazlitt, 7 January 1806, in Marrs (ed.), *Letters of Charles and Mary Anne Lamb*, vol.2, p.197.

7 *The Times*, 3, 4 and 6 January 1806.

8 *The Times*, 30 December 1805.

9 *The Times*, 9 January 1806.

10 *Ibid.*

11 *Morning Chronicle*, 8 January 1806.

12 *Ibid.*

13 *Naval Chronicle*, 15 (January–June 1806), p.143.

14 Quote from the caption to Rudolph Ackermann's print, 'This Shallop, Which brought the Body of the ever lamented Lord Nelson From Greenwich to Whitehall Stairs…', London, 21 January 1806, National Maritime Museum, PAD3935.

15 *The Times*, 9 January 1806.

16 *Morning Chronicle*, 9 January 1806.

17 Clarke, *Life of Horatio Lord Viscount Nelson*, p.506.

18 *Ibid.*, p.508.

19 *Morning Chronicle*, 9 January 1806.

20 Clarke, *Life of Horatio Lord Viscount Nelson*, p.508.

21 *Gentleman's Magazine*, 99 (1806), p.66.

22 Clarke, *Life of Horatio Lord Viscount Nelson*, p.508. See also *Naval Chronicle* 15 (January–June 1806), p.140.

23 Duncan, *Correct Narrative*, p.396.

24 *The Times*, 9 January 1806.

25 Duncan, *Correct Narrative*, pp.396–397.

26 *The Times*, 9 January 1806.

27 *St James's Chronicle*, 16–18 August 1781.

28 *Oracle*, 31 October 1797.

29 *Derby Mercury*, 18 November 1802; *Morning Chronicle*, 10 November 1802.

30 *Oracle*, 31 October 1797.

31 The 'Regulations to be attended to at Greenwich' are found in the *Morning Chronicle*, 8 January 1806.

32 *Morning Chronicle*, 9 January 1806.

33 *Ibid.*

34 Clarke, *Life of Horatio Lord Viscount Nelson*, p.507.

35 *Morning Chronicle*, 9 January 1806.

36 *The Times*, 1 February 1965, p.8.

Gloria Clifton
[pp.170–75]

1 *The Times*, 18 June 1858.

2. *Punch*, XV, 1848, p.151.

3 The Metropolis Management Act, 1855, 18 & 19 Victoria, C.120.

George R. Dalgleish
[pp.230–35]

1 Mudie, *Historical Account*, p.67.

2 *Ibid.*, p.71.

3 *Ibid.*, p.69.

4 Lockhart, *Life of Sir Walter Scott*, vol.7, p.40.

5 Brown, 'Scott in 1822: p.2.

6 *Ibid.*

7 Lockhart, *Life of Sir Walter Scott*, vol.7, p.59.

8 Caldwell, 'The Re-arming of the Clans, 1822', p.79.

9 *Blackwood's Magazine*, 68 (1822), p.273.

10 Mudie, *Historical Account*, p.132.

11 *Ibid.*, pp.168–74.

12 Myrely, *British Military Spectacle*, p.149, n.80.

13 John Gibson Lockhart, quoted in Prebble, *The King's Jaunt*, p.225.

14 Scott, *Hints*, p.12.

15 *Ibid.*, p.26.

16 Lockhart, *Life of Sir Walter Scott*, vol.7, p.421.

17 Scott, *Hints*, pp.6, 26.

18 Hugh Scott of Harden, quoted in Prebble, *The King's Jaunt*, p.269.

19 Mudie, *Historical Account*, p.131.

20 Quoted in Prebble, *The King's Jaunt*, p.269.

21 Quoted in Brown, 'Scott in 1822', p.5.

22 Mudie, *Historical Account*, p.93.

23 Norman, 'George IV and Highland Dress', p.10.

24 *Ibid.*, p.5.

25 Skinner, 'A Contemporary Account of the Royal Visit to Edinburgh, 1822'.

26 Mudie, *Historical Account*, p.325.

27 *The Scotsman*, Saturday 31 August 1822, p.271, quoted in Cadell, '1822 and All That', p.49.

28 Prebble, *The King's Jaunt*, p.364.

Jonathan Schneer
[pp.276–81]

1 Eliot and Churchill both quoted in Schneer, *The Thames*, p.4.

2 Tatham, *Aqua Triumphalis*.

3 Evelyn, *Diary*, vol.1, p.367.

4 Tatham, *Aqua Triumphalis*.

5 Corbet, *Blanket-Fair*.

6 *Ibid.*

7 Davis, *Frostland*.

8 *Ibid.*

9 Frostiface of Freeseland, *An Account*, p.5.

10 William Morris, *The Earthly Paradise*, 'August'.

11 William Morris, 'For the Bed at Kelmscott'.

12 Morris, *News from Nowhere*, pp.217–20.

13 Schneer, *The Thames*, pp.173–76.

14 *Commonweal*, vol.5, no.182, 6 July 1889, quoted in Salmon (ed.) *Political Writings of William Morris*, pp.426–30.

15 Schneer, *The Thames*, p.177.

BIBLIOGRAPHY AND FURTHER READING

The place of publication is London unless stated otherwise.

Ackroyd, Peter
Thames: The Biography (2007).

Allan, Brian
Francis Hayman (1987).

The Ambulator; or, the Stranger's Companion in a Tour Round London … Comprehending Catalogues of the Pictures by Eminent Artists (1774).

Andrews, David
'Cyclopaedia of telescope makers: part 5', *Irish Astronomical Journal*, 23 (1996), pp. 57–117.

Archer, Michael
Delftware: The Tin-Glazed Earthenware of the British Isles (1997).

Atterbury, Paul (ed.)
A.W.N. Pugin: Master of Gothic Revival (1995).

Baines, Anthony
Non-keyboard Instruments: Catalogue of Musical Instruments in the Victoria and Albert Museum (1998).

Baird, Rosemary
'Letters of Introduction: The Duke of Richmond, Prince Lobkowicz and Canaletto', *The Burlington Magazine*, vol. 149 (March 2007), pp. 182–84.

Barlow, Edward
Barlow's Journal of His Life at Sea … from 1659 to 1703, edited by Basil Lubbock, 2 vols (1934).

Beal, Peter
'Songs by Aurelian Townshend, in the Hand of Sir Henry Herbert, for an Unrecorded Masque for the Merchant Adventurers', *Medieval and Renaissance Drama in England*, 15 (2002), pp. 243–60.

Beasley, David
'Rivercraft: The History of the Goldsmiths' Company Barges', *Goldsmiths' Review* (1992/3), pp. 6–11.

Beddington, Charles (ed.)
Canaletto in England: A Venetian Artist Abroad, 1746–1755 (2006).

Bergeron, David M. (ed.)
Pageants and Entertainments of Anthony Munday: A Critical Edition (New York, 1985).

Bergeron, David M.
'The Christmas Family: Artificers in English Pageantry', *English Literary History*, 35 (1968), pp. 354–64.

Bernard, George W.
Anne Boleyn: Fatal Attractions (2010).

Birch, Thomas (ed.)
The Court and Times of Charles I, 2 vols (1848).

Bjorvand, Einar
'Prothalamion', in *The Spenser Encyclopedia*, edited by Albert C. Hamilton (1990), pp. 561–62.

Black, Jeremy
George III: America's Last King (2006).

Bold, John, with contributions from Peter Guillery, Paul Pattison, and Ann Robey
Greenwich: An Architectural History of the Royal Hospital for Seamen and the Queen's House (2000).

Bold, John
'Comparable Institutions: The Royal Hospital for Seamen and the Hotel des Invalides', *Architectural History*, 44 (2001), pp. 136–44.

Boswell, John
The Life of Samuel Johnson (1906).

Branigan, Keith
Roman Britain: Life in an Imperial Province (1980).

Brewer, John
The Pleasures of the Imagination: English Culture in the Eighteenth Century (1997).

Britland, Karen
Drama at the Courts of Henrietta Maria (Cambridge, 2006).

Brockliss, Laurence, John Cardwell, and Michael Moss
'Nelson's Grand National Obsequies', *English Historical Review*, 121 (2006), pp. 162–82.

Bronkhurst, Judith
William Holman Hunt: A Catalogue Raisonné, 2 vols (2006).

Brown, Iain Gordon
'Scott in 1822: Fugelman of Royalty', *The Scott Newsletter*, 28 (spring 1996), pp. 2–5.

Brown, L.
'Queen Charlotte's Medal for the Recovery of George III', *British Numismatic Journal*, 72 (2002), pp. 183–84.

Bryant, Julius
Finest Prospects: Three Historic Houses, A Study in London Topography (1986).

Burrows, Donald (ed.)
The Cambridge Companion to Handel (Cambridge, 1997).

Burton, Richard
Historical Remarques and Observations on the Ancient and Present State of London and Westminster (1684).

Byrne, Maurice
'The Goldsmith-Trumpet-makers of the British Isles', *The Galpin Society Journal*, 19 (1966), pp. 71–83.

Cadell, Patrick
'1822 and All That', *Scottish Archives*, 16 (2010), pp. 41–50.

Caldwell, David Hepburn
'The Re-arming of the Clans, 1822', *Review of Scottish Culture*, 21 (2009), pp. 67–86.

Callender, Geoffrey
The Portrait of Peter Pett and the Sovereign of the Seas (Newport, Isle of Wight, 1930).

Carley, James P.
The Books of Henry VIII and his Wives (2004).

Carley, James P.
'John Leland's *Cygnea cantio*: A Neglected Tudor River Poem', *Humanistica Lovaniensia*, 32 (1983), pp. 225–41.

Carnegie, David
'Galley-foists, the Lord Mayor's Show, and Early Modern English Drama', *Early Theatre*, 7 (2004), pp. 49–74.

Castle, Terry
Masquerade and Civilization: The Carnivalesque in Eighteenth-Century English Culture and Fiction (Stanford, CA, 1986).

Chamberlayne, Edward
The Second Parte of the Present State of England Together with Divers Reflections Upon the Antient State Thereof, 12th edn (1684).

'The Chantrey Ledger'
The Walpole Society, 56 (1991–92).

Clarke, Richard
The Life of Horatio Lord Viscount Nelson (1813).

Clegg, W.P.
Docks and Ports: 2. London (Shepperton, 1987).

Clements, Paul
Marc Isambard Brunel (Stroud, 2006).

Cloake, John
Palaces and Parks of Richmond and Kew II: Richmond Lodge and the Kew Palaces (Chichester, 1996).

Clowes, William Laird
The Royal Navy: A History from the Earliest Times to the Present Day, 5 vols (1898).

Coke, David
'Vauxhall Gardens', in *Rococo: Art and Design in Hogarth's England*, edited by Michael Snodin (1984), pp. 75–81.

Cook, Sir Theodore Andrea
Thomas Doggett, Deceased: A Famous Comedian (1908).

Cookson, Brian
Crossing the River: The History of London's Thames River Bridges from Richmond to the Tower (2006).

Corbet, Charles
Blanket-Fair, or the History of Temple Street, Being a Relation of the Merry Pranks Plaid on the River Thames during the Great Frost (1684).

Cordulack, Shelley Wood
'Victorian Caricature and Classicism: Picturing the London Water Crisis', *International Journal of the Classical Tradition*, 9 (2003), pp. 535–83.

Croad, Stephen
London's Bridges (1983).

Crook, J. Mordaunt, and M.H. Port
The History of the King's Works, 1782–1851 (1973).

Croucher, John S.
'An Exceptional Woman of science', *Bulletin of the Scientific Instrument Society*, 84 (2005), pp. 22–27.

Croucher, John S., and Rosalind F. Croucher
'Mrs Janet Taylor's "Mariner's Calculator": Assessment and Reassessment', *The British Journal for the History of Science* (forthcoming)

Curl, James Stevens
Spas, Wells and Pleasure Gardens of London (2010).

Currie, Ian
Frosts, Freezes and Fairs: Chronicles of the Frozen Thames and Harsh Winters in Britain from 1000AD (Coulsdon, Surrey, 1996).

Dalgleish, George, and
Henry Steuart Fothringham
Silver: Made in Scotland (Edinburgh,
2008).

Daniels, Stephen et al. (eds)
*Envisioning Landscapes, Making
Worlds: Geography and the
Humanities* (New York, 2011).

D'Aulnoy, Marie Catherine,
Baronne
*Memoirs of the Court of England in
1675*, trans. by W.H. Arthur (1927).

Davis, G.
*Frostland; Or, A History of the River
Thames in a Frozen State* (1814).

De Bellaigue, Geoffrey
'Huzza the King is Well!', *The
Burlington Magazine*, 126 (1984),
pp. 325–31.

Defoe, Daniel
*A Tour through the Whole Island of
Great Britain*, edited by G.D.H. Cole
and D.C. Browning (1974).

Dekker, Thomas
Troia Nova Triumphans (1612)

Dekker, Thomas
*London's Tempe, Or The Field of
Happiness* (1629).

Dickens, Charles
Bleak House (1994 edn).

Dickens, Charles
Sketches by Boz (1995 edn).

Dillon, Janette, and
Philip Butterworth
*Performance and Spectacle in 'Hall's
Chronicle'* (2002).

Dixon, Philip
'The Tudor Palace at Greenwich',
Court Historian, 11 (2006),
pp. 105–11.

Doran, Susan (ed.)
*Elizabeth: The Exhibition at the
National Maritime Museum* (2003).

Doran, Susan (ed.)
Henry VIII: Man and Monarch
(2009).

Downes, Kerry
Hawksmoor (1979).

Drayton, Michael
Idea: The Shepherd's Garland
(1593).

Drayton, Michael
*Idea's Mirror: Amours in
Quatorzains* (1594).

Drayton, Michael
Poly-Olbion (1613).

Duncan, Archibald
*A Correct Narrative of the Funeral of
Horatio Lord Viscount Nelson*
(1806).

Edelstein, T.J.
Vauxhall Gardens (1983).

Elton, Oliver
Michael Drayton: A Critical Study
(1905).

Esdaile, Katherine
'Bacon's *George III, The River
Thames at His Feet*, at Somerset
House', *The Burlington Magazine*,
75 (October 1939), p. 168.

Evelyn, John
*The Diary and Correspondence of
John Evelyn, F.R.S.*, edited by
William Bray, 4 vols (1850).

Farber, Harold
*Caius Gabriel Cibber, 1630–1700:
His Life and Work* (Oxford, 1926).

Fellowes, Edmund
English Cathedral Music (1969).

Fitzgerald, Brian
*Emily, Duchess of Leinster,
1731–1814: A Study of Her Life and
Times* (1949).

Frostiface, Icedore,
of Freeseland [pseud.]
*An Account of All the Principal
Frosts for Above an Hundred Years
Past* (1740).

Fry, Sir Frederick Morris,
and Roland Stuart Tewson
*An Illustrated Catalogue of Silver
Plate of the Worshipful Company of
Merchant Taylors* (1929).

Galinou, Mireille, and John Hayes
*London in Paint: Oil Paintings in the
Collection at the Museum of
London* (1996).

Gaschke, Jenny (ed.)
*Turmoil and Tranquillity: The Sea
Through the Eyes of Dutch and
Flemish Masters, 1550–1700*
(2008).

Gavin, C.M.
Royal Yachts (1932).

Goulty, George A.
'Nelson's Memorial Rings',
Genealogist Magazine (June 1990).

Gowing, Lawrence
'Hogarth, Hayman, and the Vauxhall
Decorations', *The Burlington
Magazine*, 95 (1953), pp. 4–19.

Graves, John
George III's Miniature Dockyards
(1995).

Griffiths, Ralph A.
*The Reign of Henry VI: the Exercise
of Royal Authority, 1422–1461*
(1981).

[Great Exhibition]. *Official
Descriptive and Illustrated
catalogue*, 3 vols (1851).

Grove Music Online.
Oxford Music Online.
www.oxfordmusiconline.com

Gwynn, John
London and Westminster Improved
(1766).

H., T.J.
'The Improvement of the Quality of
Iron and Steel, From Their Becoming
Rusty When Buried in the Earth',
*The London and Edinburgh
Philosophical Magazine and Journal
of Science*, 2 (1833), pp. 75–77.

Halfpenny, Eric
'Musicians at James II's Coronation',
Music and Letters, 32 (April 1951),
pp. 103–114.

Halfpenny, Eric
'Four Seventeenth-Century British
Trumpets', *The Galpin Society
Journal*, 22 (1969), pp. 51–57.

Hall, Edward
*The Union of the Two Noble and
Illustre Famelies of Lancastre and
Yorke* (1809).

Halliday, Stephen
*The Great Stink of London:
Sir Joseph Bazalgette and the
Cleansing of the Metropolis* (Stroud,
1999).

Hamilton, James
Turner: A Life (1997).

Harris, John
*The Artist and the Country House
from the Fifteenth Century to the
Present Day* (1979).

Hatton, Edward
*A New View of London;
Or, An Ample Account of That City*,
2 vols (1708).

Hawksmoor, Nicholas
*Remarks on the Founding and
Carrying on the Buildings of the
Royal Hospital at Greenwich* [1728],
repr. in *Wren Society*, 6 (1929).

Held, Julius S.
'Rubens's Glynde Sketch and the
Installation of the Whitehall Ceiling',
The Burlington Magazine, 112
(May 1970), pp. 274–81.

Hellwig, G.
*Joachim Tielke, ein Hamburger
Lauten- und Violenmacher der
Barockzeit* (Frankfurt-am-Main,
1980).

Heywood, Thomas
*A True Description of His Majesties
Royall Ship* (1637).

Hibbert, Christopher (ed.)
*Louis Simond: An American in
Regency England* (1968).

Hibbert, Christopher, Ben
Weinreb et al. (eds)
The London Encyclopaedia (2008)

Hill, David
*Turner on the Thames: River
Journeys in the Year 1805* (New
Haven, CT, 1993).

Hill, Tracey
*Pageantry and Power: A Cultural
History of the Early Modern Lord
Mayor's Show, 1585–1639*
(Manchester, 2010).

*An Historical Account of the Late
Great Frost …* (1684).

Hogwood, Christopher
*Water Music and Music for the
Royal Fireworks* (Cambridge, 2005).

Holinshed, Raphael
*The Third Volume of Chronicles,
Beginning at Duke William the
Norman, Commonly Called the
Conqueror* (1586).

Holman, Peter
*Four and Twenty Fiddlers: The Violin
at the English Court 1540–1690*
(Oxford, 1993).

Humpherus, Henry
*The History of the Origin and
Progress of the Company of
Watermen and Lightermen of the
River Thames* (1887).

Hutton, Charles
*A Mathematical and Philosophical
Dictionary*, 2nd edn, 2 vols (1815).

Impey, Edward, and
Geoffrey Parnell
*The Tower of London: The Official
Illustrated History* (2006).

Ives, Eric W.
Anne Boleyn (Oxford, 1986).

James, Henry
Portraits of Places (1883).

Jenks, Timothy
'Contesting the Hero: The Funeral
of Admiral Lord Nelson', *Journal
of British Studies*, 39 (2000),
pp. 422–53.

Jerrold, Blanchard
London: A Pilgrimage (2005).

Jones, Christopher
*The Great Palace: The Story
of Parliament* (1983).

Kelly, Stuart
*Scott-Land: The Man Who Invented
a Nation* (2010).

Knight, Roger
*The Pursuit of Victory: The Life and
Achievements of Horatio Nelson*
(2005).

Knighton, C.S., and
D.M. Loades (eds)
*The Anthony Roll of Henry VIII's
Navy* (Aldershot, 2000).

Lambert, Andrew
Nelson: Britannia's God of War
(2004).

Lancashire, Anne Begor
*London Civic Theatre: City Drama
and Pageantry from Roman Times
to 1558* (Cambridge, 2002).

Lavery, Brian, and
Simon Stephens
*Ship Models: Their Purpose and
Development from 1650 to the
Present* (1995).

Lee, Sophia
*The Worshipful Company of
Vintners: A Catalogue of Plate*
(1996).

Leland, John
De Rebus Britannicis Collectanea,
edited by Thomas Hearne, 6 vols
(1770).

Lincoln, Margarette (ed.)
Nelson and Napoleon (2005).

Lindley, David (ed.)
*Court Masques: Jacobean and
Caroline Entertainments,
1605–1640* (Oxford, 1995).

Liversidge, Michael, and Jane Farrington (eds)
Canaletto and England (Birmingham, 1993).

Lockhart, John Gibson
The Life of Sir Walter Scott, 10 vols (Edinburgh, 1902).

Longstaffe-Gowan, Todd
'Brazen Proclamations: The Deployment of Statuary in Some Early London Garden Squares', *Sculpture Journal*, 18 (2009), pp.52–66.

Lowinsky, E.E.
'A Music Book for Anne Boleyn', in *Florilegum Historiale*, edited by J.G. Rowe and W.H. Stockdale (Toronto, 1971), pp.160–235.

Lyles, Anne (ed.)
Constable: The Great Landscapes (2006).

Macalpine, Ida, and Richard Hunter
George III and the Mad-Business (1991).

MacCarthy, Fiona
William Morris: A Life for Our Time (1994).

MacCulloch, Diarmaid
Thomas Cranmer: A Life (1996).

MacLeod, Catharine, and Julia Marciari Alexander
Painted Ladies: Women at the Court of Charles II (2001).

McManus, Clare
Women on the Renaissance Stage: Anna of Denmark and Female Masquing in the Stuart Court, 1590–1619 (Manchester, 2002).

McRae, Andrew
Literature and Domestic Travel in Early Modern England (Cambridge, 2009).

McRoberts, David, and Charles Oman
'Plate made by King James II and VII for the Chapel Royal of Holyroodhouse in 1686', *Antiquaries Journal*, 48 (1968), pp.285–95.

Maidment, James, and William Hugh Logan (eds)
The Dramatic Works of John Tatham (Edinburgh, 1879).

Marrs Jr, Edwin W. (ed.)
The Letters of Charles and Mary Anne Lamb, 3 vols (1975–78).

Marsden, Jonathan (ed.)
The Wisdom of George the Third (2005).

Martin, Gregory
The Ceiling Decoration of the Banqueting Hall: Corpus Rubenianum XV–XXII (2005).

Martin, Meredith
'Interiors and Interiority in the Ornamental Dairy Tradition', *Eighteenth-Century Fiction*, 20 (2008), pp.357–84.

Martineau, Jane, and Andrew Robison (eds)
The Glory of Venice: Art in the Eighteenth Century (1994).

Matthew, H.C.G., and Brian Harrison (eds)
Oxford Dictionary of National Biography (Oxford, online edition).

Middleton, Thomas
The Triumphs of Truth … Shewing also his Lordship's Entertainment upon Michaelmas Day Last (1613).

Millar, Delia
The Victorian Watercolours and Drawings in the Collections of Her Majesty The Queen, 2 vols (1995).

Millar, Oliver
The Tudor, Stuart and Early Georgian Pictures in the Collection of Her Majesty the Queen, 2 vols (1963).

Milne, Gustave
The Port of Roman London (1985).

Mollam, Charles
Irish National Inventory of Historic Scientific Instruments (Dublin, 1995).

Monks, Sarah
'The Visual Economies of the Downriver Thames in Eighteenth-Century British Art', *Visual Culture in Britain*, 7 (2006), pp.1–20.

Morris, Christopher
The Journeys of Celia Fiennes, (1947).

Morriss, Roger, Brian Lavery, and Stephen Deuchar
Nelson: An Illustrated History, edited by Pieter van der Merwe (1995).

Morris, William
News from Nowhere (1966 edn)..

Morton, Alan Q., and Jane A. Wess
Public and Private Science: The King George III Collection (Oxford, 1993).

Morton, Lucy
Triumphs of the Silversmith's Art: Catalogue of English and Continental Silver (2008).

Mudie, Robert
A Historical Account of His Majesty's Visit to Scotland, 3rd edn (Edinburgh, 1822).

Mumby, Julian
'Queen Elizabeth's Coaches: The Wardrobe on Wheels', *The Antiquaries Journal*, 83 (2003), pp.311–67.

Munday, Anthony
Chruso-Thriambos: The Triumphes of Golde (1611).

Munday, Anthony
Metropolis Coronata: The Triumphs of Ancient Drapery; Or Rich Cloathing of England (1615).

Munday, Anthony
The Triumphs of the Golden Fleece (1623).

Murdoch, Tessa
'A Silver Cup Commemorating the Coronation of James II, 23 April 1685, and the Culture of Gifts and prerequisites in Stuart and Hanoverian Coronations', *V&A Online Journal*, 2 (2009).

Myrely, Scott Hughes
British Military Spectacle, from the Napoleonic Wars through the Crimea (1996).

Naish, George P.B.
Royal Yachts (1964).

Nead, Lynda
Victorian Babylon: People, Streets and Images in Nineteenth-Century London (2000).

Nichols, John G. (ed.)
The Progresses and Public Processions of Queen Elizabeth, 3 vols (1823).

Nichols, John G. (ed.)
The Diary of Henry Machyn: Citizen and Merchant-Taylor of London, from A.D. 1550 to 1563 (1848).

Norman, V.
'George IV and Highland Dress', *Review of Scottish Culture*, 10 (1998), pp.5–15.

Norton, Peter
State Barges (1972).

Ogilby, John, and William Morgan
London &c. Actually Survey'd (1682).

Osborne, Michael
The State Barges of the Stationers' Company, 1680–1850 (1972).

Paget, Julian
Discovering London Ceremonials and Traditions (Aylesbury, 1989).

Palmer, Kenneth Nicholls
Ceremonial Barges on the River Thames: A History of the Barges of the City of London Livery Companies and of the Crown (1997).

Pasquin, Anthony
Memoirs of the Royal Academicians (1796).

Pepys, Samuel
The Diary of Samuel Pepys, edited by R.C. Latham and W. Matthews, 11 vols (1995).

Petrides, Anne
State Barges on the Thames (1959).

Piacenti, Kirsten Aschengreen, and John Boardman
Ancient and Modern Gems and Jewels in the Collection of Her Majesty The Queen (2008).

Pike, David L.
'"The Greatest Wonder of the World": Brunel's Tunnel and the Meanings of Underground London', *Victorian Literature and Culture*, 33 (2005), pp.341–67.

Pollard, A.F. (ed.)
Tudor Tracts 1532–1588 (New York, 1964).

Porter, Stephen (ed.)
Survey of London, vol.44: Poplar, Blackwall and the Isle of Dogs (1994).

Potts, Alex
'Picturing the Modern Metropolis: Images of London in the Nineteenth Century', *History Workshop Journal*, 26 (1988), pp.28–56.

Prebble, John
The King's Jaunt: George IV in Scotland, August 1822 (1988).

Prentice, Rina
The Authentic Nelson (2005).

Preston, Harley
London and the Thames: Paintings of Three Centuries (1977).

Quarrell, W.H., and Margaret Mare (eds)
London in 1710: From the Travels of Zacharias Conrad von Uffenbach (1934).

Rackham, Bernard
Catalogue of the Glaisher Collection of Pottery and Porcelain in the Fitzwilliam Museum, Cambridge (Woodbridge, 1987).

Redford, Bruce
Venice and the Grand Tour, 1670–1830 (1996).

Reynolds, Graham
The Sixteenth- and Seventeenth-Century Miniatures in the Collection of Her Majesty The Queen (1999).

Ribeiro, Aileen
'The Exotic Diversion: The Dress Worn at Masquerades in Eighteenth-Century London', *Connoisseur*, 197 (1978), pp.3–13.

Riding, Christine, and Jacqueline Riding (eds)
The Houses of Parliament: History, Art, Architecture (2000).

Rimer, Graeme, Thom Richardson and J.D.P. Cooper (eds)
Henry VIII: Arms and the Man (2009).

Roberts, Jane
Royal Artists from Queen Mary of Scots to the Present Day (1987).

Roberts, Jane, and Christopher Lloyd (eds)
George III and Queen Charlotte: Patronage, Collecting and Court Taste (London, 2004).

Roberts, Jane, Prudence Sutcliffe and Susan Mayor
Unfolding Pictures: Fans in the Royal Collection (2005).

Robinson, James
Masterpieces: Medieval Art (2008).

Rodger, N.A.M.
The Wooden World: An Anatomy of the Georgian Navy (1988).

Rogers, Nicholas
'The Sea Fencibles, Loyalism and the Reach of the State', in *Resisting Napoleon: The British Response to the Threat of Invasion, 1797–1815*, edited by Mark Philip (Aldershot, 2006), pp.41–59.

Salmon, Nicholas (ed.)
Political Writings of William Morris: Contributions to 'Justice' and 'Commonweal', 1883–1890, (Bristol, 1994).

Sanders, Julie
The Cultural Geography of Early Modern Drama, 1620–1650 (Cambridge, 2011).

Sayle, R.T.D.
The Barges of the Merchant Taylors' Company (1933).

Schneer, Jonathan
The Thames: England's River (2005).

Scott, Robert Henry
'The History of the Kew Observatory', *Proceedings of the Royal Society of London*, 39 (1885), pp.37–86.

Scott, Sir Walter
Hints Addressed to the Inhabitants of Edinburgh and Others in Prospect of His Majesty's Visit, by an Old Citizen (Edinburgh, 1822).

Shay, Robert, and Robert Thompson
Purcell Manuscripts: The Principal Musical Sources (Cambridge, 2000).

Sheppard, Francis
London: A History (Oxford, 1998).

Sheppard, F.H.W. (ed.)
Survey of London [vols 33–34] (1966).

Shirley, James
A Contention for Honour and Riches (1633).

Shrank, Cathy
Writing the Nation in Reformation England, 1530–1580 (Oxford, 2004).

Simon, Jacob (ed.)
Handel: A Celebration of His Life and Times, 1685–1759 (1986).

Skinner, Basil C.
'A Contemporary Account of the Royal Visit to Edinburgh, 1822', *The Book of the Old Edinburgh Club*, 31 (1962), pp.65–167.

Smith, George (ed.)
The Coronation of Elizabeth Wydeville (1935).

Smith, J.
'Completing Greenwich Hospital', *Journal of the Greenwich Historical Society*, 2:4 (2001), pp.109–19.

Smith, William C.
Handel: A Descriptive Catalogue of the Early Editions (Oxford, 1970).

Smith, William C.
'The Earliest Editions of the Water Music', in *idem, Concerning Handel: His Life and Works* (1948), pp.269–87.

Solkin, David H.
Painting for Money: The Visual Arts and the Public Sphere in Eighteenth-Century England (1993).

Somerset, Anne
The Life and Times of William IV (1980).

Soo, Lydia M.
Wren's 'Tracts' on Architecture and Other Writings (Cambridge, 1998).

Spenser, Edmund
The Complete Works in Verse and Prose of Edmund Spenser (Manchester, 1887)

Stansky, Peter
Redesigning the World: William Morris, the 1880s, and the Arts and Crafts (Princeton, NJ, 1985).

Starkey, David
Six Wives: The Queens of Henry VIII (2003).

Starkey, David (ed.)
Henry VIII: A European Court in England (1991).

Stevenson, Christine
Medicine and Magnificence: British Hospital and Asylum Architecture, 1660–1815 (2000).

Strong, Roy
The Tudor and Stuart Monarchy: Pageantry, Painting, Iconography, 3 vols (Woodbridge, 1996–99).

Tate Gallery
Turner 1775–1851: Bicentenary Exhibition Catalogue (1974).

Tatham, John
Aqua Triumphalis; Being a True Relation of the Honourable the City of Londons Entertaining Their Sacred Majesties Upon the River of Thames … August 1662 (1662).

Taylor, James, and Pieter van der Merwe
The Spread Eagle Art Collection (Tonbridge, 2006).

Thames Tunnel Committee
The Thames Tunnel (1825).

Thomas, Arthur, and Isobel Thornley (ed.)
The Great Chronicle of London (1938).

Thompson, E.P.
William Morris: From Romantic to Revolutionary, 2nd edn (1976).

Thomson, Katrina
Turner and Sir Walter Scott: The Provincial Antiquities and Picturesque Scenery of Scotland (Edinburgh, 1999).

Thomson, Richard
Chronicles of London Bridge by an Antiquary (London, 1827).

Thorne, James
Handbook to the Environs of London (Chichester, 1983).

Thurley, Simon
The Royal Palaces of Tudor England: A Social and Architectural History (1993).

Thurley, Simon
Whitehall Palace: An Architectural History of the Royal Apartments 1260–1698 (1999).

Thurley, Simon
'A Country Seat Fit for a King: Charles II, Winchester and Greenwich', in *The Stuart Courts*, edited by Eveline Cruickshanks (Stroud, 2000), pp.214–39.

Thurley, Simon
Hampton Court Palace: A Social and Architectural History (2004).

Thurley, Simon
'Architecture and Diplomacy: Greenwich Palace under the Stuarts', *The Court Historian*, 11:2 (2007), pp.21–29.

Thurley, Simon, with contributions by Patricia Croot and Claire Gapper
Somerset House, The Palace of England's Queens 1551–1692 (2009).

Ticehurst, Norman
The Mute Swan in England (1957).

Toupee, S.
'An evening at Vaux-hall', *Scots Magazine* (July 1739), p.332.

Treadwell, Penelope
Johan Zoffany: Artist and Adventurer (2009).

A True Discourse of All the Royal Passages, Triumphs and Ceremonies Observed at the Contract and Marriage of the High and Mighty Charles, King of Great Britaine and the Most Excellentest of Ladies, the Lady Henrietta Maria of Bourbon (1625).

Tytler, Patrick Fraser
Life of Henry the Eighth, Founded on Authentic and Original Documents (Edinburgh, 1837).

Walker, Richard J.B.
The Eighteenth- and Early-Nineteenth-Century Miniatures in the Collection of Her Majesty The Queen (Cambridge, 1992).

Walpole, Horace
The Letters of Horace Walpole, Fourth Earl of Orford, edited by Peter Cunningham, 9 vols (1891).

Wardle, Patricia
'A Rare Survival: The Barge Cloth of the Worshipful Company of Pewterers and the Embroiderer John Best', *Textile History*, 37:1 (2006), pp.1–16.

Warner, Malcolm
The Image of London: Views by Travellers and Émigrés, 1550–1920 (1987).

Watkin, David
The Architect King: George III and the Culture of the Enlightenment (2004).

Webb, Geoffrey
'The Letters and Drawings of Nicholas Hawksmoor Relating to the Building of the Mausoleum at Castle Howard, 1726–1742', *The Walpole Society*, 19 (1930–31).

Welch, Charles
Numismata Londinensia: Medals Struck by the Corporation of London (1894).

Werlich, Robert
Orders and Decorations of All Nations: Ancient and Modern, Civil and Military (Washington, DC, 1965).

Weston-Lewis, Aiden
'Orazio Gentileschi's two versions of *The Finding of Moses* reassessed', *Apollo* (June 1997), pp.27–35.

Whipple, R.S.
'An Old Catalogue and What it Tells Us of the Scientific Instruments and Curios Collected by Queen Charlotte and King George III', *Proceedings of the Optical Convention*, part 2 (1926), pp.502–28.

Whitfield, Peter
London: A Life in Maps (2006).

Whittet, T.D.
'The Barges of the Society of Apothecaries', *Pharmaceutical Historian*, 10:1 (1980), pp.4–8.

Williams, Alan, and Anthony de Rueck
The Royal Armoury at Greenwich 1515–1649: A History of its Technology (1995).

Williams, Clare (ed. and trans.)
Sophie in London 1786: Being the Diary of Sophie v. la Roche (1933).

Wood, Julia K.
'"A Flowing Harmony". Music on the Thames in Restoration London', *Early Music*, 23 (1995), pp.553–81.

Wooding, Lucy
Henry VIII (2008).

Wriothesley, Charles
A Chronicle of England During the Reigns of the Tudors, from AD 1485 to 1559, edited by William D. Hamilton, 2 vols (1875–77).

Wroth, Warwick
'Tickets of Vauxhall Gardens', *Numismatic Chronicle*, 18 (1898).

INDEX